Glubb Pasha and the Arab Legion

During the 1950s, John Glubb and the Arab Legion became the 'cornerstone' of Britain's imperial presence in the Middle East. Based on unprecedented access to the unofficial archive of the Arab Legion, including a major new accession of Glubb's private papers, Graham Jevon examines and revises Britain's post-1945 retreat from empire in the Middle East.

Jevon details how Glubb's command of the Arab Legion secured British and Jordanian interests during the 1948 Arab–Israeli War, answering questions that have dogged historians of this conflict for decades. He reveals how the Arab Legion was transformed, by Cold War concerns, from an internal Jordanian security force to a quasi-division within the British Army. Jevon also sheds new light on the succession crisis following King Abdullah's assassination, and uses previously unseen documents to challenge accepted contentions concerning King Hussein's dismissal of Glubb, the 1956 Suez Crisis, and the nature of Britain's imperial decline.

Previously a Tutor on the Stanford Program in Oxford (teaching third-year undergraduates from Stanford University), Graham Jevon gained his DPhil from the University of Oxford. His research interests centre on twentieth-century British imperialism and decolonisation. Currently, he is working on a new project analysing Britain's construction and use of armies throughout the Arab world after the First World War.

Glubb Pasha and the Arab Legion

*Britain, Jordan, and the End
of Empire in the Middle East*

GRAHAM JEVON
University of Oxford

CAMBRIDGE
UNIVERSITY PRESS

CAMBRIDGE
UNIVERSITY PRESS

University Printing House, Cambridge CB2 8BS, United Kingdom

One Liberty Plaza, 20th Floor, New York, NY 10006, USA

477 Williamstown Road, Port Melbourne, VIC 3207, Australia

4843/24, 2nd Floor, Ansari Road, Daryaganj, Delhi – 110002, India

79 Anson Road, #06-04/06, Singapore 079906

Cambridge University Press is part of the University of Cambridge.

It furthers the University's mission by disseminating knowledge in the pursuit of education, learning, and research at the highest international levels of excellence.

www.cambridge.org
Information on this title: www.cambridge.org/9781107177833
DOI: 10.1017/9781316823125

© Graham Jevon 2017

First published 2017

Printed in the United Kingdom by Clays, St Ives plc

A catalogue record for this publication is available from the British Library.

Library of Congress Cataloging-in-Publication Data
Names: Jevon, Graham, author.
Title: Glubb Pasha and the Arab Legion: Britain, Jordan, and the End of Empire in the Middle East / Graham Jevon.
Description: New York, NY: Cambridge University Press, 2017. |
Includes bibliographical references.
Identifiers: LCCN 2016049750 | ISBN 9781107177833 (hardback)
Subjects: LCSH: Glubb, John Bagot, Sir, 1897–1986. | Jordan –
Foreign relations – Great Britain. | Great Britain – Foreign relations –
Jordan. | Jordan. Jaysh al-Arabi – History.
Classification: LCC DS154.13 .J48 2017 | DDC 355.0095695/09044–dc23
LC record available at https://lccn.loc.gov/2016049750

ISBN 978-1-107-17783-3 Hardback

Contents

Illustrations

Acknowledgements

This book is the product of a multitude of debts. For financial support I am grateful for the generous backing of the Arts and Humanities Research Council, the Barclays/British Society of Middle Eastern Studies (BRISMES) Scholarship, and St Antony's College, Oxford. Beyond the financial I am also thankful to the College and all those – too many to mention – whom I have come into contact with during my time here for their help and encouragement.

Ultimately, this book is the product of archival research and therefore the kind permission and assistance of the Trustees of the Liddell Hart Centre for Military Archives; the Bodleian Library; Rhodes House; the Leopold Muller Memorial Library at the Oxford Centre for Hebrew and Jewish Studies; the British Library of Political and Economic Science; The British Library; Hertfordshire County Council Libraries; SOAS; and The National Archives, Kew, London. I am particularly grateful to the Israel State Archives and Dorith Herman at the Haganah Archives for sending documents by email and airmail, respectively. At The National Archives I owe huge thanks to the Freedom of Information Centre for putting up with my many requests; at one point my requests made up approximately 15 per cent of the department's entire workload. Helen Potter, especially, could not have been more helpful. I am also grateful for the efficient work of the Freedom of Information teams at the Foreign and Commonwealth Office and the Treasury.

I am grateful to the editors of the *English Historical Review* for permission to reproduce my 2015 article, aspects of which appear – revised and expanded – in Chapters 2 and 3. I am particularly thankful for the feedback and assistance provided by Kim Reynolds, Martin Conway, and the two anonymous reviewers.

In different ways many people have helped shape this manuscript. Lily Eilan, Maziyar Ghiabi, and Johannes Raute translated a selection of documents. Paola Cubas Barragan provided administrative help. Nigel Ashton, James Belich, Judith Brown, John Darwin, Matthew Hughes, Bob and Deba Mcdonald, Brant Moscovitch, Ami Naramor, and the two anonymous reviewers at Cambridge University Press have read and commented on parts of this manuscript, or its earlier incarnations, offering words of advice or encouragement.

This work could not have been completed without the support of the St Antony's College Middle East Centre, not least Julia Cook, Mastan Ebtehaj, Ahmed Al-Shahi, and Avi Shlaim, who not only read an earlier version of the manuscript, but kindly made available copies of documents in his possession and gave permission to reproduce several maps.

Special mention must go to Agrima Bhasin and Seyma Afacan, who provided constant help locating sources and offered ever-insightful critiques. And, of course, Eugene Rogan, whose guidance and ever-pertinent comments have had an untold impression on this book.

Ultimately, this project would not have been possible without access to the private papers of John Glubb and Robert Melville. I am therefore immensely grateful to the Glubb family, particularly Mary and Peter, for depositing his papers at the Middle East Centre Archive. Likewise, I am extremely thankful to Robert Melville for taking the time to meet me and for subsequently making his papers available. Sadly, he passed away on 18 January 2017, shortly before publication. Bob was most helpful and very supportive of my research and it is regretful that he was not able to see the finished book.

Given the importance of the Glubb and Melville collections, I am especially indebted to the Middle East Centre's archivist, Debbie Usher, who went beyond the call of duty to make this mass of material available to me. Debbie's assistance and her interest have made an immeasurable impact on this study.

As this is my first book, I might have expected the publication process to be painfully bureaucratic. It turned out to be surprisingly straightforward. That, I am sure, is testament to the friendly professionalism of Maria Marsh and everyone at Cambridge University Press.

Final thanks go to friends and family, not least my parents, whose contribution has been incalculable.

It goes without saying, of course, that any errors and omissions are mine, and mine alone.

A Note on Transliteration

A formal method for the transliteration of Arabic names has not been rigidly applied. For individuals familiar with English readers, such as King Hussein and President Nasser, the common Anglicised form has been used. There are also occasional inconsistencies where adjustments have not been made to the transliteration in original sources. For example, in direct quotations Talal may be spelled Tellal and Tawfiq Abu al-Huda written as Tewfiq Abul Huda.

Abbreviations

AHC	Arab Higher Committee
AJJDB	Anglo-Jordan Joint Defence Board
ALA	Arab Liberation Army
BLPI	British Loaned Personnel (Iraq)
BMEO	British Middle East Office
CAB	Cabinet
CIGS	Chief of the Imperial General Staff
C-in-C	Commander-in-Chief
CO	Colonial Office
COS	Chief of Staff
DMO	Director of Military Operations
FO	Foreign Office
FRUS	Foreign Relations of the United States
GP1986	Glubb Papers (1986 accession)
GP2006	Glubb Papers (2006 accession)
HMG	His/Her Majesty's Government
IDF	Israel Defense Forces
MECA	Middle East Centre Archive, St Antony's College, Oxford
MELF	Middle East Land Forces
MOD	Ministry of Defence
RJAF	Royal Jordanian Air Force
SBO	Senior British Officer
SWB	Summary of World Broadcasts (BBC)
TJFF	Transjordan Frontier Force
TNA	The National Archives (UK)
UNSCOP	United Nations Special Committee on Palestine
VCIGS	Vice-Chief of the Imperial General Staff
WO	War Office

Introduction

Throughout the twenty-first century, and much of the twentieth, conflict in the Middle East has dominated the international news headlines. Since the 2011 uprisings, popularly referred to as the Arab Spring, different parts of the region have almost taken it in turns to lead the international segments of Western news media broadcasts: Tunisia, Egypt, Libya, Bahrain, Gaza, Syria, and Iraq have all had their moment in the spotlight. Jordan, though, has remained largely overlooked, except, if you listen carefully, as a location on which refugees have descended from other states that have dominated the headlines, such as Palestine, Syria, and Iraq. This hints at Jordan's centrality, if only geographically. However, Jordan's apparent absence within the international current affairs consciousness belies its centrality to the politics of the region, particularly its historical significance in relation both to the Arab–Israeli conflict and to Britain's imperial moment in the Middle East.

The purpose of this book is to unpack Jordan's pivotal relationship to these two critical issues during what is arguably *the* most crucial decade in the history of the Arab world.[1] Based on significant new sources, this study provides an analysis of the post–Second World War role of the Arab Legion – the Jordanian Army, as it was known until 1956 – and its British commander, John Bagot Glubb – more commonly known as Glubb Pasha. This is not a history of Jordan. Nor is this simply an account of a parochial army in a colonial backwater. At heart this is an assessment of

---

[1] Eugene Rogan posits that the first decade of the twenty-first century has a strong case for being the most significant. See: Eugene Rogan, 'A History of the West Through Arab Eyes', 8 March 2010: www.wilsoncenter.org/event/the-history-the-west-through-arab-eyes (accessed: 12 August 2014).

Jordan, the Arab Legion, and Glubb within the context of Britain's gradual retreat from empire in the Middle East during the emerging Cold War
era. Along the way, this book provides significant new revelations and
insights into key historical issues, including the partition of Palestine; the
1948 Arab–Israeli War; the royal succession crisis following the assassination of King Abdullah; the abrupt dismissal of Glubb by King Hussein;
and the 1956 Suez Crisis.

BACKGROUND / CONTEXT

Jordan first became a direct British interest as a result of the First World
War, when the Middle East became a new frontier of Britain's empire, as it
sought to uphold its interests in the region – not least, protection of the Suez
Canal and the increasing importance of oil.[2] Despite long-standing involvement in Egypt and the Persian Gulf, throughout the nineteenth century
Britain had acquiesced in the Ottoman Empire's control of the deserts east
of Suez as a means of limiting the influence of its European rivals – notably
Russia – and allowing transit to India and the East. Britain had no desire
to become embroiled in direct control of the region.[3] This changed after
the Ottoman Empire allied with Germany in 1914. This prompted Britain
to support an Arab revolt against the Ottomans, led by the Hashemite
family: Sharif Husayn of Mecca and his sons, Ali, Abdullah, Faysal, and
Zayd. As part of this wartime alliance Britain promised to support the
creation of an independent 'Arab Kingdom' ruled by Husayn. Meanwhile,
unbeknownst to the Hashemites, Britain made an essentially incompatible
agreement with another of its wartime allies: France.[4] When the moment
of truth arrived during the post-war peace negotiations, it was the Anglo–
French alliance that took precedence. At the San Remo Conference in April
1920 a new map of the Middle East was drawn; the former Ottoman
Empire was divided into British and French spheres of influence, creating
the modern Middle East state system that we know today. Two new states,
Lebanon and Syria, were established and placed under French tutelage.

---

[2] M. A. Fitzsimons, *Empire by Treaty: Britain and the Middle East in the Twentieth Century*
(London, 1965), pp. 15–16; Mary C. Wilson, *King Abdullah, Britain and the Making of
Jordan* (Cambridge, 1987), p. 45.

[3] Fitzsimons, *Empire by Treaty*, pp. 4–6; L. Carl Brown, *International Politics and the
Middle East: Old Rules, Dangerous Game* (London, 1984), pp. 107–12.

[4] Eugene Rogan, *The Fall of the Ottomans: The Great War in the Middle East, 1914–1920*
(London, 2016), pp. 275–309; Jonathan Schneer, *The Balfour Declaration: The Origins
of the Arab–Israeli Conflict* (London, 2010), pp. 64–103.

Meanwhile, Britain was granted a League of Nations mandate over Iraq and Palestine, which Britain subsequently divided in two, thus creating another new state: Transjordan, east of the River Jordan.[5]

In Palestine, west of the river, Britain retained administrative control of the mandate, effectively running it as a colony, but in Iraq and Transjordan the British installed two of Husayn's sons to rule: Faysal in Iraq and Abdullah in Transjordan. Faysal and Abdullah were not native to these regions; they were parachuted in to rule these new states as compensation for their thwarted ambitions elsewhere. Abdullah arrived in the Transjordan area in January 1921 while travelling from Mecca, in the Hashemites' Hijazi heartland, to reclaim Syria from the French. While there he formed relationships with local tribal leaders. Because this threatened to derail Britain's formative control of the area, and because of fears that his ambitions in Syria might disturb the accord with France, the British were motivated to collaborate with Abdullah in Transjordan.[6] Given Britain's broken promise to support an independent Arab kingdom, Abdullah might have been expected to avoid another alliance with the British. However, Abdullah was a pragmatist who 'saw no benefit in responding to Britain with enmity from a position of weakness'.[7] Abdullah appraised that, as a first step, his dynastic ambitions were best served by working with the British in Transjordan. And Abdullah's reliance on Britain deepened after the Saudis wrested control of the Hijaz from his father in the mid-1920s.[8] Initially the Anglo–Abdullah relationship in Transjordan was an uncertain one, largely due to British frustration at the Amir's style of administration.[9] However, by the end of the Second World War Abdullah had established himself as Britain's most reliable ally in the Middle East, a region that the foreign secretary of the new post-war Labour government described as 'of cardinal importance to the United Kingdom, second only to the United Kingdom itself'.[10] Given that Jordan had become Britain's closest ally in its most important

---

[5] Throughout this book, 'Transjordan' will be used to refer specifically to the pre-1948 state, prior to Transjordan's occupation of the West Bank of Palestine when its name changed. When referring specifically to the post-1948 state, or when referring to the state in general terms, it will be referred to as 'Jordan'. State association will be referred to as 'Jordanian' throughout, regardless of periodisation.

[6] Yoav Alon, *The Making of Jordan: Tribes, Colonialism and the Modern State* (London, 2007), pp. 38–40; Wilson, *King Abdullah*, pp. 39–53.

[7] Sulayman Musa, *Cameos: Jordan and Arab Nationalism* (Amman, 1997), pp. 128–9.

[8] Wilson, *King Abdullah*, pp. 53, 88–90.

[9] Alon, *Making of Jordan*, pp. 46–8, 57–60.

[10] Quoted in: Ron Pundik, *The Struggle for Sovereignty: Relations between Great Britain and Jordan, 1946–1951* (Oxford, 1994), pp. 41–2.

sphere of influence, the Anglo–Jordanian relationship is a crucial area of exploration for understanding the final throes of the British Empire.

Despite this, historians have largely treated Jordan's relationship with Britain with barely more attention than the mainstream Western media. The literature on British involvement in Jordan is steadily growing, but it remains largely overlooked.[11] Nowhere is this more glaringly obvious than in a recent edited collection designed to explore Britain's historical and contemporary involvement in the Middle East. While Palestine, Israel, the Levant (in this case, Lebanon and Syria), Iraq, Egypt, Yemen, and the Gulf all have at least one chapter devoted to them, Jordan – which remains a stalwart ally of Britain and the West – is conspicuous by its absence.[12] The problem, as Peter Sluglett has observed, is that historians of British imperialism in the Middle East have focused primarily on the Eastern Question, Egypt, and Palestine.[13] Yet exploring how Britain managed relations with its closest regional ally during this period of upheaval is crucial to helping us understand how Britain's role in the Middle East evolved after the Second World War.

The relative lack of attention to Jordan is not just an issue for historians of British imperialism; regional historians have also traditionally overlooked the Hashemite Kingdom. Though as Betty Anderson has highlighted, it has become something of a cliché to begin a study of Jordan by referencing this lack of scrutiny, and the paucity of Jordanian studies has started to be remedied in recent years.[14] As a general rule, the literature on the history of Jordan can be divided into two categories. In the first instance, historians have been interested in the making of the Jordanian state under Amir Abdullah (he became king in 1946).[15]

---

[11] Notable exceptions include: Tancred Bradshaw, *Britain and Jordan: Imperial Strategy, King Abdullah I and the Zionist Movement* (London, 2012); Pundik, *Struggle for Sovereignty*; Nigel Ashton, "A 'Special Relationship' Sometimes in Spite of Ourselves": Britain and Jordan, 1957–73', *Journal of Imperial and Commonwealth History*, 33:2 (2005), pp. 221–44; Stephen Blackwell, *British Military Intervention and the Struggle for Jordan: King Hussein, Nasser and the Middle East Crisis, 1955–1958* (New York, 2009).

[12] Zach Levey and Elie Podeh (eds.), *Britain and the Middle East: From Imperial Power to Junior Partner* (Eastbourne, 2008).

[13] Peter Sluglett, 'Formal and Informal Empire in the Middle East', in: Robin W. Winks (ed.), *Oxford History of the British Empire, Volume V: Historiography* (Oxford, 1999), pp. 421–3.

[14] For a pithy overview of the literature on Jordan, see: Betty S. Anderson, 'Review Essay: The Evolution of Jordanian Studies', *Middle Eastern Studies*, 12:2 (2003), pp. 197–202.

[15] Uriel Dann, *Studies in the History of Transjordan, 1920–1949: The Making of a State* (Boulder, 1984); Alon, *Making of Jordan*; Wilson, *King Abdullah*.

In the second instance historians have explored the political survival of Abdullah's grandson, King Hussein – and the inherent survival of the state.[16] There are only a handful of exceptions to this periodisation, including two general histories of Jordan by Ann Dearden and Philip Robins;[17] N. H. Aruri's study of Jordan's *Political Development*;[18] Ilan Pappé's single chapter on British rule between 1943 and 1955;[19] Joseph Massad's study of the 'production' of Jordanian national identity and culture;[20] Betty Anderson's analysis of Jordanian nationalism;[21] Kamal Salibi's pro-Hashemite *Modern History of Jordan*;[22] and Roberts Satloff's *Jordan in Transition*. However, while as the title suggests, Satloff explores the transition from Abdullah to Hussein, his primary focus is 'the years following the 1951 assassination of Abdullah'.[23] This book, however, transcends this dividing line and examines Britain's relationship with Jordan across this transitory period, thus involving the reigns of all three of Jordan's first three kings: Abdullah, Talal, and Hussein.

As instruments of control Glubb and the Arab Legion provide the ideal focal point. It is worth emphasising that Britain's global imperial interests were not maintained using one single method. For that reason historian John Gallagher coined the phrase 'British world system' to account for the broader context of Britain's imperial reach. He explained:

The 'empire', as a set of colonies and other dependencies, was just the tip of the iceberg that made up the British world system as a whole, a system of influence as well as power which, indeed, preferred to work through informal methods of influence when possible, and through formal methods of rule only when necessary.[24]

[16] Nigel Ashton, *King Hussein of Jordan: A Political Life* (New Haven, 2008); Avi Shlaim, *Lion of Jordan: The Life of King Hussein in War and Peace* (New York, 2008); Uriel Dann, *King Hussein and the Challenge of Arab Radicalism: Jordan, 1955–1967* (Oxford, 1989); Lawrence Tal, *Politics, the Military and National Security in Jordan, 1955–1967* (Basingstoke, 2002).

[17] Ann Dearden, *Jordan* (London, 1958); Philip Robins, *A History of Jordan* (Cambridge, 2004).

[18] N. H. Aruri, *Jordan: A Study in Political Development, 1921–1965* (Hague, 1972).

[19] Ilan Pappé, 'British Rule in Jordan, 1943–55', in: Michael Cohen and Martin Kolinsky (eds.), *Demise of the British Empire in the Middle East: Britain's Responses to Nationalist Movements, 1943–55* (London, 1998), pp. 198–219.

[20] Joseph A. Massad, *Colonial Effects: The Making of National Identity in Jordan* (New York, 2001), p. 1.

[21] Betty S. Anderson, *Nationalist Voices in Jordan: The Street and the State* (Austin, 2005).

[22] Kamal Salibi, *The Modern History of Jordan* (London, 1993).

[23] Robert Satloff, *From Abdullah to Hussein: Jordan in Transition* (Oxford, 1994), p. vii.

[24] John Gallagher, *The Decline, Revival and Fall of the British Empire* (Cambridge, 1982), p. 75. See also: John Darwin, *The Empire Project: The Rise and Fall of the British World-System, 1830–1970* (Cambridge, 2009), pp. xi, 12–17.

Transjordan was a quintessential part of Britain's informal empire. Britain ruled indirectly, via Abdullah, who was guided, politically, by a British resident. As Priya Satia elucidates, though, the system of indirect rule implemented in the Middle East meant that the installed rulers, such as Abdullah, were sidelined 'for all matters pertaining to "imperial security"'.[25] In Transjordan security was maintained – and Abdullah's authority backed – by the Arab Legion. This system of indirect rule continued even after Transjordan became independent in 1946. Alec Kirkbride continued to advise Abdullah – albeit his job title superficially changed from British resident to British minister – and Glubb continued to command the British-financed Arab Legion.

Glubb and the Arab Legion were absolutely central to the Anglo–Jordanian relationship and characteristic of the twentieth-century shift towards liberal counterinsurgencies. If nineteenth-century colonial pacification was characterised by mass violence and destruction, the twentieth century experienced what Laleh Khalili described as a 'constant seesawing between the idea of violently *deterring* the civilian population from supporting the insurgents and the notion that these civilians would be best *persuaded* to disavow the insurgents'.[26] This oscillation between violent deterrence, on one hand, and humane persuasion on the other was a key part of Glubb's formative imperial experience.[27]

Born in Preston, Lancashire, in 1897, Glubb began his adult life as a newly commissioned officer of the Royal Engineers serving on the Western Front, where his experiences were recorded in a meticulous diary.[28] In his autobiography Glubb recounted that: 'From my earliest childhood, it had always been assumed that I would be an officer in the Royal Engineers like my father. No alternative career had ever been dreamed of – much less discussed.'[29] This was not strictly true. At the age of twenty-three Glubb revealed, in a diary-like note, that privately he dreamed of being a writer. He put this ambition on hold, though, because he lacked confidence and had neither the money to sustain himself, nor the experiences to write about. Consequently Glubb resorted to his other

---

[25] Priya Satia, *Spies in Arabia: The Great War and the Cultural Foundations of Britain's Covert Empire in the Middle East* (Oxford, 2008), p. 7.

[26] Laleh Khalili, *Time in the Shadows: Confinement in Counterinsurgencies* (Stanford, 2013), p. 42 [emphasis in original].

[27] Massad, *Colonial Effects*, pp. 149–50.

[28] John Glubb, *Into Battle: A Soldier's Diary of the Great War* (London, 1978).

[29] John Glubb, *The Changing Scenes of Life: An Autobiography* (London, 1983), pp. 2–5, 10–12, 16–25.

love: soldiering.[30] Thus, when the First World War ended Glubb answered a War Office call for volunteers to serve in Iraq, where a rebellion had broken out against British rule in June 1920.[31] Using heavy artillery and aerial bombardment, the uprising was crushed by the British, in what Eugene Rogan described as 'scorched-earth tactics'.[32] Glubb arrived in October, with the fighting having 'practically all finished'.[33] Yet he would nonetheless become an integral tool in the maintenance of British control in this newly created state.

In 1921 the British decided that the cheapest and most efficient means of ruling the desert was to use 'air control', where '"terror" was the scheme's underlying principle'.[34] As Glubb explained:

If the tribes rose in rebellion several hundred miles from Baghdad … a military expedition might take many weeks and cost millions of pounds. But if the RAF was in control, aircraft could take off after breakfast from Baghdad, bomb the insurgents and be back in Baghdad for lunch. The cost of such an operation would be negligible.[35]

Initially this tactic proved ineffective and problematic, as RAF pilots struggled to identify correct targets. Key to this scheme was local knowledge. To that end, Glubb was seconded to the RAF as one of several intelligence officers. Selected because of the Arabic language skills he had developed, his task was to become familiar with a designated part of the desert. As Glubb explained: 'my duties were merely to know every tribe and village in my area so that, in the event of operations, I could lead aircraft to their target'.[36] By this method the British sought to ensure that the desert tribes paid their taxes and complied with the laws of the central Iraqi government. Glubb was a vital cog in this system and therefore began his career in the Middle East as a key component of Britain's strategy of violent deterrence.

Glubb was also a conduit of persuasion during his time in Iraq, a skill that saw him headhunted by the government in Transjordan. In 1926 Glubb was informed that he would have to return to England because he

[30] 'Of the Object of My Life', Glubb, 24 October 1920, Glubb Papers (2006 accession) [Hereafter: GP2006], Box 47, Middle East Centre Archive, St Antony's College, Oxford [Hereafter: MECA].
[31] Glubb recounts his career in Iraq in: John Glubb, *Arabian Adventures: Ten Years of Joyful Service* (London, 1978).
[32] Rogan, *Fall of the Ottomans*, p. 402.
[33] Glubb to Aunty, 24 October 1920, GP2006, 23.
[34] Satia, *Spies in Arabia*, pp. 246, 252–3.
[35] Glubb, *Arabian Adventures*, p. 32.
[36] Glubb, *Changing Scenes*, pp. 60–3.

could only remain on secondment from the British Army for a maximum of five years. Not wanting to leave the region, Glubb resigned his commission and accepted an offer to work as a civilian administrator contracted directly to the Iraqi government. Glubb remained in this essentially political role until March 1928, when he was transferred to the southern desert, tasked with administering Iraq's southern border region and protecting it against tribal raiding from the Ikhwan in Saudi Arabia. Believing that air control would be ineffective in this instance, Glubb sought to create a desert police force made up of local Bedouin tribesmen.[37] The problem Glubb faced was that the 'tribes were intensely resentful against the Iraqi government which made them pay taxes but did nothing to protect them'. Glubb's task, therefore, was to win their confidence and 'co-operation'. This he did. Glubb established the Southern Desert Camel Corps, armed with machine guns and made up of men from the local Bedouin tribes. With this force he successfully brought order to Iraq's southern desert.[38]

As a consequence of this success, the Jordanian government offered Glubb a contract in the hope that he could achieve the same feat in Transjordan. Prior to Glubb's arrival the authorities had relied on the Tribal Control Board – a Court of Justice based in Amman – to deal with raiding, which inflicted severe and collective punishment. The Jordanian tribes considered this treatment unjust given that they were victims of raiding by the Ikhwan, who were immune from the same treatment in Saudi Arabia. This led to a significant fracturing of the tribes' relationship with the central Jordanian government.[39] When Glubb arrived in Transjordan in November 1930 as second-in-command to the Arab Legion's founder, Frederick Peake, he was given free reign 'to take "immediate" punitive action in the desert'.[40] Yet Glubb preferred to focus on cooperation. He was given 'a free hand in raising a Bedouin police'.[41] And by distancing himself from the Arab Legion – which the tribes considered their enemy – and distributing money during what was a period of economic crisis, Glubb persuaded the Jordanian tribes to stop raiding and cooperate. With the help of Bedouin who had served with him in Iraq, Glubb was able to recruit tribesmen in Transjordan – who were also traditionally

---

[37] Glubb, *Arabian Adventures*, pp. 161–85.

[38] Ibid., pp. 172–85; Glubb, *Changing Scenes*, pp. 83–94.

[39] Alon, *Making of Jordan*, pp. 87–92.

[40] Robert S. G. Fletcher, *British Imperialism and 'The Tribal Question': Desert Administration and Nomadic Societies in the Middle East, 1919–1936* (Oxford, 2015), p. 241.

[41] Humphreys to Glubb, 9 December 1930, GP2006, 4.

suspicious of the central government – into his new force: the Desert Patrol.[42] He convinced the tribes that it was in their interest to work with him, that they would get good government pay, and, if they stopped raiding, they could breed their own flocks.[43] Moreover, by enlisting the sons of Bedouin shaykhs into his Desert Patrol, Glubb gave these tribal leaders a stake in the central government's authority. This was a crucial pacification technique in itself, and by the summer of 1932 Glubb had successfully brought tribal raiding from both sides of the border to an end.[44] In his own words, this had been achieved 'without firing a shot or sending a man to prison'.[45] Despite Glubb's cooperation with Bedouin shaykhs, the central authority's relationship with the desert tribes remained subject to moments of restlessness and punitive action was always a tool in the armoury of the Desert Patrol. Yet Glubb preferred to control the desert periphery using methods of persuasion, such as the provision of subsidies and the offer of employment.[46] In his own somewhat rosy summary: 'The basis of our desert control was not force but persuasion and love.'[47]

Glubb's construction of the Desert Patrol had a profound effect on the very nature of the Arab Legion after he replaced Peake as the force's commander in 1939. Glubb's cooperation with the Bedouin and their integration into the Desert Patrol was the very antithesis of the Arab Legion created by Peake, who had little interest in the desert periphery and considered the nomadic tribes nothing more than a nuisance.[48] He therefore excluded the Bedouin from the Arab Legion. As Peake explained: 'My policy was to raise a Force from the sedentary, or village, Arabs, which would gradually be able to check the Bedouin and allow an Arab Government to rule the country without fear from tribal chiefs.'[49] Glubb, meanwhile, was more wary of the *hadari* – men from settled towns and villages – because they tended to be better educated and therefore more inclined to be politically minded.[50] When Peake retired in 1939 the makeup of the Arab Legion therefore began to change, as the integration

[42] Alon, *Making of Jordan*, pp. 92–8; John Glubb, *The Story of the Arab Legion* (London, 1948), pp. 91–3.

[43] Alon, *Making of Jordan*, p. 99.

[44] Ibid., p. 98; Glubb, *Changing Scenes*, pp. 99–102; James Lunt, *Glubb Pasha: A Biography* (London, 1984), p. 80.

[45] Glubb, *Changing Scenes*, p. 145.

[46] Alon, *Making of Jordan*, pp. 121–4; Glubb, *Story of the Arab Legion*, p. 170.

[47] Glubb, *Changing Scenes*, p. 105.

[48] Fletcher, *Tribal Question*, p. 256; P. J. Vatikiotis, *Politics and the Military in Jordan: A Study of the Arab Legion, 1921–1957* (London, 1967), p. 69.

[49] Quoted in: Massad, *Colonial Effects*, p. 106.

[50] Peter Young, *The Arab Legion* (Reading, 1972), p. 22; John Glubb, *A Soldier with the Arabs* (London, 1957), p. 436.

of the Bedouin became a crucial component of the force that Glubb moulded.[51] He raised several all-Bedouin battalions, which became the cornerstone of Glubb's Arab Legion.[52]

This was not the only change the Arab Legion was subjected to once Glubb took charge. Under Peake's command the Arab Legion was essentially a gendarmerie, or police force, charged with maintaining internal security of this fledgling political entity.[53] But just months after Glubb replaced Peake as commander of the Arab Legion, the Second World War broke out and the Arab Legion had to adapt. Almost overnight it was revolutionised, converted from an internal security force of approximately 1,000 men in 1939 into an ad hoc army containing about 6,000 men by 1945. It is Glubb's role as commander of the Arab Legion with which he has become synonymous, and this book explores the evolving role of this newly formed army and its British commander thereafter; until Britain's formal connection with Jordan and the Arab Legion ended in 1957, twelve months after Abdullah's grandson, King Hussein, ordered Glubb to leave the country.

Hitherto the Arab Legion has largely been spared significant critical analysis. It does feature prominently in Ron Pundik's account of Anglo–Jordanian relations, as well as *The Hashemite Kingdom of Jordan*, written by former Arab Legion officer Maan Abu Nowar.[54] The nature and existence of this force, though, has often been taken for granted. As a subject it has predominantly been the preserve of its former officers.[55] Along with an account by journalist Godfrey Lias, who described his experience observing the Arab Legion while 'in search of a story of adventure', these books merely provide a narrative account of life within the force they had fond memories of serving, but offer very little in terms of critical analysis or the wider context of British policy and regional politics; they are essentially memoirs and not based on extensive archival research.[56] The most detailed analytical appraisal remains Vatikiotis's 1967 *Study of the Arab*

---

[51] Alon, *Making of Jordan*, pp. 120–1.

[52] Vatikiotis, *Politics and the Military*, pp. 72–3; Young, *Arab Legion*, p. 22; Glubb, *Soldier*, p. 436.

[53] Anderson, *Nationalist Voices*, p. 43; Vatikiotis, *Politics and the Military*, p. 75.

[54] Pundik, *Struggle for Sovereignty*; Maan Abu Nowar, *The Struggle for Independence 1939–1947: A History of the Hashemite Kingdom of Jordan* (Reading, 2001); Maan Abu Nowar, *The Jordanian–Israeli War 1948–1951: A History of the Hashemite Kingdom of Jordan* (Reading, 2002).

[55] James Lunt, *The Arab Legion, 1923–1957* (London, 1999); Peter Young, *Bedouin Command: With the Arab Legion, 1953–1956* (London, 1956); Young, *Arab Legion*; Glubb, *Soldier*; Glubb, *Story of the Arab Legion*.

[56] Godfrey Lias, *Glubb's Legion* (London, 1956), p. 7.

Legion. In this 'study in civil–military relations' he provided an intricate account of the Arab Legion's evolving structure from its inception to its demise and it contains much of continuing value. However, it was written prior to the opening of the official British archives and also scarcely looked beyond the parochial. For instance, Vatikiotis identified the Arab Legion's expansion between 1948 and 1956 as part of a coherent post-war British policy to consolidate the Arab Legion as a military force, and he linked this primarily to the border tension with Israel.[57] This claim has since remained unchallenged. Both Ilan Pappé and Ron Pundik identify the Arab Legion as a primary asset, which the British sought to cultivate.[58] This book, though, debunks this contention.

If, as a subject, the Arab Legion has remained relatively under-researched, as a component part of broader studies of imperial defence it has been almost completely overlooked. No doubt because Jordan was not a formal British colony, the Arab Legion remained excluded from Ashley Jackson's recent exploration of the role of the colonies in Britain's imperial defence system.[59] Similarly, as the Arab Legion was also not a formal part of the British military forces, it is also absent from David French's recent study, which sought to remedy the absence of the British Army from post-war British history.[60] The Arab Legion's complex status, as the army of an independent country, but funded by Britain and commanded by a British officer, has caused it to slip through the historiographical net. There thus remains a need for a more thorough account of the Arab Legion's existence and its place in the British world system. Indeed, one of the questions this book considers is: to what extent, and in what context, did the Arab Legion have a wider imperial defence function, beyond its role inside Jordan?

Within the existing literature, Glubb has been a more prominent subject of study than the force he commanded. This no doubt taps into an innate desire to personify history. During his career in the Middle East Glubb often found himself referred to as a 'second Lawrence of Arabia'. This was not an association that Glubb welcomed, and a close friend and

---

[57] Vatikiotis, *Politics and the Military*, pp. ix, 74.
[58] Pundik, *Struggle for Sovereignty*, p. 43; Ilan Pappé, 'Sir Alec Kirkbride and the Anglo–Trans-Jordanian Alliance, 1945–50', in: John Zametica (ed.), *British Officials and British Foreign Policy 1945–50* (Leicester, 1990), p. 126.
[59] Ashley Jackson, *Distant Drums: The Role of Colonies in British Imperial Warfare* (Brighton, 2010), p. 15.
[60] David French, *Army, Empire, and Cold War: The British Army and Military Policy, 1945–1971* (Oxford, 2012), p. 1.

colleague of Glubb's described this portrayal as a 'poor compliment'.[61] Nonetheless, Glubb has personified the romanticism of the Englishman in Arabia and the first two biographies of Glubb were targeted at the romantic fascination of armchair adventurers.[62] As a political figure, Glubb has polarised opinion, both amongst his contemporaries and historians. Former British officer of the Arab Legion Peter Young described Glubb as a 'deeply religious ... man of such unshakeable integrity' that he would not abuse his power over the Arab Legion to cow the Jordanian government.[63] In stark contrast, Palestinian-Egyptian writer Said Aburish described Glubb as 'a narrow-minded-Bible-thumper [who] always behaved as if he were the uncrowned king of Jordan'.[64] Jordanian historians Sulayman Musa and Kamal Salibi both provide generally positive portrayals of Glubb. Musa comments on Glubb's 'success' in his task of maintaining order and integrating the Bedouin into the state; a feat 'achieved by goodwill and by dealing with the people according to their own traditions, habits and way of life'.[65] Salibi, meanwhile, argues that: 'More than any other Englishman of his time, Glubb loved the tribal Arabs and knew how to win their affection and trust.'[66] Musa's and Salibi's appraisals both fit the pro-Hashemite slant of their work. This is at odds with Joseph Massad who portrayed Glubb as the personification of empire.[67] The crux of Massad's analysis is that Glubb followed a dual policy of de-Bedouinizing the Bedouin, on one hand, while creating a new Bedouin culture throughout the country based on his own orientalist image of what the Bedouin should be, on the other.[68] Andrew Shryock has described Massad's critique as a confusing mix of 'character assassination and hagiography ... with the odd result that Glubb emerges as the only well-rounded character, the only "actor"'.[69] Yoav Alon is also critical of Massad, to the extent that *Colonial Effects* directly prompted him to provide 'a corrective portrayal of Glubb'. Focusing on his 'work

[61] Glubb to Foot, 28 February 1944, GP2006, 83; 'Glubb Pasha', Melville to Stanley Priddle (Reuters), 9 February 1956, Melville Papers, 4/45, MECA.

[62] Lunt, *Glubb Pasha*; Trevor Royle, *Glubb Pasha: The Life and Times of Sir John Bagot Glubb, Commander of the Arab Legion* (London, 1992).

[63] Young, *Arab Legion*, p. 19.

[64] Said Aburish, *Nasser: The Last Arab* (London, 2004), p. 97. The *New York Times*, 3 March 1956, also described Glubb as 'the uncrowned king of Jordan'.

[65] Musa, *Cameos*, p. 117.

[66] Salibi, *Modern History of Jordan*, p. 116.

[67] Massad, *Colonial Effects*, p. 111.

[68] Ibid., pp. 124–5.

[69] Andrew Shryock, 'Review of Colonial Effects', *International Journal of Middle East Studies*, 38:3 (2006), p. 479.

in the desert' during the inter-war period, Alon's 'main argument' is that 'Glubb was a unique colonial administrator who tried to combine the interests of Britain with those of the local nomads'.[70] Emphasising Glubb's persuasive approach – his use of respect and cooperation – Alon explains that this led to a 'less troubled relationship between the colonizer and the colonized than in more typical colonial settings'.[71] In his efforts to counter Massad's appraisal, Alon teeters on the edge of exonerating Glubb. The historian's task, though, should be to neither blame nor absolve, but merely to understand.[72] Nonetheless, Alon convincingly debunks Massad's omnipotent portrayal of Glubb. While Massad is correct to acknowledge that Glubb used the Bedouin as a means of control, they were not merely exploited by Glubb and he was not the sole reason for the changes to their way of life and the construction of a Jordanian national identity. Glubb's relationship with the Bedouin is not a key feature of this book's analysis; the pertinence of this debate, though, is that we should be wary of viewing Glubb, like Massad does, as an all-powerful arm of the British Empire. This appraisal is too simplistic. Glubb was undoubtedly a key actor in the history of the Hashemite Kingdom, and his construction of the Arab Legion has surely contributed to Jordan's political stability in comparison to its neighbours, where military coups have been a frequent occurrence. Yet Massad has exaggerated Glubb's Machiavellian influence and underplayed his limitations. The strength of Massad's study lies in what Betty Anderson has praised as his 'excellent analysis of state construction in the colonial realm', for providing 'questions and answers about nationalism that few writers have posed before'.[73] It is unfortunate that his use of Glubb as a 'metonym for Empire' has resulted in a somewhat distorted portrayal of the former Arab Legion commander.[74]

The nub of the Glubb debate is: whom was he working for? And where did his loyalties lie? In the very first page of his memoirs, Glubb nailed his loyalty firmly to the Jordanian mast, as he recounted a pledge to Abdullah that he 'would act always as if [he] had been born a Trans-Jordanian', unless the two countries should find themselves pitted against each other

[70] Yoav Alon, 'British Colonialism and Orientalism in Arabia: Glubb Pasha in Transjordan, 1930–1946', *British Scholar*, 3:1 (2010), pp. 106–7.
[71] Ibid., p. 124.
[72] Avi Shlaim, 'The Debate about 1948', *International Journal of Middle East Studies*, 27:3 (1995), p. 290.
[73] Anderson, 'Review Essay', pp. 201–2.
[74] Massad, *Colonial Effects*, p. 111.

in war.[75] Moreover, he maintained: 'I had no official connection with the British government at all, nor did the latter ever attempt to interfere or give orders.'[76] This appraisal is not strictly true, as the Arab Legion was deeply wired into the British system. While Glubb might not have been a British stooge and Britain may not have interfered with day-to-day decisions, the Arab Legion was wholly dependent on the British Treasury for financing, and Glubb was in regular contact with the British political and military authorities. For Avi Shlaim, therefore, Glubb was 'really an imperial proconsul' and his 'primary loyalty was to Britain'.[77] Maureen Norton goes further. She asserts that Glubb's sole motivation was to further British interests; he was driven 'to seek solutions for his homeland's political and economic difficulties'.[78] Kamal Salibi disagrees, though. He contends that Glubb 'served Abdullah with loyalty, using his influence with the tribes to marshal support for the emir rather than to intrigue against him, as other British officers who had influence with the tribes often did'.[79] Similarly, Benny Morris describes Glubb as, 'above all, the Hashemite's obedient and loyal retainer and the Arabs' most successful general'. Morris argues that 'in the pivotal historical junctions he behaved like a loyal servant of the Hashemite crown rather than an Agent of Whitehall's', adding: 'Glubb felt that British and Arab interests converged and overlapped.'[80] Hatem al-Sarairah agrees that, 'When there was a compatibility in the interests of his masters, Glubb would execute his orders with enthusiasm and complete devotion to both.' However, in contrast to Morris, Sarairah posits that, when 'they disagreed on a certain issue, he would choose to follow the orders that he received from Whitehall'.[81] Ultimately, as Morris asserts, the 'truth' of Glubb's loyalty was 'complex'. Certainly more so than Norton asserts.[82] Glubb did not think in terms of Britain, the homeland, but Britain, the empire. That was his frame of reference. As Glubb saw it, Jordan was a contingent part of Britain's empire and it was best served by remaining so; what was good for Jordan was good for Britain and vice versa. Despite using the threat of resignation on several occasions, in essence Glubb was

[75] Glubb, *Soldier*, p. 19.
[76] Ibid., p. 420.
[77] Avi Shlaim, *Collusion across the Jordan: King Abdullah, the Zionist Movement, and the Partition of Palestine* (Oxford, 1988), p. 224.
[78] Maureen Norton, 'The Last Pasha: Sir John Glubb and the British Empire in the Middle East, 1920–1949' (Johns Hopkins University: PhD thesis, 1997), p. 372.
[79] Salibi, *Modern History of Jordan*, p. 116.
[80] Benny Morris, *Road to Jerusalem: Glubb Pasha, Palestine and the Jews* (London, 2002), p. 238–9.
[81] Hatem Ahmed al-Sarairah, 'A British Actor on the Bedouin Stage: Glubb's Career in Jordan, 1930–1956' (Indiana University, PhD thesis, 1989), p. 232.
[82] Morris, *Road to Jerusalem*, p. 240.

most loyal to the *role*, to the Arab Legion, as an intermediary. Glubb conceived that 'an Englishman in Arabia is a double diplomat – he must represent British interests to the Arabs, and Arab interests to the British'.[83] As this book illustrates, Glubb effectively adhered to this mantra. He was not just a man on the spot, but a man in the middle. He had his own ideas and theories about how the interests of Britain and Jordan were best served, and at times this led him to clash with both of his masters. Glubb's ultimate loyalty was to the British Empire as the umbrella organisation, but that should not distract from the fact that he was also a loyal advocate and defender of Jordan and the Hashemites.

SOURCES

What makes this assessment of Glubb and the Arab Legion particularly pertinent is its access to significant new sources, in terms of both quality and quantity. This book is based on two principal archival collections. In the first instance it relies on the official British government records held at The National Archives in Kew, London. The official records of the various Whitehall departments – principally the Foreign Office, Colonial Office, War Office, Treasury, and Cabinet – provide vital insight into the role of the Arab Legion within British policy. While much of this material – which include minutes, memos, and correspondence between Whitehall departments and the embassy in Amman – has been available to previous researchers, this book benefits from several crucial documents obtained via Freedom of Information requests. Moreover, Chapters 6–8 are based heavily on documents released in the twenty-first century under an extended fifty-year rule.

Jordanian documents, unfortunately, are not freely accessible. The Royal Hashemite Archives are not open for public use, but restricted to loyal Jordanian historians.[84] One exception to this is Nigel Ashton, who was 'afforded full and unfettered access to King Hussein's correspondence files', after eight years of perseverance, for his biography of the king. Ashton's access to official Jordanian archives was very much an exception to the rule. Moreover, he did not have access to material relating to the particularly sensitive period during the Abdullah era concerning the partition of Palestine and the 1948 War. As he acknowledged, the correspondence he did have access to primarily concerns the 1970s, 1980s,

---

[83] 'Notes on Arab Subjects', Glubb, 1 March 1944, GP2006, 95.
[84] Eugene Rogan, 'Jordan and 1948: The Persistence of an Official History', in: Eugene Rogan and Avi Shlaim (eds.), *The War for Palestine: Rewriting the History of 1948*, 2nd edn (Cambridge, 2007), p. 105.

and 1990s.[85] Despite the inaccessibility of Arab state archives, a number of important Arab sources are available. The Jordanian government has published a selection of documents from the Royal Hashemite Archives.[86] And a portion of Jordanian documents captured during the 1967 War can be found in the Israel State Archives.[87]

Media records, oral testimonies, and memoirs are also invaluable. Memoirs, just like oral recollections, must of course be treated with caution; in particular, it is important to consider the authors' motivation and the context within which they were written. The publication of both parts of Abdullah's memoirs, for example, seemingly had a political purpose, designed to legitimise the expansion of his rule. The first part was published at the end of the Second World War when Abdullah was actively pursuing his dynastic ambitions and, as Joseph Nevo points out, seems designed to legitimise Abdullah's claims to a Greater Syrian kingdom, encompassing much of what had become Transjordan, Palestine, Lebanon, and Syria.[88] It is surely for that reason that much attention is devoted to his family's role in the Arab Revolt during the First World War, and to the need for unity in the Arab world. Meanwhile, the second and final part of Abdullah's memoirs was published shortly before his assassination, when he was seeking to legitimise the recent incorporation of the West Bank of Palestine into his kingdom in the aftermath of the 1948 War. It is perhaps for this reason that Abdullah reveals scant detail about this conflict. He did discuss the 1948 War, but with the caveat that 'it is not seemly for me to go into certain confidential matters which should be kept hidden in the interest of the Arabs ... for the right to do so belongs to the Arab states as a whole'.[89] We thus have to look to other sources to build a fuller picture.

Despite their occasional omissions or biases, memoirs remain invaluable, providing useful insights into their authors' psyches, hinting at their ambitions and concerns. This is particularly pertinent for Abdullah, whose memoirs were written during the period under study. It is noteworthy, for example, that in the first part of his memoirs, written at the end of the Second World War, Abdullah described the wartime expansion

[85] Ashton, *King Hussein of Jordan*, p. ix.
[86] *The Hashemite Documents: Papers of King Abdullah* (Amman, 1995).
[87] Avi Shlaim, *The Iron Wall: Israel and the Arab World* (London, 2000), p. 85.
[88] Joseph Nevo, 'Abdallah's Memoirs as Historical Source Material', in: Asher Susser and Aryeh Shmuelebitz (eds.), *The Hashemites in the Modern Arab World: Essays in Honour of the Late Professor Uriel Dann* (London, 1995), pp. 168–9.
[89] King Abdullah, *My Memoirs Completed: 'Al-Takmilah'* (London, 1978), p. 20.

of the Arab Legion as 'a fine achievement ... due to the energy and sincerity of General Glubb Pasha'.[90] Yet in the second part of his memoirs, written a year or so after the 1948 War, Abdullah made no reference at all to Glubb, even on the two pages devoted to the Arab Legion, which he described as 'the sword and bulwark of the land, the pivot of its strength; it is the voice of the country, the scourge of those who are hostile to it, the pitfall of its enemies, and the apple of its ruler's eye'. Abdullah acknowledged 'the good work done by our British ally in providing us with needed arms and ammunition'; he thanked and praised the 'brotherhood and comradeship between the Arabs and the British who make up this army'; but Glubb was conspicuous by his absence.[91] This is no doubt evidence that Abdullah was mindful of the increasing criticism he faced throughout the Arab world for being little more than a British stooge, and a telling sign that the political climate, and Glubb's portrayal within it, had changed dramatically in five years – largely as a result of the 1948 War in Palestine and the creation of Israel. Abdullah was still determined to justify his alliance with Britain, but publicly distanced himself from Glubb: the man who personified imperial control to the rest of the Arab world.

The danger of using memoirs as a historical record is not unique to Arab participants. The point is merely made in this regard because of the lack of indigenous archival sources with which to corroborate them. Which is not to say that official archival records can be completely relied on to tell an accurate story. As Ilana Feldman warns, filing systems and in turn, the building of archives, are government constructs, subject to their own internal biases.[92] Archives, just like memoirs, are prone to both selective and inadvertent omission. The 2011 revelation that a tranche of Britain's colonial documents was hidden in a secret government archive at Hanslope Park, Buckinghamshire – with their existence previously denied – is illustrative of this problem.[93] None of the material from this 'Migrated Archive' – which has since been released – related to Jordan, but it is sobering to note that 'only 2 to 5 percent of [British] government records' are selected for permanent preservation in The National

---

[90] King Abdullah, *Memoirs of King Abdullah of Transjordan* (London, 1951), pp. 230, 241.
[91] Abdullah, *Al-Takmilah*, pp. 73–4.
[92] Ilana Feldman, *Governing Gaza: Bureaucracy, Authority, and the Work of Rule, 1917–1967* (London, 2008), pp. 31–62.
[93] David M. Anderson, 'Guilty Secrets: Deceit, Denial, and the Discovery of Kenya's "Migrated Archive"', *History Workshop Journal*, 80:1 (2015), pp. 142–60.

Archives; the other 95 per cent destroyed.[94] This has led David Anderson
to assert that: 'Archives are not in any sense primarily about transparency
and openness: they are, and have always been, the product of negotiation,
selectivity, and censorship.'[95] The rationale for this process is not always
sinister; in part it is simply a space-saving exercise. Whatever the reason
for material being hidden or destroyed, though, it is nonetheless important to maintain a healthy scepticism of the archival record also.

This has manifested itself in a recent trend in studies that have sought
to peer behind the official veneer of state archives; and to decode the
official language contained in documents 'written by individuals shaped
by a particular set of ideas and cultural concepts, a *mentalité*'.[96] Rashid
Khalidi warns that the term 'security', for example – a term particularly pertinent to this study – 'generally meant … forcible suppression'.[97]
Khalidi was speaking in reference to the 'forcible suppression of the
aspirations of the Arab majority' during the 1936 revolt in Palestine. It
would be wrong to equate this euphemism always to violent deterrence.
Laleh Khalili describes a spectrum of counterinsurgency tactics. At one
end of the scale is 'enemy-centric counterinsurgency', which 'depends on
coercive or punitive measures to deter the civilian population from supporting the unconventional forces'. Rashid Khalidi's definition is typical
of this. At the other end of the scale is 'population-centric counterinsurgency'. This 'is meant to win over that population by "securing" and
"protecting" them, as well as by providing services that would win over
that population'.[98] Glubb's role in the establishment of health and education systems in the desert fits this population-centric model, as does the
very existence of the Arab Legion, as an apparatus for security and protection, though that does not mean it could not also be used in 'enemy-
centric' practices.[99] In both cases, however, it is primarily the interests of
the imperial power that are ultimately being secured.

Archives, just like all sources, have limitations and euphemisms. They
are nonetheless indispensable wells of information. Thus, the British

[94] Edward Hampshire, '"Apply the Flame More Searingly": The Destruction and Migration
    of the Archives of British Colonial Administration: A Southeast Asia Case Study', *Journal
    of Imperial and Commonwealth History*, 41:2 (2013), pp. 335–6.
[95] Anderson, 'Guilty Secrets', p. 144.
[96] Satia, *Spies in Arabia*, p. 12.
[97] Rashid Khalidi, *The Iron Cage: The Story of the Palestinian Struggle for Statehood*
    (Oxford, 2007), p. 28.
[98] Khalili, *Time in the Shadows*, pp. 45–6.
[99] Alon, *Making of Jordan*, pp. 133–8.

National Archives is crucial to this study, and the relative inaccessibility of the Jordanian state archives is unfortunate. Yet as Avi Shlaim counselled:

> A Military historian of the Middle Ages would be green with envy at the sight of the sources available to his contemporary Middle Eastern counterpart. Historians ... would do much better to explore in depth the manifold sources that are available to them than to lament the denial of access to the Arab state archives.[100]

This book adheres to this mantra, and is able to make use of a wealth of previously unseen documents with which to calibrate existing accounts.

For while the official Arab archives remain closed, this book is able to remedy this absence via unprecedented access to what is best described as the *unofficial archive of the Arab Legion*, held at the Middle East Centre Archive at St Antony's College, Oxford. Housed in the impressive new building designed by the late Dame Zaha Hadid, this utterly vital new source material is a major driving force of this study and is principally comprised of two highly significant collections of private papers. The most important of these are the private papers of Glubb himself. Upon his death in 1986 fourteen boxes of material, pre-selected by Glubb, were deposited to the archive. Twenty years later after his wife, Rosemary, passed away, the Glubb family generously deposited the remainder of Glubb's private papers – a further 100 boxes, which complete this collection. Because of the enormous scale of this recent accession to the archive it remains uncatalogued. I am tremendously grateful, therefore, to the archivist, Debbie Usher, for expediting the re-housing of these documents and creating a draft box list, specifically to make the material available for this project.[101] The Glubb collection is a jumbled assortment of papers, where official reports and correspondence sit alongside newspaper cuttings and Christmas cards. The uncatalogued nature of this mass of hoarded material has provided one of the main challenges to this study. However, the rewards, as this book testifies, are great. When Elizabeth Monroe was establishing the Middle East Centre Archive in the 1960s, she contacted Glubb about the existence of any privately held records.[102] Glubb acknowledged that, 'I have a lot of papers', however, he downplayed their value, noting: 'I think that most of them are at a fairly humble level. Matters of local administration rather than the fate

---

[100] Shlaim, 'Debate about 1948', p. 290.
[101] To differentiate the two accessions, which are currently housed separately, they will be identified in the footnotes as: GP1986 and GP2006. The box numbers refer to the current, temporary housing of the collection.
[102] Monroe to Glubb, 9 February 1966, GP2006, 40.

of empires.'[103] It was Glubb, though, who was being humble. Admittedly, the Glubb collection contains its fair share of the mundane. But it is an exceptionally rich source for anyone interested in Britain's moment in the Middle East.

The Glubb collection is absolutely pivotal to this book. It is therefore only prudent to outline its provenance. In essence, the 2006 accession contains any and all of the paperwork found at Glubb's family home when it was being cleared following the death of Lady Glubb.[104] A substantial part of this collection thus includes material from Glubb's life after he left the Middle East – including book drafts and correspondence with publishers. The material most salient to this project concerns the working papers from Glubb's time in the Arab Legion, particularly Glubb's scattered diary-like notes and correspondence with the British political and military authorities and with other officers within the Arab Legion. While Glubb's papers are not especially well organised – it does not resemble a set of files taken directly from the office; probably because Glubb clearly reorganised this material to assist in the writing of his many books – there is nonetheless a coherent paper trail detailing its overall provenance. When he was first notified of King Hussein's decision to dismiss him on 1 March 1956, Glubb was given just two hours' notice to leave the country. However, Glubb refused to go at such short notice, and it was agreed that he could leave at 7.00 the following morning. This brief period of respite enabled Glubb time to salvage the material that forms an integral component of this study. Before Glubb departed, he and the British ambassador, Charles Duke, 'discussed what arrangements were possible for the disposal of various secret documents and other material which it would be embarrassing to leave in the possession of Jordanians'. As Duke explained:

We arranged that General Glubb should send to the Embassy certain of his papers and more precious personal possessions for safe custody, and should destroy as far as possible anything else which would be compromising. We also arranged to try and get as many as possible of the files which General Glubb kept in his own personal custody in his office. His Private Secretary and a British Officer succeeded in getting some of these, but were eventually prevented from taking the rest out of Arab Legion Headquarters.[105]

---

[103] Glubb to Monroe, 6 March 1966, Administration Records, MECA.
[104] I am grateful to Eugene Rogan and Debbie Usher for their accounts of retrieving this material.
[105] 'The Dismissal of Glubb', Duke to Lloyd, 8 March 1956, PREM11/1419, TNA.

J. R. B. Knox, an Arab Legion officer who superintended the packing of Glubb's belongings, confirmed that practically all of Glubb's papers made it to the embassy, 'though one box of papers was removed by the Arabs'.[106] It is this material that Glubb was able to salvage which forms the backbone and the driving force of this book, and which elevates this study above all previous accounts of Glubb and the Arab Legion.

Four other studies have made partial use of this material, but they have only scratched the surface. James Lunt's 1984 biography refers to Glubb's private collection in his acknowledgements. However, he clearly had only limited access, as Lunt makes no reference to much of the material on which this book has drawn.[107] Trevor Royle's biography of Glubb also mentions his private papers. Royle extols his gratitude to Glubb's wife for the 'loan of documents'. Yet Royle's belief that 'the bulk of his collection was donated to the archives of the Middle East Centre' when Glubb died reveals that he was unaware that the original accession was merely the tip of the iceberg.[108] The third study to have used any of this material is Robert Fletcher's re-orientation of British activity in the Arabian deserts during the inter-war period. While Fletcher has had access to the full collection deposited at the archive in 2006, his study addresses an earlier period and a different aspect of Glubb's career, within the context of a broader study of colonial administration in the desert peripheries.[109] A fourth study to have accessed this material was published just as the present book was going to press. *The Glubb Reports*, edited by Tancred Bradshaw, attempts to elicit Glubb's views on the political issues facing the Middle East throughout his career. However, it repeats a number of the misplaced contentions corrected here. Its main value lies simply in its full transcription of sixty-three documents written by Glubb, though it only includes a total of eight documents from the 2006 accession of Glubb's papers.[110] This is perhaps indicative of the fact that this collection, in its current uncatalogued state, is impossible to comprehensively navigate without meticulously trawling through the entire collection; the existing temporary box list can only guide you so far.

[106] 'Notes on Meeting with Brigadier Mead', VCIGS to CIGS, 12 March 1956, WO216/912, TNA.
[107] Lunt, *Glubb Pasha*, p. 237.
[108] Royle, *Glubb Pasha*, p. xv.
[109] Fletcher, *Tribal Question*, p. 273.
[110] Tancred Bradshaw (ed.), *The Glubb Reports: Glubb Pasha and Britain's Empire Project in the Middle East 1920–1956* (Basingstoke, 2016).

The second part of the unofficial Arab Legion archive is the private papers of Lieutenant-Colonel Robert Melville, which were deposited alongside the Glubb collection after I met him at his home in London in 2013. Having served with the Arab Legion since the Second World War, Melville became Glubb's man in London, where he ran the Arab Legion Staff Liaison Office between 1949 and 1956. This office was established to bridge the gap between the Arab Legion and Whitehall created by the Britain's withdrawal from Palestine in 1948. Unlike Glubb's papers, the Melville collection feels much more like an official archive than a collection of randomly hoarded private papers. While it is also uncatalogued, owing to its recent accession to the archive, the Melville collection is neatly self-structured, as it is effectively the organised files of the Arab Legion's London office, which were removed when it was shut down after Melville's dismissal, a few months after Glubb's departure in 1956. The Melville collection excels in revealing the nature of the Arab Legion beyond the 1948 War. It is particularly useful for understanding the size, shape, and purpose of the Arab Legion, and its relationship with the British government. Combined, the Glubb and Melville collections provide a unique insight into and have enabled a completely fresh assessment of Glubb Pasha and the Arab Legion.

CONTENT AND STRUCTURE

The most exciting feature of this new material is what it reveals about the partition of Palestine and the 1948 War. It has enabled a significant reappraisal of a well-worn debate, which maintains significant contemporary resonance. As Kirsten Schulze reminds us: '[T]he debate on what exactly happened in the 1948 War and who did what to whom is not just history. It cuts to the heart of the Israeli–Palestinian conflict, past and present, and remains one of the most important factors in achieving a just and lasting peace between Israelis and Palestinians.'[111] This continued contemporary resonance has helped maintain a lively historical debate. During the first three decades following the 1948 War, the historiography was dominated by an official Zionist history, written by veterans of the conflict, which pitched Israel as the underdog in a 'fight between David and Goliath, between the boys of Israel and the Arab armies backed by powerful Britain'.[112]

---

[111] Kirsten E. Schulze, 'The 1948 War: The Battle over History', in: Joel Peters and David Newman (eds.), *The Routledge Handbook on the Israeli–Palestinian Conflict* (London, 2013), p. 46.

[112] Moshe Shertok speaking on Israeli Radio, *Summary of World Broadcasts* [hereafter: *SWB*], Part III, *Western Europe, Middle East, Far East, and Americas* (BBC), 8 July 1948, p. 70. See, for example: Chaim Herzog, *The Arab–Israeli Wars: War and Peace in the Middle East* (London, 1982), pp. 21–108; Moshe Dayan, *Story of My Life* (London, 1976), pp. 65–94.

The opening of the official archives in Britain, Israel, and the United States in the late 1970s prompted a wave of revisionist histories.[113] This group of Israeli historians challenged three key issues: the causes of the refugee crisis; the military balance of the war; and the reasons why a formal peace settlement proved elusive.[114] It is the military balance issue and its three subsidiary controversies – the Hashemite–Zionist relationship; the war aims of the Arab states; and the role of Britain – that concern us here. The flag-bearer for the revisionist take on the military balance of the war is Avi Shlaim's controversial *Collusion* thesis. Like Uri Bar-Joseph, who described Israel and Transjordan as the *Best of Enemies*, Shlaim gave scholarly, archival-based credence to the charge that King Abdullah colluded with the Zionists to partition Palestine in contravention of the November 1947 UN partition plan, which proposed the creation of an independent Jewish state and an independent Arab state when the British mandate ended in May 1948. A subsidiary contention is that Britain supported this 'collusion'.[115] In his abridged paperback edition, Shlaim removed the word 'collusion' from the title, as he believed this had distracted from the crux of his argument. He maintained, though, that it was an accurate description of the British aspect of the thesis.[116] In a subsequent article Shlaim regretted omitting the term 'collusion' and reiterated that it was an apt description for both parts of his thesis.[117] Regardless of the terminological semantics, though, the significance of these negotiations, for Pappé, Shlaim, Morris, and others, was that they helped dictate the outcome of the 1948 War.[118] The most vocal critic of the revisionist accounts of 1948 is Efraim Karsh, with whom Shlaim has traded accusations of 'distorting and misrepresenting' the available evidence.[119] Karsh offers a polar opposite interpretation of the crucial meetings where agreements are alleged to have been made.[120] Another critic,

[113] Simha Flapan, *The Birth of Israel: Myths and Realities* (New York, 1987); Shlaim, *Collusion*; Benny Morris, *The Birth of the Palestinian Refugee Problem, 1947–1949*, paperback edn (Cambridge, 1989); Ilan Pappé, *Britain and the Arab–Israeli Conflict, 1948–51* (Oxford, 1988).

[114] For a historiographical overview, see: Shlaim, 'Debate about 1948', pp. 287–304; Schulze, 'Battle over History', pp. 45–55.

[115] Uri Bar-Joseph, *The Best of Enemies: Israel and Transjordan in the War of 1948* (London, 1987); Shlaim, *Collusion*, p. 1.

[116] Avi Shlaim, *The Politics of Partition: King Abdullah, the Zionists and Palestine, 1921–1951* (Oxford, 1990), p. vii–viii.

[117] Shlaim, 'Debate about 1948', pp. 298–9.

[118] Pappé, *Britain and the Arab–Israeli Conflict*, p. 209.

[119] Avi Shlaim, 'A Totalitarian Concept of History' and Efraim Karsh, 'Historical Fictions', *Middle East Quarterly*, 3:3 (1996), pp. 52–60.

[120] Efraim Karsh, *Fabricating Israeli History: The New Historians* (London, 1997); Efraim Karsh, 'The Collusion That Never Was: King Abdullah, the Jewish Agency and the Partition of Palestine', *Journal of Contemporary History*, 34:4 (1999), pp. 569–85.

Joseph Heller, has suggested that Abdullah 'was in fact too busy fighting for his own political survival to take part in collusions'.[121] Meanwhile Avraham Sela has argued that any pre-war agreements were overtaken by subsequent events.[122] More recently, Tancred Bradshaw has reopened this debate. By disputing the interpretation of existing sources, like Karsh, Bradshaw argues that neither the Jewish Agency – the de facto government of the Zionist movement in Palestine – nor the British supported Abdullah's territorial ambitions in Palestine.[123] If nothing else, Bradshaw's contribution is evidence that, almost thirty years on from the publication of Shlaim's *Collusion* thesis, this debate is stuck in a cycle of revision and counter-revision based on conflicting interpretations and emphasis of the same set of sources.

The major obstacle that has held the debate back is the lack of access to the official records of the Arab states. This, Avi Shlaim lamented, has hampered the emergence of post-revisionism.[124] Indeed, even Eugene Rogan and Avi Shlaim's relatively recent edited collection, which set out to rewrite the history of 1948, admitted: 'In many cases, the paucity of new material limits the scope of revision. The authors present their work in the hope that official documents will be made available in Arab archives to permit a more thorough revision of the Arab–Israeli conflict.'[125] Perhaps the most significant addition to the 1948 debate in recent years is Matthew Hughes's account of Lebanon's involvement in the revised edition of Rogan and Shlaim's edited collection. Previously, Lebanon's role had been either 'exaggerated militarily or relegated to a few footnotes'. Aided by the newly available papers of Farid Chehab – the Lebanese director of general security – Hughes confirmed that the Lebanese military remained inactive and apathetic, thus further negating the David versus Goliath portrayal of the conflict.[126] Laila Parsons's new book based on the recently discovered papers of Fawzi al-Qawuqji, field

---

[121] Joseph Heller, *The Birth of Israel, 1945–1949: Ben-Gurion and His Critics* (Gainesville, 2000), p. 303.

[122] Avraham Sela, 'Transjordan, Israel and the 1948 War: Myth, Historiography and Reality', *Middle Eastern Studies*, 28:4 (1992), p. 627.

[123] Bradshaw, *Britain and Jordan*, pp. 147–9, 163–7; Tancred Bradshaw, 'History Invented: The British–Transjordanian "Collusion" Revisited', *Middle Eastern Studies*, 43:1 (2007), pp. 21–43.

[124] Shlaim, 'Debate about 1948', p. 290.

[125] Eugene Rogan and Avi Shlaim, 'Introduction', in: Rogan and Shlaim (eds.), *Rewriting the History of 1948*, p. 8.

[126] Matthew Hughes, 'Collusion across the Litani? Lebanon and the 1948 War', in: Rogan and Shlaim (eds.), *Rewriting the History of 1948*, pp. 204–27.

commander of the Arab Liberation Army created by the Arab League, is also set to be a welcome addition to the 1948 opus.[127] The most important Arab army in the 1948 War, though, was the Arab Legion. It was the best trained; it did most of the fighting; and it successfully secured the West Bank, which was annexed to Transjordan when the fighting finished. A better understanding of the Arab Legion's war aims and its conduct, therefore, is what the debate really needs. On the final page of his Glubb study, Benny Morris lamented that: 'Only the opening of the Arab states' archives – all, regrettably, closed to researchers – may provide a definitive answer.'[128] Aided by Glubb's papers, this book is able to offer a more accurate appreciation of the Arab Legion's involvement than has previously been possible, including its war aims and the rationale behind key decisions. It thus provides significant new insights into the nature of this conflict, which further shatters the David versus Goliath myth.

While this book is not formally divided into parts, the first half examines the Arab Legion's relationship with the Palestine issue. Chapter 1 details how the Palestine problem helped sustain the Arab Legion's existence after 1945, thwarting Britain's intention to disband 80 per cent of that force. This meant that when the United Nations recommended the partition of Palestine in 1947, the Arab Legion was a military force, and therefore Abdullah was a political force to be reckoned with. Meanwhile the following three chapters cut to the heart of the 1948 debate by examining Glubb and the Arab Legion's involvement in the 1948 War during three consecutive stages of the conflict: the civil war between November 1947 and May 1948; the first two stages of official fighting between Israel and the Arab states during the summer; and the final stage of the conflict leading to the armistice agreements that brought the fighting to an end in the spring of 1949. Via its focus on the conduct of the Arab Legion, Chapter 2 corroborates the significance of a meeting between the British foreign secretary, the Jordanian prime minister, and Glubb in February 1948. It confirms that this meeting defined the Arab Legion's conduct thereafter as Glubb subsequently prepared to implement an alternative and secret partition scheme. Meanwhile, Chapter 3 details how the secret pre-war negotiations continued to govern Glubb's strict adherence to the scheme of occupying the Arab areas of Palestine (as defined by

---

[127] Laila Parsons, *The Commander: Fawzi al-Qawuqji and the Fight for Arab Dependence* (New York, 2016) [published while this book was in press and has therefore not been consulted]; Laila Parsons, 'Soldiering for Arab Nationalism: Fawzi al-Qawuqji in Palestine', *Journal of Palestine Studies*, 36:4 (2007), pp. 33–6.

[128] Morris, *Road to Jerusalem*, pp. 241–2.

the UN partition scheme) and acquiescing in the establishment of Israel, despite the pan-Arab pressure on Abdullah. By distinguishing between the influence of Abdullah and Glubb, Chapter 3 reconciles the fighting between the Arab Legion and the Israel Defense Forces, particularly in Jerusalem, with the Arab Legion's otherwise limited approach to the conflict. Meanwhile, Chapter 4 emphasises the rivalry between Transjordan and Egypt, revealing the extent to which the two armies worked against each other. On the Arab Legion side, Glubb sought to ensure the defeat of the Egyptian Army as a means of enabling the start of peace negotiations. Based on significant new sources, this section debunks the David versus Goliath portrayal of the conflict. It corroborates the revisionist argument that pre-war negotiations between Abdullah and the Jewish Agency and between the Jordanians and the British helped shape the 1948 War. Yet by emphasising Glubb's limited autonomy, it posits a significant nuance, which reconciles some of the principal criticisms of the 'collusion' thesis.

This detailed appreciation of the 1948 War is important in its own right, but it is also a crucial component of a broader attempt to unpack the nature of Britain's involvement in the Middle East. This book does not purport to provide a universal explanation for Britain's position in the region and its wider retreat from empire, but an understanding of the situation within one particular locale: Jordan. In his study on Britain's post-war decline, John Darwin extolled the need to focus on a broad range of relationships in order to understand the deeper causes of decolonisation. Yet he also accentuated his indebtedness to more detailed studies of bilateral relations.[129] That is the entry point at which this study seeks to contribute to the broader issues. Using Glubb Pasha and the Arab Legion as a prism, this book seeks to explain why Britain maintained an imperial presence in Jordan – even after it was granted independence in 1946 – and why that connection was eventually severed.

Within the existing literature there are three primary explanations for Britain maintaining its imperial presence in the Middle East after 1945: prestige, practical, and psychological. Spencer Mawby's account of British policy in Aden is underpinned by the notion that policy makers were motivated by a desire to maintain prestige and influence rather than 'a simple calculation of material interests'.[130] Similarly, John Kent argues that Britain's military presence in Egypt was primarily about prestige. He

---

[129] John Darwin, *Britain and Decolonisation: The Retreat from Empire in the Post-war World* (London, 1988), pp. vii–viii.

[130] Spencer Mawby, *British Policy in Aden and the Protectorates, 1955–67: Last Outpost of a Middle East Empire* (London, 2005), p. 3.

contends that the British recognised that the Suez base – the largest military base in the world – was not adequate to defend Middle East oil or Britain's treaty obligations to keep out the Soviet Union. Thus, Britain's military presence must simply have been designed to uphold British prestige and the perception that it was a world power.[131] Michael Cohen is not convinced by this argument, however, noting that it belies the 'gravity' with which both the civilian and the military leaders regarded the Soviet threat. For Cohen, the primary purpose of Britain's military presence in the Middle East was its practical strategic importance in the event of global war against the Soviet Union.[132] A third explanation for Britain's continued imperial presence emphasises a psychological or habitual driver. Piers Brendon, for example, has apprised that 'the British kept Aden because they could and because they were *conditioned by the past*'.[133] This tallies with William Roger Louis's assertion that British statesmen suffered 'from neuroses about holding what they had inherited'.[134]

Britain's withdrawal from the Middle East, meanwhile, has spawned four principal explanations. To borrow Ronald Hyam's cricketing analogy, the British were: bowled out by nationalists and freedom fighters; run out by imperial overstretch and economic constraints; retired due to loss of will; or booed off by international criticism.[135] In her seminal study of Britain's moment in the Middle East, Elizabeth Monroe emphasised Britain's loss of will. She pointed to Britain's inability to quell the drive for self-determination in Ireland in 1922 as creating a 'loss of imperial nerve'. Monroe placed this within a generalised decline in 'confidence about empire'.[136] Nigel Ashton considers this 'equally applicable' to Britain's retreat from the Middle East during the 1960s and applies this 'psychological' explanation to Britain's military intervention in

---

[131] John Kent, 'Informal Empire and the Defence of the Middle East 1945–56', in: Roy Bridges (ed.), *Imperialism, Decolonization and Africa* (Basingstoke, 2000), pp. 114–52; John Kent, 'The Egyptian Base and the Defence of the Middle East, 1945–54', in: Robert Holland (ed.), *Emergencies and Disorder in the European Empires after 1945* (London, 1994), p. 47.

[132] Michael Cohen, *Fighting World War Three from the Middle East: Allied Contingency Plans, 1945–1954* (London, 1997), pp. 84–5.

[133] Piers Brendon, *The Decline and Fall of the British Empire, 1781–1997* (London, 2007), p. 502 [emphasis added].

[134] William Roger Louis, 'Robinson and Gallagher and Their Critics', in: William Roger Louis (ed.), *Ends of Imperialism: The Scramble for Empire, Suez and Decolonisation* (London, 2006), p. 908.

[135] Ronald Hyam, *Britain's Declining Empire: The Road to Decolonisation 1918–1968* (Cambridge, 2006), p. xiii.

[136] Elizabeth Monroe, *Britain's Moment in the Middle East, 1914–1971*, 2nd edn (London, 1981), pp. 131–50.

Jordan in 1958 and Kuwait in 1961. He posits that both Britain's failures, such as the 1956 Suez debacle, and successes, such as the intervention in Jordan and Kuwait, had a negative psychological impact on Britain's willingness to act in defence of its interests in the Middle East.[137] Martin Jones's account of Britain's withdrawal from Palestine effectively accords with the loss of will argument. He asserts that 'the British Government decided to leave because it knew it had failed'.[138] Ronald Hyam, however, describes the 'failure of will' as the 'weakest' of all the explanations. Instead he emphasises international pressures and constraints as the most 'persuasive' and the 'most important'.[139] Similarly, in *The Empire Project* John Darwin's overarching argument is that the fate of the British world system was 'largely determined by geopolitical forces over which the British themselves had little control'.[140] Spencer Mawby, meanwhile, puts Britain's withdrawal from Yemen in 1967 down to the success of Arab nationalism rather than a British loss of will or the reduction of material capability.[141] Similarly, Ilan Pappé argues that Britain failed to deal with the Palestinisation of Jordan and rising anti-British Arab nationalism in the wake of its annexation of the West Bank after 1948. The result was the abrupt dismissal of Glubb in 1956, and the end of British dominance in Jordan.[142] Betty Anderson also puts the onus – perhaps unsurprisingly given the book's focus – on nationalism. In particular, she highlights the Jordanian National Movement: an umbrella movement of multiple political parties unified by the common goal of severing the British connection. Anderson describes the growing strength of this movement – established in Jordanian schools and Arab universities in the 1920s and 1930s, often as a reaction to European imperialism, Zionism, and the making of the Hashemite state – and its 'climax' in 1956.[143] Others have accentuated domestic considerations. Shohei Sato argues that Britain's withdrawal from the Persian Gulf in 1971 was a 'means to justify the Labour government's reversal of its [domestic] social policies'. Sato asserts that the economic saving of this military withdrawal was negligible and that it was

[137] Nigel Ashton, 'A Microcosm of Decline: British Loss of Nerve and Military Intervention in Jordan and Kuwait, 1958 and 1961', *The Historical Journal*, 40:4 (1997), pp. 1069–83.

[138] Martin Jones, *Failure in Palestine: British and United States Policy after the Second World War* (London, 1986), p. 343.

[139] Hyam, *Britain's Declining Empire*, pp. xiii–xiv.

[140] Darwin, *Empire Project*, p. 649.

[141] Mawby, *British Policy in Aden*, p. 3.

[142] Pappé, 'British Rule in Jordan', pp. 198–219.

[143] Anderson, *Nationalist Voices*, pp. 67–72, 140, 145, 170.

designed to 'justify' more significant social cuts in Britain, which risked harming the Labour Party's political standing.[144] Both Peter Sluglett and John Gallagher posit that it is unwise to give any single factor too much prominence.[145] Indeed, these factors are not necessarily mutually exclusive. Tom Segev, for example, has drawn a correlation between the success of nationalism and loss of will, arguing that, in Palestine, the British became 'sick' of the mandate as a result of Arab and Zionist insurrection.[146] Moreover, Gallagher maintains that at different times and in different locales, each of these factors may have been more or less significant.[147] As this book argues, even in one single locale, Jordan, all of these forces had some part to play. Though, of course, some were more significant than others.

The chronological structure of this study is designed to answer these two core questions: why did the British remain? And why did they depart? The existence of the Arab Legion was tied into the Anglo–Jordanian Treaty. This study is therefore bookended by an opening chapter on the treaty's creation in 1946 and a closing chapter on its termination in 1957. As Ronald Hyam astutely observed, 'you cannot properly understand the dismantling of the British empire unless you know how it was constructed'.[148] Similarly, on a smaller scale, it is necessary to understand the construction of Britain's treaty relationship with Jordan, in order to understand its demise. By examining how and why the treaty was constructed, within the context of the Arab Legion's intended future, Chapter 1 emphasises the ad hoc nature of Britain's post-war policy. It reveals that the treaty was drawn up with scant coordination amongst the multitude of interested departments within Whitehall and argues that the treaty was complacently constructed, as it failed to deal with Britain's desire to drastically reduce the Arab Legion. As Chapter 2 details, Britain's impending withdrawal from Palestine increased the value of the relationship with Jordan and raised Glubb's profile from marginalised man on the spot to the guardian of British interests. It also emphasises Abdullah's

[144] Shohei Sato, 'Britain's Decision to Withdraw from the Persian Gulf, 1964–68: A Pattern and a Puzzle', *Journal of Imperial and Commonwealth History*, 37:1 (2009), pp. 111–12.

[145] Sluglett, 'Formal and Informal Empire', p. 430; Gallagher, *Decline, Revival and Fall*, pp. 152–3.

[146] Tom Segev, *One Palestine, Complete: Jews and Arabs under the British Mandate* (London, 2000), p. 490.

[147] Gallagher, *Decline, Revival and Fall*, pp. 152–3.

[148] Hyam, *Britain's Declining Empire*, p. xi.

continued dependence on Britain. This argument is compounded by further detailed analysis of the 1948 War in Chapters 3 and 4.

Chapter 5 reengages with the question of the Arab Legion's proposed function via the discussions over its future role and its corresponding subsidy during the three years beyond 1948. It examines the implications of the 1948 War and Jordan's annexation of the West Bank, both for the Anglo–Jordanian connection generally and for the Arab Legion specifically. In so doing, it finds that Jordan and Abdullah emerged from the war ever more dependent on Britain. It also reveals that, contrary to popular belief, the Arab Legion was not earmarked for expansion after 1948. Rather, it was subsequent developments within the Cold War that drove the Arab Legion's reorganisation. The British only sanctioned an increase in the Arab Legion in response to the onset of the Korean War in 1950.

Chapter 6 takes a necessary detour away from the primary focus on the Arab Legion. Instead it addresses British involvement in the royal succession crisis created by the assassination of King Abdullah in 1951. Hitherto, Britain's relationship with Jordan had been founded on the staunch reliability of the kingdom's first and only ruler. His assassination thus put British influence in Jordan and its new role for the Arab Legion in doubt. The royal succession was a pivotal moment in Jordanian history. Yet it has hitherto been significantly under-researched. In his chapter on British policy in Jordan, Ilan Pappé devoted only one sentence to the brief reign of King Talal, positing only that his removal was 'probably because of mental illness, but possibly as a result of local and British intrigues'.[149] Only three studies have devoted any serious attention to the succession question and the short reign of King Talal. The benchmark study is Robert Satloff's *Jordan in Transition*. Satloff provided a laudable account of this tricky period in Jordan's history. However, as he himself pointed out, his study 'is principally a study of internal Jordanian politics'.[150] Moreover, many of the documents relevant to this period were released under an extended fifty-year rule, and therefore not available to Satloff or Pappé. Some of this material was available to Avi Shlaim and Nigel Ashton in the writing of their respective biographies of King Hussein – although only Nigel Ashton noticeably makes use of this material. Yet given the primary focus of these studies was the life and times of Talal's son, Hussein, there remains a real need to focus on Britain's approach to the crisis, and this chapter seeks to fill that gap. Aided by a large tranche of recently released

---

[149] Pappé, 'British Rule in Jordan', p. 208.
[150] Satloff, *Jordan in Transition*, p. viii.

documents, this chapter provides unique insight into Britain's role in the succession crisis and in relation to the overall study reveals the extent to which Britain sought to maintain influence in Jordan by massaging the royal succession. Indeed, understanding British involvement during this crisis is crucial to comprehending Britain's attitude towards King Hussein and his subsequent dismissal of Glubb.

The penultimate chapter directly addresses the process that led to Glubb's dismissal, focusing on the struggle for control of the Arab Legion after Hussein's accession as king. It examines the relationship between Hussein and Glubb and between Hussein and Britain within the context of the strains and stresses facing the allies, including the conflict with Israel, the rise of Arab nationalism, and the pressures of the Cold War. This chapter identifies the Glubb paradox, whereby his presence in Jordan became both integral and detrimental to Britain's position in Jordan and the wider Middle East. It also explains how this paradox affected British policy and the relationship with Jordan.

The final chapter examines the last year of the treaty's existence. It explores the relationship between Glubb's dismissal, the Suez Crisis, and the termination of the treaty in 1957. Within the existing literature the Suez Crisis is central to both these issues. Glubb's dismissal is widely considered one of the causes of Britain joining the coalition against the Egyptian president, Gamal Abd al-Nasser, in October 1956. Meanwhile, the termination of the treaty is generally regarded – to varying extents – as a product of the Suez debacle. This fits the popular theme that the Suez Crisis, to use Brian Lapping's phrase, 'wrote finis' to the British Empire.[151] This chapter challenges both these contentions concerning the relationship between events in Jordan and the causes and consequences of the Suez Crisis. With the aid of three recently released documents, this chapter posits an alternative assessment of the British reaction to Glubb's dismissal, which debunks the accepted myth that the British prime minister blamed Nasser. And regarding the consequences of Suez, this final chapter argues that the treaty was terminated primarily as a result of a review of the relationship prompted by Glubb's dismissal and the removal of the Glubb paradox; Suez merely got in the way of this review and thus delayed rather than precipitated the end of the treaty relationship. This chapter thus challenges the notion that Suez marked the end of Britain's moment in the Middle East. It accentuates a gradual process of Britain's changing relationships, in this case with Jordan.

[151] Brian Lapping, *End of Empire* (London, 1985), p. 277.

By assessing the life of the treaty, from construction to termination, and the role of Glubb and the Arab Legion therein, this book is able to answer the two core questions: why did the British remain? And why did they retreat? Via this approach, this study accords with Sluglett and Gallagher's assertions that it is unwise to emphasise any single factor too deeply. Both Britain's presence and its withdrawal were products of a multitude of forces. Prestige and neuroses were certainly factors in Britain's continued presence in Jordan and its desire to control the Arab Legion. However, both these explanations were founded on the practical purpose of securing Jordan as a geostrategic asset. Policy makers might not always have made clear-headed, balance sheet calculations of material interests, but the national interest was nonetheless the driving force. With regards to Britain's retreat, the least convincing explanation, as Ronald Hyam iterated, is the loss of will. Arab nationalism and economic overstretch were both important forces, but neither was singularly determinative. Nor were they the original seed of the treaty's demise. If one single factor helps bind these multiple explanations together, it is, as both Hyam and Darwin have contended, the changing international climate. This is at the centre of the interaction of forces involved in the treaty's construction, sustenance, and termination. The crux of the argument advanced here is that the treaty was built on and sustained by a system of mutual dependence and it was a change in the balance of this system that brought about the treaty's demise. William Roger Louis identified a fresh post-war approach of dealing with the Middle Eastern states as 'partners rather than dependents'.[152] Yet the Anglo–Jordanian relationship was a partnership based on dependence. The British remained in Jordan because they were reliant on Jordan as a geostrategic haven, and the relationship was sustained because Abdullah was equally dependent on Britain's financial and military support. The treaty relationship deteriorated as the balance of dependence shifted, owing to the changing international and geopolitical environment. The British became more dependent on Jordan, prompting them to maintain and assert more control. Meanwhile the British connection increasingly became a liability to the Hashemite Kingdom and it too desired more control to offset the threat of Arab nationalism. At the centre of this struggle were Glubb and the Arab Legion.

[152] William Roger Louis, *The British Empire in the Middle East 1945–1951: Arab Nationalism, The United States, and Postwar Imperialism* (Oxford, 1984), p. 737.

I

The 1946 Treaty, Palestine, and the Preclusion of the Arab Legion's Planned Post-War Disbandment

When the Second World War ended, Britain remained the predominant power in the Middle East. Given the end of France's mandate over Syria and Lebanon, Britain, which still held mandates in Palestine and Transjordan, was effectively the only external power with a formal political foothold in the region. The future of Britain's position in the Middle East was ominous, however. Its status as a world power was under threat from the two new global superpowers, the United States and the Soviet Union; its economy was struggling; and the Arab–Jewish conflict in Palestine had intensified. In many ways Britain's relationship with Transjordan was reassuringly reliable. Abdullah had remained loyal to Britain throughout the Second World War, and the Arab Legion had proved a useful asset: assisting in overturning the Iraqi coup in 1941; helping defeat the Vichy French in Syria; and guarding vital installations in Palestine, such as British military stores and the Iraq–Haifa oil pipeline, thus freeing up British forces for action in Europe.[1] As a consequence of its wartime role, the Arab Legion underwent a radical transformation from an internal security force to an ad hoc army. It 'expanded from a strength of about 1,450, costing £186,000 in 1940, to a strength of nearly 6,000, costing over £1,600,000' by 1945, at which point the military units of the Arab Legion consisted of a Mechanised Brigade of three regiments (each containing 732 men) and sixteen infantry companies (containing a total of 3,152 men; approximately 200 per company). The Mechanised Brigade and all but one of the infantry companies were stationed in Palestine; and even that was 'used as a reinforcement and

---

[1] Wilson, *King Abdullah*, pp. 133–4; Musa, *Cameos*, pp. 117–18.

training unit for the companies in Palestine'.[2] As the world returned to a peacetime footing, the British thus had a decision to make: should they consolidate the Arab Legion in its new form, or scale it back to its pre-war state?

Hitherto this question has not seriously been examined. Yet answering it provides a crucial insight into British strategic thinking in the Middle East. Anyone searching for an answer to this question within the existing literature will find what amounts to a misplaced assumption. Ron Pundik posited that the post–Second World War importance of Transjordan was 'by virtue of its central geo-strategic position in the area, and *the strength of its army*'.[3] This implies that Britain considered the Arab Legion a vital asset worth cultivating and tallies with Ilan Pappé's statement that: 'In order to prepare the Arab Legion for this task [a Third World War in which Palestine was considered a likely battleground], Britain had imme-diately after the Second World War strengthened this force by adding new and substantial numbers of British officers to its core.'[4] As this chapter reveals, however, neither of these statements accurately describes Britain's post-1945 appreciation of the Arab Legion. In a slightly less inaccu-rate account, Vatikiotis contended that after the 1946 Anglo–Jordanian Treaty, 'the Legion entered an entirely new phase: this was the transition from a security force with limited military operational functions to a reg-ular army, a fully-fledged military institution'. While this is not strictly incorrect, it is nonetheless misrepresentative, and is presumably the gen-esis of the subsequent misplaced assumptions. Vatikiotis implied that the 1946 Treaty was designed to formalise the Arab Legion as a military force. This was not the case, however. The problem with his argument, which was made prior to the release of the official British documents, is that, as he explicitly stated, 'most of the illustrative data [that he used] are drawn from the period of greatest expansion, 1948–1956'.[5] Effectively, Vatikiotis applied evidence of the Arab Legion's consolidation in 1948, and subsequent expansion, to posit that the 1946 Treaty initiated this process. However, as this chapter illustrates, when the treaty was signed, and for the following eighteen months, Britain's intention was to dis-band the bulk of the Arab Legion – thus reverting it back to an internal security force.

[2] Treasury to Sabben-Clare, 23 January 1945; 'The Military Units of the Arab Legion', Kirkbride, 4 June 1946, CO537/1499, TNA.
[3] Pundik, *Struggle for Sovereignty*, p. 43 [emphasis added].
[4] Pappé, 'Alec Kirkbride', p. 126.
[5] Vatikiotis, *Politics and the Military*, p. 74.

There were two reasons why the realisation of this intention was prevented. The primary factor, as the second half of this chapter details, was the deteriorating security situation in Palestine, where 80 per cent of the Arab Legion was stationed. In part, however, the 1946 Treaty also helped thwart this planned reduction. Not as a matter of policy, as Vatikiotis implied, but unintentionally. Thus, before exploring Britain's failed attempt to disband the bulk of the Arab Legion, this chapter begins by examining the manner in which the treaty was created. Analysis of the 1946 Treaty has hitherto been rather simplistic and cursory. It has traditionally been disregarded as a predominantly 'unexceptional treaty'. The emphasis has been placed primarily on the limited nature of independence it offered and the extensive strategic rights Britain maintained.[6] As Uriel Dann has asserted, this was the principal reason why the United States did not officially recognise Transjordan as an independent state until 31 January 1949.[7] Tancred Bradshaw, though, puts the US reaction down to Zionist pressure, rather than an altruistic objection to the superficial nature of independence.[8] Nevertheless, one of the limitations of the existing literature concerning the nature of the 1946 Treaty is that it has focused on the outcome of the treaty with little or no analysis of the process of its construction. The purpose of the treaty and its details have been understood as part of a single, coherent policy. William Roger Louis explains: 'The Colonial Office, Foreign Office, and Chiefs of Staff intended the treaty with Jordan to confirm both a political and a military alliance.'[9] In broad terms, this is entirely correct. However, this statement belies the extent to which the treaty was primarily drafted by the Colonial Office, with scant consultation with other Whitehall departments. The manner in which the treaty was drafted reveals important nuances that reveal much about the nature of Britain's empire, in general, and about the post-1945 foundation of the Anglo-Jordanian relationship and the future of the Arab Legion. In particular, it emphasises that British policy was severely debilitated by a lack of coordination between the various Whitehall departments. It compounds Michael Cohen's assessment that Britain did not possess 'a monolithic policy-making machine'.[10]

[6] Wilson, *King Abdullah*, pp. 148–50; Louis, *British Empire in the Middle East*, pp. 354–8.
[7] Dann, *Studies in the History of Transjordan*, pp. 93–113.
[8] Bradshaw, *Britain and Jordan*, p. 111.
[9] Louis, *British Empire in the Middle East*, p. 354.
[10] Michael Cohen, *Palestine: Retreat from the Mandate: The Making of British Policy, 1936–45* (London, 1978), p. 187.

At the outset it is important to emphasise the fractured nature of Britain's world system, not only as a whole, but also as a microcosm within the Middle East where administration was divided between the Colonial Office – which administered the mandated territories of Palestine and Transjordan – and the Foreign Office – which had responsibility for affairs relating to Egypt, Iraq, and Saudi Arabia. Until 1947, the India Office also had a significant interest in the region – notably in the Persian Gulf. After the 1946 Treaty granted independence, Transjordan came under the umbrella of the Foreign Office, but its function related to Palestine as this is where the bulk of the Arab Legion was employed. The Arab Legion, as Colonial Office Assistant Secretary Trafford Smith neatly summarised, was at the centre of a complex web of interests within Whitehall:

> [It was] a question for the Colonial Office in respect of its political aspect in Palestine, for the Foreign Office in regard to its connection with Trans-Jordan, and for the War Office as regards the possibility of replacing the Arab Legion units by other troops. The Treasury are also concerned, as they are expected to provide the funds to pay for the cost of the Arab Legion.[11]

During the Second World War, Glubb proposed the creation of 'a single service to cover the area from Cyrenaica to Persia, and Sudan to Syria'.[12] Glenday, within the Colonial Office, commented that: 'Quite apart from the probable general advantage of remedying the present system whereby much time is spent by two Depts – CO & FO – over the Palestinian problem, the ever increasing international reactions to the Jewish question there would appear to support strongly such an idea.'[13] However, the creation of a 'Levant Civil Service' did not become a reality and the diversification of responsibility only served to exacerbate the difficulty of forming truly holistic policies that would suit all of the departments' competing interests. In November 1945, Britain's new foreign secretary, Ernest Bevin, opened the British Middle East Office (BMEO) in Cairo, and its main function was 'to develop and co-ordinate British economic and social policy in the Middle East'. During its formative years, it did acquire a political function, as a hub for information and advice on Middle East issues.[14] However, it did not provide comprehensive unity for

---

[11] Trafford Smith to Baxter, 27 June 1946, CO537/1499, TNA.
[12] 'Note on Post-war Settlements in the Middle East', Glubb, 15 November 1942, CO732/88/9, TNA.
[13] Minute by Glenday, 12 January 1943, ibid.
[14] 'Functions and Organisation of the British Middle East Office', 5 May 1948, Pyman Papers, Liddell Hart Military Archives, King's College London.

Britain's Middle East policies and initiatives and it lacked the resources to become an effective institution.[15] It did not remedy the dearth of cohesion that would ultimately have an impact on the process of drafting the 1946 Treaty with Transjordan.

The absence of a coordinated policy-making machine was a problem because the treaty negotiations with Transjordan were not conducted in isolation; they were part of a broader realignment of Britain's relationship with the Middle East, conducted not by choice, but by necessity. During the inter-war period Britain had initiated a policy of 'empire by treaty' in the Middle East.[16] Bilateral treaties with Iraq in 1930 and Egypt in 1936 had granted these states nominal independence in return for unfettered access to military assets. These treaties were anathema to nationalists, who baulked at the extent of Britain's military presence and the freedom of movement the treaties afforded British forces via land, sea, and air.[17] Egyptians were further incensed when, in 1942, the British ambassador used the threat of military force to demand that King Farouk dismiss his prime minister and replace him with the more pro-British Mustafa Nahas.[18] When the Second World War ended, the Egyptians were determined to initiate the evacuation of British troops and the realisation of Egyptian sovereignty over Sudan.[19] Thus, on 20 December 1945, Egypt formally requested a revision of the 1936 Treaty. Hitherto, Britain had delayed attempts to revise the treaty, but by the end of 1945, stalling was deemed by Oriental Minister Sir Walter Smart at the embassy in Egypt to be 'no longer in our interest politically. The effect of the stalling is that a free field is being left to every kind of extremist and vociferous, half-baked politician, and nationalist claims tend to become more and more unrestrained.'[20] A similar situation had also emerged in Iraq. Although the ruling Hashemite regime was staunchly pro-British, nationalist sentiment – including the temporarily successful coup in 1941 – had shown that some adjustment to the Anglo–Iraqi relationship would be required. It was for this reason that in 1946 Britain agreed to discuss revisions to the Anglo–Iraqi Treaty even though it was not due to expire until 1957. Britain had no appetite for major changes to the existing

[15] Monroe, *Britain's Moment*, pp. 160–1; David Devereux, *The Formulation of British Defence Policy Towards the Middle East, 1948–56* (London, 1990), p. 5.

[16] Fitzsimons, *Empire by Treaty*.

[17] Louis, *British Empire in the Middle East*, pp. 229–30, 322.

[18] Aburish, *Nasser*, p. 18.

[19] Louis, *British Empire in the Middle East*, pp. 229–32; Aburish, *Nasser*, p. 21.

[20] Quoted in: Louis, *British Empire in the Middle East*, p. 231.

treaty arrangements in either Egypt or Iraq – not least because of how valuable Britain's military bases and privileges had proved during the Second World War.[21] British Prime Minister Clement Attlee was sceptical about Britain's ability to remain a major power in the Middle East and questioned the value of its military presence, but more traditional views, led by Bevin, held sway.[22] Bevin believed it was essential that Britain retained a network of bases and freedom of movement in case of war. Consequently, he hoped that Egypt and Iraq would accept cosmetic changes that reproduced the 'essential features' of the existing treaties.[23] As it turned out, attempts to revise these treaties broke down. But it was against this backdrop, and within this context, that treaty negotiations were opened with Transjordan.

The primary motivation behind Britain's decision to grant Jordanian independence was to reward Abdullah for his support for Britain during the Second World War and to consolidate the position of a proven staunch ally in the Middle East. As with Egypt and Iraq, the British had no particular appetite for altering the nature of the relationship with Transjordan. However, for a number of reasons it had become very difficult to refuse Abdullah's desire for Jordanian independence. During the Second World War, Abdullah had played his hand astutely. After war was declared in September 1939, Abdullah immediately confirmed his support for Britain and offered the unequivocal service of the Arab Legion. While both Abdullah and Glubb were somewhat disappointed that the Arab Legion did not see any action in Europe, the Arab Legion was unequivocally at Britain's disposal and did play its part in Palestine, Syria, and Iraq.[24] By committing himself to Britain from start to finish, Abdullah had proved himself utterly loyal and consequently enhanced his profile within British thinking. Throughout the war he pressed his case for reward, anxious to shake off the binds of the mandate and obtain full independence.[25] In July 1941, Abdullah explained to the British that: 'The Arabs, as other peoples, want their country for themselves and it was for that reason that they participated in the last war. They hoped for final success in

---

[21] Fitzsimons, *Empire by Treaty*, p. 56.
[22] Devereux, *Formulation of British Defence Policy*, p. 185; Cohen, *Fighting World War Three*, p. 81.
[23] Louis, *British Empire in the Middle East*, pp. 232–4.
[24] Wilson, *King Abdullah*, pp. 129–35; Salibi, *Modern History of Jordan*, pp. 148–51; Musa, *Cameos*, pp. 117–18; Abu Nowar, *Struggle for Independence*, pp. 16–19.
[25] Sulayman Musa, *Jordan: Land and People* (Amman, undated), p. 47; Abu Nowar, *Struggle for Independence*, pp. 62–3.

this war and again offered their aid.'[26] The Second World War itself provided Britain with an excuse to delay the realisation of independence and the British merely reassured Abdullah that they would consider the matter when the war was over.[27] When the conflict finally came to an end, Abdullah was ready and waiting to claim his prize. It was no doubt with that in mind that Abdullah eulogised about Britain in his memoirs – originally published in 1945. He praised the 'enormous sacrifices and hardships' that the British people endured during the Second World War and, addressing the Arab world, he asserted: 'be strong, loyal and alert and Britain will be with you and put her trust in you'.[28] Ideally he wanted British support for his ambition to rule over Greater Syria, encompassing Transjordan, Palestine, Syria, and Lebanon.[29] However, independence was an acceptable interim compromise – designed to consolidate British influence. Given Britain's support for Syrian and Lebanese independence from France in 1941 as a means of courting Arab support during the Second World War, the British were in no position to argue against Transjordan achieving equal status.[30] Thus, on 17 January 1946, Ernest Bevin announced Transjordan's proposed independence in a speech at the UN General Assembly. Two months later, on 22 March, Transjordan was granted independence via the signing of the 1946 Treaty of Alliance, and Transjordan's first ruler, Amir Abdullah, was subsequently inaugurated as the country's first king.

Although the notion of granting independence to Transjordan had been circulating for several years, it was only in mid-January 1946, just weeks before Abdullah was due to arrive to conduct negotiations, that the British government decided to start thinking about 'the agenda for discussions with the Amir and the sort of treaty we are going to conclude with him'.[31] With Abdullah due to arrive on 22 February and the British resident in Transjordan, Alec Kirkbride, a couple of weeks earlier for preliminary consultation, the proposed treaty draft was barely in its infancy less than a month before the arrival of the Jordanian delegation. At this stage the very foundation of the treaty was still largely baseless

---

[26] Quoted in: Abu Nowar, *Struggle for Independence*, p. 74.
[27] J. V. W. Shaw to Oliver Stanley (Secretary of State for Colonies), 24 July 1945, FO371/45415/E6792, TNA; Abu Nowar, *Struggle for Independence*, p. 74.
[28] Abdullah, *Memoirs of King Abdullah*, pp. 240–2.
[29] Salibi, *Modern History of Jordan*, pp. 151–2; Abu Nowar, *Struggle for Independence*, pp. 20–3, 44, 52–80; Wilson, *King Abdullah*, p. 136; Joseph Nevo, *King Abdallah and Palestine: A Territorial Ambition* (Basingstoke, 1996), pp. 205–6.
[30] Louis, *British Empire in the Middle East*, p. 124.
[31] Minute by Trafford Smith to Martin, 12 January 1946, CO537/1846, TNA.

other than that it should be 'on the general lines of the Treaty of Alliance
with Iraq of 1930'.[32] The reason for basing it on the Iraqi treaty had
more to do with convenience than content. J. S. Bennett, the head of
the International Relations Department at the Colonial Office, acknowledged: 'It may well be that the kind of Treaty relationship evolved in the
Middle East between the two world wars is now passing out of date, with
the revision of the Egyptian Treaty and the movement to the same effect
in Iraq.'[33] Yet the Colonial Office recommended little more than adding
a military annex to the core of the Iraqi treaty simply to account for the
main difference between the two relationships of Britain continuing to
subsidise the Arab Legion.[34] The 1946 Treaty was an anachronism know-
ingly set within a framework that was recognised as defunct. However,
the convenience of precedent overruled the question of suitability.

    Having failed to consider the details of the post-mandate alliance in
good time, the treaty had to be drafted in haste, and this stifled inter-
departmental coordination. Less than a month before negotiations with
Abdullah were due to start it was still undecided as to 'whether the discussions with the Amir should be conducted by the Foreign Office and the
Colonial Office jointly', or by some other combination. While acknowledging that the Treasury would have a huge interest, and that the subject
should be 'discussed with the Middle East (Official) Committee', Trafford
Smith also noted that there was clearly 'no time to be lost'. He therefore
suggested that preliminary discussions take place between the Foreign
and Colonial Offices only, thus sidelining potentially crucial input into
the discussions from other relevant departments.[35] Urgency trumped the
need for coordination. Even the Foreign Office, the department set to
assume responsibility for Jordanian affairs after independence, had minimal input into the construction of the treaty. The first discussion relating
to the drafting of the proposed treaty took place on 11 February, and the
Colonial Office intended to submit the draft treaty and annexures to the
Cabinet ten days later for approval prior to the Amir's arrival the following day.[36] Thus, when requesting the Foreign Office's input, the Colonial
Office explained that it had become 'necessary to move very fast in preparing the first rough draft'. The Foreign Office was informed that in
order to keep to this timetable, it would have to forward its views to the

---

[32] Trafford Smith to Baxter, 29 January 1946, CO537/1842, TNA.
[33] Minute by Bennett, 11 April 1946, CO537/1849, TNA.
[34] Trafford Smith to Baxter, 29 January 1946, CO537/1842, TNA.
[35] Ibid.
[36] Trafford Smith to Parker, 13 February 1946, ibid.

Colonial Office by 15 February at the latest, 'in order that higher authority and the Secretary of State may have an opportunity of considering them before the Cabinet meeting'.[37] Consequently, the Foreign Office response was 'hurriedly compiled' and of limited value given that there had 'not as yet been sufficient time to formulate any definite "Foreign Office views" on the proposed treaty'.[38] Despite being the department about to inherit responsibility for Jordanian affairs, and despite its present predominant involvement in the negotiations to renew the treaties with Iraq and Egypt, the Foreign Office had barely any input in the drafting of the treaty that would set the tone for future relations with Transjordan.

The Chiefs of Staff were also given limited time to consider their 'preliminary reactions ... on the Treaty and Military Convention', prompting the Colonial Office to apologise for presenting them 'with a problem of this magnitude at such short notice'.[39] From a bilateral perspective the Chiefs of Staff appraised that the proposed treaty and military annex more than covered Britain's strategic requirements in war and peace, which allowed some room for movement in the negotiations with Abdullah.[40] The Chiefs of Staff Committee therefore approved the Joint Planning Report with just one main amendment: to make sure that land forces could be stationed in Transjordan during peacetime. It was pointed out that such a clause 'might be deemed by U.N.O. to be incompatible with our professed intention of granting independence to Trans-Jordan', but ultimately it was decided that 'this should not prevent us trying to obtain Treaty rights of this nature if we could get them'.[41] And in article 1 of the annex to the final treaty this desire was acceded to.

The lack of time for input from the Foreign Office, the Treasury, and the Chiefs of Staff prevented the implementation of a truly coordinated or holistic regional policy, resulting in a lamentably bilateral agreement. The Chiefs of Staff felt that the treaty 'must be related to our overall needs in [the] Middle East as a whole'.[42] They warned that having the treaty run for twenty-five years and the military convention run for only five years might encourage Egypt to press for a similar short-term military arrangement relating to the much more important Suez Canal base, during the

---

[37] Trafford Smith to Baxter, 13 February 1946, ibid.
[38] Baxter to Trafford Smith, 15 February 1946, ibid.
[39] Martin to Major-General Jacob, 13 February 1946, ibid.
[40] Cabinet Offices to Commanders-in-Chief, 20 February 1946, CO537/1499, TNA.
[41] 'Extract of Minutes from: C.O.S.(46) 28th Meeting', 21 February 1946, CO537/1843, TNA.
[42] Cabinet Offices to Commanders-in-Chief, 20 February 1946, CO537/1499, TNA.

Anglo–Egyptian Treaty renewal process.[43] The commanders-in-chief of the British Army's Middle East Land Forces (MELF) added that 'all treaties with Middle East states should be negotiated on the lines set out in telegram No.25 Saving'.[44] This Foreign Office telegram, which offered guidelines for the preliminary treaty negotiations with Egypt, stipulated that the question of Egypt's defence should be transformed 'from the level of a purely bilateral understanding ... to the level of a general partnership between the Middle East states and His Majesty's Government'.[45] Clearly the intention within the Foreign Office was to establish a consistent approach to Britain's future relationship with the Arab states. However, the Colonial Office was completely unaware of this telegram until it saw reference to it in another telegram on 6 March. Bennett lamented that it was 'a pity' that the Foreign Office had not shared this telegram earlier. He went on to exclaim:

The political side of our current re-adjustments in the Middle East – e.g. Trans-Jordan, Egypt, Libya ... needs close co-ordination: the F.O. don't seem to be 100% effective in providing it: ... In my view it is becoming an urgent matter to get some improvement made in the arrangements for handling these big Middle Eastern issues.[46]

If British policy in the Middle East was to have a clear sense of direction, it was essential that the relevant departments communicated and coordinated. But this was not the case, and the 1946 Treaty was drawn up with both these bureaucratic fundamentals largely absent. The Colonial Office acted under the assumption of three basic tenets: 'that there should be an alliance between H.M.G. and Trans-Jordan, that H.M.G. must continue to give Trans-Jordan financial help, and that British strategic interests must be safeguarded'.[47] To that end the Colonial Office only really had to get a treaty agreed. This approach satisfied the ministerial requirements for the treaty. As was outlined in the Cabinet discussions, the military arrangement with Transjordan, like all the others throughout the region, was created as an 'insurance' against what was deemed the very possible failure of the newly formed United Nations.[48] The treaty was designed to give Britain as much freedom of action as possible, and article 2 of the

---

[43] 'Extract of Minutes from: C.O.S.(46) 28th Meeting', 21 February 1946, CO537/1843, TNA.
[44] GHQ Middle East to Cabinet Offices, 6 March 1946, CO537/1844, TNA.
[45] FO to Cairo, 25 Saving, 25 January 1946, ibid.
[46] Minute by Bennett, 11 March 1946, ibid.
[47] Minute by Reilly, 24 January 1946, CO537/1842, TNA.
[48] Cabinet Secretary's Notebook, 25 February 1946, CAB195/4/6, TNA.

military annex, which stipulated that Britain would be granted 'facilities at all times for the movement and training of the [British] armed forces ... and for the transport of the supplies of fuel, ordnance, ammunition, and other materials required by these forces, by air, road, railway, water-way and pipe-line and through the ports of Trans-Jordan', was deemed to be 'as wide as we can draw it'.[49] The finer details of the treaty were not considered crucial. The Colonial Office was primarily concerned with getting the treaty signed, and this precluded the time needed for proper consultation. The mere existence of a treaty and the veneer of independence were the primary objectives. The only caveat was that the treaty should not stifle Britain's strategic use of Transjordan in relation to its geopolitical significance. Just like in the process of treaty revision with Egypt and Iraq – the British were determined to maintain their existing military privileges.

Ultimately, the problem with trying to coordinate policy between several interested departments was that it was a time-consuming process, and in this instance getting the treaty signed quickly was deemed more important than dealing comprehensively with any potential problems. Acting High Commissioner for Palestine and Transjordan J. V. W. Shaw warned: 'To delay showing tangible signs of appreciation for the loyalty of Trans-Jordan would, I consider, involve the grave risk that this goodwill might be undermined by resentment and disappointment and the existing assets of friendship be dissipated in political argumentation.'[50] This haste resulted in a number of details being left unresolved. In relation to the question of whether the treaty should contain a provision relating to civil aviation, the Colonial Office lamented that 'this is only one of a great many points which have had to be covered in extremely hurried preparation for the negotiations'.[51] Moreover, Laurence Barton Grafftey-Smith, the British ambassador in Jedda, warned that independence for Transjordan would reignite disputes with Saudi Arabia regarding Transjordan's southern frontier. He cautioned: 'I fear that we will have a good deal of bad blood and friction if [the] British mandate in Trans-Jordan is terminated without some attempt at a simultaneous resolution of frontier disputes with Saudi Arabia.'[52] Indeed, King Saud himself raised the issue with Britain after he was forewarned of Transjordan's

---

[49] Cabinet Secretary's Notebook, 18 March 1946, CAB195/4/13; 'Treaty of Alliance', 22 March 1946, CO537/1844, TNA.
[50] Shaw to Oliver Stanley, 24 July 1945, FO371/45415/E6792, TNA.
[51] Minute by Martin to Bigg, 5 March 1946, CO537/1844, TNA.
[52] Jedda to FO, 12, 5 January 1946, CO537/1842, TNA.

proposed independence.[53] However, despite this warning, and despite sharing Grafftey-Smith's foreboding, High Commissioner for Palestine and Transjordan Sir Alan Cunningham exclaimed:

I trust, however, that there will be no question of holding up negotiations of the Trans-Jordan Treaty or the date of its (?execution) [sic] pending attempt to promote settlement of the dispute. Such delay, whatever the final outcome, would exasperate the Amir Abdullah and imperil the existing fund of goodwill in Trans-Jordan towards Great Britain.

The strength of Abdullah's goodwill was seemingly given precedence over the risk of exacerbating inter-Arab tensions. Kirkbride agreed that it would be preferable to leave this dispute 'for eventual settlement through the machinery of the Arab League', even though it was expected to put a huge strain on this fledgling organisation, founded in March 1945. Ultimately it was deemed preferable to allow the problem to fester and leave it to someone else to clear up rather than run the risk that Britain 'be blamed for failure of attempt at settlement'.[54] The British government had a vested interest in the outcome of this matter. As Parliamentary Under-Secretary of State for the Colonies Arthur Creech Jones told the Cabinet: 'it was to our interest that the [Jordanian] port of Aqaba should not pass into the possession of Ibn Saud'.[55] Nonetheless, it was deemed preferable to ignore any complications in the expectation that the situation would work itself out after the treaty was agreed.

This somewhat slipshod approach to constructing the treaty relationship was quintessentially apparent in Britain's handling of the future of the Arab Legion. In the interest of economising, the Treasury had instigated a review of the post-war future of the Arab Legion in 1945. It had always been the intention to eventually disband the garrison companies, which had been formed merely as a 'wartime measure' to undertake guard duties in Palestine. Indeed, their 'creation as part of the Arab Legion was primarily a matter of administrative convenience'.[56] As the Second World War drew to a close, and 'in view of the changed military situation in the Middle East', the Treasury requested that the Colonial Office seek the opinion of the War Office as to whether the current levels were still necessary.[57] The financial implications of the Second World War

53 'Memorandum from King Ibn Saud', 18 January 1946, ibid.
54 Cunningham to Hall (S. of S. for Colonies), 10 February 1946, ibid.
55 'Extract from CONCLUSIONS of a Meeting of the Cabinet held at 10 Downing Street, S.W.1., on Monday 25th February 1946', CO537/1843, TNA.
56 Minute by Garran, 8 April 1947, FO371/62203/E2014, TNA.
57 James to Sabben-Clare, 23 January 1945, CO537/1499, TNA.

set forth a candid demand for clarity over the role of the Arab Legion as a means of identifying its true value. In 1945/6, the total cost of the military units of the Arab Legion was £1,743,202. If the infantry companies were disbanded, as planned, that would reduce the cost of the Legion to approximately £1.1 million – a reduction of about 30 per cent.[58] After consulting the Middle East Command, the War Office replied: 'we are satisfied that the present strength of the Arab Legion is justified by military considerations'.[59] The War Office response that it was too early to start reducing the Arab Legion was hit by a sharp rebuff from the Treasury. It wished to know

whether the Arab Legion has or has not an Imperial role as a military force. If it has not, then we feel it should be reduced to the level required for local purposes only ... [with] its cost remaining on the Trans-Jordan estimates. If, as would seem to be the case, it is on the other hand a force with actual or potential Imperial duties, then surely the Army Votes [i.e. budget] should bear at least a part of its cost.

The Treasury felt it wrong that a civilian department – presently the Colonial Office – should bear the cost of a military force whose size and expense was set by the War Office.[60] As the intermediary in the review of the Arab Legion's future, the Colonial Office was non-committal. Having forwarded the War Office's reply to the Treasury with the comment that 'we agree generally' with those views,[61] Major F. H. Anderson of the Colonial Office felt that the Treasury's counter-argument was 'very well reasoned'.[62] In his opinion, there was 'considerable force in the Treasury argument and now that the war is over the whole matter should certainly be reviewed'.[63]

A further complication was that the Arab Legion was considered a vital quid pro quo in the relationship with Abdullah. The outgoing High Commissioner for Palestine and Transjordan, Lord Gort, argued against any reduction of the Arab Legion on the basis that Abdullah considered the Arab Legion's Mechanised Brigade a symbol of Transjordan's 'progress and prestige'. As such, he believed 'the political effect of any reduction in this Brigade at the present time would be out of all proportion

---

[58] 'Total Cost of Military Units of Arab Legion 1945/46', Kirkbride, undated, CO537/1842, TNA.
[59] D. E. Howell to J. D. Chalmers, 27 May 1945, CO537/1499, TNA.
[60] L. Petch to T. A. G. Charlton, 14 August 1945, ibid.
[61] Sabben Clare to James, 16 June 1945, ibid.
[62] Minute by Anderson, 20 August 1945, ibid.
[63] Minute by Anderson, 29 August 1945, ibid.

to any economy effected'.[64] Gort added: 'in view of their war record any unilateral reduction of the Arab Legion would be regarded by the Emir and his people, in the nature of an ungrateful and unwarranted affront'.[65] Abdullah, after all, considered the Arab Legion 'the apple of its ruler's eye'.[66] Gort, therefore, objected to reduction primarily on grounds of loyalty and political impact. How could Britain on one hand seek to maintain Abdullah's solidarity by rewarding him with independence, but at the same time massively reduce the Arab Legion – a symbol of Abdullah's power and prestige? However, the Treasury believed it would 'be difficult to justify its continued maintenance on anything like the expanded scale to which it rose during the war'.[67] This dilemma provided an unwanted complication to the process of agreeing to a swift treaty. Thus, when the process of drafting the treaty began, the Colonial Office opted to separate the two issues. Bennett suggested that talks regarding the future of the Arab Legion be conducted independently of the strategic aspects of the treaty because, in his view:

if we try to deal with the Treaty question as a 'by-product' of the Arab Legion discussions, the matter will get into the wrong perspective and may take a long time to reach finality. By asking for a new full-scale strategic appreciation on the basis of a new Treaty, we should, on the contrary, be able to mop up the Arab Legion question much more easily. The future size and role of the Arab Legion will automatically fall into place once we have worked out our own future strategic requirements in an independent Trans-Jordan, our military relations with the Trans-Jordan Government, and the amount of any subvention that may be paid to Trans-Jordan after it has become independent.[68]

The treaty did not therefore take into account the future of the Arab Legion, contrary to Tancred Bradshaw's claim that: 'The future of the Arab Legion was a key feature of the treaty negotiations.'[69] Despite being under review for almost a year, this complication was put off until after the treaty was signed.

Meanwhile, as the treaty was being finalised, a British consensus that the Arab Legion should be significantly reduced was emerging. The Chiefs of Staff believed that the Arab Legion should revert to its pre-war status as an internal security force. The future role of the Legion as set out by

[64] Lord Gort to Oliver Stanley, 23 May 1945, ibid.
[65] Minute by Anderson, 2 June 1945, ibid.
[66] Abdullah, *Al-Takmilah*, p. 74.
[67] Creech Jones to Cunningham, 30 January 1946, FO371/52605/E2099, TNA.
[68] Bennett to Reilly, 23 January 1946, CO537/1842, TNA.
[69] Bradshaw, *Britain and Jordan*, p. 109.

the Chiefs of Staff Committee was threefold: '(a) To maintain law and order in Transjordan and to safeguard the pipeline; (b) to deter neighbouring States from attacking Transjordan; (c) to prevent smuggling into Palestine.'[70] The Chiefs of Staff wanted the Arab Legion to be responsible only for maintaining security within the borders of Transjordan. This tallied with the political authorities responsible for the security of Palestine, who now wanted the 80 per cent of the Arab Legion stationed there withdrawn. While recognising the vital internal security role that the Arab Legion was performing inside Palestine, the new High Commissioner, Sir Alan Cunningham, was concerned about the political implications of employing a 'foreign force'. This, he felt, 'will inevitably give rise to a series of embarrassing questions'. In particular, if the Arab Legion became involved in incidents with 'the Jews' it would likely 'arouse considerable adverse comment in both the United Kingdom and America'. Consequently, Cunningham pleaded: 'For both constitutional and political reasons, therefore, I must urge that the War Office be asked to consider the replacement of the units of the Arab Legion now employed in Palestine by other troops.'[71] The Foreign Office agreed because: 'The continued presence in Palestine of the troops of a Foreign Power is obviously highly anomalous and is likely to get us into all sorts of difficulties.'[72] The Treasury, unsurprisingly, also 'entirely' endorsed these recommendations.[73] The War Office effectively agreed too. It wished to keep the fifteen garrison companies presently in Palestine to meet its 'imperial commitment for Garrison Companies in the Middle East'. However, as these were to be used outside Transjordan, the War Office now felt 'they should form part of the Transjordan Frontier Force rather than the Arab Legion'.[74] The TJFF and the Arab Legion were two quite different entities. As Harold Beeley of the Foreign Office succinctly explained: 'The TJFF, despite its name, is a Palestinian force, but the Arab Legion is in fact the national army of the independent State of Transjordan.'[75] Although a British national was in command of the Arab Legion, Glubb was contracted to the Jordanian government and had no official connection to the British government except for an administrative link to the Colonial

[70] 'Memorandum Drawn Up by Mr Kirkbride Explaining the Operation of Certain Claims in the Military Annex to the Draft Treaty with Trans-Jordan', 13 March 1946, CO537/ 1499, TNA.
[71] Cunningham to Hall, 8 June 1946, ibid.
[72] Thomas Wikeley to Trafford Smith, 8 July 1946, ibid.
[73] Trafford Smith to Baxter, 27 June 1946, ibid.
[74] Thelwall to Chalmers, 7 May 1946, ibid.
[75] Minute by Beeley, 22 March 1947, FO371/62203/E2014, TNA.

Service for pension purposes. Meanwhile, the TJFF was a 'Colonial Force', funded by the War Office, for which the Palestine government was responsible.[76] It was not even made up primarily of Jordanians. When the TJFF was disbanded in February 1948, the nationality breakdown, excluding its British officers, was: 1,463 Palestinians; 749 Jordanians; 130 Syrians; 113 Egyptians and Sudanese; twenty-four Lebanese; and four other nationalities.[77] Politically and constitutionally it was deemed appropriate for the TJFF to take over the Arab Legion's responsibilities in Palestine. It was believed that the TJFF would be 'less vulnerable to hostile Jewish criticism' and that it would be easier to defend its presence in Palestine.[78] Moreover, because of its greater number of British officers, the War Office considered the TJFF both more efficient and more reliable than the Arab Legion.[79] Thus, the War Office proposed an expansion of the TJFF to meet Britain's military requirements in the Middle East, and was preparing to reduce the Arab Legion into a small force dedicated solely to maintaining internal security within Transjordan.

One obstacle to this large-scale reduction of the Arab Legion, however, was the hastily considered 1946 Treaty. By separating the review of the Arab Legion from the details of the treaty, the Colonial Office had inadvertently put in place a mechanism that obstructed Britain's ability to disband the Arab Legion unilaterally. When designing the quid pro quo on which Britain's treaty rights would be based, the Colonial Office worked along the premise of giving 'assistance to the Amir in the maintenance of his armed forces, in return for his agreeing to meeting H.M.G.'s strategic requirements in Trans-Jordan'.[80] As Peter Garran of the Colonial Office observed, this meant that despite the original remit of the garrison companies and the intention to disband them, 'we probably could not maintain the view ... that the garrison companies should not be regarded as constituting military units of the Transjordan Forces within the meaning of the Treaty and its annex'.[81] The treaty inadvertently consolidated the garrison companies, which had originally been attached to the Arab Legion merely as a matter of administrative convenience, as a formal part of the military forces of Transjordan. Moreover, article 8 of the military annex to the treaty stipulated that: 'The strength of such units [the Arab

[76] Russell Edmunds to P. Garron [*sic*], 5 March 1947, ibid.
[77] Gurney to Fletcher-Cooke, 3 February 1948, CO537/3577, TNA.
[78] Cunningham to Oliver Stanley, 6 November 1946, CO537/1499, TNA.
[79] 'Comments on Reorg of Arab Legion', undated, WO191/82, TNA.
[80] Minute by Trafford Smith, 29 January 1946, CO537/1842, TNA.
[81] Minute by Garran, 8 April 1947, FO371/62203/E2014, TNA.

Legion] will be agreed upon annually by the High Contracting Parties.'[82] When Britain suggested reduction of the Arab Legion, Glubb was quick to point out that, according to this article: 'Any decision would therefore have to be a subject for negotiation on a diplomatic level.'[83] Under the terms of the new treaty any reduction in the Arab Legion would require the Jordanian government's approval. The Foreign Office acknowledged that this point had seemingly been 'overlooked'.[84] In an example of apparent complacency the British had seemingly failed to consider the full ramifications of the treaty.

There is also scope to suggest that there was some degree of manipulation from the men on the spot, because Kirkbride had not overlooked the fact that the military annex allowed for annual discussions to fix the strength of the Arab Legion. During the treaty negotiations, he reasoned that the Arab Legion's strength would effectively be dictated by Britain, although he noted that it would be 'desirable to avoid any appearance of dictation by His Majesty's Government'.[85] Kirkbride therefore approved the wording of the treaty so as to avoid any explicit statement of British control, while noting that in actual fact Britain would be able to dictate the size of the Arab Legion. However, less than two months later, Kirkbride – like Glubb – used the ambiguous wording to preclude reduction of the Arab Legion to two mechanised regiments, as proposed. He warned that it was likely to be strongly resisted by King Abdullah and the Jordanian government.[86] Owing to Britain's lack of coordination and Kirkbride's intervention Abdullah had managed to cling onto the army that had nominally been created in his country's name during the Second World War. Glubb, Kirkbride, and Abdullah were each against reduction of the Arab Legion, and the wording of the treaty gave them a lever to use. It meant the Foreign Office had in the back of its mind that 'we are not in a position to disband, or otherwise modify the strength of the Arab Legion except by agreement with the Trans-Jordan Government, in accordance with Article 8 of the Annex to the Treaty'.[87] This therefore made a mockery of the Colonial Office's belief that the future of the Arab Legion could be mopped up more easily after independence.

[82] 'Treaty of Alliance', 22 March 1946, CO537/1844, TNA.
[83] 'Account of a Meeting on 18/7/46 in Jerusalem Headquarters', Glubb, 18 July 1946, FO371/52930/E7781, TNA.
[84] Henderson (for Baxter) to Winnifrith, 24 June 1946, CO537/1499, TNA.
[85] 'Memorandum Drawn Up by Mr Kirkbride Explaining the Operation of Certain Claims in the Military Annex to the Draft Treaty with Trans-Jordan', 13 March 1946, ibid.
[86] 'The Military Units of the Arab Legion', Kirkbride, 4 June 1946, ibid.
[87] R. G. Howe to C. S. Sugden, 15 October 1946, ibid.

This oversight created an obstacle to Britain's ability to reduce the strength of the Arab Legion unilaterally, but it was not the determinant factor. The future of the Arab Legion was ultimately decided by the unstable security situation in Palestine, where the British authorities were dealing with a high level of Zionist terrorist activity, including high-profile incidents such as the bombing of the British military headquarters at the King David Hotel on 22 July 1946. Although the Arab Legion was controversial politically, militarily strong practical arguments existed for maintaining the status quo. General Officer Commanding in Palestine and Transjordan Lieutenant-General Barker warned: 'The precarious situation in Syria and the fact that Palestine is facing the gravest crisis in its history makes any suggestion of reduction dangerous to contemplate.' He concluded:

I cannot stress too strongly that this is a most inopportune moment to introduce changes and disturb a going concern. I therefore strongly recommend that [the] situation should remain as at present until next spring when we should have a clearer idea of the future.[88]

If the Arab Legion was withdrawn without replacement, it was expected to result in 'a large increase' in thefts of arms and explosives, 'both of which are already inadequately guarded'.[89] Even if Britain could unilaterally disband the Arab Legion, it was presently performing a vital function, and while the plan was to replace the Arab Legion with the TJFF, this could not be done overnight. The War Office proposed that the Arab Legion garrison companies should simply be transferred wholesale to the TJFF.[90] However, this was deemed 'out of the question' because of the 'political implications'. As one Colonial Office official explained: 'The Arab allegiance [within the Arab Legion] is to the Amir and their personal loyalty is also very strong to Brigadier Glubb.' This meant that compulsory transfer was ill-advised, and large-scale voluntary enlistment in a British unit such as the TJFF, by those disbanded from the Arab Legion, was deemed highly unlikely.[91] Kirkbride added that simply transferring the fifteen garrison companies currently in Palestine from the Arab Legion to the TJFF would also be false economy, noting that the running costs of the TJFF was even more expensive than the Arab Legion, owing to its 'much larger cadre of British officers than is the case of the

---

[88] Evelyn Barker to Mideast, 20 July 1946, FO371/52930/E8187, TNA.
[89] C-in-C MELF to WO, 7 August 1946, CO537/1499, TNA.
[90] WO to C-in-C Middle East, 23 March 1946, ibid.
[91] Chalmers to Thelwall, 31 May 1946, ibid.

Arab Legion'.[92] However, this was not a meaningful factor. Regardless of the economic aspect, the plan was for the TJFF to take over the role being performed by the Arab Legion garrison companies. The main problem was how best to handle the handover, given the 'imminent crisis' presently facing Palestine.[93]

It was decided that the replacement could only be safely arranged via a gradual handover process. The War Office requested that the Mechanised Brigade of the Arab Legion remain in Palestine with the position scheduled to be reviewed in early 1947. Meanwhile, it was all set to begin the gradual transition of disbanding the Arab Legion garrison companies and replacing them with equivalent units of the TJFF immediately.[94] This would raise the strength of the TJFF from 2,500 to 7,500 men.[95] It was expected to take about one year to recruit and train fourteen new TJFF companies. As long as there were no objections to the recruitment of Jordanian subjects, particularly those from the disbanding Arab Legion companies, the War Office proposed to instruct MELF 'to begin recruiting and training fourteen Trans-Jordan Frontier Force Companies as soon as possible'.[96] Thus, at the end of 1946 the Arab Legion was all set to undertake a yearlong disbandment that would result in its losing the bulk of its manpower.

However, the Palestine situation continued to preclude the planned reduction of the Arab Legion. Having failed to find a political solution to the Palestine problem, in February 1947 Britain handed the dilemma of finding a solution to the Arab–Jewish conundrum in Palestine to the United Nations. The uncertainty this created led the Treasury, in agreement with the Colonial Office, to suggest that, as long as the Foreign Office did not think it would affect the Palestine case in the United Nations, it would be advisable to delay the formation of new TJFF units and continue using the Arab Legion garrison companies until the situation was clearer.[97] The Foreign Office agreed with this course.[98] From a 'practical point of view', it was deemed preferable to maintain the status quo 'until the present crisis in Palestine is over'. This meant maintaining

[92] 'Memorandum Drawn Up by Mr Kirkbride Explaining the Operation of Certain Claims in the Military Annex to the Draft Treaty with Trans-Jordan', 13 March 1946, ibid.
[93] 'Account of a Meeting on 18/7/46 in Jerusalem Headquarters', Glubb, 18 July 1946, FO371/52930/E7781, TNA.
[94] Sugden to Bernard Reilly, 3 October 1946, CO537/1499, TNA.
[95] Russell Edmunds to P. Garron [sic], 5 March 1947, FO371/62203/E2014, TNA.
[96] Fitzgeorge-Balfour to Chalmers, 27 September 1946, CO537/1499, TNA.
[97] Russell Edmunds to Garron [sic], 5 March 1947, FO371/62203/E2014, TNA.
[98] Garran to Russell Edmunds, 21 April 1947, ibid.

the 'anomalous situation' of using the national army of an independent state rather than the misleadingly named Palestinian force.[99] This did not end the intention to replace the Arab Legion with the TJFF. Indeed, the British ploughed ahead with plans to rename the Transjordan Frontier Force so that it more accurately reflected its status. Abdullah had initially requested that the word 'Transjordan' be removed from its title because it created political difficulties with his Arab neighbours, who struggled to distinguish between the two forces. Britain agreed that a name change was desirable, and the first alternative recommended was the 'Palestine Legion'. The new name eventually decided on was the 'Palestine Frontier Force'.[100] However, just like the expansion of the TJFF, the announcement of this name change was put on hold while the fate of Palestine was considered, lest the reason for the alteration be misrepresented. However, after the United Nations agreed to partition Palestine in November 1947 it was decided to disband the TJFF, and the name change became redundant.[101] With the British mandate in Palestine set to end, the TJFF, which was a colonial force of the Palestine government, no longer had a purpose, and on 8 February 1948 this force was formally disbanded and the Arab Legion avoided reduction.

For two years after the Second World War ended, the Arab Legion was maintained merely on an ad hoc basis until conditions in Palestine allowed for its reduction. The Arab Legion maintained its Second World War strength after 1945 not by British design, but as a result, partly, of an uncoordinated and hastily designed treaty, yet mainly by force of circumstance. When the treaty was signed, and for the following eighteen months, the British government planned to disband 80 per cent of the Arab Legion. It was all set to revert to a mere internal security force. The British had little interest in the Arab Legion as an asset beyond its ability to maintain internal security within Transjordan and its value as a quid pro quo for securing dominant access to an important geostrategic area. The treaty gave Glubb, Kirkbride, and Abdullah a lever with which to hinder this plan, but ultimately the Arab Legion avoided reduction because it was required to meet demands inside Palestine. Within the existing literature it is a well-worn tale that the 1946 Treaty of Alliance granted only nominal independence to Transjordan and that Britain maintained significant military privileges. This chapter does not deny this. However, it

[99] Minute by Beeley, 22 March 1947, ibid.
[100] CO to Garran, 14 October 1947, FO371/62203/E9694; WO to C-in-C MELF, 5 May 1947, FO371/62203/E13321, TNA.
[101] WO to C-in-C MELF, 3 December 1947, WO32/15562, TNA.

does contend that acceptance of this truism has obscured other important nuances. Yes, Britain maintained significant privileges, but the treaty was not part of any grand strategy. Its construction was not well coordinated within Whitehall and it declined to consider any finer details. The British gave almost no consideration to the treaty's implications. They merely sought to retain the geostrategic advantages that Transjordan offered, within a new framework that would satisfy Abdullah and the wider international community. Transjordan was therefore also a key beneficiary of the treaty, as it helped consolidate its military prowess in the form of the Arab Legion. This, in turn, would help make Abdullah and Transjordan an important political and military player when the future of Palestine was decided in 1948.

2

The Partition of Palestine, the Greater Transjordan Solution, and the Newfound Significance of Glubb Pasha and the Arab Legion

Ultimately the preclusion of the Arab Legion's planned disbandment was a symptom of a much bigger problem facing the British: how to solve the Palestine question that had plagued them since they were granted a League of Nations mandate over the country in 1920. Until then Palestine had not been a state in its own right, but a vaguely defined part of the Ottoman Empire loosely administered from Jerusalem and Beirut.[1] Its population was predominantly Arab. But since the late nineteenth century Palestine was targeted by the Europe-based Zionist movement, which sought the creation of an independent state with a Jewish majority in what it considered the ancestral home of the Jewish people.[2] In subsequent decades a steady stream of Jewish immigration took place, many fleeing persecution in Russia and Eastern Europe. By 1914 approximately 10 per cent of the Palestinian population was Jewish.[3] It was a significant minority. Yet in 1917, the Zionist movement obtained a major political breakthrough when British Foreign Secretary Arthur Balfour – seeking Zionist support for the British war effort – promised to support 'the establishment in Palestine of a national home for the Jewish people', albeit with the vague caveat that 'nothing shall be done which may prejudice the civil and religious rights of existing non-Jewish communities in Palestine'.[4] This was essentially incompatible with two other

[1] Schneer, *Balfour Declaration*, pp. 3, 7–9.
[2] Shlaim, *Iron Wall*, pp. 1–5.
[3] Schneer, *Balfour Declaration*, pp. 10–12.
[4] Arthur Balfour to Lord Rothschild, 2 November 1917, in: Walter Laqueur (ed.), *The Israel–Arab Reader: A Documentary History of the Middle East Conflict* (Harmondsworth, 1969), p. 36.

54

agreements between Britain and its wartime allies: the Hashemites and France. The Balfour Declaration nonetheless found expression within the confines of the Anglo–French agreement, as it was formalised in the text of the official League of Nations mandate for Palestine.[5] Thereafter the British authorities struggled to deal with the competing demands inside Palestine, between the native Arab majority, who demanded an end to Jewish immigration, and Zionist settlers, who continued to arrive from Europe demanding an independent Jewish state. The Second World War put the problem on hold to some extent as Britain and the Zionist movement united against Nazi Germany.[6] However, in 1944 a new Zionist insurgency erupted against the British.[7] Moreover, the Holocaust in Europe had significantly compounded the immigration issue. Palestine thus emerged from the Second World War as an ever more intractable problem. After several failed attempts to find a satisfactory solution and with the continued threat of Zionist terrorism, in February 1947 Bevin announced Britain's decision to pass the problem of finding a political solution to the Palestine question on to the United Nations.

In order to find a solution, the United Nations established the UN Special Committee on Palestine (UNSCOP). While the Jewish Agency was eager to negotiate with UNSCOP, the Arab League and the Arab Higher Committee (AHC), which represented the Palestinian Arabs, refused to have any involvement.[8] This has widely been acknowledged as the Arabs' biggest mistake, as by boycotting UNSCOP's investigation they had no input in its eventual recommendations.[9] When it reported its conclusions in September, UNSCOP recommended an end to the mandate and partition, thus creating an independent Arab state and an independent Jewish state. This proposal was welcomed by the Jewish Agency, but rejected by the Arabs. The Zionist movement accepted the plan as a 'tactical step' towards the attainment of a Jewish state.[10] The Palestinian Arabs, meanwhile, were utterly opposed to any form of partition designed to meet Zionist demands at their expense.[11] As Secretary to the Arab Higher

---

[5] The British Mandate for Palestine, 24 July 1922, in: Laqueur (ed.), *Israel–Arab Reader*, pp. 54–61.
[6] Cohen, *Retreat from the Mandate*, pp. 128–9.
[7] Bradshaw, *Britain and Jordan*, p. 118.
[8] Shlaim, *Collusion*, pp. 91–2.
[9] T. G. Fraser, *The Arab–Israeli Conflict*, 3rd edn (Basingstoke, 2008), pp. 34–5; Segev, *One Palestine, Complete*, p. 498.
[10] Segev, *One Palestine, Complete*, p. 496.
[11] Walid Khalidi, 'The Arab Perspective', in: William Roger Louis and Robert W. Stookey (eds.), *The End of the Palestine Mandate* (London, 1986), pp. 120–1.

Committee Anwar Nusayba explained: 'They [the Palestinians] refused at any time to sign their own death warrant.'[12] Two months later, on 29 November, the UN General Assembly endorsed this partition plan by a two-thirds majority vote – in which Britain abstained [Map 1].[13] This decision immediately sparked a vicious civil war inside Palestine. The chaos that ensued and the impending end of the mandate had significant implications for both Britain and Transjordan, and the purpose of this chapter is to assess how the two sought to deal with this issue. At the heart of this were Glubb and the Arab Legion, both of which became crucial tools for securing British and Jordanian interests in post-mandate Palestine.

In assessing the role of Glubb and the Arab Legion during the final months of the Palestine mandate, this chapter drives at the heart of the controversial 'collusion' debate. In essence there are two facets to Avi Shlaim's 'collusion' thesis. Firstly, he argued that in a secret meeting between King Abdullah and the Jewish Agency twelve days before the UN partition plan was approved, an 'explicit agreement was reached between the Hashemites and the Zionists to carve up Palestine', whereby Abdullah would annex the areas allotted to the Arab state to create Greater Transjordan.[14] Ilan Pappé has described it as a 'tacit agreement'.[15] For Efraim Karsh, however, there was simply no agreement, tacit or otherwise.[16] A subsidiary argument advanced by Shlaim, which is the aspect this chapter is primarily concerned with, was that Britain was party to this collusion; that Britain gave Abdullah the 'green light' to use the Arab Legion to implement a Hashemite-Zionist partition of Palestine when Prime Minister of Jordan Tawfiq Abu al-Huda and Glubb met British Foreign Secretary Ernest Bevin in London on 7 February 1948. For Shlaim, this marked 'a major turning-point in Britain's policy towards the Middle East'.[17] Efraim Karsh has refuted this claim, describing it as 'the warning that Whitehall never gave'.[18] Meanwhile, Maureen Norton echoes Shlaim's argument that Britain supported the Greater Transjordan scheme, but claims that the February meeting was not a turning point, but a charade, 'staged' to hoodwink historians into believing that the Greater Transjordan scheme was a Jordanian rather than a British

---

[12] Quoted in: Segev, *One Palestine, Complete*, p. 496.
[13] Fraser, *Arab–Israeli Conflict*, pp. 29–40.
[14] Shlaim, *Collusion*, pp. 110–16.
[15] Ilan Pappé, *The Making of the Arab–Israeli Conflict* (London, 2001), p. 20.
[16] Karsh, 'Collusion that Never Was', p. 570.
[17] Shlaim, *Collusion*, pp. 1, 132–40.
[18] Karsh, *Fabricating Israeli History*, p. 109.

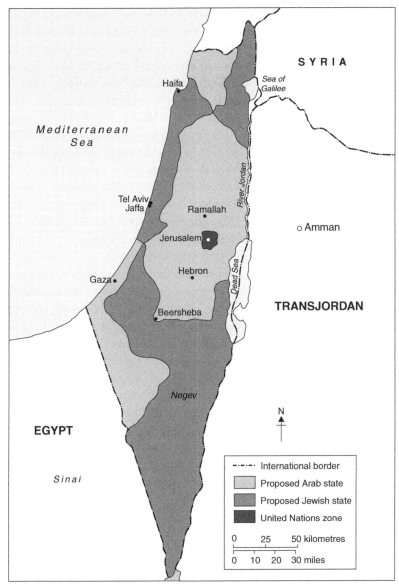

MAP 1. United Nations partition plan, November 1947.
Based on: Avi Shlaim, Collusion across the Jordan: King Abdullah, the Zionist
Movement, and the Partition of Palestine (Oxford, 1988), p. 118.

initiative.[19] Norton also contends that Glubb was the Machiavellian mastermind behind this scheme. Armed with the most significant new archival material related to the partition of Palestine to emerge since the late 1970s, this chapter is able to move this debate forward. By examining the conduct of Glubb and the Arab Legion after this meeting until the end of the mandate in May, this chapter corroborates Shlaim's 'green light' argument; it confirms that the Arab Legion was given the objective of securing the areas of Palestine allotted to the Arab state by the United Nations and acquiescing in the establishment of a Jewish state. This chapter argues that the February meeting was a watershed moment. It marked the end of a period of deliberation and the moment at which the Greater Transjordan policy was set in motion. Moreover, it defies Norton's claim that Glubb influenced high policy, but emphasises that Britain did come to rely on him to implement the scheme.

Before addressing the February meeting itself and the role of Glubb and the Arab Legion thereafter, it is important to begin by briefly detailing the genesis of the Greater Transjordan option and Glubb's ability to influence high policy. The idea of partitioning Palestine between a Jewish state and an enlarged Transjordan first became a serious option to solve the dispute in 1937, when it was recommended by the Palestine Royal Commission headed by Lord Peel, which Britain established in response to the 1936–9 Arab revolt. Abdullah welcomed this proposed expansion of his rule, arguing that the Arabs must compromise with Zionism and that 'the present situation, if it continues, will be a disaster to Palestine and the Arabs'.[20] The other Arab states, however, objected to the expansion of Abdullah's influence and the AHC was singularly opposed to partition. In an attempt to quell the intensifying Arab opposition, the British published a White Paper in 1939, which restricted Jewish immigration, and the Peel Report was discarded. The Greater Transjordan option resurfaced at the end of the Second World War when Glubb proposed it as an alternative to Jordanian independence.[21] Throughout the Second World War, Glubb had vehemently opposed partition. For Glubb, the only post-war solution was for Britain to maintain firm control of Palestine.[22] However, he also opposed Jordanian independence. Glubb explained: 'I do not deprecate complete independence because I want to make Arabia a British colony, but because I think they

[19] Norton, 'Last Pasha', p. 362.
[20] Quoted in: Salibi, *Modern History of Jordan*, p. 141.
[21] 'A Periodical Report of Trans-Jordan and the Arab Legion', Glubb, August 1945, GP2006, 92.
[22] 'A Further Note on Peace Terms in the Middle East', Glubb, 25 May 1943, GP2006, 96.

want our positive help. For us to cut our losses and clear out would be the worst thing that could happen for the Arabs.' Glubb believed that Britain should 'emphasize the increasing *inter* dependence of all nations, and the fact that even great European powers have come to the conclusion that they must sacrifice part of their independence in future'.[23] Glubb therefore posited Greater Transjordan as a means of rewarding Abdullah and enhancing his profile without independence. He backed partition more forcefully, though, after the failure of the Anglo-American Committee of Inquiry.

This committee was established at the end of 1945 to overcome Anglo-American discord concerning the future of Palestine and the problems the Holocaust had created in Europe, but it served only to highlight divisions over the issue. In August 1945 Earl G. Harrison, whom the United States had sent to Europe to seek a solution to the problem of displaced persons, reported to President Harry S. Truman that 'Palestine is definitely and pre-eminently the first choice'.[24] Subsequent to this report, Truman wrote to British Prime Minister Clement Attlee to request that an additional 100,000 Jewish immigrants be allowed into Palestine on the basis that 'no other single matter is so important for those who have known the horrors of concentration camps for over a decade as is the future of immigration possibilities into Palestine'.[25] In response, Attlee acknowledged that 'the situation in Europe' was 'one of the most horrible events in human history', but he was quick to warn that 'in the case of Palestine we have the Arabs to consider as well as the Jews and there have been solemn undertakings. ... It would be very unwise to break these solemn pledges and so set aflame the whole Middle East.'[26] Given this impasse, an Anglo-American Committee of Inquiry was formed in November 1945, consisting of six men from both countries. Yet when the Committee's report was published in May 1946, it was almost immediately thwarted after Truman emphasised the report's recommendation that 100,000 displaced Jewish immigrants from Europe be immediately admitted to Palestine, but ignored the other political recommendations.[27]

---

[23] Glubb to Owen Tweedy (Ministry of Information), 14 April 1943, GP2006, 83 [emphasis in original].

[24] Quoted in: Peter Grose, 'The President versus the Diplomats', in: Louis and Stookey (eds.), *End of the Palestine Mandate*, p. 42.

[25] Truman to Attlee, 31 August 1945, *Foreign Relations of the United States, 1945, Volume VIII* (Washington, DC, 1969), p. 738. [Hereafter: *FRUS*].

[26] Attlee to Truman, 16 September 1945, *FRUS, 1945, VIII*, p. 740.

[27] Acting Secretary of State to Secretary of State, 30 April 1946, *FRUS, 1946, VII*, pp. 588–9; Memorandum of Conversation, by the Director of the Office of European Affairs, 27 April 1946, *FRUS, 1946, VII*, pp. 587–8; Jones, *Failure in Palestine*, pp. 102–4; William Roger Louis, 'British Imperialism and the End of the Palestine Mandate', in: Louis and Stookey (eds.), *End of the Palestine Mandate*, pp. 8–9.

This angered Attlee and Bevin, who did not believe that Palestine was a solution to the problem of Jewish refugees in Europe.[28] Attlee asserted that it was necessary to examine 'the Report as a whole' before overtly acceding to any individual recommendation, and insisted that it was necessary 'to consider not only the physical problems involved but also the political reactions and possible military consequences'.[29] Allen Podet has argued that the inquiry would have proved a success, but for Britain's refusal to compromise. He describes the British as 'bankrupt in imagination, unable to comprehend that the Anglo-American group had placed in their hands what might well be the solution to their Near East problems'.[30] This, though, ignores the fact that the report was almost unanimously rejected. From the outset, the Jewish Agency believed that the committee's 'intention' was 'no doubt the elimination of Zionism'.[31] And the report's publication barely altered that view. While some moderates supported the report, others, such as David Ben-Gurion, the chairman of the Jewish Agency Executive, considered the conclusions to be even 'worse' than feared.[32] The Arabs' response was equally intransigent. They rejected nearly all of the report, leading Arab League Secretary-General Abd al-Rahman Azzam to complain: 'If ten extreme Zionists had got together in a New York room, they could not have devised anything more to the sole advantage of Zionists.'[33] Ultimately, the report in its entirety failed to cultivate the support of anyone: the Americans, the British, the Arabs, or the Zionists.

The failure of the Anglo-American Committee of Inquiry prompted Glubb to suggest, in an unsolicited memo, that partition between a Jewish state and Transjordan was the only possible solution to the Palestine problem.[34] Glubb explained that he had 'been converted to partition' based on the apparent futility of any other solution.[35] Initially Glubb

---

[28] Louis, 'British Imperialism', pp. 2, 8.

[29] Attlee to Truman, 10 June 1946, FRUS, 1946, VII, pp. 623–4.

[30] Allen H. Podet, The Success and Failure of the Anglo-American Committee of Inquiry, 1945–1946: Last Chance in Palestine (Lewiston, 1986), p. 346.

[31] Quoted in: Amikam Nachmani, Great Power Discord in Palestine: The Anglo-American Committee of Inquiry into the Problems of European Jewry and Palestine, 1945–1946 (London, 1987), p. 92.

[32] Ibid., pp. 210–12.

[33] Quoted in: ibid., p. 207. For the Arab reaction, see: Walid Khalidi, 'The Arab Perspective', in: Louis and Stookey (eds.), End of the Palestine Mandate, pp. 110–11.

[34] 'A Note on Partition as a Solution of the Palestine Problem', Glubb, 13 July 1946, WO216/207, TNA.

[35] 'A Further Note on Partition as a Solution of the Palestine Question', Glubb, December 1946, CO537/1856, TNA.

advocated a gradual process of implementing partition, whereby Britain should announce its intention to partition Palestine, with Transjordan assuming full control of the Arab areas twelve months later. However, given the return to prominence of Hajj Amin al-Husayni, Glubb revised his suggestion in a further unsolicited memo. Husayni was the figurehead for an independent Palestine and a rival of both Britain and Abdullah. In 1921, shortly after Britain assumed the mandate, the twenty-five-year-old member of one of Jerusalem's wealthiest and most powerful families was appointed as the Grand Mufti of Palestine and president of the newly established Supreme Muslim Council, after he promised to 'cooperate with the Government' and maintain 'tranquillity'. The British supported Husayni because of his popular status, in the hope that he could curb nationalist agitation in Palestine. For fifteen years he largely met Britain's expectations, and during this period he consolidated his own political and religious influence and power.[36] The Mufti's relationship with Britain was irreparably ruptured, though, by his role in the 1936–9 Arab revolt in Palestine. While he had not supported the uprising in its formative stages, he eventually bowed to popular pressure. This led to the creation of the Arab Higher Committee (AHC) with the Mufti as its head. He thus became the leading, symbolic figure of the revolt against his former master.[37] After Britain crushed the revolt, the Mufti supported the 1941 coup against the pro-British government in Iraq; when that was overturned, he fled to Nazi Germany, where he continued his fight against Britain; and in 1946 he moved to Egypt, where he once again held political sway in Palestine via the reformed AHC.[38] Given the Mufti's return to prominence, Glubb altered his partition proposal. He still advocated a fairly transparent Hashemite-Zionist division of Palestine, with the belief that 'the defection of Trans-Jordan to the side of partition would break the solid front of Arab opposition'.[39] But Glubb now suggested that partition should be implemented immediately after its announcement, rather than waiting twelve months; thus denying the Mufti an opportunity to thwart it.

[36] Philip Mattar, *The Mufti of Jerusalem: Al-Hajj Amin al-Husayni and the Palestinian National Movement* (New York, 1988), pp. 19–32, 117; Khalidi, *Iron Cage*, pp. 52–62.
[37] Mattar, *The Mufti of Jerusalem*, pp. 65–85.
[38] Ibid., pp. 109–10.
[39] 'A Further Note on Partition as a Solution of the Palestine Question', Glubb, December 1946, CO537/1856, TNA.

Glubb's proposal had little influence on British policy, though. The reaction to Glubb's recommendations on Palestine was indicative of his marginal role within Whitehall, particularly inside the Colonial Office. Glubb regularly bombarded the British government with lengthy memoranda on a multitude of Middle Eastern issues in an attempt to influence high policy. This was Glubb's ultimate ambition, but he lamented his failure to realise it. In a revealing letter to Hugh Foot, the colonial secretary in Nicosia, Glubb exposed his hopes and regrets:

> There is nothing I should like more than political influence in London. But how am I to acquire it? I do not know a single prominent person in England. The trouble is that we have to chose [*sic*] our careers when we are young, and at that time we (or I at least) are not interested in politics or in careers, but only adventure.... I took the wrong turning 15 years ago, because I was more attracted then by adventure and romance, than by official career. I see no way to rectify my mistake.[40]

Glubb was frustrated that he had got himself stuck in a 'sluggish backwater' from which he would 'never attain high rank'. Although it did not deter him, Glubb complained to his friend and confidant that 'it is [a] sheer waste of time for us out here to keep writing memos on British policy. Probably no official in any authority ever reads them in England. Even if they do, and go so far as to minute them "Very interesting", our effusions are quite ineffective.'[41] Glubb's fears were not unfounded. In one of the more sympathetic appraisals of Glubb's memoranda Bernard Reilly of the Colonial Office remarked: 'I feel that there is much that is sound in what he writes, but I doubt whether his efforts will have much effect on practical policy.'[42] Most dismissed Glubb as 'dealing with matters on which he is not in the least qualified to express an opinion'.[43] It was no surprise therefore that the reaction within the Colonial Office to Glubb's memorandum on partition was primarily one of disinterest. One Colonial Office official ridiculed it as being written in 'Glubb's usual tiresomely long-winded and repetitive style'.[44] Another remarked, several months later, how the memorandum had been filed away unread and was now out of date.[45] Contrary to Norton's contention that Glubb 'influenced policy at the highest

---

[40] Glubb to Foot, 28 February 1944, GP2006, 83.
[41] Glubb to J. de C. Hamilton, 10 June 1944, ibid.
[42] Minute by Reilly, 30 August 1946, CO537/1856, TNA.
[43] Minute by Butterhill, 15 March 1943, CO732/88/9, TNA.
[44] Minute by Martin, 20 January 1947, CO537/1856, TNA.
[45] Minute by [indecipherable], 25 June 1947, ibid.

levels of the British foreign policy establishment', Glubb's effusions had little or no impact on high policy.[46] During the Second World War, Glubb had fruitlessly advocated the creation of a Levant Office. He had also been an ineffective opponent of granting Transjordan independence. Now his views on partition were ignored. The British government sought an entirely different solution. Britain's final attempt at solving the problem, in what became known as the Bevin Plan, was a five-year trusteeship that would pave the way for an independent Palestinian state with a permanent Jewish minority.[47] However, the Jewish Agency would only accept partition and the AHC would only accept immediate independence in the whole of Palestine.[48] Consequently, the Bevin Plan was rejected and Britain lost all hope of mediating a solution. The British Cabinet therefore decided to 'refer the problem of Palestine to the judgement of the General Assembly of the United Nations'.[49]

Bevin's announcement that the future of Palestine would be handed over to the United Nations caused Abdullah to be consumed by a mixture of anxiety and excitement.[50] His fear stemmed from the likely turmoil in neighbouring Palestine; the possibility of it being overrun by his enemy, the Mufti; and the withdrawal of British forces from close proximity. Transjordan also faced losing crucial access, strategically and financially, to the Mediterranean.[51] Abdullah's excitement, meanwhile, emerged from his long-standing expansionist ambitions. Described by one of his contemporaries as a 'falcon trapped in a canary's cage', Abdullah had had a long-term goal to establish his rule over a Greater Syrian Empire.[52] Abdullah's invitation to Britain to cooperate in this desire had been consistently met with 'unavoidable official rebuff'.[53] Palestine, however, presented Abdullah with an opportunity to expand. In her advocacy of Glubb's agency Norton all but omits Abdullah from the scene. However, Abdullah was the driving force of the Greater Transjordan option. Throughout 1945–7 Abdullah had been trying to woo prominent Arab

[46] Norton, 'Last Pasha', p. 363.
[47] Michael Cohen, *Palestine and the Great Powers 1945–1982* (Princeton, 1982), pp. 217–18.
[48] Shlaim, *Collusion*, pp. 84–5.
[49] 'Conclusions of a Meeting of the Cabinet', 14 February 1947, CAB128/9/22, TNA.
[50] Shlaim, *Collusion*, p. 87.
[51] Kirkbride to Burrows, 29 October 1947, FO816/112, TNA.
[52] Shlaim, *Collusion*, p. 33; Larry Collins and Dominique Lapierre, *O Jerusalem* (New York, 1972), p. 87.
[53] Pirie-Gordon to Bevin, 10 September 1947, FO371/62226/E8679, TNA.

leaders in Palestine and boost his prestige amongst the population.[54] And it was he who sought Zionist and British support for his dynastic ambitions.

Abdullah's relationship with the Zionist movement dated back as far as the 1920s. From Abdullah's perspective, he was prompted to make this connection to combat British financial prudence and Transjordan's economic weakness.[55] Meanwhile, the Zionists were eager to procure the support of an Arab ruler as a 'counterweight' to local opposition in their pursuit of a Jewish national home in Palestine.[56] This relationship found a real purpose as the question concerning the future of Palestine intensified after 1945. The first significant talks between Abdullah and the Jewish Agency occurred in August 1946. These two meetings did not result in any agreement, but as Avi Shlaim appraised, it identified common ground and formed a basis for future negotiations.[57] A further meeting took place between King Abdullah and Golda Meir, the acting director of the Jewish Agency's Political Department, on 17 November, and the relative significance of this meeting is at the heart of the Hashemite-Zionist 'collusion' debate. There are two contemporary records of this meeting: by Ezra Danin and Elias Sassoon, two of the Jewish Agency's Arab experts who accompanied Meir at the meeting. Combined they have spawned two polarised interpretations. Shlaim argues that 'the two reports prove beyond doubt that a firm deal was concluded'.[58] Meanwhile Efraim Karsh contends that 'careful examination of the two documents ... proves that Meir was implacably opposed to any agreement that would violate the letter and the spirit of the UN partition resolution passed twelve days later. In no way did she consent to Transjordan's annexation of the Arab areas of Mandatory Palestine.' Karsh adds that Golda Meir's verbal recollection of the meeting several months later and the inferiority of her position further negate the notion that any agreement was made.[59] These two documents – alone – do not support Shlaim's claim that *a firm deal was concluded.* Yet the veracity with which Karsh has sought to deny any hint of 'collusion' has obscured the true significance of this meeting.

[54] Haim Levenberg, *Military Preparations of the Arab Community in Palestine 1945–1948* (London, 1993), pp. 212–24.
[55] Bradshaw, *Britain and Jordan*, pp. 55–65; Nevo, *King Abdallah and Palestine*, p. 200.
[56] Shlaim, *Collusion*, pp. 51–2; Yoav Gelber, *Jewish–Transjordanian Relations 1921–1948* (London, 1997), p. 2.
[57] Shlaim, *Collusion*, pp. 76–83.
[58] Ibid., pp. 110–16.
[59] Karsh, 'Collusion that Never Was', p. 570–4.

Certainly, the two parties openly discussed the possibility of reaching a Hashemite-Zionist accommodation over the future of Palestine. It is also indisputable that the Zionists confirmed that they would 'look favourably' on an attempt by Abdullah to seize the Arab areas of Palestine,

especially if it did not hinder us in the establishment of our state, if it did not lead to clashes between us and his forces, and particularly if this action were taken under a declaration that the seizure was only to ensure order and keep the peace until the U.N. could establish a government in that part.

The meeting ended with the Jewish Agency asking, and Abdullah accepting, that 'should there be a common basis – whether political, economic, or security – ... he [would] be prepared to sign a written agreement'.[60] This open-ended conclusion in itself casts doubt on the notion that a *firm* agreement was reached. It does, however, confirm that Abdullah received definite encouragement that his dynastic objectives could be achieved. The salient point that emerges from the records of this meeting is that it provided both sides with a clear comprehension of each other's main objectives; it demonstrated a mutual willingness to find a solution; and Abdullah received encouragement that the Zionists would acquiesce in the establishment of Greater Transjordan. As Golda Meir retrospectively recorded: 'If he was prepared to confront the world and us with a *fait accompli* – the tradition of friendship between us would continue.'[61] Thus, contrary to Karsh's assertion that she in no way gave consent for Abdullah's annexation of Arab Palestine, Golda Meir did, it seems, acknowledge that the Jewish Agency would acquiesce in just such an outcome. They may not have agreed on a roadmap to partition, but they did form a tacit understanding that Hashemite-Zionist partition of Palestine would be a mutually acceptable outcome.

Meanwhile, Abdullah simultaneously sought support from his patron, Britain, which, despite divesting the problem of finding a solution to the United Nations, maintained a vested interest in the outcome. Hitherto the British may have ignored Glubb's Greater Transjordan recommendation, but in light of the UN partition plan, the scheme Abdullah advocated became an increasingly attractive option. The British were fully aware that Abdullah 'was naturally anxious to ensure that the remaining Arab areas of Palestine are united to Transjordan and looks to us, as

---

[60] Ezra Danin, Report of Meeting between Golda Meir and King Abdullah, Nahayarim, 17 November 1947, in: Neil Caplan, *Futile Diplomacy, Volume II: Arab–Zionist Negotiations and the End of the Mandate* (London, 1986), pp. 277–9.

[61] Quoted in: Karsh, 'Collusion that Never Was', p. 573.

his ally, to achieve this object'.[62] As a result of Abdullah's probing, the Greater Transjordan option and possible intervention of the Arab Legion in Palestine was discussed throughout Whitehall during the second half of 1947.[63] The resulting conclusion was that the Greater Transjordan option offered the best opportunity of safeguarding British interests. This solution offered Britain two principal benefits in comparison to the UN scheme. The British were particularly keen to limit disorder and protect their strategic assets in the region, and the UN scheme threatened both these aims. If an independent Palestinian state were created, it would most likely be led by the anti-British and anti-Hashemite Mufti. Meanwhile, the alternative prospect of an enlarged Jewish state, if it was allowed to conquer more territory, was equally undesirable to the British. Both scenarios would establish in Palestine an unreliable anti-British state. It was much more favourable to see at least part of Palestine come under the influence of King Abdullah, Britain's closest regional ally. As James Eric Cable, a recent recruit at the Foreign Office, remarked: 'It would establish in a strategic and central position a state stronger than Transjordan as it now exists, but bound to us by ties not merely of friendship and obligation but also of dependence.'[64] The first benefit of the Greater Transjordan option, therefore, was that it offered the best chance of safeguarding Britain's strategic position. The second benefit was that the Arab Legion's occupation of the proposed Arab state offered the best chance of maintaining law and order. Unlike the Zionist movement, which already possessed the political, economic, and military mechanisms of a state – in the form of the Jewish Agency – the AHC was not a meaningful equivalent. The Palestinian Arabs suffered from a divided leadership that lacked any form of central organisation. For Rashid Khalidi, the Palestinians' failure to create a national structure – largely the result of suppression by British colonial rule – made the outcome of the 1948 War 'a foregone conclusion' before it had even begun.[65] The key point here for Britain's strategic thinking in 1948 is that, aside from Britain's dislike of the Mufti, the Palestinian Arabs did not have a para-state structure ready to take control of an independent state. Thus, an independent Arab state in Palestine was only likely to foment political turmoil that risked destabilising the

---

[62] 'Correspondence Between King Abdullah and the Secretary of State', J. E. Cable, 4 November 1947, FO371/62226/E10711, TNA.

[63] Minute by Burrows, 13 November 1947, ibid.

[64] 'Correspondence Between King Abdullah and the Secretary of State', Cable, 4 November 1947, ibid.

[65] Rashid Khalidi, 'The Palestinians and 1948: The Underlying Causes of Failure', in: Rogan and Shlaim (eds.), *Rewriting the History of 1948*, pp. 29–32; Khalidi, *Iron Cage*, pp. 31–64.

whole region, as the exiled Mufti competed with other potential leaders, such as his long-time rival Raghib al-Nashashibi.[66] The onset of the civil war that followed the UN resolution was considered proof that the end of the mandate would be beset by chaos. Kirkbride predicted:

If present developments are anything to judge by, the whole of Palestine is going to be in a state of disorder by the time we lay down the mandate. ... Arab Palestine will be without any central authority or police force and whoever takes over will have to compete with the jealousies and ambitions of the local leaders, bands of patriots who want to fight the Jews, bands of patriots who want to fight each other for supremacy and bands of brigands out for loot from any source whatsoever.[67]

Kirkbride was warning that the Arab Legion's task of occupying the Arab areas of Palestine would not be a smooth one. However, as the High Commissioner advised, the intervention of the Arab Legion provided 'the best chance of maintaining some semblance of order in the area of the Arab state'.[68] The Greater Transjordan option was not universally popular within Whitehall.[69] Harold Beeley, an anti-Zionist who joined the Foreign Office after serving as secretary to the Anglo-American Committee of Inquiry, scoffed at the notion that the Palestinian Arabs would support this, and he doubted whether the Arab Legion would follow such orders.[70] Ultimately, however, the Foreign Office deemed that any disadvantages of the Greater Transjordan option were outweighed by the benefits it would provide, such as the maintenance of Britain's strategic interests in a large part of Palestine and 'the only way of avoiding major bloodshed'.[71] At a meeting between the Treasury, the Foreign Office, and the War Office on 6 January it was deemed 'very much to our [Britain's] interest that conditions of security should be restored in Palestine as soon as possible after our withdrawal'.[72] The Arab Legion was considered the only possible means of filling the politico-security vacuum that the end of the mandate would create.[73]

By the start of 1948 there was a general consensus within Whitehall that it would be preferable for the Arab Legion to occupy the proposed

[66] For an account of Arab rivalries in Palestine, see: Khalidi, *Iron Cage*, pp. 65–75.
[67] Kirkbride to Orme Sargent, 5 January 1948, FO371/68367/E2095, TNA.
[68] Cunningham to FO, 2477, 20 December 1947, FO371/62226/E12317, TNA.
[69] Pappé, *Britain and the Arab–Israeli Conflict*, pp. 10–11.
[70] Minute by Beeley, 23 December 1947, FO371/62226/E12084/G; Minute by Beeley, 30 December 1947, FO371/62226/E12317, TNA.
[71] FO to Amman, 493, 11 November 1947, CO537/2107, TNA.
[72] 'Arab Legion', L. F. L. Pyman, 7 January 1948, FO371/68827/E449/G, TNA.
[73] Minute by Walker, 11 December 1947, FO371/62226/E11928/G, TNA.

Arab state. However, this preference was essentially private, and Abdullah was yet to receive British backing. Kirkbride had 'been at pains to conceal from the King' his 'own view' that Transjordan's claim to the Arab areas of Palestine was the best solution.[74] Kirkbride presumably concealed his opinion to avoid prematurely giving Abdullah the impression that he had formal British support. But for the counsel of Kirkbride Abdullah had been set to announce his intentions to claim the Arab areas of Palestine to the Arab League.[75] Kirkbride reported that 'the King had been getting increasingly restless about developments regarding Palestine and the absence of any advice about or indication of His Majesty's Government's future policy concerning Transjordan was disturbing him seriously'. Kirkbride had to impress upon Abdullah 'the importance not only of avoiding commitments but, also, of concealing his own intentions'.[76] The British realised that Abdullah wanted British backing for his desire to 'intervene in Palestine contrary to the decisions of the Arab League'. However, the British were reluctant to provide more than 'vague generalisations'.[77] In his quest for more concrete British approval, Abdullah instructed his prime minister, Samir al-Rifai, to arrange a meeting with Bevin before the end of 1947. In agitating for this meeting Rifai outlined a brief 'plan for Transjordan's action that on British withdrawal from Palestine the Arab Legion, if it had been withdrawn, should return at once'. The prime minister 'emphasised that he did not expect any agreement officially from His Majesty's Government'.[78] However, it is clear that Abdullah wanted his prime minister to engage in high-level talks with the British foreign secretary in order to gauge Britain's reaction to his intentions. When Samir al-Rifai's replacement as prime minister, Tawfiq Abu al-Huda, visited London in January 1948, to discuss a revision of the 1946 Treaty – which the Jordanians prompted for the purpose of combatting, albeit in style rather than substance, the imperialist stigma associated with the treaty – the new prime minister also requested a private meeting with Bevin to discuss the future of Palestine.[79] Abu al-Huda asked that it 'be arranged without the knowledge of the Transjordan Foreign Minister or other members of the delegation'. The purpose of the meeting was for the Jordanian prime minister to 'put to Mr Bevin certain

---

[74] Amman to FO, 321, 29 October 1947, CO537/2107, TNA.
[75] Amman to FO, 368, 6 December 1947, ibid.
[76] Kirkbride to Burrows, 8 December 1947, FO371/62226/E12416, TNA.
[77] FO to Amman, 11, 10 January 1948, FO371/62226/E12264/G, TNA.
[78] BMEO to FO, 67 Saving, 12 December 1947, FO371/62226/E11928/G, TNA.
[79] Pappé, *Britain and the Arab–Israeli Conflict*, p. 9.

opinions on possible developments in Palestine which would not be altogether acceptable to the Foreign Minister, as representing younger and more Nationalist opinion in the country'.[80] This meeting eventually took place on 7 February, and understanding what transpired at this meeting and thereafter is crucial to grasping the manner in which Palestine was partitioned and Britain's approach to its withdrawal.

The existing debate regarding the significance of this meeting – present at which were Bevin, Abu al-Huda, Glubb, and Christopher Pirie-Gordon from the British Legation in Amman – is based on scant contemporary records: Glubb's memoirs, written nine years after the event, and a handful of Foreign Office documents. In his memoirs Glubb recounted that as he was translating Abu al-Huda's message that the Jordanian government proposed to send the Arab Legion to occupy the proposed Arab state when the mandate ended, Bevin interrupted him,

saying 'it seems the obvious thing to do.' ... 'It seems the obvious thing to do,' repeated Mr Bevin, 'but do not go and invade the areas allotted to the Jews.' ... Mr Bevin thanked Taufiq Pasha for his frank exposition of the position of Trans-Jordan, and expressed his agreement with the plans put forward. We rose, shook hands cordially and took our leave.[81]

With that shake of the hands Britain had given Transjordan the 'green light' to occupy the Arab areas of Palestine.[82] Tancred Bradshaw and Efraim Karsh have challenged this argument, both emphasising that it rests on 'Glubb's memoirs alone' and that the declassified documents do not substantiate this claim.[83] Even Benny Morris, who broadly concurs with the 'collusion' thesis, concedes that 'Glubb's remembered version of that meeting is only partly confirmed by the Foreign Office documents written at the time'.[84] After the meeting, the Jordanian prime minister sent a brief account back to the king. He informed Abdullah that the meeting had taken place and that 'pure military questions were discussed'. Without going into detail, he confirmed: 'I am very pleased at the results and am proud to say that it is due to His Majesty that these results have been attained.'[85] Abu al-Huda certainly believed the meeting had been a success.

---

[80] Pirie-Gordon to Burrows, 28 January 1948, FO371/68366/E1730/G, TNA.
[81] Glubb, *Soldier*, pp. 63–6.
[82] Shlaim, *Collusion*, p. 1.
[83] Bradshaw, 'History Invented', p. 30; Bradshaw, *Britain and Jordan*, pp. 147–9; Efraim Karsh, 'Rewriting Israel's History', *Middle East Quarterly*, 3:2 (1996), pp. 19–29.
[84] Morris, *Road to Jerusalem*, p. 110.
[85] Abu al-Huda to Abdullah, 8 February 1948, FO816/112, TNA.

The question is: what had he achieved? In a telegram to Amman, recording the conversation, Bevin explained that Abu al-Huda used this meeting to inform the British government of Abdullah's view that 'it would be to the public benefit if it [the Arab Legion] returned to the Arab areas of Palestine to maintain law and order'. He added:

I asked his Excellency whether, when he spoke of the Arab Legion entering Palestine, he referred to the Arab areas as laid down in the United Nations' decision or whether he thought it would also enter the Jewish areas. Tawfiq Pasha replied that the Arab Legion would not enter Jewish areas unless the Jews invaded Arab areas.[86]

Perhaps the most striking feature of this telegram is the extent to which Bevin portrayed himself as a passive recipient of information. What Glubb described as an instruction, Bevin reported as a question.[87] Bevin added: 'In conclusion Tawfiq Pasha repeated his assurance that he did not desire to create difficulties for His Majesty's Government or to involve them in responsibility. Any action which might be taken would be purely on Transjordan's responsibility.'[88] At face value, therefore, the official record divests Britain of any blame and portrays Bevin as passively receiving information from an independent ally in whose plans he had a curious interest – hence the question – but no control and no interest in exerting influence. However, this belies the extent to which Britain did wish to exert influence; Britain's preference for the Greater Transjordan scheme; and the extent to which Transjordan was dependent on Britain, who continued to bankroll the Hashemite Kingdom.

Moreover, new sources have emerged, which further support the notion that Bevin gave active approval. The most explicit new documents are located in Glubb's papers. In reference to the account in his memoirs, it is important to acknowledge that they were not simply reliant on almost ten years of memory. The organisation of his papers demonstrates that Glubb used them when writing his memoirs, and he was able to call on contemporary documents, which support his retrospective account. These documents may not satisfy Karsh et al. because Glubb is again the author. However, it is notably corroborative that during the weeks, months, and years following the February meeting, Glubb made numerous references to an agreement being reached. For example, shortly before

---

[86] 'Conversation with the Transjordan Prime Minister', Bevin to Kirkbride, 9 February 1948, FO371/68366/E1916/G, TNA.
[87] Shlaim, *Collusion*, p. 137.
[88] 'Conversation with the Transjordan Prime Minister', Bevin to Kirkbride, 9 February 1948, FO371/68366/E1916/G, TNA.

the end of the mandate Glubb outlined the understanding when writing to the British military commander in the Middle East:

> The situation envisaged by us and by H.M.G. when we were in London, was that nothing much would happen until May 15th. The Jews would then implement the Jewish state, with the blessing of a united U.N.O., and the Arab areas of Palestine would be a vacuum, into which the Arab Legion would march.[89]

Three months later in a private letter to Kirkbride – where nothing was to be gained from misrepresenting the events and so it can surely be relied on for its accuracy – Glubb recounted what had transpired during the meeting with Bevin:

> You are of course aware that when I was in London with Tewfiq Pasha in February for the treaty negotiations, Trans-Jordan's intention to occupy part of the Arab areas of Palestine was explained to Mr Bevin. The only comment made by the latter was that we should be careful not to enter the Jewish areas.[90]

This is almost identical to the account Glubb gave in his memoirs and supports the notion that Bevin, while not urging Transjordan to send the Arab Legion into Palestine, gave his approval so long as it did not obviously defy the UN resolution by entering the proposed Jewish state.

Meanwhile, additional British documents have been released, which, while not providing a smoking gun, further support the contention that Bevin gave his agreement. The first time the question of Palestine was discussed in the Cabinet after the February meeting between Bevin, Abu al-Huda, and Glubb was several weeks later on 22 March. Hitherto the best record of this Cabinet meeting was the minutes, which provide a rather bland, homogenous account of the meeting where:

> The Cabinet agreed that ... the British civil and military authorities in Palestine should make no effort to oppose the setting up of a Jewish State or a move into Palestine from Transjordan.

The minutes summarised both these moves as things that 'might' happen.[91] The recently released Cabinet secretary's notebook provides a more revealing and slightly different appraisal. Here, Bevin is recorded as saying that the 'Jews will prob.[ably] establ.[ish] a State in some area' and, crucially, he stated that he was: 'Convinced Abdullah will put troops into parts of Pal.[estine] wh.[ich] Jews can't hold.' He added: 'That will mean a row among Arab States. But don't think we sh[oul]d. use B.[ritish]

---

[89] Glubb to John Crocker (C-in-C MELF), 24 April 1948, GP2006, 83.
[90] Glubb to Kirkbride, 4 August 1948, ibid.
[91] 'Conclusions of a Meeting of the Cabinet', 22 March 1948, CAB128/12, TNA.

troops to check this develop[men]t. of events. "Nature" may partition Palestine.'[92] No doubt Bevin was left 'convinced' of Abdullah's intentions as a result of his meeting with Abu al-Huda in February, and he was seemingly reconciled to allowing this to happen, in spite of any inter-Arab conflict that may occur. The most tantalising remark Bevin made was his final comment: '"Nature" may partition Palestine.' Bevin, it seems, was reconciled to the Arab Legion filling the politico-security vacuum inside Palestine and establishing an alternative form of partition that the international community would be compelled to accept as the new *natural* order. The intention was that the Arab Legion would enter the Arab areas of Palestine under the pretext of 'restoring order'.[93] It was understood that: 'For publicity purposes they [the king and the prime minister] say to the Arabs that they are going to try and occupy the whole of Palestine, but this is merely to forestall the accusation that they are implementing partition.'[94] It was not envisaged that the Arab Legion would enter as an invading army. As Glubb outlined: 'I may repeat that, when we were in London last February nobody envisaged a war in Palestine. A peaceful occupation of the vacant Arab areas with the tacit acquiescence of the Jews was the plan agreed upon.'[95] In February Bevin approved this scheme; he approved the use of the British-financed and -officered Arab Legion for that purpose. The official contemporary British records do not contain a formal and explicit written agreement. Yet that is not surprising. Kirkbride warned, on the very day that Abdullah met Golda Meir, that a formal agreement between 'Abdullah and the Jews would be dangerous in that secrecy would be impossible'.[96] This danger would be even more applicable to British involvement. Indeed, when discussing the pros and cons of the Greater Transjordan option in November 1947, Bevin was adamant: 'We must ... be extremely careful not to be associated with any such scheme, at any rate to begin with, as this would only increase opposition of Arab and Jewish extremists.'[97] It is not surprising, therefore, that the official records are not explicit – but British support for the Greater Transjordan scheme is nonetheless clear.

In order to allow the Arab Legion to perform this function, the British approved a reorganisation scheme, including a subsidy of £2 million,

[92] Cabinet Secretary's Notebook, 22 March 1948, CAB195/6, TNA.
[93] Minute by Walker, 14 February 1948, FO371/68367/E2095/G, TNA.
[94] Amman to FO, 90, 14 February 1948, FO371/68367/E2163/G, TNA.
[95] Glubb to Kirkbride, 4 August 1948, GP2006, 83.
[96] Amman to FO, 342, 17 November 1947, CO537/2107, TNA.
[97] FO to Amman, 493, 11 November 1947, ibid.

plus £500,000 capital expenditure, which consolidated the Arab Legion at its present strength of approximately 7,000 men.[98] In that respect, both Britain and Abdullah were fortunate that the Arab Legion had not been reduced as previously planned. Given that the main obstacle to the Arab Legion's reduction had been the vital role that it was performing in Palestine, it might have been expected that Britain's withdrawal from Palestine would have finally allowed for this reduction to be enacted. However, as Bernard Burrows explained, 'it is precisely the withdrawal of our own forces from Palestine that gives the Arab Legion its present high political value'. The case put to the Treasury to justify an increase to the subsidy was that it was 'imperative that the Arab Legion should be maintained on its present footing for the next year and in our own interest we must pay for this to be done'.[99] Aside from the Greater Transjordan objective, Britain's withdrawal from Palestine did render a reorganisation of the Arab Legion necessary. Hitherto the Arab Legion depended on the British forces in Palestine for much of its essential services and support. The imminent departure of the British forces from Palestine meant that the Arab Legion 'must in future, be able operationally and administratively to stand on [its] own feet'.[100] It also needed to be more capable of defending itself against external aggression.[101] Nonetheless, the 1948 reorganisation was considered a short-term measure. It was no coincidence that the supply of new equipment was expedited. Ordinarily the Arab Legion's reorganisation and the supply of new equipment would not have begun until after the start of the new financial year in April. However, in this instance it was vital that the Arab Legion received its new equipment well in advance of the end of the mandate.[102] The reorganisation of the Arab Legion in 1948 was primarily required as a short-term measure to cope with the immediate problems in Palestine; to enable it to *secure* the Arab areas of Palestine adjacent to Transjordan. The British still hoped the Arab Legion could be reduced once the Palestine situation

[98] Minute by Walker, 10 February 1948, FO371/68828/E1864, TNA.
[99] Burrows to Russell Edmunds, 22 January 1948, WO32/15562, TNA.
[100] 'Note on Transjordan Government's Proposal to Reorganise the Arab Legion', January 1948, FO371/68827/E1080/G, TNA.
[101] 'Appreciation by the War Office of the Military Needs of Transjordan and the Extent to Which the Proposal to Reorganise the Arab Legion (1947) Would Satisfy Them', 23 December 1947, WO32/15562, TNA.
[102] 'Minutes of a Conference Held in the War Office (Room 350) on 6 February 1948 on the Reorganisation of the Arab Legion', 11 February 1948; 'Minutes of a Meeting Held in the War Office (Room 350) on 2 February, 1948 on the Reorganisation of the Arab Legion', WO32/15562, TNA.

was resolved. As Burrows explained: 'If conditions are more settled when the problem comes to be reconsidered in twelve months' time it is to be hoped that it will be possible to reduce our contribution substantially.'[103] The fact that the 1948 reorganisation of the Arab Legion was based on Glubb's 1947 proposal, albeit with minor modifications, and that Glubb had also shown himself to be in favour of partition since 1946 has led Maureen Norton to conclude that Glubb was the Machiavellian mastermind behind the Greater Transjordan scheme.[104] However, just as his political suggestions were ignored, his original reorganisation proposal was initially written off as being 'like most of Glubb's schemes, ... somewhat ambitious'.[105] Glubb's significance lies not in the plan's inception, but in its execution, which, as the remainder of this chapter reveals, further corroborates the existence of an Anglo-Hashemite plan to implement an alternative form of partition.

After the February meeting Glubb actively sought to ensure that the ground was prepared for the smooth occupation of the proposed Arab state when the mandate ended. Principally, he sought to eliminate two problems that threatened the Greater Transjordan scheme. The first problem emerged within weeks of the February meeting when Glubb reported an unexpected development caused by the gradual infiltration of the Arab Liberation Army (ALA) into Palestine. The ALA, which the Arab League had established as a means of allowing the member states to avoid direct intervention, was dominated by Syria and led by Fawzi al-Qawuqji, who had fought for Arab nationalist causes throughout the Middle East.[106] In 1948, this career soldier was put in charge of the hastily assembled Arab Liberation Army, which by the end of January, when it began filtering into Palestine, contained almost 4,000 volunteers – some trained soldiers, many not – from across the Muslim world.[107] The ALA's entry into Palestine had the potential to cause problems for the Greater Transjordan scheme, if it gained control of areas that the Arab Legion planned to occupy. The British maintained some hope that, because of enmity between Qawuqji and the Mufti, the ALA leader might

[103] Burrows to Russell Edmunds, 22 January 1948, ibid.
[104] Norton, 'Last Pasha', pp. 250, 259–60.
[105] DMO to VCIGS, 18 June 1947, WO32/15562, TNA.
[106] Parsons, 'Soldiering for Arab Nationalism', p. 33; Fawzi al-Qawuqji, 'Memoirs, 1948. Part I', *Journal of Palestine Studies*, 1:4 (1972), p. 27.
[107] Joshua Landis, 'Syria and the Palestine War: Fighting King Abdullah's "Greater Syria Plan"', in: Rogan and Shlaim (eds.), *Rewriting the History of 1948*, p. 195; Abu Nowar, *Jordanian–Israeli War*, pp. 13–14.

'be favourably inclined towards King Abdullah's ambitions in Palestine'. However, his primary allegiance was believed to be with the Syrian president, and Kirkbride therefore concluded that the ALA's 'establishment in the Nablus area before Transjordan was in a position to move has prejudiced the chances of Transjordan being able to occupy Arab areas of Palestine without being involved in hostilities'.[108]

The irony was that Abdullah facilitated the Arab Liberation Army's entry into Palestine, despite its negative impact on his territorial ambitions. But this was indicative of the political dilemma facing the king in his pursuit of Greater Transjordan. Before entering Palestine in January, Qawuqji impressed upon the Syrian authorities the need to contact Amman in advance, 'informing it of our movements to facilitate' the ALA's passage across the River Jordan and 'to ensure that in the future we could receive supplies and provisions through Jordan'. He was therefore shocked when the first units of the ALA arrived at the Syrian-Jordanian frontier on 22 January only to be told that the Jordanian government 'knew nothing' about their intentions and 'refused to let us cross'. Only after Ismail Safwat, the General Officer Commanding the Arab League Military Committee, visited King Abdullah in Amman did they gain approval to do so, albeit on certain conditions, namely, that the ALA crossed the frontier before dawn and that it must not attack anyone until after the end of the mandate.[109] Apart from his personal ambitions in Palestine, Abdullah was wary of overtly fuelling the civil war raging in Palestine. However, as Glubb informed Kirkbride, the Jordanian authorities allowed the ALA passage through Transjordan because refusing would result in accusations of treachery in the Arab press.[110] Despite this explanation, Kirkbride issued a formal protest to Abdullah; to whit the king assured him that he would not permit further volunteers to pass through into Palestine via Transjordan. However, Kirkbride suspected that the political situation might overwhelm Abdullah once more.[111] And so it proved. Once the initial units had reached their designated positions in central Palestine, Qawuqji 'entered Palestine, on 6 March 1948, with the remaining units of the Liberation Army via Amman, not stealthily by night, and not piecemeal, but in broad daylight and actually across the Allenby Bridge'.[112]

[108] Amman to FO, 34, 24 January 1948, FO371/68365/E1088, TNA.
[109] Qawuqji, 'Memoirs, 1948. Part I', pp. 27–8.
[110] Amman to FO, 29, 21 January 1948, FO371/68365/E941/G, TNA.
[111] Amman to FO, 39, 28 January 1948, FO371/68365/E1293, TNA.
[112] Qawuqji, 'Memoirs, 1948. Part I', pp. 27–8.

Despite official Jordanian approval for the ALA's entry into Palestine, and true to Kirkbride's pre-emptive concern, its presence did appear to threaten the Greater Transjordan scheme, and it was up to Glubb to solve this problem. When he returned from London in February, Glubb reported that upon arrival in Nablus, the ALA had quickly gained control of the civil population, had proved well disciplined, and had been welcomed by the local Arabs. The ALA's influence was spreading, and Glubb warned: 'If they continue at their present rate, the Arab League army will have complete control of the Arab areas of Palestine before May 15th.' Glubb was concerned that:

In order to justify the re-entry of the Arab Legion into Palestine on May, 15th some invitation to them from the people of Palestine would be desirable. If the 'holy warriors' are already in control such an invitation will not come. Thus if Arab Legion units evacuate Palestine according to the present programme, the chance that they will return later on, will be greatly reduced.[113]

If the ALA acquired control of the proposed Arab state before the end of the mandate, the Arab Legion could hardly re-enter and fill the politico-security vacuum as planned. Indeed, there would be no vacuum to fill.

To counter the unexpected progress of the ALA, Glubb wanted to 'change the programme for the withdrawal of the Arab Legion'.[114] With the British mandate now coming to an end, it was necessary for the Arab Legion units stationed in Palestine to return to Transjordan – despite the covert intention to return. According to the original withdrawal programme, the entirety of the Arab Legion was scheduled to return to Transjordan between 1 February and 15 April.[115] However, given the progress of the ALA, Glubb was concerned that this withdrawal programme seemed 'to play into the hands of the extremists, both Fawzi and the Mufti'.[116] Due to the location of the Kirkuk–Haifa oil pipeline and the main British army installations, the Arab Legion was primarily stationed in the areas of Palestine allotted to the Jewish state, thereby enabling the ALA to gain a foothold in the Arab areas. Haim Levenberg has argued that the positioning of the Arab Legion meant that Abdullah was unable to use it to consolidate control of the proposed Arab state before the end of the mandate.[117] Yet Glubb actively sought to overcome this problem.

[113] 'A Note on the Situation in Arab Palestine on 21st February 1948', Glubb, with covering letters from Glubb to Montgomery (CIGS), Crocker, and MacMillan (General Officer Commanding, Palestine and Transjordan), 22 and 23 February 1948, GP2006, 83.
[114] Glubb to Montgomery, 23 February 1948, ibid.
[115] 'Withdrawal of Arab Legion', undated, WO191/82, TNA.
[116] Glubb to Montgomery, 23 February 1948, GP2006, 83.
[117] Levenberg, *Military Preparations*, pp. 226, 237.

According to the 'present programme' of withdrawal, when the Arab Legion units were released from duty in areas of the proposed Jewish state, they would 'return directly to Trans-Jordan, thereby [as Glubb cautioned] leaving the League army in undisputed possession of the Arab areas until May 15th'. With the Arab Legion presently absent from the areas designated to the proposed Arab state, Glubb warned: 'The Mufti and Fawzi, two of the bitterest enemies of Britain, will be free to dispute the Arab areas between them.' Glubb therefore suggested that if, instead of withdrawing directly to Transjordan as planned, 'Arab Legion units could be released from Jewish areas and stationed in Arab areas, the situation would be reversed'. He added:

In Ramallah, Hebron and Beersheba, the Arab Legion could still get in before the League army influence spreads there. In Nablus, the Arab Legion could easily attain influence equal to that of the League army, and would gradually eclipse it.

Glubb proposed: 'If Arab Legion units were to move to Arab areas now, they would of course *ostensibly* do so under the orders of the British army, to help to maintain order and keep the roads open.' In reality, though, the Arab Legion was being redeployed to prepare the Arab areas of Palestine for occupation by the Arab Legion after the end of the mandate. Glubb did not suggest that the promise to withdraw the Arab Legion from Palestine before the end of the mandate be broken – although the fact that at least one unit never withdrew back to Transjordan suggests that may have been a part of Glubb's thinking. What he suggested was strategic redeployment of Arab Legion units to 'establish local contacts' and consolidate their position before a last-minute withdrawal and almost immediate re-entry. Rather than allow the ALA to fill the void, Glubb proposed to counteract this by moving the Arab Legion forces from locations inside the proposed Jewish state into the areas they planned to occupy first.[118] General MacMillan, the General Officer Commanding British Troops in Palestine and Transjordan, 'agreed', and proposed that Arab Legion units be transferred to Nablus, Hebron, and Ramallah.[119] The War Office also had 'no objection ... provided, of course, it is all withdrawn by 15th May 1948'.[120] The British authorities did not propose this plan to Glubb, and their main operational concern remained an efficient and safe withdrawal of British forces from Palestine. However, the

[118] 'A Note on the Situation in Arab Palestine on 21st February 1948', Glubb, GP2006, 83 [emphasis added].
[119] Chief of Staff (Milpal) to Glubb, GO530, 25 February 1948, ibid.
[120] War Office to C-in-C MELF, 6 March 1948, WO32/15562, TNA.

British military was in favour – from a strategic perspective – of the emergence of Greater Transjordan and was therefore willing to acquiesce in Glubb's plan for the Arab Legion's temporary redeployment to the areas that the Arab Legion planned to occupy when the mandate ended.[121]

In his object of eclipsing the ALA and establishing local contacts in the Arab areas of Palestine, Glubb was ultimately successful, though this was not solely due to Glubb's redeployment of the Arab Legion. It was also a consequence of the Liberation Army's deficiencies, as it proved not to be as efficient as Glubb initially surmised. With the ALA overstretched, under-resourced, and suffering from inadequate training, it struggled to cope with the Haganah's military superiority and the devastating impact of Plan D – a series of military operations the Haganah designed to secure control of the proposed Jewish state in preparation for the end of the mandate.[122] Fawzi al-Qawuqji made repeated requests to the High Command in Damascus for more financial and material support, but to no avail. Moreover, Qawuqji complained that failures to pay wages on time 'caused us to lose control of the troops'.[123] The ALA's plight was further compounded by a failure to generate popular support in Palestine. Many Palestinian Arabs in towns such as Jaffa and Haifa – from labourers to the upper middle classes – did not support the war being waged by either the ALA or the Mufti's Holy War Army. Their main concern was public order and economic security.[124] The ALA experienced difficulties enlisting just 'a few hundred Palestinian volunteers'. As a result of these deficiencies, Ismail Safwat concluded: 'Our forces in Palestine – whether trained volunteers or armed Palestinian guerrillas – cannot achieve a decisive military victory.'[125]

---

[121] This is contrary to Ronen Yitzhak's claim that General MacMillan 'removed the Arab Legion companies from areas of Jewish settlement and stationed them elsewhere in order to avoid further clashes between the Arab Legion and the Jews'. Yitzhak, *Abdullah al-Tall*, pp. 28–9.

[122] Qawuqji, 'Memoirs, 1948. Part I', pp. 45–58; 'A Brief Report of the Situation in Palestine and Comparison Between the Forces of Both Sides', Ismail Safwat, 23 March 1948, in: Walid Khalidi (ed.), 'Selected Documents on the 1948 Palestine War', *Journal of Palestine Studies*, 27:3 (1998), pp. 62–72; 'Plan D', 10 March 1948, in: Kirsten Schulze, *The Arab–Israeli Conflict* (London, 1999), pp. 117–22.

[123] Fawzi al-Qawuqji to High Command, 9 May 1948, in: Fawzi al-Qawuqji, 'Memoirs, 1948. Part II', *Journal of Palestine Studies*, 2:1 (1972), p. 5.

[124] Itamar Radai, 'Jaffa, 1948: The Fall of a City', *Journal of Israeli Studies*, 30:1 (2011), pp. 30–3, 36–7.

[125] 'A Brief Report of the Situation in Palestine and Comparison Between the Forces of Both Sides', Ismail Safwat, 23 March 1948, in: Khalidi (ed.), 'Selected Documents', pp. 62–72.

Given these difficulties, Kirkbride deemed the atmosphere ripe for securing Jordanian interests. Throughout March Glubb held talks with Arab notables in Hebron and Gaza.[126] And by mid-April Kirkbride reported that the notables in Gaza, Hebron, and Ramallah were openly in favour of Arab Legion occupation when the mandate ended. Nablus was more cautious, owing to the presence of the ALA, but had not shown any opposition to the scheme. Meanwhile Beersheba, terrorised by Zionist forces, would welcome any saviour, according to Kirkbride.[127] A few days later Kirkbride added: 'Arab Legion sources of information report a general collapse of Arab morale in Palestine extending to the Army of Liberation whose commander is stating his position is critical and that he needs more troops urgently.'[128] Fearful that the situation could easily change in the space of a month, Kirkbride asked whether the end of the mandate could be brought forward. His request was refused.[129] But the ALA's situation did not improve. Just two weeks before the end of the mandate it was reported that: 'The morale and value of the Liberation Army in the Nablus-Jenin-Tulkarm area is falling rapidly. Fauzi has gone to Damascus and may not return.'[130] Qawuqji communicated to his HQ that 'the population's only source of reassurance' was the 'presence' of the Arab Legion and 'the hope that other armies would come in'.[131] The Arab Legion was now deemed the only force capable of protecting the Arabs in Palestine.[132] In that respect, the Arab Legion was used as part of a quintessential 'population-centric counterinsurgency' tactic, designed 'to win over [the] population by "securing" and "protecting" them'.[133] That was Glubb's aim and his target was met; the Arab Legion had eclipsed the ALA as the best hope for saving Arab Palestine. Glubb commented subsequently: 'The first *contre temps* was the arrival of the Arab Liberation Army.'[134] This problem he had overcome.

The second obstacle to realising the Greater Transjordan scheme was maintaining the adherence of and coordinating with the Zionists. During the final few weeks of the mandate, Colonel Goldie, commander of the

[126] Levenberg, *Military Preparations*, p. 228.
[127] Amman to FO, 225, 13 April 1948, FO371/68852/E4687, TNA.
[128] Amman to FO, 227, 16 April 1948, FO371/68852/E4783, TNA.
[129] Amman to FO, 230, 17 April 1948, FO371/68852/E4805, TNA.
[130] 'Note', most likely by Glubb, 29 April 1948, GP2006, 90.
[131] Fawzi al-Qawuqji to High Command, 8 May 1948, in: Qawuqji, 'Memoirs, 1948. Part II', p. 15.
[132] Levenberg, *Military Preparations*, p. 209.
[133] Khalili, *Time in the Shadows*, pp. 45–6.
[134] 'The Trans-Jordan Situation', Glubb, 12 August 1948, GP2006, 83.

Arab Legion Mechanised Brigade, made two clandestine visits to meet
with Zionist officials. These meetings were initiated by Glubb, who was
'consciously turning to the Haganah and not to the statesmen'.[135] The
purpose was 'to ensure' that the Arab Legion's planned 'occupation of the
range of hills from Nablus to Hebron ... would be peaceful'.[136] Previous
accounts of the Goldie mission referred to a single meeting between
Goldie and the Haganah held in Naharayim on 2 May.[137] Indeed, in an
interview almost forty years later, Goldie himself claimed 'there was only
one meeting'.[138] However, we now know that Goldie met with Zionist
representatives at least twice before the end of the mandate. The first of
these, as Benny Morris has noted, was a meeting held in Afula on the
10 April attended by Goldie and a Haganah 'district officer' codenamed
'Barkai'.[139] Hitherto the only record of this meeting was a report located
in the Haganah Archives. We now have access to the Arab Legion account
of this earlier meeting, which provides fresh insight into this meeting and
the role of Glubb and the Arab Legion during 1948. Norman Lash, the
Arab Legion divisional commander, provided Glubb with a nine-point
'gist' of what transpired, which reveals three primary aims of the meeting
in Afula, each geared towards avoiding conflict. Principally Goldie had
been sent on a fact-finding mission. Glubb wanted to ascertain what the
Haganah's intentions were. The first point Lash reported, which points
to the principal fact-finding objective, was that: 'It is quite definitely the
Jewish policy to avoid hostilities with the Arab Legion. They refer to the
opening of hostilities with us as "the third bent" which they are anxious to avoid (at this stage anyway).' Presumably this was the number
one enquiry that Goldie was instructed to make. The second reason for
this meeting was that Goldie had been sent to request that the Haganah
be instructed to 'lay off' Arab Legion transport; something that Barkai
agreed to instruct, although he warned that 'it was impossible to arrange
for immunity of our transport when engaged in protecting Arab *civilian*
transport'.[140] The third purpose of the meeting was to prepare the way
for further talks as and when they might be required. Indeed, Goldie's
second meeting on 2 May was initiated within that context. Benny

---

[135] 'Meeting with Brigadier Goldie', 10 April 1948, Haganah Archives, 105–54.
[136] Glubb to Kirkbride, 4 August 1948, GP2006, 83.
[137] Lunt, *Glubb Pasha*, pp. 136–7; Royle, *Glubb Pasha*, pp. 350–2; Shlaim, *Collusion*,
    pp. 179–86; Collins and Lapierre, *O Jerusalem!*, pp. 312–13.
[138] Interview with Goldie, 15 September 1985, Avi Shlaim's Private Collection.
[139] Morris, *Road to Jerusalem*, p. 140.
[140] Lash to Glubb, 11 April 1948, GP2006, 90 [emphasis in original].

Morris emphasised that a three-week delay existed between the two meetings.[141] However, the delay was not surprising. After the first meeting Lash reported: 'The D.O. [Barkai] said that he had no doubt that a meeting could be arranged between a senior British officer on our side and a senior officer of the Hagana General Staff *if we thought it useful.*'[142] But at this point Glubb was seemingly satisfied with the gist he had received.

The Arab Legion account of the first meeting indicates that it was more productive than the Haganah report suggests. The Haganah account reveals little more than that Glubb sent Goldie to initiate discussions 'about not attacking from both sides' after 14 May.[143] The Arab Legion account is more revealing, however. Goldie's meeting with Barkai had reassured Glubb that the two sides shared similar goals and that partition could be implemented with minimal conflict. Indeed, he had learned that the Haganah planned to avoid hostilities and that, in Lash's words: 'The Jews fully expect us to go into Arab Palestine next month and are on the whole in favour of it: they have a pretty good idea as to where we are going.' The Haganah apparently had no intention of obstructing Glubb's task of occupying the areas allotted to the Arab state, meaning the Greater Transjordan scheme and the fate of the Arab Legion both appeared reasonably secure. Moreover, Glubb learned that Haganah policy would work in the Arab Legion's favour. Goldie was informed by Barkai that: 'Their policy at present is: 1) Picquet L of C [picket lines of communication]; 2) Kill Arab leaders; 3) Drastic local reprisals.' In relation to the second point, the Haganah had 'appreciated that the Arabs have no good junior leaders and think that if a few outstanding men are disposed of they will become a complete rabble'.[144] The elimination of the Arabs as an effective fighting force would indeed play into the hands of the Arab Legion's principal objective of entering Arab areas of Palestine under the pretext of establishing law and order. The Haganah's policy of drastic local reprisals was also convenient for the strategic plan being followed by Glubb because it would surely increase the demand for Arab Legion protection. Glubb was not intending on staging a mock battle. He was seeking to launch a 'police operation', which the international community would hopefully ratify.[145] Thus, a second meeting between Goldie and the Haganah was not immediately deemed necessary.

[141] Morris, *Road to Jerusalem*, p. 140.
[142] Lash to Glubb, 11 April 1948, GP2006, 90 [emphasis added].
[143] 'Meeting with Brigadier Goldie', 10 April 1948, Haganah Archives, 105–54.
[144] Lash to Glubb, 11 April 1948, GP2006, 90.
[145] 'The Trans-Jordan Situation', Glubb, 12 August 1948,GP2006, 83.

The Haganah's policy of killing Arab leaders was proven effective within days of the Goldie meeting, following the death of Abd al-Qadir al-Husayni – cousin of the Mufti and commander of the Holy War Army – during an attempt to retake the village of Qastal, six miles west of Jerusalem. According to Ben-Gurion, Abd al-Qadir's death was not an intentional consequence of the Haganah policy revealed to the Arab Legion. Ben-Gurion explained: 'He raised his hands and pleaded for his life. Our boys didn't know who he was and they shot him. Only when they had checked his papers did they realize whom they had shot.'[146] Whether or not his death was intentional, it certainly justified the Haganah's logic, as it initiated the effective collapse of the force he commanded.[147] Bahjat Abu Gharbiyya, who fought alongside Abd al-Qadir, described his loss as 'irreparable. He was the standard around which the fighters rallied.' Abd al-Qadir's death was keenly felt in Jerusalem.[148] It 'caused confusion in the whole area', prompting his followers to turn to Fawzi al-Qawuqji for leadership and reinforcements.[149] Initially the ALA did step in, but after several days of fighting, military supplies were depleted and the High Command in Damascus ordered Qawuqji to retreat.[150] The ramifications of Abd al-Qadir's death were not limited to Jerusalem, though. As Bahjat Abu Gharbiyya explained, it had a 'depressing effect' throughout the country.[151] Abd al-Qadir was revered as a hero in Palestine.[152] Jaffa resident Ishaq Khurshid said: 'The truth is, that after the battle of al-Qastal and the fall of Abd al-Qadir al-Husayni, a general collapse occurred. The collapse was said to take place throughout Palestine, but I felt it most acutely in Jaffa.'[153] When Zionist forces attacked Jaffa on 25 April, following the Zionist capture of Haifa, the town's leaders fled, its resistance capitulated, and a mass exodus followed, before the few remaining inhabitants surrendered.[154] Within weeks of Abd al-Qadir's death and less than a month

[146] Ben-Gurion's Diary, 14 April 1948, in: David Ben-Gurion, *Israel: A Personal History* (London, 1972), p. 84.

[147] Avi Shlaim, 'Israel and the Arab Coalition', in: Rogan and Shlaim (eds.), *Rewriting the History of 1948*, p. 86.

[148] Bahjat Abu Gharbiyya, *Memoirs of a Freedom Fighter, 1916–49* (Beirut, 1993), in: Khalidi (ed.), 'Selected Documents', pp. 72–84.

[149] Amin Ruwayha to C-in-C and Inspector General, 8 April 1948, in: Qawuqji, 'Memoirs, 1948. Part I', p. 41.

[150] Qawuqji, 'Memoirs, 1948. Part I', pp. 45–9.

[151] Abu Gharbiyya, *Memoirs of a Freedom Fighter*, in: Khalidi (ed.), 'Selected Documents', pp. 72–84.

[152] Segev, *One Palestine, Complete*, pp. 505–6.

[153] Quoted in: Radai, 'Jaffa, 1948', p. 23.

[154] Morris, *Birth of the Palestinian Refugee Problem*, pp. 95–101.

before the mandate had ended, therefore, the irregular forces operating in Palestine – both the ALA and the Holy War Army – were in dire straits.

The plight of the Palestinian forces and the Haganah's comparative success was not entirely good news for the prospects of the Greater Transjordan scheme, as it caused unanticipated problems for the strategic plan being followed by Glubb. Despite seeking to eclipse them, the Arab Legion commander lamented that the irregular Arab forces were 'proving helpless'. They had no organisation, no plan, and scant resources, which meant: 'The result is that Arab resistance inside Palestine is almost at an end already.' This posed a significant problem for the Arab Legion's planned re-entry into the Arab areas of Palestine in order to effect partition. The scheme required a political and security vacuum for the Arab Legion to enter and protect. As Glubb acknowledged: 'I think that the Trans-Jordan Government would not be justified in re-invading Palestine against Jewish resistance, if all other Arab resistance were already at an end.'[155] Glubb was treading a fine line between nullifying the threat of effective Arab resistance and simultaneously maintaining sufficient resistance for Arab Legion support to be required when the mandate ended.

The Greater Transjordan scheme's predicament was further compounded by the uncertainty of the accord with the Zionists. Towards the end of April – two weeks after Abd al-Qadir's death – Glubb observed that the situation on the ground in Palestine had changed. He remarked that, in comparison to February:

The situation has recently developed very rapidly and in quite a different manner. The Jews have taken the initiative and shown their hand, presumably in order to show the world that they can implement partition, before U.N.O. has time to cancel it.

Despite his willingness to communicate with the Haganah, Glubb still did not trust the Zionists to honour any agreement if they found an opportunity to achieve further territorial gains. Glubb was concerned that:

What we do not know is whether the Jews will then have the self-control to limit themselves to the boundaries of the Jewish state, or whether they will get drunk with victory, and try and seize more.

Glubb did concede, though, that: 'On the other hand, the situation may still arise in which the Jews voluntarily withdraw within the boundaries of the U.N.O. Jewish state, and the Arab areas are left empty.'[156] One

---

[155] Glubb to Crocker, 24 April 1948, GP2006, 83.
[156] Ibid.

thing that seems clear from Glubb's dialogue is that he and the Arab
Legion were not working according to a fixed Hashemite-Zionist agenda.
As Avi Shlaim acknowledged, though, there was not a 'precise and definitive political and military agreement' akin to the Anglo-French-Israeli
conspiracy against Egypt in 1956.[157] Glubb nevertheless acted according
to an assumption – no doubt borne out of Abdullah's tacit understanding
with the Jewish Agency – that the Zionist forces would not violate the
UN boundaries. This, however, could not be guaranteed, and the uncertainty created by the plight of the irregular forces in Palestine left Glubb
hugely concerned.

By the beginning of May Glubb surmised that these fears would not
be realised. His appreciation of the situation, as of 1 May, was that
the Haganah was 'securing undoubted control' of the proposed Jewish
state, but had 'not penetrated much to Arab areas', except for Jerusalem.
Glubb therefore predicted: 'If this goes on until May 15th, the Jews will
by then more or less have control of their areas, and we can then take
over the Arab areas. In other words, partition will have come into existence.'[158] With the end of the mandate just two weeks away, implementation of the Greater Transjordan partition scheme appeared to be in sight.

One substantial problem remained, though. Glubb believed: 'The snag
is Jerusalem.' Under the UN partition plan, the holy city was designated
an international zone; it was scheduled to be an island within the Arab
state [Map 1]. This meant it lay outside Glubb's objective as defined in
February, to effect partition based on the lines drawn by the United Nations.
Despite the improved prospects for the Greater Transjordan scheme, Glubb
remained distrustful of the ambitions of the Zionist authorities with regard
to Jerusalem. He predicted that, 'if no international force has arrived, the
Jews will certainly try to capture the whole city from the Arabs. They will
probably succeed.' Moreover, despite Glubb's desire to avoid genuine conflict, he was to some extent a hostage to popular pressures. Indeed, he
reported that:

Passionate excitement about Jerusalem already exists in Trans-Jordan. The idea
of the Jews occupying the Holy Places is working everyone into a frenzy. I am
afraid that if this takes place on May 15th, I shall be unable to resist Arab pressure to put the whole Arab Legion into Jerusalem. This will almost destroy the
Arab Legion, will certainly destroy Jerusalem, and will spoil all our plans for

---

[157] Shlaim, *Politics of Partition*, pp. vii–viii.
[158] Glubb to Crocker, 1 May 1948, GP2006, 83.

settlement. If it were not for the Jerusalem snag, I think the prospects after May 15th might not be too bad.[159]

Glubb's principal objective during the remaining few weeks of the mandate, therefore, was to try to eliminate this complication.

Glubb attempted two different tactics to remedy the Jerusalem problem. The ideal solution was to obtain international protection for the city. To that end, Glubb wrote to MELF Commander-in-Chief General John Crocker, in the hope that he could use his influence to secure international assistance to enforce a truce in Jerusalem. After detailing the likely destruction that fighting in Jerusalem would cause, Glubb proposed that the only feasible solution was to threaten retaliation against residential areas by British, American, and French rocket-firing jets. He suggested:

> both sides could be told that any attack by either party would be dealt with by fighter aircraft. As Jews and Arabs live in separate quarters of Jerusalem, the residential areas of the attacking community would be shot up by fighters. Town fighting is so confused that it would be impossible to stop the 'front line advance' by air action. But retaliation of residential areas would probably do it.[160]

The use of air power was a familiar tactic to Glubb from his days as an RAF intelligence officer in Iraq during the 1920s.[161] No doubt with that experience in mind, Glubb hoped to use the threat of violent deterrence and the promise of international protection for Jerusalem to enable the Arab Legion to re-enter Palestine and effect partition with minimal conflict, as planned.[162] This option, however, was out of Glubb's hands, and his request for international protection was made more in hope than expectation. Indeed, the fact that Glubb made this request to Crocker was an indication of his sense of isolation from the government in London. The MELF commander-in-chief did not have the power to acquire the international protection that Glubb sought, but, presumably, Glubb felt Crocker was in a better position to influence the British government, which did.

The second means by which Glubb sought to avert the problem of Jerusalem was to invoke the option of further talks with the Haganah. A follow-up meeting was therefore now deemed useful, and Glubb accordingly sent Goldie to meet with Shlomo Shamir, who was due to become the commander of the Haganah's newly created 7th (Armoured)

[159] Ibid.
[160] Ibid.
[161] Satia, *Spies in Arabia*, pp. 239–63.
[162] Glubb to Crocker, 1 May 1948, GP2006, 83.

Brigade. On 2 May Goldie travelled to Nahayarim, where he was to pass on a verbal message from Glubb to the Haganah.[163] The most reliable account of this meeting is the Haganah report, written the following day. This account hints strongly that the purpose of this meeting was to solve the issue that concerned Glubb most: the Jerusalem snag. After a brief discussion about how to arrange future meetings, Goldie began by stating: 'We want contact with you for preventing a collision. Is this possible?' And, after Shamir replied in the affirmative, Goldie brought up what was surely the crux of the meeting: 'We are worried about the situation in Jerusalem. How can we prevent collision there?'[164] Indeed, it was later recorded that 'they [the Arab Legion] were anxious particularly to avoid any clash with us in Jerusalem'.[165] These talks between the Haganah and the Arab Legion did not result in a mutual restraint pact. However, they did provide the two forces with an understanding of each other's post-mandate objectives and intentions. This left Glubb concerned about possible complications in Jerusalem, but confident that otherwise the Greater Transjordan scheme was achievable. As agreed in February, the Arab Legion was well placed to occupy the proposed Arab state with the tacit acquiescence of the Zionists.

For this to happen, however, it was vital that Glubb and the British officers remained in control of the Arab Legion. With the mandate about to end and the prospect of an Arab–Israeli War imminent, the position of British officers in the Arab Legion became a major source of debate in London. The Colonial Office, which was presumably unaware of the Greater Transjordan scheme, considered it impossible to leave Glubb in command of the Arab Legion if it were to become involved in operations against the new Jewish state.[166] Moreover, back in October 1947 the Foreign Office opined that if King Abdullah sent the Arab Legion back into Palestine,

we should probably have to withdraw those British officers who are seconded to the service of the Transjordan Government and we should also have to consider to what extent we would continue payment of the subsidy.[167]

---

[163] Interview with Goldie, 15 September 1985, Shlaim's Private Collection.

[164] 'A Report from a Meeting with the Representatives of the Arab Legion: Transmitted by SH.R', 3 May 1948, FM/2513/2, Israel State Archives.

[165] 'Meeting: M. Shertok, E. Epstein – G. Marshall, R. Lovett, D. Rusk (Washington, 8 May 1948)', *Political and Diplomatic Documents, December 1947-May 1948* (Jerusalem, 1979), p. 759.

[166] Minute by Mathieson to Martin, 5 May 1948, CO537/3579, TNA.

[167] FO to Amman, 470, 25 October 1947, FO371/62226/E10711, TNA.

However, British involvement within the Arab Legion was crucial to the subsequently approved Greater Transjordan scheme, and Bevin understood this.[168] Bevin was aware of Goldie's negotiations with the Haganah and understood that 'the object of these top secret negotiations is to define the areas of Palestine to be occupied by the two forces'. Bevin therefore confirmed:

I am reluctant to do anything which might prejudice the success of these negotiations which appear to aim at avoiding actual hostilities between the Arabs and the Jews. Since their conduct, and no doubt also their implementation, seems to depend to a considerable extent on British officers serving with the Arab Legion, I feel we ought not to withdraw the latter prematurely.[169]

Bevin and the Foreign Office therefore agreed with Kirkbride's suggestion that the removal of British officers from the Arab Legion should only be considered in the event 'of a Transjordanian attack on the Jewish State within its frontiers as laid down by the Assembly', which would contravene the scheme agreed in February.[170] Bevin therefore ensured that those responsible for implementation remained able to carry out this task.[171]

When the mandate ended, the Greater Transjordan option was the unspoken policy of both Britain and Transjordan. Contrary to Maureen Norton's assertion, Glubb was not the mastermind of the scheme; he may have supported it, but its origins lay in a convergence of Abdullah's and Britain's hopes and fears. Glubb was nonetheless crucial to its implementation. In February Glubb was given the task of securing central Palestine and acquiescing in the creation of a Jewish state in accordance with the UN partition resolution. Glubb was tasked with exploiting the lack of authority in the proposed Arab state. To that end he did all he could during the final few months of the mandate to maintain a politico-security vacuum in the Arab areas of Palestine – to combine muted Arab resistance that would require Arab Legion intervention and Jewish acquiescence of this fait accompli. These efforts, moreover, are particularly revealing in relation to the controversial 'collusion' debate. Glubb's concerns and the nature of the Arab Legion's meetings with the Haganah demonstrate that any Hashemite-Zionist understanding was unstable and imprecise, but they confirm that the two sides were actively communicating at the

---

[168] 'British Officers in the Arab Legion', Walker, 11 May 1948, FO371/68852/E6008, TNA.
[169] FO to Amman, May 1948; Bevin to Minister of Defence, 13 May 1948, CO537/3579, TNA.
[170] 'British Officers in the Arab Legion', Walker, 11 May 1948, FO371/68852/E6008; FO to Amman, May 1948; FO to Amman, 382, 14 May 1948, CO537/3579, TNA.
[171] Shlaim, *Collusion*, pp. 221–2.

military level in an effort to avoid conflict. It also confirms that both sides had a good comprehension and were broadly in favour of each other's objectives and intentions. The conduct of the Arab Legion shows that the Greater Transjordan solution was pursued on the premise that the Zionists would acquiesce in the Arab Legion's occupation of central Arab Palestine and it confirms, beyond a shadow of doubt, that the Arab Legion was governed by a Greater Transjordan objective – approved by Bevin.

In the broader context of Anglo-Jordanian relations, the Greater Transjordan scheme shows that despite obtaining independence, Transjordan remained a British dependency. Several historians have highlighted Abdullah's negotiations with Golda Meir in November 1947 and his pursuit of Greater Syria as evidence that Abdullah was not a British 'pawn' or 'puppet'.[172] Abdullah undoubtedly had his own ambitions, and to some extent the Greater Transjordan scheme is consistent with L. Carl Brown's theory that so-called puppet states often manipulated the great powers, 'at least as much as the other way round'.[173] This should not distract us, though, from the fact that Abdullah remained dependent on Britain. The British, as Kirkbride reminded the king and Abu al-Huda, 'had never urged Transjordan to intervene in Palestine'.[174] Abdullah nonetheless required and received British approval for use of the British-officered and -financed Arab Legion. The Greater Transjordan option became policy because it suited both Britain and Abdullah. Britain was relinquishing the Palestine mandate because it did not have the resources or means to sustain its position. Moreover, the international climate precluded direct imperial intervention. Nonetheless, Britain's desire to maintain as much influence as possible in an important geostrategic location compelled it to contrive in a policy of indirect intervention via an informal asset: Glubb and the Arab Legion. Despite its retreat, the British sought to ensure that post-mandate Palestine was pro-British and stable. To that end, Glubb and the Arab Legion, which had been on the cusp of being severely marginalised, proved valuable tools.

---

[172] Jon and David Kimche, _Both Sides of the Hill: Britain and the Palestine War_ (London, 1960), p. 60; Bradshaw, _Britain and Jordan_, pp. 128, 200; Pundik, _Struggle for Sovereignty_, p. 4.

[173] Brown, _International Politics and the Middle East_, p. 212.

[174] Amman to FO, 687, 28 August 1948, FO816/128, TNA.

3

The 1948 War and Glubb's Management of the Greater Transjordan Scheme

In February both Britain and Transjordan pinned their hopes for a satisfactory resolution to the Palestine problem on Glubb and the Arab Legion occupying central Palestine with the tacit acquiescence of the Zionists. It was not expected, however, that the end of the mandate would descend into a full-blown war involving the regular armies of the neighbouring Arab states. Not until the final week of the mandate did this become certain, and at midnight on 14/15 May, when the British mandate ended, the Arab Legion marched across the Allenby bridge as part of the invading Arab coalition, ostensibly to prevent the creation of a Jewish state and to facilitate the creation of an independent Arab Palestine.[1] Yet when the war came to an effective end in 1949 with the signing of a series of bilateral armistice agreements between Israel and the Arab states, the Greater Transjordan objective had largely reached fruition [Map 5]. The Arab Legion controlled the bulk of central Palestine allotted to the Arabs under the UN partition resolution. Thus, two states – two apparent enemies – emerged from the war territorially victorious. This begs two questions: how did this come about? And what was the significance of the pre-war preparations? This chapter addresses these questions by assessing the role of Glubb and the Arab Legion during the course of the two rounds of official fighting, between May and July.

The key to understanding the Arab Legion's conduct during the 1948 War is to distinguish between the influence of Glubb and Abdullah. Avi Shlaim made little distinction between the conduct of the Arab Legion and the will of the king. Shlaim portrayed Abdullah as an 'independent

[1] Amman to FO, 331, 15 May 1948, FO371/68372/E6304, TNA.

actor' who dictated Jordanian policy. He emphasised that 'Abdullah fulfilled his part of the original agreement with Golda Meir despite the
apparent collapse of this agreement by the time of the second meeting
[between the two in May 1948]'. Shlaim acknowledged that Glubb was
'fully behind this limited strategy', yet he seemingly underplayed the significance of Glubb's role in waging the limited war that the Arab Legion
fought.[2] Meanwhile, Maureen Norton has argued too far in the opposite
direction. Norton is right to emphasise Glubb's significance, but she casts
Abdullah as an almost completely passive nonentity and explains almost
every action as exposing the will of Glubb's grand design.[3] Understanding
the true dynamic of the Arab Legion's role in the 1948 War can be understood only by recognising the balance of power between Glubb and the
king over the Arab Legion, rather than associating the actions of the
Arab Legion as representing the whim of merely one or the other. By
acknowledging this dynamic this chapter corroborates the notion that
the Arab Legion conducted a limited campaign, which merely sought to
occupy the areas of Palestine allotted to the Arab state by the United
Nations and accept the emergence of Israel, but places the emphasis for
this on Glubb's adherence to the Greater Transjordan scheme approved
in February, rather than on Abdullah's adherence to an agreement with
the Jewish Agency.

Although Greater Transjordan was Abdullah's desire, as a more
achievable alternative to his Greater Syria ambition, the climate created
by the civil war, including high-profile incidents such as the massacre
of the Arab population in Deir Yassin (9/10 April), and the expulsion
and flight of Arab inhabitants from Tiberias (17/18 April), Haifa (21/22
April), and Jaffa (25–27 April), put increasing pressure on Abdullah to
act in pan-Arab solidarity.[4] While Benny Morris has convincingly argued
against the suggestion of a coherent Zionist plan for the expulsion of
Palestinian Arabs, it was undoubtedly the case that attacks on Arab
towns and villages contributed to a vicious circle of mass panic and flight
that helped fuel the Palestinian refugee crisis.[5] Under the weight of this
pressure, Kirkbride observed that Abdullah alternated between 'moods
of lucidity and something approaching a complete nervous breakdown'.[6]
Abdullah still hoped to enlarge his kingdom, but was wary of appearing

[2] Shlaim, *Politics of Partition*, pp. 422–9.
[3] Norton, 'Last Pasha', p. 307.
[4] Amman to FO, 234, 21 April 1948, FO371/68852/E5013, TNA.
[5] Benny Morris, *1948 and After: Israel and the Palestinians* (Oxford, 1990), p. 31.
[6] Kirkbride to Burrows, 29 April 1948, FO816/118, TNA.

to undermine the Arab cause.[7] It was within the context of this dilemma that he had a second meeting with Golda Meir on 10/11 May – just days before the mandate ended. The fact that the meeting took place was in itself evidence that Abdullah still hoped to ratify an agreement with the Zionists. However, the mounting pan-Arab pressure compelled him to attempt to alter the premise of their discussion in November 1947. This pressure was visibly evident to Meir, who observed: 'He is very worried and looks terrible.' After the meeting she informed Ben-Gurion: 'He did not deny that we had agreed on a mutually satisfactory arrangement.'[8] However, when asked by Golda Meir if he had broken his original promise, Abdullah replied: ' "When I made that promise, I thought I was in control of my own destiny and I could do what I thought right. But since then I have learned otherwise." ' Abdullah then, Meir recalled, 'went on to say that before he had been alone, but now, "I am one of five" '.[9] Owing to the surge in Arab passions provoked by the violence in Palestine it had become difficult for Abdullah to break from the veneer of a united Arab front.

Abdullah's change of heart did not alter the Arab Legion's war aim, though. Avraham Sela's principal criticism of the 'collusion' thesis is that even if an agreement had been reached between the Jewish Agency and Abdullah in November 1947 and approved by Britain in February 1948, the evolution of events between then and May had rendered the agreement 'antiquated and impractical'.[10] This appreciation, however, is too rigid. Yes, the full-scale Arab–Israeli war that materialised in May had not been anticipated in February. However, the Arab Legion's war aim remained consistent with the target of the scheme approved by Bevin. Abdullah might have wavered, but Glubb, who spent the previous three months preparing to implement partition, remained an active adherent to the Greater Transjordan scheme. Thus, on the last day of the mandate Kirkbride was able to report that, despite Abdullah's misgivings, 'tonight … the Arab Legion will adhere to their original scheme and will establish themselves in Hebron, Ramallah and Nablus and then extend the sector over Arab areas'.[11] Glubb's initial war aim was governed by the original objective agreed in February: simply to occupy the Arab areas of Palestine.

[7] Amman to FO, 302, 8 May 1948, CO537/3579, TNA.
[8] Ben-Gurion's Diary, 11 May 1948, in: Ben-Gurion, *Israel*, p. 91.
[9] Golda Meir, *My Life* (London, 1989), p. 178.
[10] Sela, 'Transjordan', p. 627.
[11] Amman to FO, 326, 14 May 1948, CO537/3579, TNA.

The Arab Legion entered Palestine with the intention of avoiding a conflict with the Zionist forces; yet, while it largely remained faithful to this objective, it nonetheless engaged in bouts of fierce fighting. One of the perennial questions hanging over the 'collusion' thesis concerns the intense fighting that occurred in Jerusalem: why did Abdullah and the Jewish Agency not come to an agreement over Jerusalem?[12] There is credence to Uri Bar-Joseph's principal contention that a degree of conflict, even if not authorised by Glubb, was inevitable in the fog of war.[13] This certainly explains a number of skirmishes. But how can we explain the larger context of the Arab Legion's inconsistent conduct? The answer is not simply, as Pappé suggests, that the two parties decided that their difference of opinion over Jerusalem was so great that they would leave it to be decided on the battlefield.[14] Equally unsatisfying is Shlaim's suggestion that: 'One explanation of this paradox is that within the context of the tacit understanding between the two sides, there was plenty of scope for misunderstandings.'[15] The conduct of the Arab Legion is best explained by acknowledging the significant, but limited nature of Glubb's autonomy.

Glubb was determined to avoid conflict with the Zionist forces and adhere to the original Greater Transjordan scheme, but he was being hounded from above. Within days of the mandate ending Kirkbride reported that Abdullah 'realises that he has now embarked on an enterprise which may carry him beyond the original scheme for occupation by Transjordan of some of the Arab areas of Palestine'. Still aware of his dependence on Britain, Abdullah therefore sought British 'support or at least acquiescence' to go beyond the approved scheme. Abdullah did not detail his specific intentions, but made express reference to 'his national and religious duties in regard to Palestine as a whole and Jerusalem in particular'.[16] At Bevin's insistence, Kirkbride warned Abdullah that 'any departure from the original scheme of things would necessitate a reconsideration by His Majesty's Government of their own position'.[17] Yet Abdullah, who had been subjected to repeated pleas to help the Arabs in Palestine, wanted Glubb to send the Arab Legion to save Jerusalem.[18] At noon on 17 May the king sent written orders to Glubb to that

[12] Sela, 'Transjordan', p. 626; Pappé, *Britain and the Arab–Israeli Conflict*, p. 32.
[13] Bar-Joseph, *Best of Enemies*, pp. 77–8.
[14] Pappé, *Britain and the Arab–Israeli Conflict*, p. 32.
[15] Shlaim, 'Israel and the Arab Coalition', p. 92.
[16] Amman to FO, 341, 17 May 1948, FO816/120, TNA.
[17] Kirkbride to Abdullah, 22 May 1948, ibid.
[18] Sela, 'Transjordan', p. 650.

effect.[19] When Glubb met Fawzi al-Qawuqji later that day, as the ALA commander handed over responsibility for Jerusalem and central Palestine to the Arab Legion, Glubb omitted to mention this order. Qawuqji said that he 'found [it] impossible to explain ... why the Jordanian Army units took so long to enter Jerusalem', despite the fact that 'they were stationed on the outskirts of the city and ... thanks to our having eliminated the Naqi Ya'qub settlement in the night of May 15, the road to Jerusalem was open to them'.[20] The reason is that Glubb was determined, as far as possible, to adhere to the original Greater Transjordan scheme. He was also reluctant to engage the Arab Legion in street fighting, for which it was ill prepared; the Arab Legion was 'trained to fight in the desert, not in major towns and cities'.[21] Glubb feared that conflict in Jerusalem would 'almost destroy the Arab Legion'.[22] Consequently, Glubb visited the Arab Legion units at Nablus and Ramallah on 17/18 May, 'principally in order to escape from the insistence of the King and Prime Minister for immediate action'.[23] However, Glubb could only ignore Abdullah's orders for so long.[24] While he was in Nablus visiting the 1st Brigade headquarters, Glubb was informed by Salih al-Sharaa and Maan Abu Nowar that the men of the Legion were 'frustrated', asking: 'Why are we here in Nablus while the battle is in Jerusalem?' It was made clear to Glubb that the men were restless.[25] Meanwhile, those inside Jerusalem were desperate for military assistance. On 18 May Fadel Rashid, the commander of the Jerusalem garrison, cabled Fawzi al-Qawuqji, whose Arab Liberation Army had already withdrawn. Rashid advised that the situation in Jerusalem was 'grave' and warned: 'We must have reinforcements or [we will] be wiped out. Wiped out. I repeat wiped out or the city will fall.' These pleas were forwarded on to the Jordanian authorities.[26] Meanwhile, Ahmad Hilmi, chairman of the High Committee in Jerusalem, appealed to Abdullah directly, prompting the king to send Glubb another demand to send a force to Jerusalem.[27] According to Ali

---

[19] Glubb, *Soldier*, p. 110; Yitzhak, *Abdullah al-Tall*, p. 40.

[20] Qawuqji, 'Memoirs, 1948. Part II', pp. 27–9.

[21] Nigel Bromage, *A Soldier in Arabia: A British Military Memoir from Jordan to Saudi Arabia* (London, 2012), p. 18.

[22] Glubb to Crocker, 1 May 1948, GP2006, 83.

[23] Amman to FO, 348, 19 May 1948, FO816/120, TNA.

[24] Glubb, *Soldier*, pp. 109–13.

[25] Abu Nowar, *Jordanian–Israeli War*, p. 93.

[26] 'Most urgent from Fadel to Qahtan', 18 May 1948, in: Qawuqji, 'Memoirs, 1948. Part II', pp. 31–2.

[27] Abu Nowar, *Jordanian–Israeli War*, p. 94.

Abu Nowar, a young captain in the Arab Legion: 'The King said to Glubb "you either now send troops inside Jerusalem to save it within the walls and outside the walls or I am going to go and give the order myself." '[28] As a result of the pressure from above and below, Glubb, as he had always feared, could not hold back from sending the Arab Legion into Jerusalem. As he explained to Kirkbride:

The excitement was intense, and the King issued repeated orders for the Arab Legion to enter Jerusalem, which orders I ignored. Eventually you yourself agreed that we could resist no longer.[29]

Thus, late on 18 May, Glubb ordered the Arab Legion into the holy city. Just as he feared during the month prior to the end of the mandate, Jerusalem proved the snag.

Glubb's decision to send the Arab Legion into Jerusalem was primarily, albeit, as he admitted, 'not due solely to political reasons'. There was also a military rationale. As Glubb explained:

If the Jews had captured the whole of Jerusalem, they could have driven down the main road to Jericho, and the whole Arab Legion in the Nablus, Ramallah and Hebron areas would have been cut off. Having once crossed into Palestine as a military formation, we could not help intervening in Jerusalem to cover our own lines of communication, once the Jerusalem truce was broken by the Jews.[30]

Ultimately, though, Glubb sent the Arab Legion into Jerusalem because of the political pressure to take offensive action. As Kirkbride explained:

Glubb had the choices of turning outwards on operations which might ultimately lead him into a Jewish area or inwards to relieve the Arab areas of Jerusalem. He chose the latter, I think wisely.[31]

A crossed-out Foreign Office minute concurred with Kirkbride's appraisal, noting: 'Brigadier Glubb's decision is almost certainly a wise one, I should say.'[32] It is significant that both Kirkbride and the Foreign Office referred to Glubb having had a choice. Both the decisions initially to ignore Abdullah's orders and eventually to relent, by sending troops into Jerusalem, were Glubb's. He was not acting on orders dictated from London; Glubb was acting on his own initiative, in accordance with the policy agreed in February. Although Jerusalem was designated an

[28] Interview with Ali Abu Nowar, 20 June 1990, Geyelin Papers, MECA.
[29] Glubb to Kirkbride, 4 August 1948, GP2006, 83.
[30] Ibid.
[31] Amman to FO, 348, 19 May 1948, FO816/120, TNA.
[32] Minute by Beith, 20 May 1948, FO371/68829/E6577/G, TNA.

international zone by the United Nations, it was to be located within the Arab state. The fighting in Jerusalem was thus, in itself, pursued by Glubb to prevent a breach of the original scheme approved by Bevin – by avoiding encroachment on the designated Jewish state.

When it started, the fighting in Jerusalem was real and fierce. Indeed Glubb remarked: 'In Jerusalem we immediately got into real fighting of an intensity equal to that of European warfare, although we had not meant to fight at all.'[33] The intense nature of the fighting in Jerusalem should not obscure the nature of what transpired in 1948, though. Rather, it further reveals the dynamics of the conflict, as the Arab Legion's objectives in Jerusalem remained limited. It was confined to securing the area of Jerusalem east of Notre Dame: the Old City, in the centre, and the Arab City, in the east.[34] The Arab Legion eventually conquered the Old City on 28 May, by which point the 'Legion's total casualties were 90 killed and 201 wounded'.[35] Barring a few minor skirmishes in the Jewish colony in the west of Jerusalem, such as in Rememeh on 1 June, the Arab Legion made no attempt to infiltrate the western Jewish part of the city.[36] Most of the Arab Legion's battles during this period were defensive as it fended off repeated attacks at Latrun, the main stronghold protecting the road to Jerusalem from Tel Aviv.[37] The fighting in and around Jerusalem was therefore still indicative of the limited nature of the Arab Legion's objectives.

The fighting that occurred in Jerusalem and its environs did not prevent the implementation of the tenets of the Greater Transjordan scheme. Rather, it proved a useful smokescreen for the real objective. As Kirkbride apprised, the 'original Transjordan plan was upset', but not broken, by the breaking of the truce covering Jerusalem 'by the Jews'.[38] Indeed, it may even have saved the scheme. Kirkbride reasoned that:

To have saved the Holy Places of Jerusalem would give Transjordan great merit in the Arab world and the troops can be given the battle for which they are

---

[33] Glubb to Kirkbride, 4 August 1948, GP2006, 83.
[34] HQ Arab Legion to British Minister *et al.*, COSI Nos. 30, 32, 34, and 42, 19–31 May 1948, GP2006, 85; HQ 1 Div to HQ Arab Legion, COSI No. 11, 20 May 1948, GP2006, 97.
[35] 'The Part Played by the Arab Legion in the Arab–Jewish Hostilities in Palestine 1948–1949', FO Research Department, redrafted by Glubb, 21 October 1950, FO816/170, TNA.
[36] 'War Diary: Arab Legion Operational Log', GP2006, 85.
[37] Ben-Gurion, *Israel*, pp. 105–6.
[38] Amman to FO, 370, 22 May 1948, FO371/68373/E6897, TNA.

clamouring without the risk of being involved in what might be described as an act of aggression against the Jewish state.[39]

Moreover, it provided an unexpected advantage. Kirkbride surmised that the

Unforeseen commitment of Jerusalem was however in a sense a benefit for it would have been impossible for the Arab Legion having arrived at the border of the Jewish State to remain inactive both on account of the attitude of the men themselves and because of Arab public opinion which would have described the attitude as due to a British plot to effect partition.[40]

Thus, the unexpected fighting in Jerusalem provided a convenient alibi for the implementation of partition.[41] The fighting in Jerusalem did not satisfy everyone. This defensive posture infuriated Ali Abu Nowar, who felt that the 'usage' of Arab Legion troops in Jerusalem was 'treacherous' on the part of its British officers, as it made it 'impossible to achieve anything'. He complained that after the Arab Legion's initial successes, the British officers halted its advance:

When they [the Israeli forces] were defeated, unsuccessful in their attack and they were withdrawing, we were begging the brigade and division commander to finish them. They were in a bad condition. They [the British officers] would say no, we will wait for them to come and fight in here.[42]

In order to quell the desire for offensive action, Glubb circulated 'propaganda' within the Arab Legion, spreading the message that 'there is no good fighting, because we might suddenly be attacked and have to fight like hell'.[43] From Glubb's perspective, regardless of the Greater Transjordan scheme, the Arab Legion 'had not sufficient resources to wage war on the Jewish state'.[44] The 1948 reorganisation of the Arab Legion and the military supplies it received was primarily designed to occupy and secure the proposed Arab state, not to wage war. Indeed, it was only the Mechanised Regiment that was trained to fight. Much of the reorganised Arab Legion was made up of the old garrison companies, which had been hurriedly converted into an infantry brigade.[45] This, combined with the Greater Transjordan scheme, meant Glubb was

[39] Amman to FO, 348, 19 May 1948, FO816/120, TNA.
[40] Amman to FO, 370, 22 May 1948, FO371/68373/E6897, TNA.
[41] Norton, 'Last Pasha', p. 348.
[42] Interview with Ali Abu Nowar, 20 June 1990, Geyelin Papers.
[43] Glubb to Lash, 9 July 1948, GP2006, 90.
[44] 'The Trans-Jordan Situation', Glubb, 12 August 1948, GP2006, 83.
[45] Sarairah, 'British Actor', p. 157.

reluctant for the Arab Legion to engage in direct conflict, if it could be avoided.

Initially this policy proved largely successful, as within two weeks of the mandate ending, the Arab Legion had gained effective control of the areas allotted to the Arab state – except for western Galilee and Gaza – without violating any non-Arab territory. Consolidating Greater Transjordan was always going to be the most difficult part of the process, though, and it was the aspect most affected by the unexpected intervention of the Arab states. To that end, Britain sought to arrange a truce, and on 29 May the UN Security Council adopted a British proposal for a ceasefire in Palestine after Britain 'gave an assurance' that it 'would suspend the deliveries of all war-like materials to the Arab Governments'.[46] Tancred Bradshaw has emphasised the British-inspired arms embargo as proof of Britain's non-involvement in attempting to establish Greater Transjordan.[47] However, Bradshaw's argument that Britain did all it could to restrict the Arab Legion's role in the war and that therefore it was not party to the Greater Transjordan scheme skews the rationale for British approval. It was not simply about territorial aggrandisement, but minimising conflict. Thus, Britain's attempt to reduce the supply of arms was a continuation of policy within this context. Moreover, it is telling that the embargo was not posited until after the Greater Transjordan territorial objectives had largely been achieved. Until that point Glubb was utterly content with Britain's support. After the first truce began on 11 June – at which point the territorial aspect of the Greater Transjordan objective had essentially been achieved – Glubb expressed his deep appreciation for the 'magnificent support' of the MELF commander-in-chief and added that: 'Actually H.M.G. have also done us very well.'[48] During the opening weeks of the conflict, Bevin had been 'under the strongest pressure from America ... and from sections of public opinion here with regard to the continuation of assistance to the Arab Legion by means of the subsidy, the loan of officers and the supply of war material'. He explained that, 'I have so far been able to resist this pressure'.[49] For example, after 'serious fighting' began in Jerusalem, Britain issued the Arab Legion with 'sufficient ammunition of all calibres, for one month's contact with the enemy'.[50] However, after the Arab Legion had 'successfully

---

[46] COS to Glubb, 79908SDIB, 'For the Eyes of Glubb Pasha Only', 2 June 1948, GP2006, 90.
[47] Bradshaw, *Britain and Jordan*, p. 142.
[48] Glubb to Crocker, 13 June 1948, GP2006, 83.
[49] FO to Amman, 421, 24 May 1948, FO816/121, TNA.
[50] 'The Trans-Jordan Situation', Glubb, 12 August 1948, GP2006, 83.

carried out the greater part of its objective of occupying the central Arab areas of Palestine', Bevin now pressed for a ceasefire as a means to end the conflict and to consolidate the fait accompli of Greater Transjordan.[51] To that end, after the Egyptians requisitioned a shipment of ammunition bound for Transjordan the British opted not to make good this loss of ammunition so as 'to do nothing to prejudice the success of the negotiations for the truce'.[52] The Foreign Office believed that a restriction on arms supplies was the only means to 'forestall the lifting of the American arms embargo' and prevent an influx of Soviet arms, which otherwise 'would undoubtedly have enabled and encourage the Jews to invade Arab territory outside Palestine'.[53] Ultimately, this proved futile as Israel ignored the embargo, but the British believed an arms embargo would help secure the Arab Legion's territorial gains.

Once a ceasefire had been agreed, the UN mediator, Count Folke Bernadotte, sought to arrange a longer-term settlement. But one of the main obstacles to this and to the realisation of Greater Transjordan was a unanimous rejection of the resolution proposal that the UN mediator submitted on 28 June. True to Bevin's original desire that *nature* would partition Palestine, Bernadotte was 'instructed to carry out his functions of seeking a peaceful settlement of the situation *without any reference to previous decisions or attempts* to find a settlement'.[54] This is essentially what Bernadotte did when he proposed that the Arab-held areas of Palestine, including Jerusalem, which was the most coveted prize of the conflict, should be incorporated into Transjordan. He also suggested Israel and Transjordan should form a union to deal with economic, defence, and foreign policy issues.[55] This solution, however, only suited those behind the Greater Transjordan scheme, which led David Ben-Gurion, Israel's first prime minister, to consider it evidence that the UN mediator was little more than 'a Bevin agent'.[56] The Israelis made clear that 'under no circumstances will we consider any proposal that diminishes Israel's sovereignty, permits outside interference in her immigration policy or envisions placing Jerusalem *in any way at all* under an Arab regime'.[57] The Israelis, after all, were fighting for statehood, not union

[51] FO to Amman, 421, 24 May 1948, CO537/3579, TNA.
[52] Crocker to Glubb, 9 June 1948, GP2006, 83.
[53] Foreign Office note attached to: Pirie-Gordon to Tawfiq Pasha, 31 May 1948, FO816/121, TNA.
[54] Ibid. [emphasis added].
[55] Kimche and Kimche, *Both Sides of the Hill*, pp. 221–2.
[56] Ben-Gurion's Diary, 29 June 1946, in: Ben-Gurion, *Israel*, p. 185.
[57] Ben-Gurion, *Israel*, p. 199.

with Transjordan.[58] The Arabs were equally intransigent. The Mufti asserted that 'no Arab would accept these proposals as a basis for discussion of the Palestine question'.[59] Meanwhile, the other Arab states had long been opposed – almost singularly – to Abdullah unilaterally gaining from the conflict.

Publicly Abdullah also rejected Bernadotte's proposal, though privately he and Britain sought to consolidate the Arab Legion's occupation of central Palestine. Abdullah sought to strengthen his grip on the West Bank by appointing military governors to the main cities.[60] And the Jordanian prime minister kept the Greater Transjordan option open by confirming that, after liberation, Palestine's inhabitants would be able to choose between 'establishing an independent State of Palestine or joining Transjordan'. Abu al-Huda nonetheless expressed public resentment at Bernadotte's inclusion of Transjordan in his proposal, and asserted that Transjordan had no territorial ambitions in Palestine.[61] In that respect, Transjordan adhered to the chorus of criticism directed at Bernadotte from the Arab world. Abdullah's predicament, which the British acknowledged, was that to proffer a lone dissenting voice in the resolution negotiations would not have affected the Arab League's course; it would merely have exposed Abdullah's true desire and put him in the firing line for criticism throughout the Arab world.[62] For that reason, the arms embargo became another useful tool towards the consolidation of Greater Transjordan. Convincing the other Arab states to accept Hashemite-Zionist partition was the principal obstacle to securing a satisfactory resolution. The British hoped that by denying the Arab states the means to wage war they could be persuaded, or compelled, to cease fighting 'and possibly even of their eventually acquiescing in some modified form of the Mediator's proposals'.[63] Fearing that the Arab world had got into the habit of ignoring Britain's advice, Kirkbride felt that UN sanctions might also be very useful in convincing the Arab states of the need to comply. Much to his surprise, he found that Abdullah and the Jordanian prime minister would 'welcome the idea of the imposition of sanctions on Transjordan also'. Clearly they recognised their isolated position and were desperate for a

---

[58] Rogan, 'Jordan and 1948', p. 113.

[59] *SWB, Part III*, 8 July 1948, p. 63.

[60] Yitzhak, *Abdullah al-Tall*, p. 50.

[61] *SWB, Part III*, 8 July 1948, p. 63.

[62] Amman to FO, 386, 24 May 1948; Amman to FO, 390, 25 May 1948; Amman to FO, 399, 26 May 1948, FO816/121, TNA.

[63] BMEO to FO, 228, 5 July 1948, FO371/68374/E9072/G; FO to Amman, 648, 6 July 1948, FO371/68375/E9168/G, TNA.

solution to be imposed.[64] In order to 'extricate Transjordan from the present position', the Jordanian prime minister felt: 'What was now wanted were sanctions by the Security Council against all the Arab states including Trans-Jordan.' He even posited that withholding the subsidy 'would also be useful pressure'.[65] Indeed, the 12 July subsidy payment was duly withheld for a short time.[66] At the political level Britain and Transjordan remained at one. They both sought to find a way of consolidating Greater Transjordan. For Britain that meant toeing the line of the United Nations, and for Transjordan that meant aligning with the Arab League.

With the UN mediator's proposals unanimously rejected by all parties, focus turned to Bernadotte's call to extend the truce, to provide more time to find an acceptable solution. The Arab League Political Committee met to discuss the situation in Cairo during the first week of July. Owing to rumours that the Arab League may reject the truce extension, Glubb visited Abdullah to warn about the lack of artillery and mortar ammunition. Glubb reported that Abdullah, alarmed by this, 'sent [a] letter to Taufiq [Abu al-Huda] in Cairo by special aircraft'.[67] Abdullah instructed his prime minister 'that under no circumstances should the first armistice be broken ... until the army had obtained the light and heavy material it needed'.[68] The Arab League, though, had 'already rejected [the] truce'.[69] Glubb was informed by his second in command, Colonel Abd al-Qadir al-Jundi, that 'the Arabs were absolutely insistent on rejecting everything. ... The military experts, Abdul Qadir [al-Jundi] and [General] Sabbar [of the Egyptian Army] etc., were not even asked their opinion.'[70] The Egyptian military had never wanted to enter the fight in Palestine. As Uthman al-Mahdi Pasha, the Egyptian chief of staff, explained: 'I opposed entering the war for lack of military supplies but they [the politicians] forced us to fight. ... I almost had a stroke when they ignored my opinion.'[71] The first round of fighting compounded this view as the initial excitement of the rank and file on the eve of war was quickly deflated when they found themselves overstretched, under-resourced, and lacking leadership

[64] Amman to FO, 547, 9 July 1948, FO816/125, TNA.
[65] Amman to FO, 546, 9 July 1948, ibid.
[66] L. F. L. Pyman to H. G. Downie, 29 July 1948 FO371/68830/E7548, TNA.
[67] 'Note', Glubb, 7 July 1948, GP2006, 83.
[68] Abdullah, *Al-Takmilah*, pp. 22–3.
[69] 'Note', Glubb, 7 July 1948, GP2006, 83.
[70] Glubb to Kirkbride, 8 July 1948, GP2006, 83.
[71] Quoted in: Fawaz Gerges, 'Egypt and the 1948 War: Internal Conflict and Regional Ambition', in: Rogan and Shlaim (eds.), *Rewriting the History of 1948*, pp. 156, 161.

and organisation.[72] However, the Egyptian prime minister broadcast a statement asserting that there was 'no alternative but to send the Arab armies to establish peace and restore justice to preserve the Arab character of Palestine'.[73] Public opinion and regional ambitions persuaded the politicians to wage war.[74] The Arab states had portrayed the first round of fighting as an almost unadulterated success. Typical of the information being fed to the Arab public was this Egyptian communiqué issued on 20 May:

> Our light forces, during their daring advance towards Beersheba, met with stiff resistance near Birket al-Amara, but our forces entered Beersheba after overcoming the enemy's defences. The inhabitants of this town welcomed the Egyptian forces; they carried Egyptian flags and acclaimed King Farouk.[75]

The Arab press portrayed the Israelis as being 'in a humiliating position as they have lost battle after battle on different fronts and their capital, Tel Aviv, is exposed to imminent disaster'.[76] When the ceasefire began in June, the Arab League Political Committee emphasised that it had agreed to the truce, 'at a time when the Arab armies held the initiative'.[77] This made it very difficult for Arab politicians to be seen making concessions in the negotiations. They had backed themselves into a corner. Internal rivalries and political ambitions had compelled them to renew the fighting.

The end of the truce infuriated Glubb. Once a ceasefire had been achieved, he, like the British, was determined that fighting should not be renewed, but this decision was completely beyond his control. Glubb was incensed that the fighting had been resumed because politicians in Syria and Egypt made 'fanatical demands for war' as a sop to 'their city mobs'.[78] This was a view shared by the commander of the ALA, Fawzi al-Qawuqji, who complained that the Arab coalition's war effort was hampered by the 'fact [that] for the most part, the 1948 fighting was directed by senior Arab politicians from behind their office desks, and in accordance with their own personal interests, ambitions and whims'.[79]

---

[72] Gamal Abd al-Nasser and Walid Khalidi (ed.), 'Nasser's Memoirs of the First Palestine War', *Journal of Palestine Studies*, 2:2 (1973), pp. 3–32.

[73] *SWB, Part III*, 15 July 1948, p. 52.

[74] Gerges, 'Egypt and the 1948 War', pp. 151–63.

[75] *SWB, Part III*, 27 May 1948, p. 70.

[76] Ibid., 10 June 1948, p. 66.

[77] Ibid., p. 64.

[78] Glubb to Lash, 9 July 1948, GP2006, 90.

[79] Qawuqji, 'Memoirs, 1948. Part II', p. 24.

Such was Glubb's fury, he felt 'the best solution would be a really good bombing of Damascus and Cairo' in order to frighten them into peace.[80] Ultimately this was hyperbole, but Glubb was deeply frustrated that the Jordanian government was subject to the collective whim of the Arab League. As Glubb summarised:

The stages by which we have been led into a real war against the Jews are familiar to you. I think that you will agree that I did everything I could to prevent a war, and ever since it began, I have done everything in my power to stop it, to avoid a renewal of hostilities or to make or prolong a truce. I have again and again told Taufiq Pasha that our resources are inadequate for war, but (under possibly irresistible pressure from the Arab League) he has again and again just drifted into war, and then rejected truces or the extension of truces.[81]

Abdullah was equally opposed to the renewal of fighting. He described the decision to end the truce as 'the most glaring example of the Arab League's mishandling of affairs', causing him 'indescribable distress and worry'.[82] But he had little choice but to acquiesce.

When the second round of fighting officially began at 8 AM on 9 July, the Greater Transjordan objective was put at serious risk. As a result of Britain's adherence to, and Israel's flouting of the arms embargo, the balance of forces had been radically altered during the first truce.[83] Given its limited objectives, the Arab Legion had nothing more to gain from a continuation of fighting; it merely had its existing gains to lose. Moreover, the fate of the Arab Legion and therefore Transjordan was also jeopardised. Consequently, Kirkbride began exploring the possibility of extricating Transjordan from the conflict. As Glubb explained:

Kirkbride is thinking out some means of getting T.J. [Transjordan] out of it altogether, but he thinks that we could not have a private truce in Pal[estine] – it would not work. He thinks the only way would be to withdraw the Arab Legion from Pal[estine] entirely, but he is afraid that this might lead to a mutiny of the Arab Legion itself.[84]

With that problem in mind, Glubb instructed Lash to find out whether Arab officers of the Legion, such as Ahmad Sudqi and Ali al-Hiyari were 'still mad to fight or would they secretly be rather glad to see it all over?' Personally, Glubb felt that withdrawal from Palestine 'for political reasons would be too difficult, and that it would be easier to stay in Palestine but

---

stop fighting, but of course this depends rather on the Jews'. The problem with overtly abandoning Palestine was that it would look very much
'like treachery'.[85] Although Glubb had hitherto been pursuing the Greater
Transjordan objective, clinging onto the gains inside Palestine was the least
important of three priorities for the Arab Legion commander, which also
included safeguarding the original Transjordan state and protecting the
Arab Legion itself. Goldie certainly believed that Glubb's 'primary concern was to spare the Arab Legion. He did not want his little army to get
a bloody nose.'[86] With those three priorities in mind, Glubb's intention,
after the truce ended, was, as Kirkbride reported, to 'make (in his own
words) arrangements for a phoney war to follow a phoney truce'.[87] Glubb
announced that 'the policy now is to have a war of passive defence'. The
arms embargo made it very difficult to go on the offensive in any case, but
this policy of 'passive defence', as Glubb admitted, was 'really going back to
the original scheme before May 15th, of holding the Arab areas and doing
nothing'.[88] In the main, this policy was consistent with the intentions of the
Jordanian government, with the prime minister having informed Kirkbride
that 'the Arab Legion would be ordered to play a purely defensive role
and would not fire unless attacked'.[89] The Arab Legion therefore entered
the second round of fighting with the intention of merely safeguarding the
gains made during the first round. Events may have moved beyond what
had been initially envisaged back in February, but the Greater Transjordan
concept continued to govern the Arab Legion's instruction.

Yet owing to competing pressures affecting them, Glubb and the
Jordanian government had subtly, but crucially different comprehen-
sions of the Arab Legion's defensive role. When the fighting resumed,
Glubb was given a written order by the Jordanian government to 'hold
on at all costs'.[90] This was not something Glubb was prepared to adhere
to, however. With the safety of the Arab Legion and the protection of
lesser Transjordan in mind, Glubb considered contingencies in case 'complete withdrawal from Palestine [became] necessary', thus abandoning
the original, yet least important objective of holding the Arab areas of
Palestine. Fearing that the Arab Legion's evacuation routes might be
blocked by refugee traffic, Glubb even queried: 'Could we demobilise all

---

[85] Ibid.
[86] Interview with Goldie, 15 September 1985, Shlaim's Private Collection.
[87] Amman to FO, 548, 10 July 1948, FO816/125, TNA.
[88] Glubb to Lash, 9 July 1948, GP2006, 83.
[89] Amman to FO, 546, 9 July 1948, FO816/125, TNA.
[90] Amman to FO, 555, 12 July 1958, ibid.

civilian vehicles in Ramallah by removing some vital part?'[91] This action was neither feasible nor seriously considered, but it reveals the extent to which safeguarding the Arab Legion and lesser Transjordan was Glubb's first priority. In a subtle, but significant difference to the Jordanian government, Glubb's approach to a 'passive defence' policy was much more flexible. Glubb was not committed to clinging to the gains made during the first round of fighting. He was not prepared – as the Jordanian government ordered – *to hold on at all costs*.

The archetypal expression of Glubb's 'passive defence' policy was the infamous evacuation of the Arab towns of Lydda and Ramle close to the border of the new Jewish state, which Glubb claimed was previously agreed with the Jordanian prime minister – although it contravened the government's order to hold on at all costs.[92] When the first truce ended, Brigadier 'Teal' Ashton, commander of the Arab Legion 3rd Brigade in Latrun, was informed by Arab Legion headquarters that the Jordanian government did not want war and that Jerusalem should be kept closed. Ashton therefore issued orders to both regiments in his sector not to open fire unless in reply to the enemy and that only small arms fire could be used without reference to him.[93] When the Israel Defense Forces (IDF) launched Operation Dani – designed to open the road from Tel Aviv to Jerusalem – on 9 July, the Arab Legion opted to consolidate the defensive stronghold along that road at Latrun. As Fawzi al-Qawuqji, who was responsible for protecting this area before the mandate ended, observed: 'The Latrun-Bab al-Wad area is of great strategic importance; throughout history these hills have been the scene of the battles that have decided the fate of the Holy City. ... If the enemy succeeded in occupying and controlling either of these roads he would be able to attain his objective by getting through to the city.'[94] The Arab Legion did not have the manpower or the resources to defend Lydda and Ramle against attack.[95] Thus, in the face of overwhelming Israeli force and after the surrender of the local inhabitants, Lash gave the order for the Arab Legion companies besieged in the Lydda and Ramle police stations to withdraw to Latrun.[96] Losing these towns was far from ideal strategically. As Glubb

[91] Glubb to Lash, 13 July 1948, GP2006, 83.
[92] 'The Trans-Jordan Situation', Glubb, 12 August 1948, ibid.
[93] Diary of 'Teal' Ashton, p. 36 [not clearly labelled], GP2006, 84.
[94] Qawuqji, 'Memoirs, 1948. Part II', pp. 17–25.
[95] Ronen Yitzhak, 'British Military Supplies to Jordan during the 1948 War: How the Anglo-Jordanian Treaty Was Put to the Test', *Middle East Critique*, 24:4 (2015), p. 351.
[96] Diary of 'Teal' Ashton, pp. 36–42, GP2006, 84.

explained: '[It] doubled the length of our front ... [thus leaving] the two regiments at Latrun in a very dangerous salient.'[97] Crucially, though, it meant the Arab Legion came away undefeated and the strategic stronghold at Latrun was consolidated – albeit left more exposed. Both of these considerations were more important to Glubb than retaining every gain made during the first round of fighting. This contravened the Jordanian government's order to hold on at all costs, but it was consistent with the order to ensure that the road to Jerusalem be kept closed.

The loss of Lydda and Ramle created immense political difficulties for Glubb and the British connection. It was immediately followed by anti-Glubb and anti-British demonstrations. When Glubb visited the front, he was persistently spat at and called a traitor by the inhabitants of villages he passed through, both in Palestine and Transjordan.[98] In describing the immediate fallout, Glubb remarked: 'On 14 July crowds demonstrated in Amman. They shouted down with Britain down with Glubb. What a life.' The previous day, Glubb 'was summoned before session of King and Cabinet', at which Abdullah suggested Glubb 'resign'. Glubb recounted that ministers suspected him of sabotaging 'the Transjordan war effort on secret orders from Britain'.[99] It was 'made clear that his stories of ammunition shortages were disbelieved as being part of British propaganda'.[100] An hour later Glubb was called to see the prime minister, who told Glubb that he 'understood [the] military situation and approved of my action but [the] King and Ministers [are] very angry. He asked me not to resign.'[101] As a result of his predicament, Glubb asked Kirkbride:

Do you think it would carry any influence if I resigned. If it were accepted it would be difficult because Abdul Qadir [al-Jundi] has not got a clue! On the other hand, if ruin were inevitable would it be best to have it with an Arab i/c [in command]?[102]

In order to help salvage British prestige – though also to relieve some of the unpleasantness associated with his scapegoat status – Glubb was prepared to abandon the Arab Legion. Kirkbride's view was 'that of the two evils the lesser one would be to remain on to the end', and Glubb was informed by the British Legation that if Abdullah asked him to resign

---

[97] Glubb to Lash, 13 July 1948, GP2006, 83.
[98] Pirie-Gordon to Burrows, 25 July 1948, FO371/68822/E10325, TNA.
[99] Glubb to H. E. Pyman, undated, GP2006, 86.
[100] Pirie-Gordon to Burrows, 25 July 1948, FO371/68822/E10325, TNA.
[101] Glubb to H. E. Pyman, undated, GP2006, 86.
[102] Glubb to Kirkbride, 13 July 1948, GP2006, 90.

again, he should insist on being dismissed.[103] Losing Glubb was a serious issue. As Malcolm Walker warned:

Once the Arab Legion ceases to have a British commander it is goodbye to our influence in Transjordan, and perhaps also in the whole Arab World. The effect of Glubb's dismissal on our prestige in the Middle East would be incalculable: if the puppet state of Transjordan were able to throw off the chains of the imperialist, how much more then should states such as Egypt or Iraq be rid of their last shackles?[104]

Bevin suggested the 'best course' was for Glubb to call the king's bluff.[105] Consequently, when Glubb saw Abdullah on 17 July, he duly offered to step down and 'serve His Majesty in any other capacity', if the king felt it advisable to defuse the hostile propaganda by replacing him as commander. However, having given Glubb the opportunity to stand down just four days earlier in front of the Council of Ministers, Abdullah asked Glubb to remain in his post.[106] Privately Abdullah knew Glubb was needed to secure Greater Transjordan and Glubb was a convenient scapegoat for the Arab Legion's defensive posture. Moreover, Glubb was deemed a vital component in maintaining the British connection. As Kirkbride explained: 'It is undoubtedly the case that ... King Abdullah and his Ministers considered removing those officers [Glubb and other British officers] from positions of executive authority and retaining their services in the form of a military mission.' However, as Kirkbride added, this idea was 'dropped because it was feared that His Majesty's Government would be offended' and the subsidy consequently reduced.[107] For both allies, Glubb was considered the key to accessing the fruits of the alliance.

In order to offset the negative ramifications of surrendering Lydda and Ramle, Glubb launched a minor, and considered a major, military offensive. In the first instance, the executive British officers of the Arab Legion were concerned at the impact the withdrawal had on morale. Thus, on 13 July, Goldie passed Ashton a plan from Lash designed to boost morale after the Ramle loss. This took the form of 'an attack to capture some place with a name'. There were two suggestions: re-conquer either the

[103] Amman to FO, 570, 14 July 1948, FO816/126, TNA.
[104] Minute by Walker, 16 July 1948, FO371/68574/E9573/G, TNA.
[105] Norton, 'Last Pasha', p. 356.
[106] Amman to FO, 586, 18 July 1948, FO816/126, TNA. This is at odds with Tancred Bradshaw's unsubstantiated claim that 'there is clear evidence that in light of these events, King Abdullah would have accepted his resignation without demur'. Bradshaw, *Glubb Reports*, p. 6.
[107] Kirkbride to Bevin, 25 September 1948, FO371/68832/E12875, TNA.

village of Qubab or Qula, both in the sub-district of Ramle. Lash, Goldie, and Ashton agreed that Qula should be the target because Qubab might lead to another embarrassing 'withdrawal', while Qula was 'not important' and 'after a famous attack [it] could sink into oblivion again'. On the 16 July a successful operation was launched against Qula, with Arab Legion casualties totalling three killed and nine wounded.[108] This success was only temporary, as the village changed hands several times over the course of the next few days.[109] The significant point, though, is that the attack on Qula was not designed to defeat the enemy or gain new ground; the motive was merely to give the appearance that the Arab Legion was actively fighting and to boost morale within the Arab Legion with a winnable offensive operation; it had no other tactical or strategic significance.

Glubb also explored the feasibility of launching a more significant offensive operation, again for political reasons, rather than for the purpose of defeating the enemy. The rationale was to rebuild his and the British officers' standing. Given the political fallout of withdrawing from Lydda and Ramle, Glubb asked Lash if it would be possible 'to mount a bigger operation during the last 48 hours', in the event of a truce being agreed. Glubb apprised:

It is important if there is a truce to whiten our faces before it begins. Otherwise when all the war is over, there may be political pressure to get rid of all British from the A.L. [Arab Legion] which would be against [the] policy of HMG.[110]

On this occasion, as on others, Glubb did not act on British orders, but he was conscious of the political necessity – in the interests of British prestige – of taking offensive action. With that in mind, Glubb proposed seizing an opportunity 'to recapture Lydda'. That was his preferred option, though he also posited that an 'alternative might be an objective more to the north'. The most important criterion for operation 'Glucose' – as it was codenamed – was to be seen to be taking some form of major offensive operation – in the interests of British prestige. However, Glubb was adamant: 'We could not do it unless a truce were imminent because we have not enough men [or ammo] to hold the ground taken.' Indeed, military supplies were a major limiting factor for the Arab Legion. Despite

---

[108] Diary of 'Teal' Ashton, pp. 44–8, GP2006, 84.

[109] Susan Slyomovics, 'The Rape of Qula, a Destroyed Palestinian Village', in: Ahmad H. Sa'di and Lila Abu-Lughod (eds.), *Nakba: Palestine, 1948, and the Claims of Memory* (New York, 2007), p. 33.

[110] Glubb to Lash, 15 July 1948, GP2006, 86.

the embargo, it did obtain 250 twenty-five-pounder shells from the Egyptians on 15 July. However, this was not enough to alter the military balance, and without the protection of a truce, retaking Lydda would only replicate the problem that prompted the Legion to retreat in the first place. Consequently, the key to such an operation would be timing. It was dependent on a truce being agreed with two or three days' notice. With such a safeguard, Glubb suggested: 'Consequently we could poop off most of our 25 p[oun]d[e]r [ammunition].'[111] On 16 July it was announced that a second truce had been agreed and would begin in two days' time.[112] Despite receiving forty-eight hours' notice, operation 'Glucose' was not launched. It nevertheless reveals a great deal about Glubb's mind-set. In particular, it confirms the extent to which he planned military offensives in terms of political outcomes, rather than as a means of destroying the supposed enemy, and it demonstrates that he was thinking in terms of British interests.

When the second truce began on 18 July, after a disastrous ten days' fighting for the Arabs, Glubb's fear that he and the British officers would need to *whiten their faces* proved well-founded [Map 2]. During the following weeks, Glubb became an ever more explicit scapegoat, and the fall of Lydda and Ramle became the symbol of his alleged treachery. The contradictory predicament that Glubb was in vis-à-vis Abdullah and the Jordanian government left him in a 'very unsatisfactory' position. Glubb resented that:

The King and the Prime Minister continue to ask me in private not to resign, but they do nothing publicly to express their satisfaction with my services, or to exhonerate [*sic*] me from the charge of having treacherously handed over Lydda and Ramle to the Jews. In other words, they seem to wish to continue to take advantage of my services and of those other British Officers, but they are not loth to see the blame for all reverses laid on me and British Officers alone.[113]

Glubb lamented: 'One can stand any amount of fighting with the enemy, but this war on two fronts is depressing.'[114]

Glubb's isolation was compounded after he revealed the Arab Legion's dire financial predicament. On 4 August Glubb visited Kirkbride to report what Kirkbride described as 'an almost incredible state of affairs financially'.[115] As of 9 August 1948, only £185,000 of the annual subsidy

[111] Ibid.
[112] Ben-Gurion's Diary, 16 July 1948, in: Ben-Gurion, *Israel*, p. 188.
[113] Glubb to H. E. Pyman, 1 August 1948, GP2006, 83.
[114] Glubb to H. E. Pyman, 27 July 1948, ibid.
[115] Amman to FO, 634, 5 August 1948, FO371/68830/E10466/G, TNA.

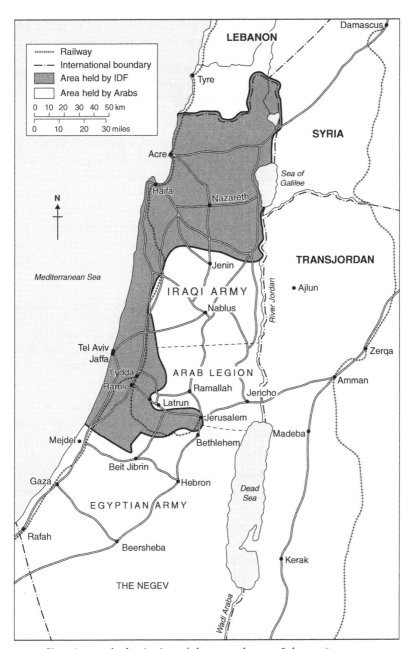

MAP 2. Situation at the beginning of the second truce, July 1948.
Based on: Avi Shlaim, Collusion across the Jordan: King Abdullah, the Zionist
Movement, and the Partition of Palestine (Oxford, 1988), p. 268.

remained for the rest of the financial year. The other £2.315 million had already been spent – in just four months.[116] Kirkbride reported:

The most astounding feature of the matter is that Glubb did this without any reference to the Transjordan Government either as regards promise of cash or actual expenditure. This Legation was kept equally ignorant until yesterday.

The Jordanian government was furious with Glubb, and Kirkbride 'was unsympathetic'.[117] Upon resuming duty – after a period of leave – one of the first things Kirkbride did was to 'reproach the King and the Prime Minister on the subject of the accusations or worse which had been levelled against British officers of the Arab Legion and against Glubb in particular after the occupation of Ramleh and Lydda by the Jewish forces'.[118] But Kirkbride reported that 'this latest development cuts the ground from under my feet and I do not feel able to defend him on this particular issue in which he is entirely in the wrong'.[119] Kirkbride clinically informed Glubb that,

while I have transmitted all the explanations you give for the over-expenditure I have not found myself able to give any support for the 'fait accompli' with which we have now been faced. ... I realise that this policy will inevitably cause considerable embarrassment and will involve you in complete re-organisation in order to effect the necessary economies but I think we shall be fortunate if we can persuade the Treasury to go even as far as I have recommended.[120]

Glubb's over-expenditure – as a result of having to manage a war on a peacetime budget – exasperated Kirkbride. In his view, Glubb ignored discrepancies within the budget and heard what he wanted to hear in meetings with the War Office and the Treasury so that he could act as he pleased.[121] The financial situation strained Glubb's relationship with Kirkbride and compounded the friction between himself and the Jordanian government.

The exigencies with which Glubb had to cope during the 1948 War increasingly made his role seem like a poisoned chalice. In order to resolve his predicament, one way or another, Glubb turned to Britain. Instinctively, Glubb exclaimed: 'These various factors give me a personal inclination to hand a written resignation to the Trans-Jordan

[116] Charteris to L. F. L. Pyman, 9 August 1948, FO371/68830/E10610/G, TNA.
[117] Amman to FO, 634, 5 August 1948, FO371/68830/E10466/G, TNA.
[118] Amman to FO, 635, 5 August 1948, FO371/68830/E10502, TNA.
[119] Amman to FO, 634, 5 August 1948, FO371/68830/E10466/G, TNA.
[120] Kirkbride to Glubb, 10 August 1948, GP2006, 83.
[121] Kirkbride to Bevin, 9 August 1948, FO371/68830/E10894/G, TNA.

Government.' Glubb hoped it would be refused, meaning: 'I would thereby be exhonerated [*sic*] from the charges of treachery now circulating, and my position would be much stronger.' However, he understood that 'there is the risk of it being accepted'. Because this would have wider ramifications for Britain, Glubb explained:

I have, therefore, asked the Legation to cable H.M.G., and to ask them to what extent they consider this an imperial interest. If it is such, I think they should give me a clear directive, in which case I will of course carry on, whatever personal unpleasantness and humiliation may result. If on the other hand, H.M.G. say that they are indifferent, and the matter is merely a personal one for myself, then I can with a clear conscience take what action is necessary to defend myself from libellous propaganda.

Glubb's threat of resignation was primarily designed to secure British support. He therefore painted a gloomy picture of his departure being followed by all the other British officers and the Arab Legion therefore collapsing. The ultimate consequence being that: 'In the end Trans-Jordan herself might disappear.'[122] Glubb wanted British support to ease the burden he was facing, and when he departed for London on 13 August this was at the forefront of his mind.

Glubb's visit to London had initially been arranged, at his instigation, to discuss the Legion's 'pressing' financial situation.[123] However, as Glubb explained to MELF Chief of Staff General Pyman on the day he departed Amman, what he really wanted to know was:

'What importance does H.M.G. attach to Trans-Jordan and the Arab Legion?' This is what I want to ask in London. If H.M.G. say that this is a most important strategic or political asset, then we will put our pride in our pockets and try all we can to salvage the situation. If, on the contrary, H.M.G. say they could not care less, then I may make enquiries in London to find another job.[124]

Glubb made a similar request – for a job in London – in May 1946. Glubb feared that Jordanian independence would soon result in his services being dispensed with, and he preferred to find a new job to support his family while he was still young enough to do so. However, on that occasion also, he accepted that: 'Should His Majesty's Government be of [the] opinion that I am best employed in Trans-Jordan, I will continue in my present post without complaint.'[125] Ultimately, Glubb considered

[122] Glubb to H. E. Pyman, 1 August 1948, GP2006, 83.
[123] Glubb to Kirkbride, 4 August 1948, ibid.
[124] Glubb to H. E. Pyman, 13 August 1948, ibid.
[125] Glubb to Kirkbride, 27 May 1946, FO371/52931/E10014, TNA.

himself a servant of the British government, and although his visit to London in August–September 1948 had initially been instigated as a result of a financial crisis, by the time of his departure Glubb was as much, if not more, concerned about his personal authority and the value of the Arab Legion. Since February he had been guided by the Greater Transjordan scheme, but in the three months since the mandate ended and the war began he increasingly found himself to be the only active adherent. Now Glubb needed further guidance and reassurance.

Glubb's visit to London proved the fillip that he required. Given the rollicking Glubb received from Kirkbride and the Jordanian government concerning the accumulated debt, Glubb might have expected a similar rebuke in London. However, Britain was strikingly uncritical of Glubb. In the Foreign Office discussions that followed, it was the practicalities of dealing with the over-expenditure that were discussed rather than Glubb's role in it. Moreover, the Foreign Office laid the blame for the over-expenditure at the door of the War Office for not keeping its accounts in a clearer manner and MELF for not presenting its bills in good time. Glubb was not the subject of Foreign Office criticism.[126] Meanwhile, he received positive news regarding future instalments of the subsidy. Prior to his arrival Glubb warned: 'If H.M.G. do not release any money during August, the Arab Legion will dissolve. It may dissolve in mutiny and anarchy.'[127] To Glubb's relief, he was given 'an assurance to the effect that for the present the subsidy (including the equipment grant) will continue to be paid to meet the recurring expenditure and the re-equipment expenditure of the Arab Legion in accordance with the agreement reached last January'.[128] The over-expenditure was accounted for by converting it into an indefinite interest-free loan of £1.5 million.[129] This allowed for future instalments of the previously agreed subsidy to continue being paid, though the existence of the debt proved troublesome to successive British governments. The debt was recorded in the British Army accounts without reference to Jordan, and when it was subsequently discussed in Whitehall correspondence, the British were careful how they referred to it.[130] In one instance, a description of the debt as being 'for the purpose of waging war' was deleted

---

[126] Minute by Burrows, 12 August 1948, FO371/68830/E10610/G, TNA.
[127] Glubb to Kirkbride, 4 August 1948, GP2006, 83.
[128] FO to Amman, 821, 20 August 1948, FO371/68831/E11168, TNA.
[129] FO to Amman, 124, 5 February 1949, FO371/75299/E1264/G, TNA.
[130] Emmett to Bancroft, 13 November 1952, FO371/98883/ET1202/28; Russell Edmunds to Hunter, 26 November 1952, FO371/98883/ET1202/29, TNA.

and replaced with the more benign phrase: 'in excess of the provision in the subsidy'.[131] The British knew and accepted that the Jordanians would never pay it back. Yet year after year they were reluctant to wipe the debt for fear of bringing attention to it in Parliament.[132] With the immediate problem of over-expenditure dealt with, though, Glubb was satisfied with the British position, from a financial perspective.[133]

From a military perspective, it was explained to Glubb that in order to keep up the appearance of non-aggression, Britain could not supply the Arab Legion with much-needed war materiel. This provoked an equally agreeable response from Glubb, who concurred that it would be 'unwise' to send war materiel immediately, although he warned of the need for speed as the Arab Legion could hold off a renewed attack for only a few days.[134] Glubb's relaxed acceptance of Britain's decision to continue adhering to the embargo is somewhat surprising, given his repeated pleas for more ammunition, but it can be explained by strong indications that Glubb was able to circumvent this problem by procuring war materiel from elsewhere. While there is not a concrete paper trail confirming completed transactions, Glubb's papers contain enough material to indicate that the Arab Legion did make productive efforts to rearm. While Glubb was in London he received a letter from Lieutenant-Colonel Charles Coaker, from Arab Legion HQ, in which he remarked: 'I hear from the Def[ence] Minister that you have been fairly successful over money and rations [from the British] and that Pakistan may help with ammo, so perhaps you have not had quite such a thankless trip as you had feared.'[135] Glubb was seeking to order '15,000 hand grenades' and 30,000 anti-aircraft rounds from Switzerland to be paid for in dollars and shipped via Karachi. Moreover, Glubb wanted to 'enquire into [the] possibility [of] entering into contract with a Swiss or Belgian company, in conjunction with the Iraq Government for the manufacture of [25,000 rounds of] 3" Mortar ammunition', 25,000 rounds of twenty-five-pounder ammunition, and an unspecified amount of 3" mortars, plus ammunition on a scale of 1,000 rounds per mortar.[136] Glubb may also have initiated contacts related

---

[131] Harvey to Rance, 6 March 1950, T220/522, TNA.
[132] FO to Treasury, 25 September 1952, FO371/98883/ET1202/21; see folder: T220/522, TNA.
[133] FO to Amman, 821, 20 August 1948, FO371/68831/E11168, TNA.
[134] Ibid.
[135] Coaker to Glubb, 29 August 1948, GP2006, 83.
[136] 'Switzerland', undated [in a bundle of papers dated August 1948], ibid.

to the Nigerian government while in London. Certainly negotiations to that effect took place shortly after Glubb's return to Amman. Reporting back to Glubb, the Jordanian military attaché in London, Major Kemal Hamoud, explained: 'The Nigerian representative who arrived in London two days ago is the expert in important export for purchasing mission who are expected to arrive in London any day. This man assures me that the Nigerian Government wants to help us and that our goods will be bought and shipped with theirs.'[137] A week or so later Kemal further reported: 'Great hope. Effort continuing all repeat all our requirements. ... When Nigerian representative secures necessary papers suggest authorize former [to] proceed [to] Amman to report personally.'[138] Whether or not deals via Pakistan, Europe, and Nigeria were agreed and arms received is not confirmed. However, it is certain that Glubb had productive communication towards that end. Whether or not the British government was aware of this is also uncertain. However, it would seem highly unlikely that the British could be oblivious to such a transaction, especially involving Nigeria, which did not obtain independence until 1960. Any such procurement of arms was not enough to significantly alter the military balance and offer the Arab Legion the means to go on the offensive. Indeed, Glubb vented renewed desperation for military materiel in November/December.[139] The prospect of new military supplies that would help consolidate the Arab Legion's ability to maintain its defensive line was, however, enough to ease the pressure on Glubb in September. Consequently, when Glubb left London in mid-September, not only had he received financial assurances from Britain, but he also had seemingly made progress towards the procurement of much-needed military supplies. When he initially arrived in London, one journalist reported: 'He looks a tired, sick man, his eyes heavy and bloodshot.'[140] However, Glubb returned to Amman with new vigour. He seemed to get the reassurance he craved, and with his position stabilised, Glubb was able to focus his efforts on securing a satisfactory resolution to the conflict.

Meanwhile Glubb's month-long absence seemed to have a positive effect of easing the tension between himself and the Jordanian government. When he left Amman in August it appeared that the Jordanians

---

[137] Kemal to Glubb, undated [25 of unspecified month, but most likely October], GP2006, 97.
[138] Kemal to Glubb, 5 November 1948, GP2006, 86.
[139] Glubb to unknown [second page missing], 9 November 1948, ibid.
[140] Newspaper Cutting, *Evening Standard*, 16 August 1948, GP2006, 83.

were attempting to edge Glubb out – or at least to diminish the extent of his power. As an alternative to removing Glubb, which risked damaging relations with Britain, Kirkbride explained that the Jordanian government created a separate Ministry of Defence, headed by Fawzi al-Mulki, seemingly with the intention of 'concentrating all authority in the hands of the Minister', thus sidelining Glubb as a mere adviser.[141] Glubb likewise suspected that one reason the Jordanian government had approved his visit to London was to enable the new minister of defence to get 'himself dug in' in Glubb's absence. He believed:

They are afraid to dismiss me lest H.M.G. cut off the subsidy, but they might like to reduce my power but still keep me as a figure-head so that they will still get the money. It is not however clear to what extent the King would support this idea.[142]

Glubb arrived back in Amman on 17 September, and a few days later he reported that: 'The appointment of the Defence Minister has not led to any catastrophic results.' Instead, he described it as little more than 'perhaps a minor annoyance'. He added:

I am still inclined to think that when the Defence Minister was created, in the hysterical days of July, he was meant to oust me. But the excitement has now subsided, and in fact some of the Trans-Jordanians are a little ashamed of their attacks on us. As a result, the Defence Minister has not developed offensively.[143]

Similarly, Kirkbride reported that the Jordanian government's antipathy towards Glubb and the British officers had dissipated as it became generally accepted that previous criticism had been 'unjustified'.[144] By the end of October Glubb reported: 'The position of the Arab Legion and the British Officers in Trans-Jordan has been more or less re-established as it was a year ago.' Though he added that it was 'still widely believed that, without it's [sic] British Officers it would have done much more [in Palestine]'.[145] This belief was not unfounded. As Glubb acknowledged: 'They [the men of the Legion] were so frightfully keen to fight on May 15th.'[146] The supply situation certainly limited the Arab Legion's capabilities, but it was Glubb and the British officers in executive command positions

---

[141] Kirkbride to Bevin, 25 September 1948, FO371/68832/E12875, TNA.

[142] Glubb to H. E. Pyman, 13 August 1948, GP2006, 83.

[143] Glubb to H. E. Pyman, 22 September 1948, ibid.

[144] Kirkbride to Bevin, 25 September 1948, FO371/68832/E12875, TNA.

[145] Glubb to Brigadier O'Connor (Acting Chief of Staff, MELF), 27 October 1948, GP2006, 86.

[146] Glubb to Lash, 9 July 1948, GP2006, 90.

who ensured the Arab Legion maintained its adherence to the Greater Transjordan scheme.

But for Glubb's presence, it is unlikely that the Arab Legion could have been restrained, as it was, in the interests of partition. Several Arab officers, including Ali Abu Nowar and Abdullah al-Tall, suggested – fruitlessly – that the Arab Legion should end its defensive posture and go on the 'offensive' in Jerusalem.[147] British officers were also eager to fight. Nigel Bromage, whom Maan Abu Nowar described as an 'English Bedouin', recounted his efforts to strengthen the defences of Lydda and Ramle shortly before the end of the first round of fighting. Bromage proposed capturing the Israeli colony at Ben Shemen.[148] When this request was 'refused' by brigade headquarters, Bromage set about capturing and destroying the Israeli colony at Gezer, which overlooked the main road to Jerusalem. Fearing the same response from HQ, Bromage launched the attack 'without the authority of the Brigade'. Despite the initial success of the attack, Bromage withdrew his men because they did not have the resources to repel the inevitable counterattack. When he returned to brigade headquarters Bromage was severely reprimanded by Ashton for 'incurring unnecessary casualties' in this unsanctioned offensive, which was illustrative of the will to fight amongst both Arab and British men of the Legion.[149] When the second truce began, Glubb reported that the 'rank and file of the Arab Legion were rather annoyed'. This was because: 'They were unaware of the strategic plan or the supply situation, but were elated at having killed lots of Jews!'[150] It would have been almost impossible for the Arab Legion to adhere to the *strategic plan* of securing Greater Transjordan and acquiescing in the establishment of Israel but for the control of Glubb.

When the mandate ended, the Arab Legion entered Palestine merely with the objective of occupying the proposed Arab state and acquiescing in the establishment of Israel. The plight of the Palestinian Arabs and the groundswell of pressure throughout the Arab world compelled Abdullah to err beyond the scheme approved by Bevin. Abdullah did not lose his original desire to expand his authority, but it was difficult for him to go it alone. Thus, on the eve of the mandate Abdullah made one final attempt to coax the Jewish Agency to acquiesce in a scheme that would be more presentable to the rest of the Arab world. He also tried to obtain

[147] Lt. Col. [Abdullah al-Tall's handwriting] to Comd 4 Bde, undated, GP2006, 86.
[148] Abu Nowar, *Jordanian–Israeli War*, pp. 145–7.
[149] Ibid., pp. 145–52; Bromage, *Soldier in Arabia*, pp. 21–2, 60.
[150] Glubb to H. E. Pyman, 25 July 1948, GP2006, 83.

British approval for more expansive Arab Legion involvement. But both these diplomatic manoeuvres proved fruitless. Nonetheless, Abdullah was under pressure to come to the aid of the Arab Palestinians, particularly in Jerusalem, and had he been in sole control of the Arab Legion, its role would have been much less limited than it actually was. Yet, with Glubb in charge, the Arab Legion was largely able to restrain itself and stick to the *strategic plan* of occupying the Arab areas of Palestine and accepting the creation of Israel. The situation may have been altered between February and May, as Sela has emphasised, but the February meeting did help shape the 1948 War. The Greater Transjordan scheme approved at that meeting continued to govern the actions of Glubb and therefore the Arab Legion.

Had it not been for Glubb's significant, but limited autonomy over the Arab Legion, it is likely that it would not have acted in accordance with the restrained object of securing the Arab areas of Palestine in the interest of Abdullah's dynastic ambitions. A memorandum, most likely written by Glubb, stated: 'Unfortunately His Majesty is a good political strategist, but a bad tactician. His blueprints are excellent but they rarely go into production.'[151] This description of Abdullah neatly summarises the fate of the Greater Transjordan scheme. It was based on Abdullah's blueprint, but reliant on Glubb to put it into production. He ensured that the Arab Legion conducted limited war with Israel. Glubb did so in the interests of both Britain and Transjordan, but without much support from either. Glubb later complained: 'In the moments of worst stress, both Governments let the Arab Legion down. The Trans-Jordan Government tell me that it is my job to get the money from my compatriots the British, who are bound by treaty to do their stuff. H.M.G. say that they have nothing to do with operations in Palestine and will only pay at peace time rates.'[152] Glubb was caught between a Jordanian government that wanted to appear to fight and a British government that would not provide the means. Yet all the time Glubb's mission remained to secure Greater Transjordan. Glubb was effectively left alone to navigate a way through the fast-changing pattern of events. During the first round of fighting this was manageable, and when the first truce ended, the Arab Legion had successfully assumed control of central Palestine without encroaching on land designated to the new Jewish state. The Greater Transjordan scheme's lack of exit strategy is what put the most strain on Glubb. His visit to London during the second truce eased the pressure somewhat. Yet when he returned to Amman in September, this conundrum remained.

---

[151] 'The External Relations of Jordan', unsigned, 25 October 1949, GP2006, 47.
[152] Glubb to H. E. Pyman, 13 April 1949, GP2006, 22.

4

Bringing the 1948 War to an End: The Ad Hoc
Consolidation of Greater Transjordan

Glubb's return to Amman in September 1948 both marked and coincided with a significant shift towards seeking a resolution to the conflict. By September the front lines had been established and both sides had signed corresponding maps.[1] The war was eventually resolved by a series of bilateral armistice agreements negotiated and signed between Israel and the Arab states – except Iraq – during the first half of 1949. This chapter assesses the role of Glubb and the Arab Legion in bringing the conflict to an end, firstly by analysing their role in enabling the start of formal negotiations and, secondly, by focusing on the armistice negotiations themselves. As the war assumed an increasingly political nature after September 1948, Glubb's ability to influence events inevitably decreased. Uri Bar-Joseph has gone as far as to suggest that Glubb 'played virtually no role in the political negotiations throughout this period ... with the exception of certain phases in the armistice negotiations'.[2] Benny Morris quite rightly suggests Bar-Joseph's statement seems to be an exaggeration.[3] Morris concedes that the 'continued inaccessibility of contemporary Arab documentation' makes it 'difficult to assess Glubb's actual input in the armistice negotiations: How important was his advice in the shaping of Jordan's positions and concessions? A definitive answer must await the opening of Jordan's state archives.'[4] Although they still do not provide the full picture, Glubb's papers nonetheless help us understand his continued importance during this period. As this chapter demonstrates,

[1] Pappé, *Britain and the Arab–Israeli Conflict*, p. 57.
[2] Bar-Joseph, *Best of Enemies*, pp. 163–4.
[3] Morris, *Road to Jerusalem*, p. 283.
[4] Ibid., p. 202.

Glubb made a significant contribution to the myriad of uncoordinated and ad hoc approaches that searched for and eventually found a resolution to the conflict, a process that was arduously complicated by inter-Arab competition. Although these rivalries had been a feature of the Palestine conflict from the outset, this issue really came to prominence, particularly between Transjordan and Egypt, as the first Arab–Israeli war came to a close.

The difficulty of finding a solution to end the 1948 War was classically illustrated during the time it took Glubb to pack his bags and travel from London back to Amman in mid-September. On 16 September the UN mediator, Count Folke Bernadotte, put together a second resolution proposal. Similar to his first suggestion, Bernadotte proposed partition between Israel and Transjordan, with the Negev forming part of the Arab state and Galilee part of the Jewish state. This was again unpalatable to both Israel and the Arabs.[5] The Egyptians were particularly appalled that the Negev, which they presently occupied, was to be handed to Transjordan. Bernadotte's proposal was therefore quite literally short-lived. On 17 September, while Glubb was still travelling back to the region, Zionist terrorists assassinated Bernadotte in Jerusalem. The UN mediator had failed to meet the impossible challenge of finding a solution that would satisfy all parties, and before he had a chance to publish his second plan, both he and his proposal were dead. His assassination had shown that it would be up to the warring parties themselves to enforce a resolution to the conflict, and one of the key sticking points over the Bernadotte scheme, the Negev, would prove the political and military battleground where the 1948 War would be decided.

Understanding exactly what transpired in the Negev and why, between October 1948 and January 1949, is absolutely crucial to understanding the dynamics of the 1948 War, the interplay that brought it to an end, and the nature of Glubb's role. On 15 October the Israelis brought the 'shooting truce' – as the second truce became known – to an end when they launched Operation Yoav, an offensive against the Egyptians, who held a defensive front in southern Palestine from Isdud in the west to Hebron and Bethlehem in the east [Map 3]. Behind this line lay the vast area of the Negev, including a small cluster of Jewish colonies, which provided the casus belli for Operation Yoav to begin. The Israelis sent a convoy of military supplies to the Jewish colonies in an attempt to coax the Egyptian

---

[5] Kimche and Kimche, *Both Sides of the Hill*, pp. 235–7; Shlaim, *Politics of Partition*, p. 216.

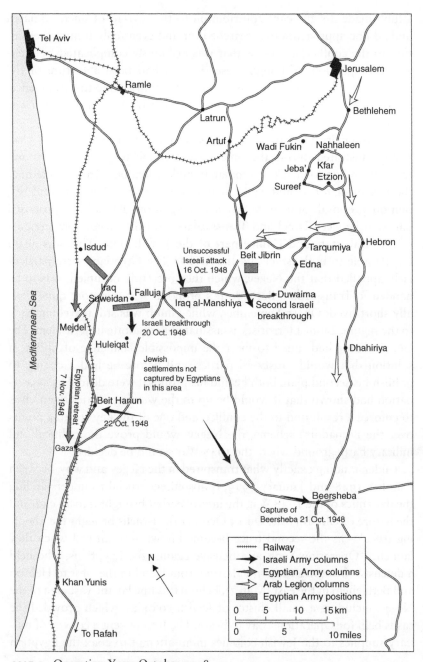

MAP 3. Operation Yoav, October 1948.
Based on: Avi Shlaim, Collusion across the Jordan: King Abdullah, the Zionist
Movement, and the Partition of Palestine (Oxford, 1988), p. 322.

Army into firing on the convoy. The Egyptians refrained, but not to be deterred, the Israelis fired on themselves and blamed the Egyptians, thus providing the pretext they needed to launch an offensive in the Negev.[6] The military governor of Jerusalem, Abdullah al-Tall, who defected from the Arab Legion in 1949, later claimed in his memoirs that King Abdullah knew and approved of Operation Yoav in advance. However, as Shlaim notes: 'No evidence can be found in any Israeli sources to corroborate this charge of a deliberate war plot against Egypt.'[7] Nor is there any such evidence in Glubb's papers. Yet while Glubb and Abdullah were not involved in or aware of the instigation of the Jewish offensive, the Arab Legion reaction remains a point of significant contention. At the height of the conflict, on 1 November 1948, the Egyptian newspaper *Al-Ahram* published an article titled 'Where are the Arab armies?', which questioned how long the other Arab states would allow the Egyptian Army to fight Zionism alone.[8] Fawaz Gerges has emphasised that, 'one of the intriguing questions is why Transjordan did not come to the aid of Egypt? Egyptians believed they were stabbed in the back.'[9] This question is not just intriguing; it is absolutely crucial to understanding not only the role of Glubb and the Arab Legion, but also the process of resolving the conflict. Thus, the first half of this chapter is devoted primarily to answering this question.

Regarding Transjordan's failure to come to Egypt's aid, King Farouk's initial complaint was that he had expected the Arab Legion and the Iraqi Army to relieve the pressure on the Egyptian front by engaging the Israelis elsewhere. The Egyptians did not want direct assistance. The Egyptian media continued to report only military victories against Israel and falsely denied the loss of territory.[10] And when the Arab League Political Committee met in Amman on 23 October, the Egyptian prime minister was adamant that 'the Egyptian government does not ask [for] help from anyone. I came here to know why the other Arab states have not attacked so far to relieve the pressure on the Egyptian army. Where is the Iraqi army and where is the Arab Legion?'[11] In his memoirs Glubb complained that the Arab Legion was unable to act because 'we did not know of the

---

[6] Shlaim, *Collusion*, p. 321.
[7] Ibid.
[8] *SWB, Part III*, 11 November, p. 69.
[9] Fawaz Gerges, 'Egypt and the 1948 War', in: Rogan and Shlaim (eds.), *Rewriting the History of 1948*, p. 166.
[10] *SWB Part III*, 21 October, p. 70; 28 October, pp. 73–87.
[11] Quoted in: Gerges, 'Egypt and the 1948 War', p. 165.

Egyptian defeat until after it had occurred [by 22 October]'.[12] Contrary to this assertion, however, it seems that Glubb was aware of the Egyptian Army's impending doom. Already on 18 October Glubb reported:

It seems possible that present op[eration]s in South Palestine may be a major offensive by Jews against Egyptian Army. If Jews can move large forces to area west of Beersheba they may try and cut off Egyptian Army from Egypt. In such an event Egyptians may meet with major defeat.[13]

The following day Glubb informed Kirkbride that: 'Unless U.N.O. can stop the fighting quickly, it looks as if the Egyptian Army in Palestine may be destroyed.'[14] Glubb was not certain about the likely fate of the Egyptian Army, and his insistence in his memoirs that 'the Egyptian Army never informed us of its operations', appears true.[15] Indeed, his information of the Egyptians' predicament came not from the Egyptians, but from claims made by the Israelis. Glubb's understanding was that the '*Jews claim* to be astride [the] main Jaffa Gaza road' and '*they claim* [a] large Egyptian force [was] hemmed in with its back to the sea at Isdud and Mejdel'. Glubb concluded: '*If these claims are true* it looks as if [the] Egyptian Army in Palestine may be destroyed unless UNO stops the fighting.'[16] So why did Transjordan not come to the aid of its Arab ally when Glubb was aware of its likely defeat? Apart from the fact that Glubb was evidently uncertain of the situation, which was fluid and fast moving, two factors were at play. Firstly, Glubb's actions relate to his three priorities outlined in the previous chapter: first, protect Transjordan; second, protect the Arab Legion; third, protect the gains in Arab Palestine. With regards to his first priority, Glubb was not unduly concerned. He was certainly wary that Amman was vulnerable to an attack by air.[17] But he 'assumed that the Jews would not violate the basic frontiers of Trans-Jordan for fear of bringing in the Anglo-Trans-Jordan treaty'.[18] Regarding his second and third priorities, Glubb was less confident. He had a number of concerns about the precarious position he was trying to hold. The Arab Legion was spread too thin and lacked ammunition and air capabilities.[19] As Glubb explained to Kirkbride: 'The Iraq Army

[12] Glubb, *Soldier*, p. 199.
[13] Glubb to H. E. Pyman, 18 October 1948, GP2006, 86.
[14] Glubb to Kirkbride, 19 October 1948, GP2006, 91.
[15] Glubb, *Soldier*, p. 199.
[16] Glubb to H. E. Pyman, 19 October 1948, GP2006, 91 [emphasis added].
[17] Glubb to Minister of Defence, 'Military Situation in Palestine', 25 October 1948, GP2006, 86.
[18] Glubb to O'Connor (Acting Chief of Staff, MELF), 27 October 1948, ibid.
[19] 'An Appreciation of the Position of the Arab Legion in Palestine', 7 November 1948, ibid.

is not in a condition to fight seriously, and thus the Arab Legion will be hopelessly outnumbered and short of ammunition.'[20] Glubb suggested that 'the worst disadvantage under which we laboured, was not having unity of command' within the Arab coalition. Though he also acknowledged that: 'If we had had unity of command, we should undoubtedly have been ordered to hold Ramle and Lydda, so perhaps it was well we had not!'[21] At the start of the conflict in May, King Abdullah had been appointed commander-in-chief of the Arab armies, but this 'unity of command existed in name only'.[22] Ultimately, the Arab states were not working in unison, and launching a diversionary offensive to save the Egyptian Army was too great a risk for Glubb to consider.

The second reason why Glubb was loath to aid the Egyptians was because Operation Yoav had the potential to promise great rewards, which Glubb undoubtedly sought to capitalise on. There was no love lost between the two Arab states, and Egypt's demise in the Negev provided an opportunity to force it into submission, thus removing the main obstacle that would enable a convenient exit strategy for Transjordan and the Arab Legion. Glubb already blamed the political motives of politicians in Egypt and Syria for ending the first truce. And when he returned to Amman in September, the principal obstacle to peace and British and Jordanian interests, as he saw it, came from inter-Arab rivalries.[23] The figurehead of the anti-Hashemite bloc was the Mufti and his Arab government of All-Palestine. The Gaza government, as it was otherwise known, was established in September by the Egyptian-dominated Arab League to challenge Transjordan's authority to annex Arab Palestine.[24] Abdullah 'vigorously refused' to recognise the Gaza government.[25] He told Azzam Pasha that Transjordan 'disagreed with the act of imposing a partisan government on the people of Palestine without giving them a chance to express their wishes'.[26] And in a telegram to Ahmad Hilmi, military governor of Jerusalem, Abdullah insisted:

The Transjordan Hashemite Government will not permit the function of any organisation which will curtail the right of Palestinians to self-determination, after the settlement of the present problem. It will also never permit the formation

[20] Glubb to Kirkbride, 19 October 1948, GP2006, 91.
[21] Glubb to H. E. Pyman, 25 July 1948, GP2006, 83.
[22] Abdullah, *Al-Takmilah*, p. 10.
[23] Glubb to Chapman Walker; Glubb to Kirkbride, 25 September 1948, GP2006, 83.
[24] Gerges, 'Egypt and the 1948 War', p. 164; Salibi, *Modern History of Jordan*, pp. 163–4.
[25] Abdullah, *Al-Takmilah*, p. 24.
[26] *SWB, Part III*, 7 October 1948, p. 66.

of any organisation in the interests of certain persons within the area it controls militarily from the Egyptian to the Syrian and Lebanese borders. It will only recognise the responsibilities shouldered by the Arab countries in their respective military areas, and will recognise the latter's commanders only.[27]

Shortly after receiving this telegram, Ahmad Hilmi accepted an offer to become prime minister in the Gaza government, as the Mufti sought to subvert Abdullah's ambitions in Palestine.[28] Abdullah, meanwhile, considered the Gaza government an obstacle to his own plans and therefore sought to undermine it politically by arranging a conference in Amman, held on 1 October. The Jordanian-controlled Radio Jerusalem announced that the Amman conference would 'enable the Palestine Arabs, with the assistance of the Arab countries, to realise their objectives in the final liberation of their country'.[29] At the Amman meeting, and at a follow-up conference in Jericho on 1 December, the gathered delegates denounced the Gaza government, proclaimed Abdullah as the representative for the future of Palestine, and demanded unity between Palestine and Transjordan with King Abdullah as the sovereign ruler of a united state.[30] However, these congresses were a rather crude and transparent attempt to legitimise Greater Transjordan and failed to sway Abdullah's main rivals within the Arab League; not least Azzam Pasha, King Farouk, and the Syrian president, Shukri al-Quwatli, who all considered these 'small' gatherings unrepresentative.[31] The military aspect of the conflict still had a significant part to play and, therefore, so did Glubb.

His first task was to neutralise the Mufti and his powerbase. After several years in exile in Cairo, the Mufti secretly re-entered Palestine at the end of September. As Husayni explained:

Together with our brethren we began organising the Palestine jihad warriors, equipping them and enlisting all those who were qualified to fight in the towns and villages of Palestine not yet occupied by the Jews, from Rafah to Jenin. Delegations of Palestinian warriors poured into Gaza from different areas, ready to renew the jihad against the enemy.[32]

[27] Text of the telegram broadcast on Jordanian-controlled 'Jerusalem Radio' on 17 September, *SWB, Part III*, 23 September 1948, p. 67.
[28] Yitzhak, *Abdullah al-Tall*, p. 58.
[29] *SWB, Part III*, 7 October 1948, p. 66.
[30] Musa, *Jordan: Land and* People, pp. 53–4; Salibi, *Modern History of Jordan*, p. 164; Bradshaw, *Britain and Jordan*, pp. 173–4; Khalidi, *Iron Cage*, pp. 67, 134; Massad, *Colonial Effects*, pp. 227–8.
[31] *SWB, Part III*, 16 December 1948, pp. 63–5; Aqil H. H. Abidi, *Jordan: A Political Study, 1948–1957* (London, 1965), pp. 55–6.
[32] Zvi Elpeleg (ed.), *Through the Eyes of the Mufti: The Essays of Haj Amin Translated and Annotated*, paperback edn (Elstree, 2015), p. 72.

This posed a problem for the Greater Transjordan scheme, but Glubb believed that if the Mufti and the Gaza government could be eliminated, Transjordan would be in a much stronger position to claim the Arab areas of Palestine.[33] On 3 October Glubb received a written order from the minister of defence to disband and disarm all bodies of armed men not under orders of the Arab Legion.[34] To that end, the Arab Legion produced a detailed plan, codenamed 'Operation Beer', to capture the headquarters of approximately 200 armed men who were 'actively supporting' the Mufti and the Gaza government 'by refusing to co-operate with the' Jordanian authorities in Ramallah.[35] Just a few days later, the Mufti returned to Cairo. He explained that he left Palestine – reluctantly – at the insistence of the Egyptian authorities. However, he also asserted that the Arab Legion hounded his force out. The Mufti complained that 'the Jordanian military forces under the command of General Glubb ... dissolved the Holy Jihad Army', denying it 'freedom of action'.[36] Glubb successfully thwarted the Mufti's efforts to establish a political foothold in Palestine. Yet as far as he was concerned, this merely amounted to cutting the tail of the snake that threatened Greater Transjordan.

What was really needed was an opportunity to cut off the head. Glubb suspected the Mufti was being supported by Egypt and Syria with a view to instigating a revolt against the Arab Legion. Glubb warned that 'the Mufti with strong Egyptian support, is apparently about to start a rebellion against the Arab Legion in Palestine, like the Arab rebellion against the British in 1936'.[37] The Mufti certainly saw Glubb and the Arab Legion as the 'real obstacle' to his ambitions in Palestine. And while the Mufti claimed that the Egyptian prime minister and the minister of war 'objected' to his military activities, he also had undoubted political support from the Egyptian government and sympathy from the nationalist movement emerging within the Egyptian Army.[38] As a result of this connection, Glubb believed: 'If the Egyptians withdrew from the south, the Gaza Government would probably collapse, and thus the problem would solve itself.'[39] Operation Yoav therefore presented Glubb with an opportunity to eliminate this problem. Immediately Glubb expressed his hope

---

[33] Glubb to Chapman Walker; Glubb to Kirkbride, 25 September 1948, GP2006, 83.
[34] Glubb, *Soldier*, p. 192.
[35] 'Op: Beer', 8 October 1948, GP2006, 91.
[36] Elpeleg (ed.), *Through the Eyes of the Mufti*, p. 77.
[37] Glubb to Chapman Walker, 25 September 1948, GP2006, 83.
[38] Elpeleg (ed.), *Through the Eyes of the Mufti*, pp. 73–7.
[39] 'Transjordan and Palestine', Glubb, 5 October 1948, GP2006, 83.

that this 'Jewish offensive … may finally knock out the Gaza government and give the gyppies [Egyptians] a lesson'. This opportunity to knock out Egypt and the Gaza government was exactly what Glubb had been waiting for. Thus, Glubb decided: 'if the Jews are going to have a private war with the Egyptians and the Gaza Government, we do not want to get involved. The Gyppies and the Gaza Govt are almost as hostile to us as the Jews!'[40] If the Arab Legion's achievements in Palestine were to be consolidated and a resolution to the conflict found, it was clear that the submission of the other Arab forces would be necessary. The Arab League had to be cajoled into ceasing its desire to fight. It was the only way Transjordan could exit the war without being accused of treachery.

With the Egyptians on the back foot, Glubb sought to capitalise by coercing the British into driving home a solution. When Glubb first heard of the Israeli offensive, he predicted 'the Jews are going to try at U.N.O. to get both Galilee *and* Negeb'. Glubb initially lamented: 'The Mufti and the Gyppies have given them just the chance they wanted.'[41] However, within days Glubb was willing to acquiesce and promote the same outcome. With the Egyptian Army seemingly close to destruction, Glubb was at pains to point out: 'I think H.M.G. should understand clearly that unless a final settlement can be made quickly, it is within the power of the Jews to conquer the whole of Palestine.' He therefore suggested that the British and American delegations at the United Nations 'should accept Jewish amendments to Bernadotte's plan – namely [Negev] and Galilee to the Jews'.[42] Glubb believed the United Nations was split between two factions: Britain, who wanted the Bernadotte plan, which it did;[43] and 'the Jews' who wanted the 1947 UN partition resolution. Glubb proposed a 'compromise between the two schemes', which he suggested that Kirkbride, if he liked it, could send off to the Foreign Office as his own idea, believing this would carry more weight.[44] And Kirkbride duly obliged.[45] Glubb's view on how the Arab areas of Palestine should be divided fluctuated as the war progressed, reflecting a largely pragmatic, and perhaps somewhat erratic, attitude to the balance of forces of the moment. When he left for London in August, Glubb believed the

[40] Glubb to Goldie, 16 October 1948, Shlaim's Private Collection.
[41] Ibid. [emphasis in original].
[42] Glubb to Kirkbride, 19 October 1948, GP2006, 91.
[43] Glubb to Kirkbride, 21 November 1948, GP2006, 100; FO to Amman, 1076, 18 November 1948, FO816/133, TNA.
[44] Glubb to Kirkbride, 21 November 1948, GP2006, 100.
[45] Amman to FO, 910, 26 November 1948, FO816/134, TNA.

annexation of the Arab areas of Palestine would make Transjordan 'a more valuable ally'.[46] While in London during August/September, Glubb proposed that Gaza and Beersheba should be annexed by Egypt, and the rest to Transjordan.[47] After returning to the Middle East, he now claimed that the Palestinian Arabs – based on the few villagers he talked to – would prefer the Arab areas of Palestine not to be partitioned further and that they favoured complete takeover by Transjordan.[48] And now that the IDF was close to defeating the Egyptian Army, Glubb was prepared to accept Israeli occupation of the Negev as a means of enabling a settlement.

Allowing the Egyptians to be defeated was not without its risks, but the risk-reward ratio was heavily in favour of the Arab Legion remaining passive. Although Glubb welcomed the Egyptians' downfall, he was wary that it might give the Israelis confidence to turn on the Arab Legion. His main concern was that: 'We don't want the Jews to capture Hebron too.' Moreover, here lay a further opportunity. Glubb reasoned: 'If we step in and occupy Hebron, we shall have no further political complications in the Hebron area! We shall appear as saviours, to rescue Hebron from the Jews when the Egyptians have run away.'[49] Hebron had proved a source of tension between Egypt and Transjordan, as the two supposed allies wrestled for control.[50] In June both countries had appointed military governors to Hebron. Initially the mayor of Hebron welcomed the Arab Legion governor, while the Egyptian appointee was turned away. Some notables disagreed with this policy, though, which led to the implementation of a 'dual administration' in Hebron in which the Egyptian governor assumed the 'upper hand'.[51] Given this situation, the Egyptian Army's plight created an opportunity for Glubb to kill two birds with one stone: to take the Egyptians out of the equation and to obtain legitimacy for Jordanian control of Palestine by appearing as its saviour. The problem was that this would leave the Arab Legion defensive line even further stretched, and in preparation for a potential Israeli offensive, Glubb was concerned that the Arab Legion would have to 'hold each [road to Hebron] with one squadron, and at the same time cover the southern

[46] 'The Trans-Jordan Situation', Glubb, 12 August 1948, GP2006, 83.
[47] Glubb to Burrows, 22 September 1948, GP2006, 83.
[48] Amman to FO, 769, 30 September 1948; Glubb to Kirkbride, 29 September 1948, FO816/129, TNA.
[49] Glubb to Goldie, 16 October 1948, Shlaim's Private Collection.
[50] Shlaim, *Collusion*, p. 300.
[51] Superintendent of Police (Hebron) to Glubb, 8 December 1948, GP2006, 85.

front of Jerusalem!!'[52] On 19 October Abdullah 'ordered' Glubb to send a regiment to Hebron. However, just as he had done in Jerusalem in May, Glubb initially ignored these orders.[53] It is difficult to be certain exactly what Abdullah's motivation was. Did he seek to protect Hebron to gain territorially, or did he seek to be seen to be aiding his Egyptian allies? It was most likely related to the appeals he received from Arab notables, including the mayor of Hebron, to save the town from attack.[54] Ultimately, Abdullah wanted to be seen as the protector of Palestine, and responding to calls for support helped legitimise his rule. What does seem certain, though, is that Glubb ignored this order to ensure the safety of the Arab Legion and allow the Egyptians to be defeated. Throughout the first week Glubb was uncertain as to whether the Israelis were launching a major operation or whether they only had a limited objective. His first call was not to get involved, but simply to preserve the Arab Legion and allow Israel to defeat the Egyptians.

In a further example of Glubb's limited autonomy, he could only ignore Abdullah's order for so long, and on 22 October he sent a small force of 350 men, led by Major Geoffrey Lockett, to protect Bethlehem and Hebron.[55] This force was not sent to aid the Egyptian forces. Glubb and Kirkbride had two primary motives. Firstly, Glubb realised that if he did nothing:

Politically we should have another Lydda and Ramle as the king ordered me to send a regiment 2 days ago! It would again be me who betrayed the Arab cause.

Secondly, he noted: 'Economically it would mean another 50,000 to 100,000 refugees.'[56] A token Arab Legion force was therefore moved south for primarily political purposes: to strengthen the Anglo–Jordanian connection in Palestine and to halt any further Israeli expansion and resulting instability. Just like the original Greater Transjordan scheme, it was designed to uphold the status quo and, further, it was designed to enhance the legitimacy of Greater Transjordan. Glubb expected Israel to accept a ceasefire in two to three days. His immediate objective, therefore, was: 'It is really essential to hold Bethlehem and if possible Hebron for those 3 days.'[57] As it turned out, the Arab Legion did not have to hold out that long, as a ceasefire was agreed that very same day.

---

[52] Glubb to Goldie, 16 October 1948, Shlaim's Private Collection.
[53] Glubb to Goldie, 21 October 1948, ibid.
[54] Abu Nowar, *Jordanian–Israeli War*, p. 241.
[55] Glubb, *Soldier*, p. 200.
[56] Glubb to Goldie, 21 October 1948, Shlaim's Private Collection.
[57] Ibid.

After the 22 October ceasefire we have to look beyond Glubb's opportunism as an explanation for the role of the Arab Legion and its failure to aid the besieged Egyptian forces. By the time the ceasefire was agreed, the Israelis had captured two crucial strategic junctions on the road south: Beit Hanun on the main western road and Beersheba on the main eastern road. This left the Egyptian forces in three separate positions: Gaza, which remained connected to Egypt; and Falluja and the Bethlehem-Hebron sector, both of which were now cut off and isolated.[58] After visiting Jerusalem and consulting with other senior officers within the Legion, Glubb concluded that 'the discipline and morale of the Egyptian Army in Hebron and Beersheba have been so far destroyed that there is really no hope of their fighting any more'. The Arab Legion therefore had little motivation to use its scarce resources to aid the Egyptians. Indeed, the Arab Legion was holding the Hebron-Bethlehem sector with 'light forces' that would not be 'strong enough to hold it', in the event of an IDF attack.[59]

Egyptian intransigence was also important in the Arab Legion's failure to aid these isolated pockets. Contrary to the suggestion that the Egyptians were stabbed in the back, inter-Arab rivalry was not one-sided. The Iraqi Parliamentary Commission of Inquiry challenged the Egyptian account that the Hashemites did little or nothing to help the besieged Egyptian forces. It claimed that Egypt refused offers to collaborate because of political suspicions of its Hashemite allies. This appraisal is contradicted by many Arab historians and by former Iraqi soldiers.[60] However, new evidence from the Jordanian side challenges the notion of a one-sided betrayal. Indeed, when two Egyptian companies were besieged in Beit Jibrin, in late October, Glubb reported that an 'Arab Legion patrol contacted them and offered to escort them out but they refused [to] leave [the] fort'.[61] This is supported by a Haganah transmission on 26 October, which reported that the Egyptian prime minister, Mahmud Nuqrashi, 'had not agreed to the terms "dictated" by King Abdullah regarding help for the besieged Egyptian forces in Southern Palestine'.[62] Speaking on the Jordanian-controlled Jerusalem Radio, an Amman spokesman explained

---

[58] Glubb, *Soldier*, pp. 197–202.
[59] Glubb to Minister of Defence, 'Military Situation in Palestine', 25 October 1948, GP2006, 86.
[60] Gerges, 'Egypt and the 1948 War', p. 166.
[61] Glubb to O'Connor, 27 October 1948, GP2006, 84, 86.
[62] *SWB, Part III*, 4 November 1948, p. 80.

that 'when the Transjordan Government was surprised by events in Southern Palestine', it asked the Egyptians if they required assistance, but received no reply.[63] The Arab Legion may not have launched a diversionary offensive elsewhere, but it did offer to help the besieged Egyptian forces escape. Maan Abu Nowar and Captain Sadiq al-Saharaa, who were 'sent to Bethlehem and Hebron to obtain information regarding the state of the Egyptian force in the sector ... were baffled by the lack of interest and cooperation shown by the Egyptian officers – especially in Bethlehem'.[64] It would seem, though, that the Egyptians were loath to allow the Arab Legion to appear as their saviours. The Egyptian media portrayed the fighting in the Negev as hugely successful and maintained the fiction that all Israeli offensives, including attacks on Beit Jibrin, were being convincingly defeated.[65] On 23 October, for example, Radio Cairo quoted the Egyptian prime minister falsely denying that Beersheba had been captured by the Israelis. Perception and appearances within the Arab coalition were deemed all-important – and proved a significant factor sustaining the war.

One of the keys to resolving the conflict was to not be the first to negotiate. With that in mind, the Egyptian stance took a curious turn. As the Egyptians came closer and closer to destruction, during the first week of November they sent out peace feelers to the Israeli delegation in Paris, where the UN Security Council was in session. The Egyptians were prepared to abandon their Hashemite ally by agreeing to sit out of any renewed warfare between Israel and any other Arab state.[66] Moreover, concurrent with these peace overtures, the Egyptians allegedly sought to betray the Jordanians directly in their efforts to seek a reprieve from becoming the first to negotiate. On 3 November, General Sabbar of the Egyptian Army gave Abdullah a personal message from the Egyptian defence minister, Hayder Pasha, 'begging him [Abdullah] to propose to King Farouq to make peace'. This was an odd request, which Glubb interpreted as follows:

[The] Egyptians will of course double cross us. Having begged us to propose peace they will denounce us in the end as the people who let down the A.[rab] League by first proposing peace![67]

---

[63] Ibid., 28 October 1948, p. 75.
[64] Abu Nowar, *Jordanian–Israeli War*, p. 242.
[65] *SWB, Part III*, 4 November 1948, pp. 68–71.
[66] Shlaim, *Collusion*, pp. 346–7.
[67] '2/11/48, 11-00 hrs', diary-like note by Glubb, 3 November 1948, GP2006, 86.

Glubb was in no doubt that the Egyptians wanted Abdullah to make himself a scapegoat to enable them to formalise the peace agreement with the Israelis that they so desperately needed. It would have been easy to fall into this trap – if that is what it was – as by the beginning of November both Glubb and Kirkbride noticed a 'change in the attitude of the public and of senior Arab Officers of the Arab Legion' in favour of securing the best terms possible before the situation worsened.[68] Glubb reported that: 'Large numbers of Palestinians, in Amman and Pal[estine], [are] openly asking for peace at any price.'[69] Indeed, the mayor of Hebron insisted that the Palestine Arabs merely wanted a settlement, and that if the Arab League could not provide one, militarily or peacefully, 'we will negotiate ourselves even without the approval of our leaders'.[70] The first Glubb heard of this Egyptian request that Abdullah propose peace was when the king read out his reply in front of the Jordanian Cabinet. Glubb was relieved to hear that Abdullah's reply was 'elastically worded'.[71] Nonetheless, this evident and vociferous mistrust of Egyptian intentions was sure to influence Glubb's actions over the coming weeks.

This was followed by an even more curious incident, which while well known, requires a retelling based on new evidence, which compounds the issue of power politics between Egypt and Transjordan. In his memoirs Glubb recounted the Arab Legion's attempt to assist the Egyptian forces besieged in Falluja. In mid-late November Geoffrey Lockett, an Arab Legion officer, volunteered to visit the besieged Egyptian troops to find out their real situation. Accordingly, he walked across enemy lines, stayed for two days, and reported upon his return that the Egyptian troops were being mortared day and night. After the Arab League failed to produce a feasible plan to rescue the besieged troops, Glubb decided to act. He recounted:

I accordingly sent Geoffrey once more to walk through the Jewish lines to Falluja and offer them a plan. Our proposal was that, on a night agreed upon, the Egyptians should walk out of Falluja to the east. We should advance to meet them and engage from the rear any Jewish forces attempting to bar their way. The distance between us was about twelve miles. The Egyptian garrison was a weak brigade group, about 2,500 strong. They would have had to abandon or destroy their heavy stores, but I still believe that eighty per cent of the personnel would have reached our lines in safety. Geoffrey passed successfully through

[68] Amman to FO, 844, 2 November 1948, FO816/132, TNA.
[69] '2/11/48, 11-00 hrs', diary-like note by Glubb, 3 November 1948, GP2006, 86.
[70] *SWB, Part III*, 11 November 1948, p. 55.
[71] '2/11/48, 11-00 hrs', diary-like note by Glubb, 3 November 1948, GP2006, 86.

Israeli lines, but the Egyptian commander rejected the proposal. This was the end of our attempts to relieve Falluja.[72]

Within the existing historiography this is the accepted account of events. And an Arab Legion evacuation plan, dated 17 November, corroborates this narrative.[73] Surprisingly, some key texts have omitted to mention this event.[74] Perhaps this reflects Glubb's straightforward, uncontested narrative, the gist of which was briefly corroborated in Kirkbride's memoirs also.[75] However, newly available sources provide fresh details about this sequence of events in late November, which necessitates a retelling. Frustratingly, these new sources raise questions for which definitive answers are elusive, but they strongly intimate at a very different story to the one Glubb told. At the very least, it reveals subtle and significant nuances regarding the final stage of the 1948 War and the interplay between two apparent allies: Egypt and Transjordan.

That Lockett made two visits on foot to the besieged troops in Falluja is confirmed by two contemporary documents. Lockett's first trip is corroborated almost word for word.[76] The document recording the second expedition, though, poses the first serious challenge as, curiously, it contains no mention of Lockett proposing an evacuation plan, let alone its refusal by the Egyptians. The entire signal simply records:

[An] Arab Legion NCO returned yesterday having walked through Jewish lines to Falluja and back. [A] Convoy of fifty camels reached Falluja with rations and ammunition but Jews now tightened siege. Rank and file mostly Sudanese and morale fairly good. Garrison seem to have rations for about a fortnight at least but they refuse to tell us. Jews should have withdrawn to truce line on November Nineteenth and abandoned siege but had not done so yesterday. Jews shell and mortar Egyptians constantly but latter make little reply to save ammunition.[77]

If Glubb did send Lockett to offer the besieged Egyptian troops a way out of Falluja, it is hard to fathom why he made no mention of the offer or the refusal in this signal to the MELF Chief of Staff, as he had done exactly a month before in relation to Beit Jibrin.

[72] Glubb, *Soldier*, pp. 215–16.
[73] Rogan, 'Jordan and the 1948 War', pp. 115–16, 124; *Hashemite Documents*, p. 295; Kimche and Kimche, *Both Sides of the Hill*, pp. 254–5.
[74] Shlaim, *Collusion*; Morris, *Road to Jerusalem*.
[75] Alec Kirkbride, *From The Wings: Amman Memoirs 1947–1951* (London, 1976), pp. 65–6.
[76] Glubb to COS MELF, 24 November 1948, GP2006, 86.
[77] Glubb to COS MELF, 27 November 1948, ibid.

So, did Glubb actually provide the besieged Egyptian forces in Falluja with a withdrawal plan, which they refused? It is difficult to be certain, but a huge question mark has been raised over the validity of this claim. On the whole, Glubb's memoirs are an accurate portrayal of events, but on this occasion it is difficult to see past the fact that Glubb makes no mention of this withdrawal plan in the contemporary documents. Moreover, we have already established that a month earlier, an Arab Legion officer – most likely Lockett because he was the commanding officer in the area at the time – had offered an escape route for Egyptian forces besieged in Beit Jibrin, east of Falluja, on the road to Hebron, which was refused. Curiously, this rejected withdrawal plan did not make it into the memoirs. Glubb did reproduce a detailed account, written by an unnamed Arab Legion officer, of a reconnaissance mission in Beit Jibrin led by Lockett on 28 October, but there is no mention of the withdrawal plan offered and refused sometime before 27 October, when it was recorded in a signal to the MELF Chief of Staff. It seems pertinent to point out that the dates of these signals are not clearly marked. They merely record the date and the time that the signal was sent, but not the month. It is possible – perhaps even likely – that Glubb's apparent error regarding the seemingly non-issued Falluja withdrawal plan can be attributed to Glubb accidentally merging the two separate, but similar incidents into one single memory based on two documents from the twenty-seventh of two different months. Yet even if we accept this, it still does not solve the curious puzzle of exactly what did transpire in Falluja in late November.

If we go back to the beginning, the whole incident was initiated by the most curious feature of all. Having suspiciously asked the Arab Legion to get Abdullah to propose peace on 3 November, two weeks later the Arab Legion received another odd request from General Sabbar. Lash reported:

Sabour Bey [the Egyptian general] had invited Lockett to go and com[man]d the B[riga]de G[rou]p at Faluja! Lash has told Lockett to hold his horses on this one for the moment, while it was being referred to you.[78]

This raises the ultimate curiosity: why, if Lockett had offered the Egyptians a withdrawal plan, did they reject it, if they had originally requested Lockett to come and command the brigade? According to an uncited source quoted by Kimche and Kimche, the Egyptian reply given by General Faud Sadeq, the commander-in-chief at Gaza, to Brigadier

[78] Coaker to Glubb, 15 November 1948, GP2006, 97.

Taha Bey, the Sudanese commander of the besieged Egyptian force, when confronted with the withdrawal plan, was that:

It is impossible to rely on a plan whose initiator is Glubb Pasha, and it is impossible to keep the details of the plan from the Jews if it originated in Amman. The evacuation of the troops by foot through areas held by Jews means a massacre for these troops. Reject the plan and drive out the mercenary Lockett. Defend your posts to the last bullet and to the last soldier as befitting Egyptian soldiers.[79]

If we accept the increasingly unreliable claim that a withdrawal plan was offered and refused, as recorded in a document cited by Kimche and Kimche, the Egyptians are seemingly revealed as double-crossers who first asked Lockett to command them, before turning him away when he tried. If Lockett's withdrawal plan was to be dismissed so unceremoniously, presumably there was no genuine will to have Lockett command the besieged force. What is more likely is that Glubb suspected the Egyptians were intending to double-cross the Arab Legion via their offer for Lockett to command the Brigade, just as Glubb suspected when General Sabbar requested Abdullah propose peace. For that reason, this withdrawal plan was probably never put on the table – at least not seriously. Whether or not the Egyptians were actually seeking to double-cross their Jordanian allies, that is what Glubb believed and is surely why Glubb decided to keep out of the fighting between Israel and Egypt – his utter distrust of the Egyptians and his recognition that Egypt needed to be knocked out of the war by Israel in order to pave the way for peace.

The fate of the Egyptian forces besieged in Falluja *was* a concern to Glubb. He explained unambiguously that: 'The matter affects us rather intimately owing to the great quantities of British equipment the Jews are likely to get, if the Fallujah garrison surrenders. This equipment will be used against us.'[80] This is where the issue of a withdrawal plan would make sense from Glubb's perspective. Contrary to the claim in Glubb's memoirs that the besieged Egyptian force was a 'weak brigade group', Glubb was of the opinion that this force was so well armed that it 'should be able to march up and down Palestine with impunity, but the Egyptians cannot make up their minds to come out'.[81] Glubb put its predicament down to poor leadership and perhaps sought to call the Egyptians' bluff by sending Lockett to ensure the Egyptian Army's defeat by making sure they destroyed their weapons and retreated. Whether or not Glubb offered

[79] Kimche and Kimche, *Both Sides of the Hill*, pp. 252–5.
[80] Glubb to O'Connor, 18 November 1948, GP2006, 85.
[81] Ibid.

the Falluja brigade a serious escape route has been brought into question. But what is certain is that a welter of intrigue and suspicion between two apparent allies surrounded this whole episode and that Glubb's primary objective was to ensure the Egyptian Army's presence in Palestine came to an end, in order to allow peace negotiations to begin.

What Glubb and the Arab Legion were doing, or not doing, on the military side also has to be considered within the context of the political situation. While Glubb was busy attempting to manufacture a scenario conducive to peace, Abdullah was re-establishing his connection with Zionist politicians and Transjordan–Israel negotiations over a Jerusalem ceasefire were progressing. Having reluctantly distanced himself from the Greater Transjordan scheme during the height of the conflict, Abdullah's previous impatience resurfaced. He was eager to come to an agreement with Israel, and on 9 November King Abdullah sent a message to the Israeli delegation in Paris informing them of his desire to reignite cooperation.[82] Meanwhile, Glubb was aware that the Israelis were keen on negotiating with Abdullah and that:

[T]he Jews three days ago suggested a *real* cease fire with the Arab Legion in Jerusalem. As a result the last 48 hours in Jerusalem have been the quietest for several weeks![83]

On the same day Glubb reported Lockett's first trip to Falluja, he also reported that a meeting was being arranged in the next few days between the Arab Legion's military governor in Jerusalem, Abdullah al-Tall, and the Israeli commander, Moshe Dayan, under UN auspices.[84] The meeting eventually took place on 29 November and the following day an 'absolute and sincere ceasefire' was agreed.[85] Given that Jerusalem had always been the key snag in Glubb's view, it is understandable that he would have been reluctant to get involved in the war between Israel and Egypt at such a critical moment.

Despite Abdullah's renewed contact with the Israelis, this failed to transform into formal peace negotiations, and this was partly because of a split in the Anglo-Jordanian camp on how to proceed. The Israelis wanted a 'formal peace treaty'.[86] Glubb recorded that: 'For six weeks past [the] Jews have been angling for negotiations with King Abdulla.'[87]

[82] Shlaim, *Collusion*, p. 348.
[83] Glubb to O'Connor, 18 November 1948, GP2006, 85 [emphasis in original].
[84] Glubb to COS, 24 November 1948, GP2006, 86, 100.
[85] Dayan, *Story of My Life*, p. 100; Shlaim, *Collusion*, p. 354–5.
[86] Dayan, *Story of My Life*, pp. 104–5.
[87] Glubb to COS, 24 November 1948, GP2006, 86, 100.

Abdullah also wanted to negotiate, but was 'deterred' by his prime minister and Britain.[88] The British were still absolutely committed to seeing Greater Transjordan emerge, but had to tread a fine line between active support, on one hand, and undermining its legitimacy, on the other. The British also adhered to the mantra that it was imperative not to be the first to negotiate. As its principal ally in the region, the British were determined that King Abdullah should not fall victim to that fate. Britain did not have an alternative strategy to Abdullah's desire to negotiate. Thus, British policy was, in effect, to wait and see how things developed. In the meantime, both the British and their proxy, Transjordan, just had to hold on and do nothing obtrusive, which included not openly negotiating with Israel. By the beginning of December the Foreign Office questioned whether it should stop restraining the Jordanians from negotiating directly with the Israelis and encourage them instead 'to obtain the best settlement they can by any means they like', regardless of the policy of the Arab League.[89] However, the Foreign Office felt: 'We cannot advise him [Abdullah] until we have reached agreement with the Americans.'[90] A significant factor contributing to Britain's wait-and-see policy was a reluctance to do anything that may upset its transatlantic partner. The British position continued to be affected by the wider international concerns, including the Arab League, the United Nations, and the United States, that had inhibited its freedom of action at the height of the conflict. This led Britain to advise the Jordanian government not to negotiate a resolution with Israel openly. It was deemed imperative that Transjordan not expose itself, and by implication Britain, to charges of treachery. Not only would this damage British prestige, but it would also harm the chances of ratifying Greater Transjordan. This put Glubb in an awkward position. He lamented that: 'H.M.G. have asked the Trans-Jordan Government through diplomatic channels, not to negotiate with the Jews and not to withdraw the Arab Legion from Palestine.'[91] Faced with this dichotomy, it is not surprising that Glubb was keen to allow the Egyptians to be defeated to enable the start of peace negotiations that would put an end to the threat facing the Arab Legion.

As December progressed, the men on the spot, Glubb and Kirkbride, became increasingly anxious that Abdullah must be allowed to negotiate

---

[88] Glubb to O'Connor, 18 November 1948, GP2006, 85.

[89] FO to UK Delegation, UN General Assembly, 767, 3 December 1948, FO371/68822/ E15531/G, TNA.

[90] Minute by Hector McNeil, 15 December 1948, FO371/68862/E16002, TNA.

[91] Glubb to unknown [second page is missing], ALC/53(a), 9 November 1948, GP2006, 86.

regardless of the political ramifications. Kirkbride believed it was time to 'cease to check any tendency of Transjordan to come to terms with the Jews if they can'.[92] Previously Kirkbride had also advised against Abdullah negotiating with Israel because he was 'not really in a strong enough position to ride out the storm which such action would cause in the Arab world'.[93] However, he had since changed his mind owing to the increasing vulnerability of the Arab Legion. Kirkbride requested that Transjordan required positive advice from Britain.[94] Glubb also considered it 'very important to get a decision from H.M.G.', in order to prevent the Jordanians from postponing negotiations indefinitely. Glubb was frustrated that 'at present we keep having meetings and saying nothing and the Jews suspect we are playing with them'. He lamented:

I have been trying to get them to make peace since last June and I usually only make them angry and suspicious. But sometimes I feel we shall drift on like this for ever, until the Jews get all Palestine – but still Tawfiq Pasha will not negotiate![95]

Like Britain, the prime minister was also conditioned to *wait and see*. As Robert Satloff has observed, Tawfiq Abu al-Huda was of the mindset that: 'To procrastinate was to gain time, and time was the essence of survival.'[96] This trait was deeply evident in his approach to extricating Transjordan from the 1948 War. According to Glubb, the prime minister 'said that it would be better for the Arab Legion to be destroyed in Palestine, rather than that we should open negotiations with the Jews. He was afraid of the Egyptian Papers and also he said of the verdict of history!' After telling Kirkbride this,

[Kirkbride] said he thought it was time to take a stand with the T.J. Govt to make peace. If necessary, it might be the time 'to chop Tawfiq', he [Kirkbride] said. The difficulty was to find another P.M. to undertake the task of opening negotiations.[97]

In order to initiate consolidation of the Greater Transjordan scheme – or, at least, to secure extrication from the conflict – both Glubb and Kirkbride deemed a change of government necessary. Glubb reported that on 12 December the Israelis threatened to cease their meetings in Jerusalem if the Jordanian government did not agree to formal peace negotiations.

---

[92] Amman to FO, 931, 6 December 1948, FO371/68822/E15533/G, TNA.
[93] Amman to FO, 693, 31 August 1948, FO371/68822/E11532/G, TNA.
[94] Amman to FO, 952, 14 December 1948, FO371/68862/E15867/G, TNA.
[95] Glubb to Kirkbride, 14 December 1948, GP2006, 85.
[96] Satloff, *Jordan in Transition*, p. 23.
[97] '2/11/48, 11-00 hrs', diary-like note by Glubb, GP2006, 86.

However, the Jordanian government, as Glubb explained, 'hesitate[s] [to] open direct negotiations owing to [the] hostility [of] other Arab countries. T.J. Govt also hope[s] for advice from HMG but so far British Govt has preserved silence.'[98] The Jordanian government was swayed by Egyptian propaganda and the inter-Arab political ramifications of negotiating with Israel. Glubb was exasperated by the influence of the other Arab states – most notably Egypt. Despite Glubb explaining 'that steel and lead were more important than talk', the minister of defence was adamant that 'the political situation was more important than military matters'. Fawzi al-Mulki told Glubb

that he believed H.M.G. did not want us to negotiate with the Jews, and thus we could not do so unless the British and Iraq govts *both* agreed. The Iraq govt, he said, have asked for time in order to 'break it gently' to the public in Iraq.[99]

While the British and Jordanian governments preferred to wait and see how things developed, Glubb wanted to be proactive. He was adamant that, in terms of obtaining a satisfactory resolution to the conflict: 'The longer we wait, the worse our situation becomes and the worse terms we shall have to accept in the end.'[100] And contrary to the notion espoused by Shlaim that Abu al-Huda was believed to have 'changed his tune' in favour of taking an independent line, the prime minister's stance, despite the deteriorating situation, became ever more intractable.[101] By the turn of the year Glubb reported: 'The King is anxious to negotiate, but the present Prime Minister has made a row that he will never negotiate with the Jews.'[102] In opposition to the policy emanating from London, both Glubb and Kirkbride were in favour of Abdullah's desire to initiate peace negotiations with Israel and were anxious for negotiations to begin as soon as possible. But all Glubb and the Arab Legion could do was hope that the Israelis could knock out the Egyptian Army. Thus, when the Israelis asked what the Arab Legion reaction would be to a renewed offensive against the Egyptian Army, Abdullah al-Tall replied: 'Hit the Egyptians as much as you can. Our attitude will be completely neutral.'[103] Meanwhile Glubb could only wait, either for the Egyptians to be defeated, thus enabling the start of negotiations, or for Abdullah to subvert the will of Britain or force a change of government to initiate peace negotiations with Israel.

98 Glubb to COS MELF, 14 December 1948, GP2006, 85.
99 Glubb to Kirkbride, 14 December 1948, ibid. [emphasis in original].
100 Glubb to H. E. Pyman, 30 December 1948, ibid.
101 Shlaim, *Collusion*, p. 366.
102 Glubb to H. E. Pyman, 30 December 1948, GP2006, 85.
103 Quoted in: Shlaim, *Collusion*, p. 363; Yitzhak, *Abdullah al-Tall*, p. 63.

The problem with forcing a change of government, as Glubb observed, was that it risked making the outgoing government heroes and would leave Abdullah 'with the full responsibility of being the first to negotiate'. Thus, Glubb explained: 'The King cannot make up his mind to do this, nor is it easy to find a new Prime Minister willing to come in on such terms.' This left the king paralysed by the dilemma, which meant: 'As a result of the above, we continue to drift without any policy.' At the turn of the year, Glubb felt Transjordan and the Arab Legion were in limbo:

Unless the King can harden his heart to get rid of this Prime Minister, we seem likely to drift on – unable to make war and unwilling to make peace – until the Jews get impatient and the war begins again.[104]

Glubb was powerless to influence Abdullah in the face of opposition from the British and Jordanian governments. By the end of 1948 Abdullah had two options open to him. He could either avert military defeat by biting the bullet and negotiating openly with the Israelis, despite the political ramifications, or he could wait and hope that one of his Arab rivals would negotiate first. Without the support of either Britain or even his own government, Abdullah was not strong enough to take that leap. Glubb understood this, and not aiding the Egyptian forces besieged in Falluja was a means to that end.

As it turned out, the uncoordinated and ad hoc approach exhibited by Glubb, on one hand, and the British and Jordanian governments, on the other, enabled Arab–Israeli armistice negotiations to begin in a manner that suited the interests of Greater Transjordan. Their wait-and-see policy was neatly complemented by Glubb's efforts to position the Egyptians into submission. On 22 December, barely a week after Abdullah al-Tall informed the Israelis that the Arab Legion welcomed the destruction of the Egyptian Army, the IDF launched Operation Horev as a final push to destroy Egyptian resistance in the Negev. True to Abdullah al-Tall's word, the Arab Legion – just like all the other Arab armies – gave the Egyptians no assistance. Despite Israel backing down in response to an ultimatum issued by Britain under the terms of the 1936 Anglo–Egyptian Treaty, on 4 January 1949 Egypt announced its intention to begin formal armistice negotiations. The Egyptians had avoided all-out defeat in Falluja and Gaza, but the Israeli onslaught had finally taken its toll.[105] Bilateral negotiations between the two, under UN auspices, began on 13 January on the neutral island of Rhodes and a month later, on 24 February, they

[104] Glubb to H. E. Pyman, 30 December 1948, GP2006, 85.
[105] Shlaim, *Collusion*, pp. 367–8.

signed a formal armistice agreement in which Israel accepted an Egyptian military presence in the Gaza Strip, while Israel consolidated its control of the northern Negev.[106] Egypt became the first Arab state to negotiate an armistice with Israel, thus allowing the Jordanians to begin formal and public armistice negotiations free of the charge of treachery.[107] The process of bringing the conflict to the point of resolution was, as much as anything, an inter-Arab power play. The aim was not to be the first to negotiate, and to that end Transjordan had been successful.

This did not mark the end of the conflict's inter-Arab struggle. On the day before armistice talks between Israel and Transjordan opened in Rhodes, Glubb reported that the Egyptian government was being 'obstinate as a face-saver' in its promise to withdraw from Hebron and Bethlehem. Owing to a story circulated in Egypt that the Arab Legion was going to push them out, Glubb reported:

As a result the Gyppy Govt. got on it's [*sic*] dignity and said it would *never* leave, if we tried to push it out but would leave before the end of April if we were polite! As a result, the Prime Minister wants everyone to be extremely polite and cordial to the Egyptians and talk a lot about our brave allies, in the hope that the brutes will go away quickly!

This prompted Glubb to instruct Goldie, rather sarcastically, 'to inform everybody of the form – "cordial friendship for our gallant allies"'.[108] If Transjordan were to negotiate the best terms possible, unhindered by its Arab allies, it would have to pander to Egyptian pride. However, during the final month of the conflict inter-Arab rivalries took a backseat as Israeli belligerence became the dominant concern for Transjordan during the armistice negotiations.

The Israel–Transjordan negotiations lasted exactly one month, beginning on 4 March and concluding on 3 April. As the war entered the final diplomatic phase, Glubb's influence and involvement inevitably declined, but contrary to Uri Bar-Joseph's suggestion that he became largely non-existent, Glubb remained a central figure. Yes, Glubb had little involvement in the post-armistice pursuit of a formal peace settlement, but he was integral to the armistice negotiations. Glubb was not part of the Jordanian delegation sent to Rhodes, but this was hardly surprising. Glubb had proved careful in April 1948 not to associate himself directly with the Zionists – even in secret, let alone in public. Moreover,

---

[106] Shlaim, *Iron Wall*, p. 42; Gerges, 'Egypt and the 1948 War', pp. 168–9.
[107] Rogan, 'Jordan and the 1948 War', p. 118.
[108] Glubb to Goldie, 3 March 1949, GP2006, 3 [emphasis in original].

it was essentially a puppet delegation that was sent to Rhodes. It is well known that the real negotiations secretly took place behind closed doors in King Abdullah's winter palace in Shuneh. However, the decisive negotiations in Shuneh were not set in motion until the middle of the month. At the outset the Jordanians sought to conduct the negotiations not elsewhere, but in Rhodes, albeit via Amman. The middleman in this setup was Glubb. Although telegrams to the delegation were signed from the minister of defence, this was a mere bureaucratic technicality.[109] The telegrams being sent to the delegation in Rhodes were drafted in Glubb's handwriting. While the official negotiations in Rhodes may have been a sideshow to the real bargaining behind the scenes in Shuneh, the Rhodes negotiations were nonetheless important. Israel and TransJordan did not from the outset concert to conduct the negotiations at Rhodes as a front for real negotiations elsewhere. The Israelis clearly approached the Rhodes negotiations at face value and appointed an appropriately senior delegation, including Moshe Dayan, who had overseen the November 1948 ceasefire agreement in Jerusalem. It was Transjordan that sent a puppet delegation, which initially angered the Israelis, who believed that the Jordanian delegation was not empowered to sign an armistice. It did have this power, but it was made clear that: 'Actually you are empowered to sign but you must submit the text to this Government before doing so.'[110]

Managing the negotiations in Rhodes from Amman proved not as practicable as the Jordanians presumably hoped. Moshe Dayan described negotiations with the official delegation as a 'tragi-comedy'. He observed that the Jordanian 'delegation had been sent to fulfil orders they would be receiving from Amman – and not to move a single step outside those orders. If there was a garbled word in a cabled instruction, they would ask for an adjournment so they could clarify it.'[111] The real powerbrokers in Amman soon became concerned that they might be bypassed by events in Rhodes. Thus, a week into the negotiations – after some worrying silences – Glubb informed the delegation that: 'From now onwards you will report progress every day by signal. Even if there is no meeting you will report the fact.'[112] There was concern that the delegation in Rhodes

[109] Tawfiq Pasha [Glubb's handwriting] to Transjordan Delegation Rhodes, 9 March 1949, GP1986, 10/2.

[110] Ibid.

[111] Dayan, *Story of My Life*, p. 110.

[112] Minister of Defence [Glubb's handwriting] to Transjordan Delegation Rhodes, 10 March 1949, GP1986, 10/2.

may have been given too much responsibility. Indeed, after the opening exchanges Glubb had to reprimand the delegation and inform it that:

[The Jordanian] Government was greatly disturbed at reports that negotiating nearly broke down because officers refused to shake hands. Transjordan is the only country which won military victories over [the] Jews. Now you must win diplomatic victories. This public duty is much more important than your personal feelings.[113]

Transjordan's intention to conduct negotiations via a puppet delegation in Rhodes, directed by strings stretching back to Amman, proved completely impractical. The Jordanians therefore shifted their approach to higher-level contacts behind the scenes.

The secret Shuneh talks only began, however, after two principal obstacles left the Rhodes negotiations in deadlock. Ultimately the lack of progress during the opening two weeks of negotiations had almost nothing to do with the inferiority of the Jordanian delegation, or the system of direction from Amman, and everything to do with Israeli belligerence. Glubb, Kirkbride, and Abdullah had been so keen on beginning negotiations since the autumn of 1948 because of the vulnerability of the Arab Legion's position. Transjordan thus entered the negotiations from a position of relative weakness, and during the negotiations Israel immediately exploited this. The day after the armistice negotiations began, the Israelis launched Operation Uvda (fait accompli), a military offensive against the Arab Legion in the south-eastern Negev. They delayed signing a general ceasefire agreement with Transjordan and instead drove south toward Eilat, on the Red Sea, in two columns: from Beersheba on the western approach and down the Wadi Araba on the eastern border with Transjordan [Map 4].[114] In the original 1947 UN partition resolution the Negev had been awarded to the proposed Jewish state and the Israelis were determined that it would be included, in its entirety, in the Israeli state as part of the final settlement. Although they had reached agreement regarding the Negev in the armistice with Egypt, the Arab Legion occupied a wedge of land at the south-eastern tip of the Negev. In order to reverse the situation on the ground, the Israelis opted to use their military superiority to conquer this area by force. On 7 March the Jordanian government made a formal complaint to the armistice commission, but by 10 March Israel's fait accompli was complete. The Negev

---

[113] Qiada [Glubb's handwriting] to Transjordan Delegation Rhodes, 8 March 1949, ibid. This turned out to be a misunderstanding, rather than a genuine refusal to shake hands.
[114] Arab Legion [Glubb] to Mideast; GP2006, 3.

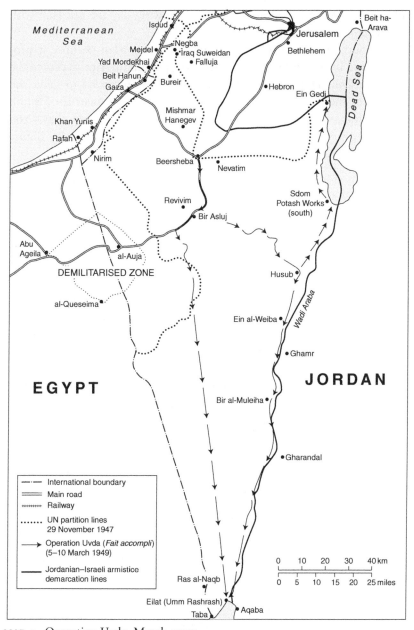

MAP 4. Operation Uvda, March 1949.
Based on: Avi Shlaim, *Collusion across the Jordan: King Abdullah, the Zionist Movement, and the Partition of Palestine* (Oxford, 1988), p. 403.

had been successfully captured, and the following day the ceasefire with Transjordan was finally signed.[115]

The southern Negev was important to Transjordan because it provided a land bridge to Egypt and, therefore, potentially vital access to the Mediterranean. Thus, despite the ceasefire Glubb intended to make life difficult for the Israeli forces. The following day Glubb instructed South Force, commanded by Nigel Bromage to defend the Negev, that: 'You will not repeat not begin guerrilla warfare until further orders.'[116] Before subsequently instructing:

As soon as possible you will organise guerrilla ops to keep all Jewish L[ines] of C[ommunication] cut permanently. This will mean western track as well as main road. Suggest you close main road again immediately as soon as Jewish force has passed. Suggest you employ dismounted forces along West track. They can block track wherever possible and resist passage of all convoys.[117]

This instruction followed the advice of Lockett, who, after reporting that he had 'watched' an Israeli brigade drive down to Eilat on the night of 10 March, suggested that they 'cut the Wadi Araba R[oa]d at a convenient place', lay mines, and conduct ambushes. Lockett believed they could cut off the Israeli brigade in Eilat or, at the very least, 'make its maintenance precarious'.[118] Glubb was adamant: 'No Jewish veh[icle] must get through without a battle.'[119] Yet this bravado proved futile. Operation Uvda was a dramatic demonstration of Israel's military superiority, which proved irreversible. Moreover, during the first two weeks of the armistice negotiations it effectively precluded the possibility of fruitful discussion regardless of the seniority or setup of the Jordanian delegation.

During the second half of the month-long armistice negotiations Israel's fait accompli in the Negev, combined with the second obstacle – the Iraqi front – would prove decisive toward the outcome of negotiations. Indeed, Glubb exclaimed: 'These two factors have revolutionised the situation.'[120] No sooner had the ceasefire been agreed in the Negev than the armistice talks came to a 'standstill' over the Iraqi front. The Iraqis 'refused to negotiate' with Israel, but the Arab Legion planned to take over their front by 18 March.[121] However, the Jordanians were wary

---

[115] Rogan, 'Jordan and the 1948 War', p. 119; Shlaim, *Iron Wall*, p. 44.
[116] Qiada [Glubb] to Southcol, 12 March 1949, GP2006, 3.
[117] Qiada [Glubb] to Southcol, undated, ibid.
[118] Lockett to Glubb, 10 March 1949, ibid.
[119] Qiada [Glubb] to Southcol, undated, ibid.
[120] Glubb to Pirie-Gordon, 17 March 1949, ibid.
[121] '1 Div Operational Order No. 10/49', 11 March 1949, ibid.

of doing so 'unless the Israeli Delegation first sign a temporary cease fire'.[122] The Israelis, however, 'categorically refused'.[123] They considered the Arab Legion's takeover of the Iraqi positions 'a flagrant violation of the truce' and that, therefore, 'discussion of this matter falls outside the purview of the armistice talks at Rhodes'.[124] This created a 'deadlock'.[125] Israeli aggression in the Negev provided an ominous precedent if a cease-fire was not agreed before the Arab Legion took over the Iraqi front. Glubb genuinely believed that the Israelis were planning an attack in the triangle at the northern tip of the Iraqi front, between Nablus, Tulkarm, and Jenin. A planned Israeli offensive against the Iraqis in October was deemed 'absolutely confirmed' by the Arab Legion and was apparently only delayed by 'bad weather' and a decision to deal with the Egyptians first. This, combined with a series of other points of circumstantial evidence, led the Arab Legion to conclude: 'It seems probable that the Jews will now postpone their attack until the Arab Legion takes over from the Iraqis.'[126] Two weeks into the armistice negotiations Transjordan had lost the south-eastern Negev as a result of an Israeli military offensive, and it feared suffering the same fate in the Iraqi sector of central Palestine.

Transjordan was therefore placed very much on the back-foot in the armistice negotiations and left short on options. Glubb remained confident that: 'On the main front – from the present southern flank of the Iraq army through Jerusalem and round to [the] south of Hebron – such an armistice should be attainable.' However, he was wary that the south-eastern Negev, which the Israelis had conquered during the negotiations, could cause a problem, as he expected Israel to demand that Transjordan agree that this be included in the new Jewish state. The predicament this created, as Glubb explained, was that:

Trans-Jordan can scarcely do this, when her troops have just been driven out by an outstandingly flagrant piece of treachery during the negotiations. At the same time, Trans-Jordan is not in a position to try and reconquer it. Some formula must be found to cover this.[127]

Using force to regain the lost land was not an option. Transjordan either had to negotiate a solution with the Israelis or rely on the United Nations

[122] Glubb to Ahmad Sudqi al-Jundi, ALC/31(B)1, 15 March 1949, ibid.
[123] 'The Palestine Situation', Glubb, 15 March 1949, ibid.
[124] Dayan, *Story of My Life*, p. 112.
[125] 'The Palestine Situation', Glubb, 15 March 1949, GP2006, 3.
[126] 'Evidence of Jewish Intended Attack on Tulkarm-Jenin-Nablus Triangle', unsigned, undated [but clearly mid-March 1949], ibid.
[127] 'The Palestine Situation', Glubb, 15 March 1949, ibid.

to arbitrate. However, Israel's use of force meant it was unlikely to relent willingly. Indeed, on 15 March Transjordan was compelled to make a further protest to Acting UN Mediator Ralph Bunche, this time relating to the Israeli occupation of Ein Gedi on the west shore of the Dead Sea, which was behind the Arab defensive line.[128] Transjordan relied on the fledgling United Nations to prove its worth. However, Glubb had almost zero faith in this organisation. He described it as being,

in practice an arrangement for helping the strong to oppress the weak. UNO is too weak to tackle anyone influential but forms a pretext by which powers can evade their obligations. Before UNO, Britain would have been obliged to help us. The existence of UNO provides her with an excuse for doing nothing. Bunche, when asked what T.J. should do in face of the Jewish offensive in the W[adi] Araba, replied 'get a friendly majority in the [UN] Sec.[urity] Council.' But meanwhile T.J. is not even a member of UNO, *because* she is an ally of Britain. Britain pleads that UNO is solving the problem and she cannot interfere – but UNO is the most shameless truce server of all.[129]

Transjordan was therefore left alone to reach an agreement with Israel.

Israeli intransigence over the Negev and the Iraqi front set the tone for the secret talks that followed in Shuneh. With the Rhodes talks in deadlock, Moshe Dayan was recalled from the Greek island in order to initiate meaningful discussions away from the official armistice negotiations.[130] On 22 March the two sides met at Shuneh, where the Israelis made their demands and a written agreement was drafted, subject to King Abdullah's approval – though the Israelis made it clear that they were not prepared to negotiate further. It was, in effect, an ultimatum.[131] The next day, Glubb was 'called to an urgent consultation' at Shuneh. When he arrived, Glubb already understood that Transjordan could not fight. It either required help from Britain and the United States or else they would be forced to 'accept whatever [the] Jews give us'.[132] Presumably he would have proffered this advice during the consultation prior to Abdullah's meeting with the Israelis later that evening. Indeed, according to Abdullah al-Tall, Glubb informed the king: 'we are alone in the field and it is unthinkable to fight the Jews after they have concentrated their forces against us.... Sir, the Jews are greedy, they want to increase their occupation of lands by every means.'[133]

[128] Glubb to Ahmad Sudqi al-Jundi, ALC/31(B), 15 March 1949, ibid.
[129] '18/3/49', diary-like note by Glubb, ibid. [emphasis in original].
[130] Shlaim, *Collusion*, pp. 407–11; Dayan, *Story of My Life*, p. 112.
[131] Shlaim, *Collusion*, pp. 411–12; Bar-Joseph, *Best of Enemies*, pp. 221–2.
[132] Glubb to Pirie-Gordon, 23 March 1949, FO816/144, TNA.
[133] Quoted in: Abu Nowar, *Jordanian–Israeli War*, p. 300.

That night the Israeli delegation returned to Shuneh, where King Abdullah was waiting, and a secret agreement with corresponding maps was signed.[134] Glubb declined to take part in this meeting, apparently not wanting to look into the eyes of the Jews.[135] That may well have been true, but knowing how politically conscious Glubb was, it is highly plausible – and more likely – that he deduced that his presence at these negotiations, where it was clear that the Israelis held all the aces, could only have negative consequences for his personal position as well as that of Britain generally. Glubb sent Charles Coaker in his stead, just as he had during the Goldie mission. Glubb was intimately aware that: 'If a single village is lost, bitter criticism is directed against the Arab Legion.'[136] He could not avoid this criticism if a village was lost in the military theatre, but he could limit his association to losses made in the political realm. It is not surprising that Glubb wanted to keep his distance from involvement in negotiations that he knew Transjordan would have to submit to Israeli demands. In July 1948 it had relinquished the towns of Lydda and Ramle. Now it had ceded territory in the Negev and the Little Triangle – a strip of land along the northern border of what had been the Iraqi front line. It was not the end that Abdullah wanted, but as Glubb explained: 'To secure [the] armistice we were obliged [to] surrender [the] following villages now held by [the] Iraqis. ... In return we got [a] small concession west of Hebron.'[137]

This land was conceded in conjunction with the genuine belief that it could be reclaimed. In the first instance Abdullah – fruitlessly – contacted President Truman in the hope that he could use his influence to counsel moderation and overturn Israel's demand for territory in the Little Triangle.[138] Secondly, the armistice was intentionally worded with later reversing it in mind. On 26 March the Rhodes delegation queried with Amman as to whether Transjordan's pre-war 'international' border with Palestine, between the Dead Sea and the Gulf of Aqaba, should be considered the armistice line.[139] Glubb replied with an emphatic instruction:

When you come to draw [the] line on [the] map it may coincide with [the] Transjordan frontier in time of mandate. We do not want to refer to it as the

[134] Eytan to Sharett, 24 March 1949, quoted in: Shlaim, *Collusion*, pp. 414–16; 'Agreement Between the Hashemite Jordan Kingdom and the State of Israel', 23 March 1949, in: Shlaim, *Collusion*, pp. 625–6.

[135] Shlaim, *Collusion*, p. 414; Abu Nowar, *Jordanian–Israeli War*, p. 300.

[136] Glubb to Pirie-Gordon, 17 March 1949, GP2006, 3.

[137] Glubb to H. E. Pyman, 5 April 1949, GP2006, 22.

[138] Abdullah to Truman, 25 March 1949, FO816/145, TNA.

[139] Transjordan Delegation Rhodes to Minister of Defence, 26 March 1949, GP1986, 10/2.

international boundary because we retain our rights to claim it in the final settlement because it was seized by a breach of the truce. Is this understood?[140]

The Jordanians may have ceded territory to Israel because of its position of weakness, but it remained intent on reclaiming this land in the final peace settlement. For that reason, article II of the armistice stated:

[N]o provision of this Agreement shall in any way prejudice the rights, claims and positions of either Party hereto in the ultimate peaceful settlement of the Palestine question, the provisions of this Agreement being dictated exclusively by military considerations.[141]

As it turned out, a conclusive peace settlement proved elusive, but when the armistice was signed, a formal peace settlement was genuinely believed to be the next – attainable – step.

The final armistice aptly reflected the nature of events since September. Abdullah and Glubb had got the formal end to the conflict they had been desperate to obtain and Greater Transjordan had effectively come into existence – albeit formal annexation did not occur until April 1950. Moreover, this had been achieved without Transjordan having to negotiate first. The armistice, though, also reflected Transjordan's vulnerability. After Glubb's return to Amman in mid-September attentions were geared towards seeking a solution to the conflict, and this period proved a continuing example of Glubb's limited autonomy. Ultimately, the political decision-making was in the hands of King Abdullah and the prime minister. Yet Glubb was in control of the military sphere and he maintained political influence. Glubb and the Arab Legion's approach to the fighting in the Negev was a key component enabling the start of the armistice negotiations, where Glubb again had a significant input. Kimche and Kimche portrayed Glubb as completely out of the loop regarding the Shuneh discussions. So much so that 'Glubb criticised Abdullah for making this deal with the Israelis'.[142] On the contrary, Glubb was pragmatic not angry. He knew Transjordan was at the mercy of Israel and after the event he surmised that: 'In view of [the] fact we have no ammunition, aircraft or tanks and Iraqis are already withdrawing it might have been worse.'[143] Glubb may not have been involved directly in the Shuneh negotiations,

[140] Minister of Defence [Glubb's handwriting] to Transjordan Delegation Rhodes, 26 March 1949, ibid.
[141] 'Hashemite Jordan Kingdom – Israel General Armistice Agreement', 3 April 1949, GP2006, 36.
[142] Kimche and Kimche, *Both Sides of the Hill*, pp. 269–72.
[143] Glubb to H. E. Pyman, 5 April 1949, GP2006, 22.

MAP 5. Palestine after the armistice, June 1949.
Based on: Avi Shlaim, *Collusion across the Jordan: King Abdullah, the Zionist Movement, and the Partition of Palestine* (Oxford, 1988), p. 429.

but it was Glubb who was communicating with the Jordanian delegation in Rhodes. At the very least, Glubb was the intermediary in this setup. Moreover, he had the opportunity to partake in the meeting at Shuneh on 23 March, where the preliminary armistice agreement was made, but he chose not to and was involved in the private consultation held in Shuneh earlier that day. While the inner-workings of the Jordanian government's decision-making process may be locked in the Royal Hashemite Archives, Glubb's advice was surely crucial. Glubb was fully aware of the negotiations with Israel at Shuneh, which enabled him, secretly, to brief the British government.[144] Moreover, nobody in Transjordan understood the military situation like Glubb did, and ultimately it was a military – rather than a political – armistice, which reflected the balance of forces in the field.

The resolution process provided a continuing example of the limited autonomy not just of Glubb, but of all the parties in the Anglo–Jordanian alliance. Abu al-Huda and the Jordanian government were subservient to pressure from the other Arab states; Britain was restrained by its need to appear neutral and in particular its reliance on US support; and Abdullah was beholden to Britain and, to a lesser extent, his own government. Perhaps more than any other actor in this affair, Abdullah was a hostage to others. He knew what he wanted, but he did not know how to achieve it. Avi Shlaim described the November–December period as 'Abdullah's game of playing for time'.[145] But in actuality it was Britain and the Jordanian prime minister who compelled Abdullah to play by these rules. This critical final stage of the 1948 War thus further reveals the spectre of British influence over Abdullah. Britain did not directly control Abdullah or dictate Jordanian policy, but the British presence loomed over Abdullah's decisions. Abdullah had required British acquiescence over the Greater Transjordan scheme back in February, and during the final throes of the conflict he required British approval in his efforts to extricate himself. While Britain advised against it, Abdullah reluctantly avoided negotiations with the Israelis until Egypt had become the first to openly negotiate, by which time it was made clear to him that 'His Majesty's Government are of the opinion that it would now be advisable to associate your Government in your discussions with the Jews'.[146]

[144] Glubb to Pirie-Gordon, 15 and 23 March 1949, FO816/144; Glubb to Kirkbride, 3 April 1949, FO816/145, TNA.
[145] Shlaim, *Collusion*, p. 366.
[146] 'Aide-Memoire', 21 January 1949, FO816/143, TNA.

Competition between the Arab states further complicated the conflict between the Arabs and Israel. Both the war and its resolution were
dictated as much by political considerations as they were military. And
the final act in this saga aptly reflected this. In a diary-like note, Glubb
described the return of the Jordanian delegation from Rhodes:

When the T.J. Delegation returned to Amman airport after signing the Rhodes
armistice, they expected to be met by reps of [the] King and Govt and thanked
for their weary efforts. Instead they were greeted by an officer and Amman police,
who whispered to them that their lives were in danger and warned them to slip
away individually to their homes.[147]

It was a rather muted end to a muted conflict, which encapsulated the
driving force of events since Glubb returned to Amman in September.
Formal negotiations with the Israelis were not something that anyone
wanted to be directly associated with. All parties, particularly on the
Arab side of the conflict, were eager to see the fighting brought to an
end, but nobody was willing to be seen negotiating with Israel. Between
September 1948 and January 1949 the war had been sustained by a battle
of wills between Transjordan and Egypt over who would negotiate first.
In this battle the Jordanians emerged victorious, but as the Arab state set
to gain most from the conflict it remained in the spotlight. Thus the true
powerbrokers sought to distance themselves from the negotiations with
Israel. For that reason a set of junior scapegoats was sent to act as the
face of the negotiations. Neither Glubb nor Abdullah wanted to be seen
to be involved. But they were; both of them were crucial. Distance from
the armistice negotiations did not remove all traces of criticism. However,
it was not as intense as it might otherwise have been. At the height of the
conflict Glubb, who was desperate for peace, was particularly sensitive to
criticism, but the relief of having the war brought to a close was palpable.
Glubb was now able to laugh off blame falsely attributed to him, remark-
ing that: 'I was glad to read a few days ago in a British paper, that the
only obstacle to peace in Palestine was the presence of "bellicose British
Generals in Amman". A little light relief should always be included in a
tragedy.'[148]

---

[147] '10/4/49', diary-like note by Glubb, GP2006, 3.
[148] Glubb to H. E. Pyman, 13 April 1949, GP2006, 22.

5

Beyond 1948: The Arab Legion, Arab Nationalism, and the Cold War

The end of the 1948 War heralded the start of a new era in the Middle East and no state was affected more than Transjordan, which was completely redefined: geographically, via the annexation of central Palestine – leaving it with an extensive border with Israel – and demographically, via the incorporation of 400,000 Palestinian Arabs living in the West Bank plus 500,000 additional Palestinian refugees.[1] Although this territory was not formally annexed to Transjordan until April 1950, Greater Transjordan's existence was effectively consolidated by the signing of the 1949 armistice, which bore the first official usage of Transjordan's new name: 'The Hashemite Jordan Kingdom'.[2] So began a period of transition, which culminated with the assassination of King Abdullah on 20 July 1951. The king's murder had its roots in the 1948 War, which was undoubtedly a major factor shaping the future of Jordan, the modern Middle East, and Britain's position in the region. However, a full understanding of British policy and the Anglo–Jordanian connection beyond 1948 requires a much broader appreciation of the prevailing international factors.

As the principal link between the two allies, the Arab Legion provides an ideal barometer for assessing the nature of British policy and the status of Anglo–Jordanian relations between 1949 and 1951. Just like the end of the Second World War, the Arab Legion emerged from the 1948 War in a rapidly expanded form and, again, a decision on its future size and shape had to be made. It is an established myth that the 1948 War led to

[1] Pappé, 'British Rule in Jordan', pp. 206, 218.
[2] 'Hashemite Jordan Kingdom – Israel General Armistice Agreement', 3 April 1949, GP2006, 36.

an expansion of the Arab Legion. Vatikiotis observed the Arab Legion's growth between 1948 and 1956 and related this simply to the 1948 War and the 'armed truce' with Israel that followed.[3] Tancred Bradshaw also argues that the Arab Legion's expansion was designed to counter the threat of an Israeli invasion.[4] Of course, the 1948 War and the changed size and shape of the Hashemite Kingdom did have an impact. However, the Arab Legion's expansion after 1948 was not sanctioned until 1951 because it related primarily to the emerging Cold War and, in particular, the onset of the Korean War. Previous studies have noted that the Korean War prompted a review of Britain's Middle East defence strategy, making its defence more essential and strengthening the Chiefs of Staff's resolve to hold on to Suez as a main base.[5] Yet the significance of the Korean War in relation to the Arab Legion has hitherto been largely overlooked, with the exception of Ron Pundik.[6] However, it is important we recognise and emphasise this trend, because it illustrates the interaction between British imperial policy and the onset of the Cold War. In this instance, Cold War concerns dictated British policy in Jordan where, despite its independent status, British involvement became increasingly formal and direct, and this jarred with the counter-trend of Arab nationalism that increased simultaneously. Combined, these two factors significantly contributed to, and therefore help explain, a deterioration of the Anglo–Jordanian alliance during the 1950s in addition to the more recognisable consequences of 1948.

One of the paradoxes of the 1948 War was that it enabled the creation of Greater Transjordan, which Abdullah desired as an achievable alternative to Greater Syria in order to increase his power and status, but this served to make the Hashemite Kingdom even more dependent on Britain. As part of the general shift towards resolution of the conflict in September 1948, the British finally sought to assess the implications of creating Greater Transjordan.[7] All those best placed to make an estimation – Kirkbride, the BMEO, and the Jerusalem Consulate – agreed that

---

[3] Vatikiotis, *Politics and the Military*, p. 91.

[4] Bradshaw, *Glubb Reports*, pp. 13, 122, 126–7, 172.

[5] Devereux, *Formulation of British Defence Policy*, p. 40; Michael Cohen, 'The Strategic Role of the Middle East after the War', in: Cohen and Kolinsky (eds.), *Demise of the British Empire*, pp. 30–2; Peter L. Hahn, 'Discord or Partnership? British and American Policy toward Egypt, 1942–56', in: Cohen and Kolinsky (eds.), *Demise of the British Empire*, p. 165.

[6] Pundik, *Struggle for Sovereignty*, pp. 238–62.

[7] FO to Amman, 892, 17 September 1948; Minute by Burrows, 15 September 1948, FO371/68861/E12205, TNA.

Greater Transjordan would not be financially viable.[8] Britain nonetheless remained committed to supporting the Hashemite Kingdom, despite
the likely increased burden for two reasons. Firstly, Britain relied on
Transjordan as a strategic hub. The loss of Palestine, which had effectively been run as a colony, left a significant hole in Britain's position in
the Middle East that Greater Transjordan would fill.[9] Secondly, British
support for Transjordan was self-perpetuating. As J. M. Troutbeck, head
of the BMEO, observed: 'H.M.G. are now so committed in the public eye
to the support of Transjordan that it would be difficult for them, even
if they so wished, to leave her to her fate. Their prestige is by now too
deeply involved.'[10] Transjordan was effectively an advertisement for the
British connection, and the decline of its closest ally would leave a huge
stain on British prestige and power. Britain did not have an equally reliable alternative to the pro-British connection of Abdullah's kingdom. As
Kirkbride outlined:

So long as the other Arab states continue to protest their friendship for Great
Britain and, at the same time, consistently disregard our advice and, in some
cases, frustrate our policy, it seems worthwhile taking some trouble to keep
Transjordan alive and on our side.[11]

In an era and region where Britain's word was becoming increasingly
less powerful, Transjordan stood out as a uniquely reliable collaborator. It was the bastion of Britain's regional presence, status, and influence. Despite the general need for financial stringency, for both practical
and prestige reasons it was therefore deemed worth paying for. Indeed,
Bernard Burrows concluded: 'If we can get a viable Greater Transjordan
for this expenditure, we shall have made a good bargain.'[12]

   With Greater Transjordan having been effectively established by the
signing of the armistice, with implicit British support and despite the negative financial implications, the true test of its place in the British world
system, and the extent of British investment in the Hashemite Kingdom,
ultimately manifested itself in the size and shape of the Arab Legion,
which was completely dictated by Britain. As stipulated in a secret letter attached to the treaty, the Arab Legion subsidy was supposed to be

[8] Kirkbride to Bevin, 67, 28 September 1948, FO371/68862/E12910/G; Jerusalem
    Consulate-General to FO, 9 October 1948, FO371/68862/E13502/G; Troutbeck to
    Burrows, 20 December 1948, FO371/68862/E16467/G, TNA.
[9] Templer to Glubb, 6 October 1948, GP2006, 91.
[10] Troutbeck to Bevin, 16 October 1948, FO371/68862/E13635, TNA.
[11] Kirkbride to Burrows, 21 October 1948, FO371/68864/E13843, TNA.
[12] 'Transjordan Finances', Burrows, 22 October 1948, FO371/68862/E15249/G, TNA.

'agreed upon annually by the High Contracting Parties'.[13] Despite some initial concerns in 1946 that this would obstruct Britain's ability to act unilaterally, in practice the Jordanians had no say. Ultimately it was the various Whitehall departments that had to agree. The Chiefs of Staff would recommend an order of establishment, taking into consideration imperial defence requirements, which the Foreign Office would consider from a political perspective before submitting a proposal to the Treasury, with additional comments from the War Office and occasionally other Whitehall departments, such as the Air Ministry. After agreement had been reached in Whitehall, Britain would then put forward a 'proposal' to the Jordanian government to avoid the accusation that Britain was 'dictating', but there was no room for negotiation.[14] Abdullah, Glubb, and the Jordanian government were beholden to London as regards the subsidy and had to resort to pleas, threats, and scaremongering if they wanted to influence the British government's internal subsidy negotiations.

The 1948 War enhanced the Arab Legion's reputation and provided it with significant new challenges, but this did not lead to expansion. Hitherto the Arab Legion was justified primarily for political, as opposed to military, reasons and the 1948/9 subsidy was symbolic of this fact. The 1947/8 subsidy was £2 million, split between the Foreign Office (£700,000) and the War Office (£1.3 million).[15] The War Office contribution in 1947 reflected the Arab Legion's deployment in mandatory Palestine. Yet since Britain's departure from Palestine, the Foreign Office had borne the full cost.[16] The 1948 War raised the Arab Legion's military profile and enhanced its reputation as an effective fighting force. The War Office acknowledged that 'the Arab Legion have, by all accounts given a very good account of themselves in the fighting, and have thereby proved their ability to be of valuable assistance to us in war'.[17] Consequently the Chiefs of Staff envisaged an 'important role' for the Arab Legion in its 'plans for the defence of the Middle East in an emergency' and recommended it be maintained at its present unauthorised strength of 14,000, to which it had risen during the 1948 War.[18] However, the War Office was

[13] 'Anglo–Transjordan Treaty of Alliance', Exchange of Letters, No. 5, Kirkbride to Abu al-Huda, 15 March 1948, FO371/68820/E3673, TNA.
[14] FO to Amman, 153, 18 February 1949, FO371/75299/E1919/G, TNA.
[15] 'Future of the Arab Legion', L. F. L. Pyman, 26 January 1948, FO371/68827/E1344/G, TNA.
[16] Minute by Minshull, 31 August 1949, FO371/75301/E10604/G, TNA.
[17] Charteris to L. F. L. Pyman, 4 August 1948, FO371/68830/E10506/G, TNA.
[18] 'Size and Shape of the Arab Legion for 1949/50: Note by the War Office', 31 December 1948, FO371/75299/E296/G, TNA.

adamant that 'there can be no question whatever of any expenditure on the Arab Legion being borne on Army Votes in 1949/50'. The War Office was prepared to 'accept the consequence that in the absence of any War Office contribution the size of the Legion may be something less than would be desirable from the Imperial defence aspect'.[19] The War Office was therefore reluctant to back the Arab Legion's needs too strongly, lest it be compelled to foot the bill, and ministers decided that the 1949/50 subsidy would be based on the force of 7,000 agreed the previous year. In 1949 the subsidy was increased from £2.5 million to £3.5 million – again including £500,000 for capital equipment expenditure – and within the existing historiography the myth pervades that a gross increase in the subsidy reflected Britain's reinforcement of the Arab Legion.[20] Yet this merely reflected an increase in prices and fell well short of the Foreign Office's request for £5 million. Nonetheless, Kirkbride still made political capital out of the apparent increase by

not reveal[ing] to the Transjordan Government that three and a half millions this year had about the same buying power as two and a half million last year and left them to cherish the belief that they would be better off.[21]

The reasons for not consolidating the Arab Legion were threefold. Firstly, it was felt that, even in its expanded form, British troops would offer better resistance against an Israeli attack than the Arab Legion. Secondly, it was considered that: 'If additional money were available for defence purposes, it might be better employed on additional British forces rather than on subsidising the Arab Legion.' Thirdly, it was believed that the political situation in the Middle East had changed since the end of January, which offered 'greater hope of a measure of stability' in the region.[22] Ultimately, these three reasons were justifications for financial stringency.

In order to save money, the British gambled on two outcomes. Firstly, that the border tension with Israel would settle down and, secondly, that the Jordanian government would be compelled to contribute financially to maintaining the Arab Legion. MELF and the War Office warned that the previous year's approved strength of 7,000 men was deemed 'totally inadequate'.[23] Moreover, Kirkbride exclaimed that it was folly to budget

[19] Key to Russell Edmunds, 24 December 1948, FO371/68832/E16464/G, TNA.
[20] Bradshaw, *Britain and Jordan*, pp. 176–7.
[21] Kirkbride to Burrows, 9 March 1949, FO371/75300/E3381/G, TNA.
[22] 'Subsidy for the Arab Legion in 1949', Minutes of a Cabinet meeting held on 1 February 1949, FO371/75299/E2249/G, TNA.
[23] 'Size and Shape of the Arab Legion for 1949/50: Note by the War Office', 31 December 1948, FO371/75299/E296/G, TNA.

for a force half the size that was presently overstretched, particularly with the Arab–Israeli conflict unresolved. Yet an annotation by Bevin indicated that the 'intention' was to compel the Jordanian government to make a financial contribution.[24] When the 1949/50 subsidy was agreed it was explained to Glubb that 'you will be maintaining the Arab Legion at a strength greater than you can afford' and that unless the Jordanian government contributed, the strength of the force would have to drop below that required during the latter part of the year, in order to make up for the initial over-expenditure.[25] Consequently the subsidy was no longer linked to a 'predetermined' size of 7,000. Instead the subsidy was now provided to fund the Arab Legion at as large a size as was possible.[26] In 1949 the subsidy was set at £3.5 million unofficially for a force of 7,000. In practice it had more than 14,000 men and was expected to be reduced to 11,000 by the beginning of 1950. Yet there was to be no real increase in the subsidy. Nor was there an increase in the size of the Arab Legion, but, rather, a planned reduction. British policy was to maintain the Arab Legion at the bare minimum level deemed necessary to maintain internal Jordanian security and to induce the Jordanians to stump up the cash if they wanted a larger force.

Both these risks were misjudged, however. Firstly, it had already been established that Greater Transjordan was likely to be even less financially viable than the original pre-1948 state, making a Jordanian contribution highly unlikely. Secondly, the political decision makers had underestimated the day-to-day struggle that the Arab Legion continued to face. The armistice had not brought about a complete cessation of hostilities. Rather, Glubb lamented: 'There has been more shooting in the front line since the Rhodes Armistice was signed than before it!'[27] Between December 1949 and October 1950, Glubb reported 117 incidents of Israeli forces either crossing or shooting across the demarcation line.[28] A Mixed Armistice Commission – involving two delegates each from Jordan and Israel, chaired by a UN mediator – was set up to deal with such incidents, but it proved largely ineffective.[29] The process of reducing the Legion's establishment had begun immediately after the armistice was

[24] Amman to FO, 76, 8 February 1949, FO371/75299/E1919/G, TNA.
[25] H. E. Pyman to Glubb, 31 March 1949, GP2006, 4.
[26] WO to C-in-C MELF, 24 February 1949, FO371/75299/E1919/G; Minute by Walker, 19 February 1949, FO371/75299/E1933/G, TNA.
[27] Glubb to H. E. Pyman, 13 April 1949, GP2006, 22.
[28] Glubb, *Soldier*, p. 285.
[29] Abu Nowar, *Jordanian–Israeli War*, p. 365.

concluded, but Israeli aggression 'put an abrupt stop to this process'. Just as it had after the 1946 Treaty, the situation on the ground in Palestine hindered plans to reduce the Arab Legion. Even at its present strength of 14,000 regulars and 3,000 irregulars, the Arab Legion was 'extremely thin on the ground'. Later that year, therefore, the Foreign Office recommended that the present size of the Arab Legion should be the approved strength for the rest of the financial year, with a £1 million supplementary subsidy to support it.[30] The Foreign Office warned that failure to do so would result in an 'embarrassing' reduction of the Arab Legion.[31] Yet the Treasury remained unconvinced. Moreover, the Jordanian government declined to contribute financially. Instead it threatened to demobilise 4,000 men unless Britain increased the subsidy.[32] Although the Foreign Office and the War Office did not want to see the Arab Legion reduced, they accepted the consequences of the ultimatum, given the difficulty of trying to obtain a supplementary grant from the Treasury.[33] In the event it was reduced by 2,000 men, though further reductions were deemed likely.[34]

Despite the 1949/50 subsidy being proved inadequate, the British stubbornly stuck to the principle of financial stringency throughout the year and continued in this vein when deciding on the 1950/1 subsidy. In 1950 the Chiefs of Staff estimated that the Arab Legion required a strength of 25,000 men to defend Jordan for one month until British reinforcements from the Canal Zone could arrive, in the event of a 'hot' war.[35] Yet they suggested a minimum force of 12,000 men to 'ensure the security of Jordan'.[36] The Chiefs of Staff, therefore, recommended £5.764 million as the amount

which will most effectively [enable the Arab Legion to] carry out its function for the local defence and internal security of Jordan and play its part with other States in the stability of the Middle East and defence against external aggression.[37]

[30] 'Arab Legion Finance', Chadwick, 25 August 1949, FO371/75301/E11052/G, TNA.
[31] Bevin to Attlee, 26 August 1949, FO371/75301/E11052/G, TNA.
[32] Amman to FO, 540, 21 October 1949, FO371/75302/E12726, TNA.
[33] Minutes by Brinson, 22 and 24 October 1949, FO371/75302/E12726, TNA.
[34] Kirkbride to Bevin, 8 November 1949, FO371/75302/E13631, TNA.
[35] 'Arab Legion Subsidy 1950/51', Furlonge, 13 May 1950, FO371/82752/ET1202/33/G, TNA.
[36] 'Chiefs of Staff Committee: Size and Shape of the Arab Legion 1950/51, Note by the Secretary', 21 January 1950, FO371/82751/ET1202/4/G, TNA.
[37] 'Arab Legion Subsidy: Note by the War Office', 25 May 1950, FO371/82752/ET1202/40/G, TNA.

It was reasoned that 'the paucity of British troops in the Middle East will not allow us to honour effectively at the start of operations our existing obligations to Jordan in the event of the Anglo–Jordan treaty being invoked'.[38] Strengthening the Legion would render 'more remote the possibility of His Majesty's Government having to go to the aid of Jordan in accordance with their Treaty obligations'.[39] However, the Arab Legion was still primarily considered a political factor, and the Treasury remained extremely reluctant to use Foreign Office funds for military purposes. The Treasury was concerned that, 'in our view at least we have in this case got a contribution to Imperial Defence which is not subject to the ordinary controls of defence expenditure or scrutinised in relation to general defence requirements'.[40] The Treasury wanted to limit the subsidy to £4 million, but a £4.9 million compromise was reached, subject to repayment of a £650,000 debt. Thus, the subsidy for 1950/1 was effectively £4.25 million and a 50 per cent rise in War Office equipment prices negated any real increase.[41] However, with this amount Glubb felt the Arab Legion could 'scrape through without disbanding any major units'.[42] During the two years immediately following the 1948 War, the Arab Legion was intended to maintain Jordan's security, and the subsidy was merely set at the minimum necessary to avoid significant reduction. The War Office director of finance, Charles Key, acknowledged that 'the maintenance of the Arab Legion, whatever its size, is an advantage from the Imperial defence point of view'.[43] Yet despite incidental advantages to imperial defence, the Arab Legion was not at all organised with this in mind.

Things changed, however, after the Korean War began. This brought into focus the Cold War and for the first time the threat of the Soviet Union became a significant consideration affecting the size, shape, and cost of the Arab Legion. War broke out in Korea when the communist North invaded the South on 25 June 1950. Two weeks later the United

---

[38] 'Subsidy for the Arab Legion: 1950', Brinson, 30 January 1950, FO371/82751/ET1202/8/G, TNA.

[39] 'Chiefs of Staff Committee: Size and Shape of the Arab Legion 1950/51, Note by the Secretary', 21 January 1950, FO371/82751/ET1202/4/G, TNA.

[40] Humphreys-Davies to Care, 24 February 1950, FO371/82751/ET1202/9/G, TNA.

[41] 'Arab Legion Subsidy: Note by the War Office', 25 May 1950, FO371/82752/ET1202/40/G; Shaw to Tomkins, 24 May 1950; Tomkins to Shaw, 26 May 1950, FO371/82753/ET1202/43; 'Arab Legion Subsidy', Furlonge, 19 January 1951, FO371/91819/ET1201/5/G; 'Chiefs of Staff Committee: Size and Shape of the Arab Legion 1950/51, Note by the Secretary', 21 January 1950, FO371/82751/ET1202/4/G, TNA.

[42] Glubb to Furlonge, 14 June 1950, FO371/82753/ET1202/48/G, TNA.

[43] Key to Russell Edmunds, 24 December 1948, FO371/68832/E16464/G, TNA.

Nations agreed to send a force, commanded by American General Douglas MacArthur, to support the South.[44] Believing that it would be advantageous to have at least one Arab state providing active support, the United States intimated that it wanted the Arab Legion to send at least a token force to Korea.[45] The Foreign Office believed that Abdullah was unlikely to agree owing to the Arab Legion being too busy dealing with issues on the border with Israel.[46] Yet, apparently unprompted, Abdullah expressed his own desire to send a 1,500-man force from the Arab Legion to assist.[47] Owing to anticipated disapproval within the Jordanian Parliament, Abdullah requested that Glubb put forward this proposal – demonstrating that the king considered Glubb a useful shield against unpopular policies. For that same reason, Kirkbride warned that Britain – which was not opposed as long as the United States bore the cost – must not propose the idea.[48] However, despite the United States initially suggesting it was prepared to finance the Arab Legion's involvement in Korea, it gradually lost faith in the notion, causing it to shy away from financing the deployment. Thus, due to financial constraints, the British also lost interest and the idea fizzled out.[49]

The conflict in Korea would nonetheless have a direct impact on the future of the Arab Legion, after it prompted Britain to reconsider its plans for the defence of the Middle East. The Foreign Office believed the Soviet Union was involved in North Korea's decision to invade and the day after the invasion expressed concern about Soviet aggression elsewhere, including the Persian Gulf.[50] In the aftermath of the Second World War, the British produced their first emergency global war plan, codenamed Doublequick. Out of this emerged Sandown, a plan for the defence of the Middle East, which was drawn up in August 1948. This plan prioritised all available forces to defend the Suez base, which meant other areas, including the oil-producing regions, would be unsupported.[51] In June 1950, however, as a result of the conflict in Korea, Sandown came

44 Cohen, 'Strategic Role of the Middle East', p. 30.
45 Pundik, *Struggle for Sovereignty*, pp. 256–7.
46 FO to Amman, 425, 18 August 1950, FO371/82711/ET1025/1, TNA.
47 Amman to FO, 287, 19 August 1950, FO371/82711/ET1025/2, TNA.
48 Amman to FO, 292, 23 August 1950, FO371/82711/ET1025/3, TNA.
49 'Arab Legion and Korea', 28 August 1950; FO to Amman, 130 Saving, 29 August 1950, FO371/82711/ET1025/5, TNA.
50 M. L. Dockrill, 'The Foreign Office, Anglo–American Relations and the Korean War, June 1950–June 1951', *International Affairs*, 62:3 (1986), p. 459.
51 Devereux, *Formulation of British Defence Policy*, p. 22; John Kent, 'Britain and the Egyptian Problem, 1945–48', in: Cohen and Kolinsky (eds.), *Demise of the British Empire*, p. 156.

under review, under the codename Celery.[52] Talks in Washington between the US and British Chiefs of Staff concluded that Middle East oil production would be vital in a war of any duration.[53] Accordingly, Britain's Middle East defence plans were expanded to include the Persian Gulf. While planning the build-up of forces to protect Abadan, home of the world's largest oil refinery, it was accepted that a complete division could not be found from MELF and that the United States could not be relied on to assist while the Korean War was ongoing. If Russia moved into the Middle East, it was considered that, in view of Britain's many other present defence commitments, not least Korea, there would be a shortage of available British forces to counter Russian moves.[54]

Increasing the Arab Legion was seen as one way to help alleviate this problem.[55] As part of the post-Korea reappraisal, the Chiefs of Staff approved two papers, titled *A Review of Middle East Policy and Strategy* and *Persia*, both of which concluded that 'the *strength* and *efficiency* of the Arab Legion should be increased'.[56] Lieutenant-Colonel Melville, the Arab Legion staff liaison officer in London, was given advanced notice by the War Office, which he passed on to Glubb in confidence. He explained: 'The Ministry of Defence and the Foreign Office consider that steps should be taken now "to increase the size and efficiency of the Legion with a view to adding to the *security of the Middle East*".' He added that the rationale was:

If a 'Korea' occurs in Persia or Iraq, UNO troops will go to help. These troops are likely to be British in the initial stages. The British will wish to use Legion troops if they are available.[57]

Specifically, the Arab Legion was earmarked for deployment in the south Persian Gulf area, Abadan, and elsewhere to 'support law and order' and to 'support British/United Nations forces in cold war counter measures'.[58] The Arab Legion was now expected to be ready 'for employment

---

[52] Cohen, 'Strategic Role of the Middle East', p. 30.

[53] Brownjohn to Robertson, 31 October 1950, WO216/718, TNA.

[54] Chiefs of Staff Committee to H. A. A. Hankey, 3 August 1950, FO371/82753/ET1202/56/G, TNA.

[55] Ibid.

[56] Brian Calvert to Furlonge, 8 September 1950, enclosed draft letter from WO to MELF, FO371/82753/ET1202/59/G; 'Arab Legion Subsidy', Brinson, 10 January 1951, FO371/91819/ET1201/5/G, TNA [emphasis added].

[57] Melville to Glubb, 28 September 1950, Melville Papers, 11/71 [emphasis in original].

[58] Brian Calvert to Furlonge, 8 September 1950, enclosed draft letter from WO to MELF, FO371/82753/ET1202/59/G; Minute by Redman (DMO), 'The Arab Legion', 3 October 1950, FO371/82755/ET1204/18/G, TNA.

as required by the general allied war plan for the defence of the Middle East', under the allied commander-in-chief.[59] As Melville informed Glubb, MELF intended the 'Legion to be used in all those roles in the M.E. which the British Army usually took'. Melville was told: 'Apparently MELF think we are good enough to do any job which would be entrusted to a British force of up to one B[riga]de Group.'[60] The increased threat of war with the Soviets, highlighted by Korea, finally provided a motive for Britain to build on the reputation that the Arab Legion had built in 1948 and, to a lesser extent, during the Second World War. It was decided that the Arab Legion needed to be expanded because its present size did 'not take into account the possibility of war with Russia'.[61] As a direct consequence of the Korean War, the 'threat from Russia' became 'a new factor' influencing the organisation and cost of the Arab Legion.[62]

This was music to the ears of Glubb, who had been desperate for an increase to the Arab Legion since 1948. Glubb had become increasingly irritated at Britain's apparent ignorance of the Arab Legion's plight. He had been unsatisfied with the 1949 subsidy, prompting Kirkbride to comment that Glubb 'seems to entertain illusions on the subject of what His Majesty's Government can and will do of a nature which I can remember suffering from when I was in my teens'.[63] Meanwhile, towards the end of September 1950, while Glubb was unaware of the impact Korea was having on the British government's thinking in relation to the future of the Arab Legion, Glubb vented his obvious frustration:

Every time I see a British General he tells me how much they all need the A.L. in war. But without giving any money. ... I am not particularly keen to die a martyr's death in the next war. I am getting near to the point when I shall write to the W.O. and tell them that the Arab Legion will NOT repeat NOT fight against the Russians in the next war. Do you think it would be good policy to get cross? After all, only the superhuman efforts of the BO's [sic] [British officers] here can make it fight the Russians. If we say we are not playing, the party is definitely off. The Jordan Govt will not do it if the B.O.'s [sic] here do not push it.[64]

Glubb clearly saw himself as a vital facilitator of Anglo–Jordanian cooperation.[65] Glubb refrained from issuing his threat, though, as Melville

---

[59] Minute by Redman, 'The Arab Legion', Appendix B, 'Expansion of the Arab Legion', WO to MELF, 3 October 1950; FO371/82755/ET1204/18/G, TNA.

[60] Melville to Glubb, 14 September 1950, GP2006, 57.

[61] Minute by Redman, 7 November 1950, FO371/82754/ET1202/67/G, TNA.

[62] 'Arab Legion Subsidy', Brinson, 10 January 1951, FO371/91819/ET1201/5/G, TNA.

[63] Kirkbride to Burrows, 9 March 1949, FO371/75300/E3381/G, TNA.

[64] Glubb to Melville, 17 September 1950, Melville Papers, 11/71.

[65] Pundik, *Struggle for Sovereignty*, p. 270.

advised him to hold his tongue because he had received positive news that: 'Almost certainly some increase will materialise.'[66] It was thanks to Korea, and the apparent increased threat from the Soviet Union, that the Arab Legion was set to receive the increased funds Glubb had long desired.

The Arab Legion was now intended to have a genuine dual function and a reorganisation plan was created to enable this. The War Office vision for the Arab Legion was that: 'In peace and during the armistice with Israel the Arab Legion is disposed as required by the Jordan Government for internal security and the defence of Jordan's frontiers. This is the force subsidised as an act of Foreign policy.'[67] But it was also required that it should 'be capable of providing at short notice one brigade group or equivalent units for employment on Middle East cold war security tasks outside Jordan'. In a major war the Arab Legion would effectively become a division within the British Army.[68] As Furlonge explained: 'Plans were therefore worked out by G.H.Q., M.E.L.F., in consultation with Lt. General Glubb, to reorganise the Legion so as to make it more capable of fulfilling its role in conjunction with British forces.'[69]

The key to establishing a cost-efficient force capable of performing this dual role was the creation of a reserve scheme.[70] In 1950 two-thirds of the Arab Legion's regular units were deployed along the border with Israel, 'preventing minor Jewish incursions or [as Glubb sardonically put it] arresting Arabs who have stolen a cow'. Apart from the fact that this was keeping the Arab Legion regular forces occupied, it also meant it was 'impossible' for them to do any training. If the Arab Legion were sent away to fight the Soviets, another force would have to be found to take over its day-to-day duties along the border with Israel. Indeed, the Jordanian government's focus was Israel, and it wanted the whole of the Arab Legion to be deployed along the border.[71] This meant the peacetime strength had to be increased to free up regular units.[72] Owing to its current

---

[66] Melville to Glubb, 28 September 1950, Melville Papers, 11/71.

[67] 'Expansion of the Arab Legion', Mcleod (DMO) to MELF, 31 May 1951, WO216/178, TNA.

[68] Minute by Redman, 'The Arab Legion', Appendix B, 'Expansion of the Arab Legion', WO to MELF, 3 October 1950, FO371/82755/ET1204/18/G, TNA.

[69] 'Arab Legion Subsidy', Furlonge, 19 January 1951, FO371/91819/ET1201/5/G, TNA.

[70] 'Minutes of a Meeting: Arab Legion Reserve Units Scheme', Leonard, 16 March 1951, FO371/91820/ET1201/20/G, TNA.

[71] Glubb to Melville, 17 September 1950, Melville Papers, 11/71.

[72] 'Expansion, Organisation and Employment of Arab Legion in Event of War', 17 September 1950, ibid.

defensive vulnerabilities, the Soviet Union was deemed unlikely to start a major war until 1954. For that reason, a three-year plan was initiated to reorganise the Arab Legion from a force comprising one armoured car regiment, one infantry brigade group, and two infantry brigades, at the end of 1950, into a force containing two infantry brigade groups, one mobile desert force, a training organisation, and the necessary administrative and internal security units, by April 1954.[73] The reorganisation plan set out that the Arab Legion's regular units would be given authorisation for a 2,000-man increase up to a maximum of 13,500. To make up the required 24,000–25,000 men, it was 'proposed that this additional strength should be found in a reserve adequate to produce 11,000 men'. The system introduced in 1947 had created a reserve by 1951 of just 2,000 men. The Army Council believed that expanding the reserve would create at

a very small cost ... an effective and strong fighting force available for service outside the State of Jordan; and by 1954 the Arab Legion could provide, if need arose, a fully mobile division for remote defence of the Middle East.[74]

Having previously been organised primarily to maintain internal security and defend Jordan from attack by Israel or its Arab neighbours, now the Arab Legion was designed to be capable of supporting the British Army in the event of war with the Soviet Union in the Persian Gulf or elsewhere.

The upshot of this re-evaluation and the perceived increased Soviet threat that Korea represented was that both the War Office and the Foreign Office pressed much more strongly for an increase in the subsidy. Obtaining Treasury approval, for what was described as 'a heavy increase', was not expected to be easy.[75] Given the scale of increase desired, Furlonge remarked: 'The battle for next year's Arab Legion Subsidy is about to begin and, as I have mentioned before, is going to be a stiff one.'[76] Just getting the minimum required to avoid reductions had proved tough the previous two years. This year, however, as Melville informed Glubb, the War Office and Foreign Office intended to take a strong line with the Treasury. He was informed: 'on this occasion, I understand the Israelis will not be quoted to the Treasury as the reason for an increased

73 'Expansion of Arab Legion', MELF to WO, 15 November 1950, FO371/82754/ET1202/
    64/G; 'Arab Legion Subsidy', Furlonge, 19 January 1951, enclosing: 'Cost of the
    Organisation', FO371/91819/ET1201/5/G, TNA.
74 G. W. Lambert to Secretary to the Treasury, 9 March 1951, FO371/91819/ET1201/17/
    G, TNA.
75 'Arab Legion Subsidy', Furlonge, 19 January 1951, FO371/91819/ET1201/5/G, TNA.
76 Furlonge to Kirkbride, 19 December 1950, FO371/82753/ET1202/60, TNA.

subsidy – but the Russians!'[77] Bevin indeed emphasised that the previous year the subsidy had been calculated to deal only with the threat from Israel and its Arab neighbours, but the international situation was now different. It was hoped that the May 1950 Tripartite Declaration – in which Britain, France, and the United States agreed to limit the influx of arms into the region – had reduced the threat emanating from other Arab states, but he emphasised to Chancellor of the Exchequer Hugh Gaitskell that 'the risk of aggression against Jordan by Russia has become much greater than a year ago'.[78] Owing to more vociferous support from both the War Office and the Foreign Office, as well as a more easily recognisable enemy, the Treasury finally backed the expansion of the Arab Legion that the military had desired, but not wholeheartedly supported since 1948. For 1951/2 the Treasury agreed a subsidy of £6.5 million based on the £7.265 million requested.[79] The subsidy was not cut from the amount requested because the expansion was not fully approved, but merely because the rate of expansion was not deemed attainable. The subsidy was merely reduced to reflect a gradual increase in strength over the course of the year.[80] However, Glubb succeeded in obtaining both the men and vehicles required in the original expansion scheme without delay. Accordingly, an £800,000 supplementary grant was requested and approved.[81] Thus, the full amount was eventually provided over the course of the year, in stark contrast to previous years – not least 1949/50 when a £1 million supplementary grant was refused. Moreover, the War Office was now prepared to help fund the Arab Legion in addition to the Foreign Office subsidy. The British Army would therefore provide £1.6, £1.12, and £1.15 million to fund the maintenance of the Special Reserve for the next three years.[82] This meant that in 1951/2 Britain spent a total of £8.9 million on the Arab Legion as compared to just £4.25 million the previous year – more than double. The 1951 subsidy thus proved a realisation of the post-Korea recommendation that the *strength* of the Arab Legion be increased.

The other post-Korea recommendation was an increase in the Arab Legion's *efficiency*, and this led to even greater cooperation with the

[77] Melville to Glubb, 14 September 1950, GP2006, 57.
[78] Bevin to Gaitskell, 23 January 1951, FO371/91819/ET1201/5/G, TNA.
[79] Russell Edmunds to Brinson, 31 March 1951, enclosing: 'Note of a Meeting Held at the Treasury on Friday, 16th March, 1950 [*sic*], to Discuss the Arab Legion Estimates for 1951/52', FO371/91819/ET1201/18/G, TNA.
[80] Ibid.
[81] Russell Edmunds to Furlonge, 3 January 1952, FO371/91822/ET1201/71/G, TNA.
[82] Melville to Glubb, 15 March 1951, Melville Papers, 4/43.

British Army.[83] In an attempt to make the administration more efficient, the Arab Legion became much more closely associated with MELF, under whose command it would fall in the event of a major war. In terms of the Arab Legion's integration into Britain's broader Middle East defence structure, this represented a significant change. Glubb observed that:

Until the autumn of 1950, the Arab Legion has had very little to do with G.H.Q. M.E.L.F., and has always corresponded direct with the War Office. Since the commencement of the war in Korea, however, and the danger of a third World War, in which the Arab Legion would come under the operational command of the C-in-C [commander-in-chief] M.E.L.F., relations between the Arab Legion and G.H.Q. have become very close.[84]

Both Melville and Glubb agreed that this had a negative impact on the day-to-day administration of the Arab Legion because while Cairo – where MELF general headquarters was located – was closer to Amman geographically, in truth it was much easier for the Arab Legion to connect with London, via daily available flights, because Cairo was out of bounds owing to the Egyptian government refusing to provide visas to Arab Legion officers. Moreover, since 1948 the Arab Legion had had an office in London, which made liaison directly with the War Office much easier than liaison via MELF, which had little understanding of the Arab Legion setup.[85]

The more significant consequence of the Arab Legion's greater integration into the structure of the British Army was the by-product of weighting military efficiency over political sensitivities. In order to prepare for a major war, when the Arab Legion would come under the command of MELF, closer cooperation began in earnest, and this contributed to an increasingly rapid Anglicisation of the Arab Legion. Kirkbride had been concerned about Anglicisation even before the onset of the Korean War. In May 1950 Kirkbride observed that since 1948 'practically no locally engaged British officers have been recruited to the establishment'.[86] In September 1949 the Arab Legion had forty-five British officers, of whom twenty-two were seconded from the British Army.[87] In May 1950, forty-nine British officers were serving with the Arab Legion, of whom thirty-seven were seconded.[88] The gross number of British officers may not

[83] Glubb to Robertson, 17 May 1951, GP2006, 93.
[84] Glubb to Kirkbride, 10 August 1951, Melville Papers, 4/43.
[85] Ibid.
[86] Kirkbride to Furlonge, 20 May 1950, FO371/82753/ET1202/47/G, TNA.
[87] 'Staff List of British Officers', September 1949, GP2006, 57.
[88] Kirkbride to Furlonge, 20 May 1950, FO371/82753/ET1202/47/G, TNA.

have increased much, but the proportion of seconded, as opposed to contracted, officers did. Kirkbride had warned that it was 'necessary to have more permanent British officers [who understood the language and mentality of the Arab troops] employed under contract by the Jordan Government and identified in a permanent manner with the Legion and the men'. MELF Commander-in-Chief Brian Robertson, however, was 'against contract officers as there was no guarantee either of their efficiency or standards of personal conduct. He preferred the carefully chosen seconded officer who was under a definite obligation to learn Arabic and to get to know his men.'[89] Kirkbride understood some of the technical benefits from the War Office perspective, but warned that the political effects of over-Anglicisation could prove counterproductive.[90]

While Robertson and Kirkbride held polarised positions, Glubb took up an intermediate stance as he hoped to benefit from greater military efficiency while warding off any political dangers. Since the end of the 1948 War Glubb had been in favour of Anglicisation as a means of bringing the Arab Legion up to speed after it unofficially and rapidly doubled in size during the course of the conflict. This left him at odds with Kirkbride. As Glubb explained to Lash: 'You are aware that Kirkbride is carrying on a war against us for over Anglicization.'[91] Glubb felt that British officers were needed to manage the proposed expansion: to oversee the technical changes in the Arab Legion's role and to train Arab officers.[92] After two years of under-funding and a persistent conflict along the border with Israel, Glubb became increasingly frustrated and desperate for the Arab Legion to obtain greater resources. He therefore welcomed the planned reorganisation of the Arab Legion – including increased Anglicisation. This is an aspect of Glubb's attitude that Ron Pundik has overlooked. He has suggested that Glubb was at one with Kirkbride on this issue.[93] In fact, Glubb was much more pragmatic – at least initially.

Glubb was keenly aware of the dangers of Anglicisation, and he did not promote permanent Anglicisation of the Legion. Glubb acknowledged Kirkbride's concern, noting: 'There is a good deal in what he says. It is such an easy and slippery slope, and has I think been responsible more than anything for the tragedies of India and Egypt.'[94] Glubb continued to

---

[89] Rapp to Furlonge, 27 November 1950, FO371/82754/ET1202/66/G, TNA.
[90] Kirkbride to Furlonge, 20 May 1950, FO371/82753/ET1202/47/G, TNA.
[91] Glubb to Lash, 17 June 1950, GP2006, 47.
[92] Glubb to Robertson, 10 February 1951, Melville Papers, 2/26.
[93] Pundik, *Struggle for Sovereignty*, p. 270.
[94] Glubb to Lash, 17 June 1950, GP2006, 47.

work along the premise that 'as soon as an Arab Officer is available to do any job, we want to get rid of the corresponding British Officer'. Glubb thus advocated to MELF that a fixed establishment should not set the number of British officers. Rather, the establishment should be flexible so that they could be replaced by Arab officers as and when appropriate.[95] Moreover, Glubb was wary that military efficiency could not be the sole criteria driving the reorganisation. The future of Brigadier 'Teal' Ashton was a case in point. After visiting the Arab Legion in autumn 1950, the MELF commander-in-chief came away hugely impressed, but he was concerned about the quality of some British officers. Robertson picked out Ashton as having 'gone to seed' and requested: 'He should not stay there any longer, and Glubb Pasha will take steps to bring his appointment to an early end.'[96] Glubb did not completely concur, however. He opined that 'he is actually extremely useful to us'. Glubb explained:

I agree [Ashton] is not fit to command a brigade in war. On the other hand, he is extremely competent at training infantry up to battalion level. He was Chief Instructor at the Middle East training centre during the last war. He also now speaks Arabic and has a thorough knowledge of the country and has worked on the National Guard since it's [sic] inception. It is essential for me to have someone in the static headquarters in West Jordan who has local contacts, speaks Arabic, liaises with the police and can organise the National Guard in villages.[97]

In short, the military efficiency of officers seconded from the British Army could not compensate for the value of having locally engaged officers. Glubb understood this and hoped to find a balance between military efficiency and morale.

Glubb had already had success since the end of the 1948 War with a military initiative, which had a positive political effect. In May 1949 Glubb proposed the formation of 'a sort of village home guard'.[98] And within a month the 'National Guard' was created, which provided basic training to villagers in the areas of Palestine occupied by Jordan, and armed them with rifles. The primary rationale behind its creation was to protect the frontier against Israeli incursions. Given its length, the Arab Legion could not adequately secure the entire border.[99] Yet within a year of its establishment the National Guard was 'no longer [just] an

[95] Glubb to Robertson, 10 February 1951, Melville Papers, 2/26.
[96] Robertson to Brownjohn, 24 October 1950, WO216/718, TNA.
[97] Glubb to Robertson, 10 February 1951, Melville Papers, 2/26.
[98] 'Trg for Local Def of Villages in Palestine', 26 May 1949, GP2006, 45.
[99] 'A Plan for the Military Training of the People', presumably by Glubb, 25 June 1949, GP2006, 36.

organisation for teaching villagers to defend their homes'; it had 'become the main source of supply for recruits for the regular army'.[100] By 1951 the National Guard meant the Arab Legion had a pool of men from which it could raise several thousand new recruits in twenty-four hours.[101] This is what enabled Glubb to raise the Arab Legion establishment to 13,500 so quickly in April 1951. The creation of the National Guard had a second effect, however. As well as providing a rudimentary military force for the defence of Jordan's frontier with Israel, the programme of popular military training had the political effect of rallying Palestinians to the Jordanian administration.[102] Maan Abu Nowar, who was 'deeply involved in the organisation and training of the National Guard', recalled that the 'many villagers' who volunteered were 'full of enthusiasm' and displayed 'genuine and wholehearted keenness to serve with discipline and honour'.[103] The National Guard was another example of 'population-centric counterinsurgency' tactics being used to unite Palestine and Transjordan, to win over the public by providing security and protection.[104] Arming the West Bank villages was an effective means of providing a cheap first line of defence against Israeli incursions, on one hand, and a method of integrating the Palestinians into the Hashemite state on the other.[105] As a result, Glubb reported a marked improvement in the internal security situation in Palestine by mid-July 1949. During the National Guard's infancy Glubb surmised: 'The immediate military value of these activities has been small, but the political effect has been remarkable.' This initiative appeared to successfully counter much of the propaganda disseminated by the neighbouring Arab states.[106] The National Guard thus proved a successful defence initiative, which also had a positive political effect; it helped galvanise the enlarged Jordanian state and offset some of the potential problems of integrating a Palestinian majority.

Anglicisation of the Arab Legion was something quite different, however, and much less likely to have the same positive political effect – unless, perhaps, the increased military efficiency would prove successful in a conflict with the Israelis – a scenario which never materialised. The key to its success, therefore, was to keep any political issues in

[100] Glubb to Cooke, 25 April 1951, GP2006, 19.
[101] Glubb to Wardrop, 21 April 1951, FO371/91820/ET1201/25, TNA.
[102] 'Trg Directive Palestine: Irregulars and National Guard', 27 June 1949, GP2006, 55.
[103] Abu Nowar, *Jordanian–Israeli War*, pp. 356–7.
[104] Khalili, *Time in the Shadows*, pp. 45–6.
[105] Glubb, *Soldier*, p. 289.
[106] 'The Situation in Palestine', presumably by Glubb, 10 July 1949, GP2006, 37.

check. In Glubb's view, ensuring the right men were found could eliminate the potential dangers. Shortly after the 1948 War ended Glubb
complained that: 'The selection of British Officers for the Arab Legion
has not, during the past 3 years, been entirely satisfactory.' Glubb considered it 'most important at the present time that the best and most
efficient British Officers should be posted to the Legion which has rapidly expanded in the last year and is short of fully trained officers'.[107]
With the British Army taking a keener interest in the military efficiency
of and compatibility with the Arab Legion, in 1951 it was seemingly set
to provide Glubb with the better-quality officers he had long desired.
In a memo to the vice-chief of the imperial general staff, Robertson
asserted: 'I hope that special efforts will be made to provide first class
officers for these jobs. Even second class is not good enough and can do
us more harm than good.' While recognising that the Arab Legion was
technically a 'foreign army', Robertson argued that owing to Britain's
'special interest' in it, it should not be treated as such. Robertson urged
most strongly that 'the requirements of the Arab Legion should be handled as expeditiously as those of our own forces'.[108] Moreover, Glubb
was given further encouragement by the chief of the imperial general
staff, Field-Marshall Sir William Slim, who wrote: 'I can assure you
that I wish to send you the best possible officers and will do all that I
can to do so. ... Rest assured that the provision of first-rate British officers for the Arab Legion and for similar forces is having my personal
attention.'[109]

In reality the Arab Legion did not get the first-class officers Glubb
desired, and he quickly came to realise that the 1951 reorganisation was
not as positive as he hoped. Although Slim had promised to give the
search for first-rate British officers his personal attention, he was also
advised to consider the Arab Legion's needs within the context of the
broader British military requirements lest they fall prey to pressure from
Glubb, who was described as a 'most persuasive and persistent chap'.
Slim was advised: 'the Arab Legion should have its share of nuggets, but
that will not work out at 100%'.[110] Although the Arab Legion was getting greater attention as a quasi-British division in the event of war with
the Soviet Union, the Arab Legion remained subordinate to a genuine

---

[107] Glubb to Adjutant General (WO), 'Selection of British Officers for the Arab Legion', 22
June 1949, GP2006, 55.
[108] Robertson to Brownjohn, 24 October 1950, WO216/718, TNA.
[109] Slim to Glubb, 30 November 1950, ibid.
[110] B.G., A.G. [indecipherable] to Brownjohn, 23 November 1950, WO216/719, TNA.

British division and would have to accept at least some British officers of 'average quality'.[111]

Having considered Kirkbride's 'anxiety' over Anglicisation 'groundless' in June 1950, a year later, and less than two months after the reorganisation began, Glubb took 'fright at the same issue'.[112] Glubb and Kirkbride were now united in their concern that the decreasing number of contract officers risked weakening the 'close relationship which must exist between the officers and men of the Legion'.[113] As Glubb explained: 'One always has to remember that the high morale of the Arab Legion is due to the fact that they think themselves an Arab Army.'[114] In that respect, the Arab Legion was a typical example of what Laleh Khalili has identified as the maintenance of imperial control using 'the appearance of independence'.[115] However, Glubb and Kirkbride seemed more aware of this than London. Ron Pundik described the competition between contract versus seconded officers as a battle between the 'sentimental' and the 'professional'.[116] This appraisal, however, does scant justice to Kirkbride's astute political acumen, and his and Glubb's awareness of Jordan's precarious political balance in an age of Arab nationalism and anti-imperialism. Neither of them was motivated by a rustic fantasy of the past. Both were singularly concerned with the pragmatic reality of raising the standards of the Arab Legion in due consideration of the politics of the day. Glubb became particularly concerned that Arab Legion correspondence was increasingly being conducted in English, which served to isolate non-English-speaking Arab officers and placed a disproportionate amount of power in the hands of interpreters.[117] This, Glubb warned, was likely to arouse criticism from anti-British elements. He added: 'This "rule of the interpreters" has been one of the major causes of the downfall of many other regimes – e.g. the French in Syria.'[118] Wary of the 'dangers of too much anglicization', Glubb warned: 'If the Arab Legion were to become a T.J.F.F. it would end up in a similar fiasco.'[119] As a British colonial force dominated by a large cadre of British officers, the Transjordan Frontier

---

[111] 'Expansion of the Arab Legion', Mcleod (DMO) to MELF, 31 May 1951, WO216/718, TNA.
[112] Kirkbride to Furlonge, 21 May 1951, FO371/91820/ET1201/29/G, TNA.
[113] Wardrop to R. A. Fyffe, 17 July 1951, FO371/91821/ET1201/43, TNA.
[114] Glubb to Robertson, 17 May 1951, GP2006, 93.
[115] Khalili, *Time in the Shadows*, p. 25.
[116] Pundik, *Struggle for Sovereignty*, pp. 270–1.
[117] Glubb to Robertson, 17 May 1951, GP2006, 93.
[118] Glubb to Lash, 17 June 1950, GP2006, 47.
[119] Glubb to Melville, 19 May 1951, Melville Papers, 4/43.

Force lacked the *esprit de corps* associated with the Arab Legion and was the subject of a mutiny amongst the Arab non-commissioned officers and a plot to seize arms and turn against the British during the Second World War.[120] In May 1950, during his battle with Kirkbride, Glubb was at pains to point out that while the TJFF 'should certainly be a lesson to us, it should not be assumed that we are repeating their mistake'.[121] Twelve months later, however, with the reorganisation in full swing, Glubb now took fright at the very issue he had previously downplayed. This prompted Glubb to keep a watchful eye on the situation: 'At the moment we are moving steadily, if unconsciously, towards becoming a unit of the British Army.' Glubb was fully aware that: 'The Arab Legion will be more loyal as an equal ally than it would ever be as a paid servant!'[122] He warned: 'It is not possible to have a first class army based on a politically hostile country. It is therefore absolutely essential for us to avoid the development of anti-British feeling in Jordan.'[123]

Yet increasing Anglicisation of the Arab Legion coincided with an increasing anti-British Arab nationalist sentiment throughout the Middle East and within Jordan and the Arab Legion. In part, Glubb's initial support for Anglicisation was a reaction against this trend. Glubb felt that since the Legion's rapid expansion after 1941, young Arab officers had been promoted too quickly, thus giving these officers 'swollen heads'. In consultation with the Jordanian minister of defence he noted: 'We are now in a period of reaction against too rapid promotion.'[124] The most ardent dissenter in the immediate post-1948 era, and the swollen head Glubb particularly had in mind, was Abdullah al-Tall. With the support of the king – and against Glubb's wishes – Tall rose through the ranks in 1948, playing a key role in the events of the conflict.[125] Abdullah al-Tall spent most of his time in Jerusalem during the war. As the second truce began Tall suggested that the Arab Legion should 'change from the defensive [*sic*] to the offensive'.[126] As far as he was concerned, Jerusalem was the most important objective, and as the most senior Arab commander in Jerusalem, whom, Tall said, people thought was 'in charge of all the Arab forces in the city', he pleaded that he be given the support he requested.

[120] Wilson, *King Abdullah*, p. 134; Abu Nowar, *Struggle for Independence*, p. 54.
[121] Glubb to Kirkbride, 27 May 1950, FO816/165, TNA.
[122] Glubb to Melville, 19 May 1951, Melville Papers, 4/43.
[123] Glubb to Robertson, 17 May 1951, GP2006, 93.
[124] Glubb to Kirkbride, 27 May 1950, FO816/165, TNA.
[125] Glubb, *Soldier*, p. 255.
[126] Lt. Col. [Abdullah al-Tall's handwriting] to Comd 4 Bde, undated, GP2006, 86.

If not, he wrote, 'I beg you to release me from this great responsibility and transfer me to any where else so that the responsibility of defending J[eru]s[ale]m does not rest on me'.[127] This perhaps explains why Tall kept copies of secret correspondence between Abdullah and the Israelis, which he later passed onto the Egyptian press after his resignation from the Arab Legion in 1949. Glubb believed that this action 'proved he was contemplating treachery even when he was high in the King's favour'.[128] Yet perhaps his initial motivation for making copies was less about betrayal and more about stockpiling evidence to absolve himself of responsibility for the Arab Legion's defensive posture. From Tall's perspective, Glubb's accusation of 'treachery' must surely have seemed ironic. The 1948 War was clearly a turning point for Abdullah al-Tall, who believed that Glubb and Abdullah had themselves been treacherous. In 1947 Tall published a book, titled *Journey to Britain*, which showed no signs of being anti-British.[129] Yet after defecting to Egypt in 1949 he became an outspoken critic of the Anglo-Abdullah regime and a year after Glubb published his own memoirs in 1957, Tall followed suit, but with a very different, anti-British account.[130]

The primary threat facing the Anglo-Abdullah regime from nationalist enemies was assassination. Abdullah had already been the subject of a failed assassination attempt while the armistice negotiations were still taking place. On 26 March 1949 an improvised explosive device was discovered on the road to the king's palace in Shuneh. According to Glubb, the two men arrested had received their orders from two of the Mufti's supporters and they 'confessed that they had been sent from Damascus to murder King Abdulla'.[131] The arrested men alleged that the Mufti, the chief of the Damascus police, and the Syrian president, Shukri al-Quwatli, were all involved in the assassination plot. Moreover, they provided a list of other assassination targets, which included Glubb, the regent of Iraq, and six other prominent Hashemite and pro-Hashemite Arabs.[132] In April 1950 Glubb reported that Jordan's new Palestinians greeted King Abdullah with immense popularity and that the general situation in Jordan was more favourable than they would have dared hope

---

[127] 'Defence of Jsm.', Abdullah al-Tall to OC 4 Bde, undated, ibid.
[128] Glubb, *Soldier*, pp. 255–7.
[129] Yitzhak, *Abdullah al-Tall*, pp. ix–x.
[130] For a reconciliation of the two texts' account of 1948, see: Rogan, 'Jordan and 1948', pp. 104–24.
[131] Glubb to Pirie-Gordon, 29 March 1949, GP2006, 4.
[132] Glubb to H. E. Pyman, 31 March 1949, ibid.

a few months ago.[133] Yet there remained an ever-increasing undercurrent of antipathy towards the Anglo-Hashemite clique in Jordan, and the threat from external enemies remained ever-present. At the end of April 1950 Kirkbride, who was not known for hysteria or falling foul of idle gossip, informed Glubb:

> I have heard, from what has proved to be a fairly reliable source in the past, that the pro-Mufti elements in Syria and Beirut are considering embarking on a campaign of assassination of British Officers of the Arab Legion. They have decided that murdering Arabs would probably react against their party but that British Officers ruling an Arab reactionary force would be fair game and would create disorder here without necessarily attracting any disapproval from the Arab world.[134]

British officers provided a convenient target for the enemies of the Anglo-Hashemite regime, and increasing Anglicisation of the Arab Legion merely added fuel to the fire.

It was arguably only a matter of time before the assassination campaign caught up with Jordan, and on 16 July 1951 the country was rocked by the assassination of the former prime minister of Lebanon, Riyadh al-Sulh, who was shot in Amman. His assassination on Jordanian soil had a 'profound effect on the country', provoking sadness, anxiety, and anger.[135] Two days later Abdullah 'received an anonymous letter warning him that he and I [Glubb] were about to be killed'.[136] Forty-eight hours after this, on 20 July, the king was shot in the head at point blank range by a Palestinian Arab as he entered the Al-Aqsa Mosque in Jerusalem. Six men were found guilty of conspiracy to murder the king, including a distant relative of the Mufti, and, convicted in absentia, Abdullah al-Tall.[137]

Abdullah's assassination was a catastrophic failure for the Arab Legion. It was 'normal practice' that 'any place visited by the King should be thoroughly inspected 24 hours beforehand and a police guard be on permanent duty in the place during the 24 hours before the King arrives'. However, it was noted that: 'For some reason, perhaps connected with the religious body, this does not appear to have been done in this case.' Consequently the assassin was able to lie in wait inside the doors of the mosque. Moreover, as the king approached the entrance, he was able to move away from the escort of officers surrounding him and enter

[133] 'The State of Jordan', Glubb, 25 April 1950, FO816/162, TNA.
[134] Kirkbride to Glubb, 28 April 1950, GP2006, 38.
[135] King Hussein, *Uneasy Lies the Head: An Autobiography* (London, 1962), p. 2.
[136] Glubb to Kirkbride, 7 August 1951, FO371/91823/ET1201/75, TNA.
[137] Glubb, *Soldier*, pp. 280–1; Wilson, *King Abdullah*, p. 211–13.

alone – leaving him completely at the mercy of the assassin. The Arab Legion's failings continued in the immediate aftermath. An Arab Legion officer, 'Rocky' Walsh, reported:

There was pandemonium and the King's escort, which was not his normal one from the Hash[emite] Regiment but came from the 8th Regiment, became completely out of hand. I do not have all the facts of the case but it seems that a considerable number of people were shot. Radi Ennab [chief of police, Jerusalem district] himself was shot and is still seriously wounded. Whether or not he and the others were shot by the assassin as he fell down or by mistake by the escort, I do not know.

It was a disaster for the Arab Legion, although it must be qualified that Abdullah was a reluctant subject of protection, even in such difficult circumstances. Glubb instructed the escort 'to take special precautions as to his security'. However, in the event, it was 'extremely difficult to make everything absolutely secure in view of the large crowds and the Old City itself'. Moreover, Abdullah proved himself impatient and 'requested to be left alone' so that he could speak to members of the crowd.[138] It is somewhat ironic that Abdullah's final moments played out like a microcosm of his whole life. Abdullah, the 'falcon trapped in a canary's cage', was eager to spread his wings, but relied on the British cage for his security, and, having escaped the cage of the security that surrounded him during his visit to Jerusalem, the falcon was shot dead.

Politically and strategically Abdullah's death was a huge blow to the status quo that Britain had been trying to maintain via Jordan ever since it had decided to withdraw from Palestine. It was a huge blow personally for Glubb, who 'wept almost throughout' at the king's funeral.[139] Yet more importantly, it plunged the whole country and its relationship with Britain into unchartered territory. The 1951 reorganisation of the Arab Legion had been enabled because of the certainty of the Abdullah connection. Right to the end Abdullah was supportive of British intentions with regard to the Arab Legion. In one of his final acts, Abdullah helped counter opposition to the 1951 Arab Legion reorganisation plan. Glubb emphasised that,

the King and Cabinet are 100% on our side. The fact that they dissolved Parliament when some members got 'fresh', is proof of the fact. What they do say to us is 'we will deal with these trouble-makers. But meanwhile please help us by not doing anything which gives them too obvious a chance to criticize us.'[140]

[138] 'Rocky' to Melville, 24 July 1951, Melville Papers, 6/57.
[139] Ibid.
[140] Glubb to Robertson, 17 May 1951, GP2006, 93.

Since the unity of Transjordan and Palestine Abdullah's freedom of action had been somewhat curtailed.[141] As Kirkbride described it:

'In the old days, the Trans-Jordanians were mostly ready to accept without question decisions taken by King Abdullah. ... [He] is now unable to enforce his wishes, and the Palestinian members of the Council of Ministers and of both houses of Parliament have demonstrated their readiness to resist Palace pressure and to express disapproval of the King's action publicly.'[142]

It was nonetheless a feature of British policy in the region that: 'As long as King Abdullah lives, the Arab Legion is almost certain to be entirely at the disposal of Britain in an emergency.'[143] Abdullah proved this when he dissolved the Jordanian Parliament and when he 'assured' General Robertson that 'in the event of trouble with Russia his forces would be unreservedly at our disposal from the start'.[144] Abdullah welcomed the Arab Legion's expansion on the basis that: 'As it grows so does security increase, and as its experience increases so does its ability to shoulder responsibility.'[145] He recognised that the more Britain relied on the Arab Legion, the more support he would receive. Abdullah and the Jordanian government, like Glubb, had, for a long time, been attempting to coax out additional British support, and one of their primary tools had been to emphasise – and often exaggerate – the communist threat. Just a month before the Korean conflict began, as the 1950/1 subsidy was being discussed, the Jordanian government warned, while requesting more money, that:

In the last two years, communism has made great progress in the Middle East, based on Israel and Lebanon, and has permeated actively into Jordan. The Russians aim to bring ruin and confusion to the Arab countries, as they have China, Burma, Malaya, and Greece.[146]

This warning was designed to encourage increased British assistance, yet it had no bearing on the British subsidy in 1950. Charles Tilly has written that: '"governments themselves commonly simulate, stimulate, or even fabricate threats of external war" for their own ends'.[147] This is

---

[141] Abu Nowar, *Jordanian–Israeli War*, pp. 367–73.
[142] Kirkbride to Attlee, 5 October 1950, quoted in: Abu Nowar, *Jordanian–Israeli War*, pp. 367–8.
[143] 'A Note on the Employment of Arab Armies', unsigned, 30 October 1949, GP2006, 47.
[144] Robertson to Brownjohn (VCIGS), 24 October 1950, GP2006, 57.
[145] Abdullah, *Al-Takmilah*, p. 74.
[146] Royal Hashemite Government of Jordan to Bevin, 3 May 1950, GP2006, 30.
[147] Quoted in: Lawrence Tal, 'Jordan', in: Yezid Sayigh and Avi Shlaim (eds.), *The Cold War and the Middle East* (Oxford, 1997), p. 111.

essentially what Abdullah and Glubb had been doing in order to coax out increased British support. They may have been largely unsuccessful – except in as far as convincing the British that Jordan was worth supporting because of its loyalty – but Abdullah was well primed to accept and support the 1951 reorganisation and Anglicisation of the Arab Legion. For many years British policy in and around Jordan had been framed around the reliable loyalty of King Abdullah, but in July 1951 that anchor was removed.

In comparison to its size and wealth, the Hashemite Kingdom became an increasingly disproportionate part of Britain's position in the Middle East, but the British emerged from the 1948 War committed to Greater Transjordan despite its financial unviability because of the reliability of the Abdullah connection, especially given the weakness of Britain's relationship with the other Arab states. In 1951 the Abdullah alliance proved its worth, as Britain was able to bolster the defence of its overseas interests by reorganising the Arab Legion into a quasi-British division. The onset of the Cold War raised the stakes in the race for world power status, and although the Soviet Union and the United States emerged as the benefactors of the changing post-war global order, Britain had no intention of relinquishing its status as a world power and very much saw itself as a key Cold War competitor. The British were determined to hold onto their empire and were equally determined to make greater use of it as a source of self-preservation. The changing role of the Arab Legion between 1948 and 1951 provides a clear indicator of this trend. An important point worth emphasising, which emerges from Britain's post-1948 attitude towards the Arab Legion, is that it shows that until 1951 Britain did not support Jordan because of the Arab Legion. Rather, it supported the Arab Legion because of the Jordanian connection. Despite proving its military worth in 1948, only in 1951 did the Arab Legion assume greater responsibilities beyond Jordan's borders. This was a radical turnaround from 1946 when the Arab Legion was set to be disbanded and its role in Palestine was to be replaced by the TJFF because it was deemed politically expedient to use the Jordanian Army for purposes beyond its own borders.

The fate of the Arab Legion during the two years following the 1948 War provides further evidence of Abdullah's dependence on Britain. Until the summer of 1950 Abdullah and Glubb had been the most ardent advocators of Arab Legion expansion, but despite the border tension with Israel and the use of the Soviet threat, they failed to coax out additional British support. After the start of the Korean War, however, this changed and Britain became the driving force. Both Abdullah and Glubb were therefore receptive to this, which enabled their dream of Arab Legion expansion to become a reality. The problem, however, was that this reorganisation was driven by military efficiency, which jarred with rising anti-British Arab nationalism. The post-Korea reorganisation of the Arab Legion blurred the lines between internal security and imperial defence. As an item in Britain's Cold War order of battle, the Arab Legion became indicative of the notion espoused by Laleh Khalili that counterinsurgency practitioners ignore politics and think only in terms of the 'technical problems to be solved'.[148] Kirkbride – and eventually Glubb – warned against this, when faced with increased Anglicisation, but the British military authorities thought only in terms of the practical Cold War countermeasures they wanted the Arab Legion to perform. This problem was compounded by the fact that these changes in the Arab Legion were initiated at the most inopportune moment. The reorganisation began in April 1951, and within four months the Hashemite Kingdom was plunged into uncertainty. Just as Britain became more reliant on the Arab Legion, Abdullah, the man who helped allow the British to do almost as they pleased, was assassinated. In an instant Jordan had become a canary's cage without a falcon.

[148] Khalili, *Time in the Shadows*, p. 5.

6

A Puppeteer in Search of a Puppet: The Royal Succession and Britain's Policy of Selective Non-Intervention

While the focus during the months prior to Abdullah's assassination was on the reorganisation of the Arab Legion for Cold War purposes, the king's assassination provided the British with a much more pressing concern: how to maintain the 'special' relationship with Jordan that they had been able to depend on with Abdullah. His death on 20 July 1951 initiated a period of uncertainty for both parties of the Anglo–Jordanian relationship. This chapter therefore digresses from the primary focus on the Arab Legion to assess Britain's involvement during the succession crisis. This is important not only because of Britain's strategic interests, but also because, despite Jordan's independent status, the British connection still loomed large over internal Jordanian politics. Both Glubb and Kirkbride had been on the scene so long that, as the future King Hussein apprised, 'our political leaders tended to turn to him [Glubb] or the British Embassy before taking the slightest decisions'.[1] And in the wake of Abdullah's assassination crucial decisions would have to be made. Not the least of which was: who should succeed Abdullah?

This sudden and tragic event opened up the Pandora's box of Jordan's future at a particularly inopportune moment. Not only was Jordan forced to face a future without its founding ruler, but also his successor was far from clear-cut. His son, Talal, eventually succeeded Abdullah on 6 September, seven weeks after his father's assassination, but Talal's reign lasted less than a year. He was deposed on 11 August 1952, and Talal's teenage son, Hussein, was immediately proclaimed king before formally acceding the throne on 2 May 1953, during which time a Regency Council

---

[1] Hussein, *Uneasy Lies the Head*, p. 115.

179

dominated by Prime Minister Tawfiq Abu al-Huda held the reins. There is a surprising dearth of literature on the question of succession and the short reign of King Talal. Only three studies broach this topic.[2] Yet none of these explores the British angle in any great depth. This chapter seeks to fill this gap, and, by detailing Britain's manipulation of events after Abdullah's assassination, this chapter identifies Britain's will to influence high policy in Jordan in order to ensure that it remained a reliable geostrategic asset, despite the loss of the relationship's principal prop.

When Abdullah passed away, the question of who would succeed him was far from straightforward. Abdullah left behind two sons: Princes Talal and Naif. Constitutionally, Talal, as the eldest son, was the natural and rightful heir to the throne. However, Talal's long-held heir status had been an uneasy one owing to a fractious relationship with his father, the result of what appeared to be a clash of personalities, but in hindsight was a consequence of Talal's tragic mental illness. During a period of intense dispute between the pair, at the height of the Second World War, Abdullah stripped Talal of his right to succeed via a secret *irade* (royal command). By the end of the war, however, relations had improved, the *irade* was cancelled, and Abdullah publicly confirmed Talal as heir to the throne.[3] This was merely a temporary rapprochement, though. The main problem was that Talal suffered from schizophrenia, but as his son, Hussein, recounted:

my grandfather never really realised until the end of his life how deeply afflicted my father was. He could not conceive that a man at times gentle and sensible, but at other times very ill, was not just being awkward or difficult. My grandfather was so healthy and tough he could not appreciate what illness was. ... He [Abdullah] had wanted a brave, intrepid, Bedouin son to carry on the great tradition of the Arab revolt, and was incapable of accepting an invalid in place of his dream.[4]

During the weeks immediately preceding his assassination, Abdullah was again seriously reconsidering Talal's status as heir. At the end of 1950 Kirkbride reported a renewed deterioration in their relationship.[5] And when Abdullah visited Turkey during May 1951 – just two months before his assassination – he preferred to appoint Naif as regent in his absence, as he and Prime Minister Samir al-Rifai had become angered

[2] Satloff, *Jordan in Transition*, pp. 3–57; Shlaim, *Lion of Jordan*, pp. 40–60; Ashton, *King Hussein*, pp. 13–36.
[3] Kirkbride to Baxter, 25 March 1947, FO371/62220/E2874, TNA.
[4] Hussein, *Uneasy Lies the Head*, p. 14.
[5] Kirkbride to Furlonge, 27 December 1950, FO371/91836/ET1941/1, TNA.

with Talal due to him compiling huge, unexplainable debts. Kirkbride advised against such a public rebuke of the heir to the throne, and reluctantly Abdullah appointed Talal regent on the proviso that he made a 'signed undertaking either to do or not do certain things in which the King took a personal interest'.[6] Within hours of Abdullah's departure to Turkey, however, Talal telephoned Kirkbride and asked a series of questions that made Kirkbride believe 'something serious had happened to his mind'. Showing signs of paranoia, Talal told the prime minister that he believed Abdullah had been sent into exile as part of a plot to make Naif king and he believed that he himself would shortly be killed to make way for Naif. As Kirkbride explained: 'This was bad enough, but worse was to come.' The following day Talal attempted to murder his wife, Sharifa Zein, while she was in hospital with their three-day-old baby, Princess Basma. In Kirkbride's account: 'At 3 am ... Talal forced his way into [the] hospital, and after announcing that he was not the father of the baby, attacked his wife with a dagger.' He was disarmed before he had a chance to hurt her, but later that day he was found using violence to 'extort information' from his ten-year-old son, Prince Muhammad.[7] As a result of this episode, the prime minister, the minister of health, and Kirkbride agreed that Talal should be sent to Beirut to be seen by a mental health specialist and, still believing there was a plot to assassinate him in Amman, Talal willingly departed.[8] This episode merely compounded Abdullah's concerns about Talal's suitability to rule. Despite what the Jordanian constitution said, Abdullah felt the throne was in his gift. Samir al-Rifai suggested that Abdullah should immediately remove Talal from the line of succession, but after a talk with Kirkbride Abdullah decided to wait until Talal returned from the holiday he had taken to recover from this recent episode before making a final decision. Kirkbride explained: 'I agreed to this, with the hope (unexpressed) that nothing would happen in the meanwhile to His Majesty.'[9] Yet within just three days of returning to Amman, 'Talal made another murderous attack on his wife and children'. Consequently, on 10 July he departed for further treatment in Geneva.[10] Ten days later, while Talal was still convalescing in Switzerland, Abdullah was assassinated, and as such, Talal, constitutionally at least, remained heir to

[6] Kirkbride to Furlonge, 9 May 1951, FO371/91836/ET1941/3, TNA.
[7] Kirkbride to Furlonge, 17 May 1951, FO371/91836/ET1941/4/G, TNA.
[8] Ashton, *King Hussein*, pp. 21–2.
[9] Kirkbride to Furlonge, 2 June 1951, FO371/91836/ET1941/9, TNA.
[10] Walker to Furlonge, 11 July 1951, FO371/91836/ET1941/25, TNA.

the throne. However, Talal's present incapacity and Abdullah's apparent wishes put Talal's succession in serious doubt.

In Talal's absence Naif was installed as regent after Abdullah's death. Officially he was holding the fort in his brother's absence, but within days of the assassination Kirkbride noticed that Naif was 'showing signs of wanting the throne for himself'.[11] Under the influence of his wife's family and other palace officials, Naif was soon openly expressing his designs on the throne.[12] According to Kirkbride, the whole palace had become 'a welter of intrigue'.[13] This state of affairs left a bitter taste in the mouth of Hussein, who lamented that 'rapacious politicians fought for the crumbs of office like money-hungry relatives that gather for the reading of a will'. He added: 'Within a matter of hours the politicians had started their intrigues. There were those who whispered, was my father well enough to succeed the throne? There were those who hoped he would never reign simply because they themselves wanted power.'[14] Naif's claim to the throne had some credence. Unlike Talal, Naif had a stable relationship with his father, and on the eve of his assassination, Abdullah had, in the presence of Naif, told Malcolm Walker, from the British Legation in Amman, that in Arab tradition, 'the bravest, wisest, strongest and, generally, the most suitable member of the reigning family should succeed'. He added: 'since Talal was incapable and Talal's eldest son was an untried boy, the only man who fulfilled all the requirements was the Amir Naif'. Abdullah made clear that he

did not propose to take any definite action until Sir Alec Kirkbride returned but [prophetically] he wanted His Majesty's Government to know that if in the meanwhile anything should happen to him, those were his wishes.[15]

When Abdullah was murdered Kirkbride was still absent on leave, and so no definite action was taken, but it is pertinent to note that: firstly, Abdullah deemed it necessary that the British be informed of his wishes – apparently he believed that they had a role as kingmaker; secondly, he required – or at least desired – Kirkbride's approval; and, thirdly, this meant it was apparently clear to the British that Abdullah wanted Naif to succeed him.

11 Amman to FO, 259, 25 July 1951, FO371/91838/ET1942/28, TNA.
12 Kirkbride to Furlonge, 23 August 1951, FO371/91837/ET1941/51, TNA.
13 Amman to FO, 264, 27 July 1951, FO371/91838/ET1942/33, TNA.
14 Hussein, *Uneasy Lies the Head*, p. 20.
15 Walker to Furlonge, 11 July 1951, FO371/91836/ET1941/25, TNA.

Meanwhile, the Iraqis, who also had designs on the throne, muddied the royal succession waters further. Like Naif, they could point to tangible indicators that Abdullah intended to forge a stronger union of the two Hashemite kingdoms. In the spring of 1951 Abdullah put forward a proposal that would make King Faysal II of Iraq his heir. The Iraqi government returned with a counterproposal that would allow for steps to be taken over the following five years to align the two countries in such a way that they could be united under Faysal II upon Abdullah's death.[16] With Abdullah's passing, however, this dialogue was cut short.[17] That was not the end of the matter, though. On the morning after Abdullah's assassination, his nephew, Abd al-Ilah, who was regent of Iraq, notified Minister of State Kenneth Younger at the Foreign Office of these plans, and requested he inform Foreign Secretary Herbert Morrison of the situation. He was sounding the British out, testing the water to see if this proposal might become a reality.[18] The Iraqis also, it seems, considered the British kingmakers. Within twenty-four hours of Abdullah's assassination, Jordan was faced with a serious succession struggle. The natural heir to the throne was incapacitated in Europe. Meanwhile, two other Hashemite contenders had tangible and competing evidence seen by the British that suggested Abdullah wanted them to succeed him.

Before the question of royal succession could be resolved, however, Jordan went through a prime ministerial change, which the British had been tempted to halt. After learning of Naif's desire to remove him, just days after Abdullah's death, Samir al-Rifai tendered his resignation. Before accepting it, however, Naif, like his father, sought Kirkbride's counsel. Kirkbride much preferred not to see any changes take place so soon. However, Rifai requested that Kirkbride not intervene for fear that he would appear to be kept in power by the British.[19] Local convention meant that regime change required the resignation of the existing government.[20] Consequently, Kirkbride muted his disapproval, Rifai's resignation was accepted, and Jordan's other perennial prime minister, Tawfiq Abu al-Huda, replaced him.[21] The Foreign Office later commented that Rifai's decision to 'refuse the British support that might have kept him

[16] Kenneth Younger to Eastern Department (FO), 21 July 1951, FO371/91797/ET10393/3, TNA.
[17] Satloff, *Jordan in Transition*, pp. 19–20.
[18] Kenneth Younger to Eastern Department (FO), 21 July 1951, FO371/91797/ET10393/3, TNA.
[19] Kirkbride to Furlonge, 25 July 1951, FO816/172, TNA.
[20] Satloff, *Jordan in Transition*, p. 22.
[21] Kirkbride to Furlonge, 25 July 1951, FO816/172, TNA.

in power, but embarrassed him and us' was 'wise and important' and 'should not be overlooked'.[22] Indeed, seemingly it was not overlooked, because this was to set a tone of selective non-intervention that would characterise British policy throughout the next twelve months as Britain helped guide Jordan through two royal successions.

With the change of government complete, the full attention of the Jordanian government and the British could be given to the royal succession. Eventually Talal did succeed his father. How and why this occurred provides a fascinating insight into the nature of British involvement in independent Jordan. The existing literature has tended to gloss over Britain's role in these events, but Britain's attitude and influence were crucial and worth identifying. While Nigel Ashton surmises that events during the five weeks between Abu al-Huda's appointment and Talal's succession 'remain somewhat murky', he asserts that 'the basic outline of what transpired can be deciphered'. He explains that:

For various reasons, including an improvement in his health, the vigorous sponsorship of his wife Zein [a sophisticated political operator with her own private communication channels with the British], the backing of the Saudis and the political ineptitude of Nayif, Talal emerged as Abu'l Huda's favoured candidate for the throne.[23]

Curiously he omits to mention arguably the most significant factor and the one that we have most information about: Britain. The official records in London show beyond doubt that the British quickly favoured Talal and why it discounted the other options. Avi Shlaim does intimate that 'Kirkbride and Glubb Pasha together played a critical part in resolving the crisis of the succession in favour of Prince Talal and ultimately his son Hussein'.[24] However, he does not go into any detail of their involvement. This chapter delves into this hidden detail to reveal the nature of British interests and influence during this pivotal moment in Jordan's history.

The British were certainly opposed to the first alternative to Talal: Naif.[25] Ashton notes that: 'To date no evidence has come to light as to why the British government failed to act on King Abdullah's final wishes regarding the succession and support Nayif's persistence in pursuing his claim to the throne.'[26] However, there is pretty clear evidence that the British had no faith in Naif as being good for either Jordan or Britain.

[22] Minute by Hunter, 9 August 1951, FO371/91789/ET1015/17, TNA.
[23] Ashton, *King Hussein*, pp. 25–6, 381.
[24] Shlaim, *Lion of Jordan*, p. 52.
[25] Ibid., p. 53.
[26] Ashton, *King Hussein*, p. 381.

Throughout the Middle East it was widely believed that Britain was supporting Naif against Talal. The Israeli media reported that Naif was 'more acceptable to the British, who support him'.[27] And Egyptian newspaper *Al-Misri* speculated that Talal's rightful succession might be obstructed 'for political reasons'.[28] Within the Egyptian and Syrian press, Naif was labelled 'weak-minded and entirely subservient to British influence'. Meanwhile, Talal was heralded as a 'great patriotic anti-imperialist'.[29] When it was put to the nationalist Arab Legion officer Ali Abu Nowar that the British opposed Naif, his reply was adamant: 'No. They liked him very much. They thought it would be easier to deal with Prince Naif than with Prince Talal.'[30] This was not true, however. The archival record demonstrates that the British considered Naif utterly undesirable. He was thought to be 'irresponsible' and heavily involved in the trading of contraband.[31] Kirkbride described him as 'quite unsuited for responsibility. He is feather headed and too susceptible to the immediate influence around him.'[32] Naif was unlikely to bring stability to the Hashemite state, because he was an unconstitutional heir and because he was criticised for being a British stooge. Coupled with Britain's general dislike of Naif and the expectation that he was unlikely to be a reliable conduit for British policy due to his apparent susceptibility to intrigue, it is far from surprising that the British offered no encouragement for Naif's claim to the throne, despite Abdullah's apparent wish.

The Hashemite union option, on the other hand, did offer at least some attraction to Britain. Prior to Abdullah's death the Foreign Office was open to all possibilities with 'the suggestion of some form of "Commonwealth" relationship' with Iraq being described as 'one of the best yet'.[33] However, in the final analysis the Foreign Office opposed union for two reasons. Firstly, it would upset the status quo in the Middle East and stir up Arab intrigue. Secondly, it was feared Britain's position in Jordan might be weakened if it came under the domination of Baghdad.[34] Iraqi Foreign Minister Salih Jabr suggested that a Hashemite union

---

[27] *SWB: Part IV, The Arab World, Israel, Greece, Turkey, Persia*, 27 July 1951, p. 38.
[28] Ibid., 27 July 1951, p. 37.
[29] Kirkbride to Furlonge, 23 August 1951, FO371/91836/ET1941/51, TNA.
[30] Interview with Ali Abu Nowar, 20 June 1990, Geyelin Papers.
[31] 'Likely Reactions in the Middle East on the Death of King Abdulla in Jordan', undated, FO371/91839/ET1942/40, TNA.
[32] Kirkbride to Furlonge, 23 August 1951, FO371/91836/ET1941/51, TNA.
[33] Minute by Hunter, 18 June 1951, FO371/91836/ET1941/11, TNA.
[34] FO to Baghdad, 720, 22 July 1951, FO371/91797/ET10393/3; Minute by Hunter, 25 July 1951, FO371/91797/ET10393/4, TNA.

would benefit Britain as Iraq could protect Jordan from Israel and from
the intrigue of other Arab states and therefore enable Britain to secure its
interests in Jordan 'without being held responsible as at present for everything' that went wrong.[35] The Foreign Office, however, believed that
payment of the subsidy would mean that Britain would continue to be
blamed for everything and that Jordan's protection from Israel was better
guaranteed by Britain and the Arab Legion.[36] Moreover, the head of the
BMEO, Thomas Rapp, warned against the Arab Legion coming under
the orders of Baghdad and the complication that would arise regarding
the maintenance of British influence within the Legion.[37] This was particularly important given the increased significance of the Arab Legion as a
constituent part of Britain's global defence strategy since the onset of the
Korean War.

Britain's objection to a Hashemite union was not unanimous, however, and the debate that ensued revealed a key feature of British policy
during this period of upheaval: a fear of Arab republicanism and the
need to appear neutral. Troutbeck, the British minister in Baghdad, was
critical of Rapp and the Foreign Office. He agreed that the disadvantages of union outweighed the advantages, but was quick to point out
that this evaluation was predicated on the basis that it was possible to
maintain an independent and friendly Jordan. This, Troutbeck felt, was
a 'dubious proposition' that had been taken for granted. In Troutbeck's
view, the notion that Britain could 'avoid serious repercussions in the
Middle East merely by trying to ossify the present situation from which
the principal prop [Abdullah] has been eliminated' was wishful thinking
in the extreme. In Troutbeck's opinion, British policy regarding the royal
succession should be shaped less by the question of which scenario was
preferable, but instead more consideration should be given to the feasibility of Jordan remaining independent and friendly. Troutbeck counselled:

If we played our cards well we might conceivably not only retain our position
in Jordan but strengthen it in Iraq. Conversely, if we were to put a spoke in the
wheel of union, we might seriously weaken our position in Iraq, and a strong position in Jordan would in that event surely be of much less use to us.[38]

At the core of this conflict of opinion was a striking commonality, which
Hunter, within the Foreign Office Eastern Department, observed. He

[35] Amman to FO, 253, 24 July 1951, FO371/91797/ET10393/4, TNA.
[36] Minute by Hunter, 25 July 1951, ibid.
[37] Rapp to Furlonge, 1 August 1951, FO371/91797/ET10393/17, TNA.
[38] Troutbeck to Furlonge, 15 August 1951, FO371/91798/ET10393/27, TNA.

considered Troutbeck to have reached the same conclusion as the Foreign Office, but via a different route. At present, Britain's interests were best served by continued control of the Arab Legion and by an independent Jordan. While Hunter recognised that at some point in the future Britain may be forced to take sides, he maintained that the tenet of British policy should be 'to remain as far as possible on good terms with all concerned, and neutral as long as we can'.[39] Troutbeck's position was built on the same premise. He warned that in order to avoid antagonising Iraq, 'great care should be taken not to express our policy of neutrality, with which I agree, in such a way as to create suspicion that it masks a positive hostility towards a closer association between the Hashemite kingdoms'.[40] With Abdullah gone and the prospect of Jordan being sucked into the orbit of one of its Arab neighbours, the Foreign Office concluded: 'The best guarantee of Jordan's independence is clearly our continued support, and our continued abstention from taking sides in any of the schemes of union.'[41] It was effectively agreed that Britain should avoid direct interference and avoid publicly endorsing the question of union either way. The main difference of opinion was merely that Troutbeck advised neutrality so as not to ostracise the Iraqis, while the Foreign Office and the BMEO favoured neutrality as a means of enabling the preferred option of sustaining the existing 'special' relationship with Jordan. Ultimately, the British feared Arab republicanism and all approaches to solving the crisis were geared towards sustaining the Anglo-Hashemite axis at the heart of the Middle East.

With Naif and the prospect of union with Iraq discounted by Britain, this left two royal succession options: the constitutional heir, Talal, and his seventeen-year-old son, Hussein. In the immediate aftermath, Prime Minister Rifai was in favour of Talal being overlooked as Abdullah's successor. He suggested to Kirkbride that 'the best solution' was for Talal to forego his rights willingly and for the next in line, Hussein, to be proclaimed king with Naif as regent.[42] However, as Hunter minuted: 'It may not be quite so simple', because Arab League Secretary-General Azzam Pasha had issued a statement 'suggesting that Talal, as the rightful heir and opponent of Britain ... was being improperly deprived'.[43] Talal's breakdown in May – shortly before Abdullah's assassination – had led

[39] 'Jordan–Iraq Union', Hunter, 30 August 1951, FO371/91798/ET10393/30, TNA.
[40] Troutbeck to FO, 612, 31 July 1951, FO371/91797/ET10393/11, TNA.
[41] Minute by Hunter, 2 August 1951, FO371/91839/ET1942/40, TNA.
[42] Amman to FO, 246, 22 July 1951, FO371/91836/ET1941/22, TNA.
[43] Minute by Hunter, 24 July 1951, ibid.

Kirkbride to conclude that Talal was 'not fit to succeed to the throne'.[44] However, when the moment of truth arrived the British, including Kirkbride, very quickly hung their hat on Talal as the most suitable immediate successor. Just a week before Abdullah's assassination, Pirie-Gordon concluded that Talal had 'the makings of a good constitutional monarch', who 'is always willing to take advice from the British provided he is on some terms of personal friendship'. He added: 'we should have a reasonable chance of getting from Talal the same support for our policy we have had from his father, without the same strained relations with other Arab states which is such a feature of his father's administration'.[45] The British were utterly opposed to Naif, preferably opposed to union with Iraq, and the 'present public line', within a week of the assassination, was 'hope that Talal *will* be able to assume his responsibilities' as king.[46] In his assessment of how Talal came to be the preferred choice for succession, Ashton observed that it is not clear if Abu al-Huda already favoured Talal before he became prime minister.[47] What is clear, however, is that the British had reached this conclusion by the time Abu al-Huda was appointed. It was surely no coincidence, therefore, that when Kirkbride met the new prime minister on the day he replaced Samir al-Rifai, they 'agreed' to keep things constitutional and to promote the accession of Talal subject to 'the Doctor's report on Talal at the end of the five weeks treatment'.[48] Of the three immediate candidates to succeed Abdullah, the British unquestionably favoured Talal. He ticked all the boxes. His succession was constitutional, and he was deemed pro-British, apolitical, and popular.

Britain promoted Talal primarily because it believed he would be a benign ruler who would allow the teenage Hussein to accede to the throne when he came of age after a period of grooming at school in Harrow and later at the British military academy in Sandhurst. Hussein provided the best opportunity for Britain to mould a long-term collaborator akin to Abdullah and thus uphold the status quo of the alliance and its strategic value. The principal problem of supporting the immediate accession of Hussein was his youth, a fact that was exacerbated by the equally young age of the heir to the other Hashemite line, Faysal II

---

[44] Kirkbride to Furlonge, 17 May 1951, FO371/91836/ET1941/4/G, TNA.
[45] Pirie-Gordon to Burrows, 12 July 1949, FO371/75316/E8782/G, TNA.
[46] Minute by Hunter, 26 July 1951, FO371/91838/ET1942/25, TNA [emphasis in original].
[47] Ashton, *King Hussein*, p. 25.
[48] Kirkbride to Furlonge, 27 July 1951, FO816/172, TNA.

of Iraq.[49] The question of succession therefore became not just a matter of who was most suitable or who had the constitutional right, but was as much about who was ready. British hopes for the future of Hashemite rule in Jordan were pinned on Hussein. And as Kirkbride noted, 'the surest way of ensuring Hussein's ultimate accession is for Talal to become the King first'. While Kirkbride feared that Talal's popularity would 'not survive his enthronement for long', this mattered not.[50] The British saw Hussein as the future of Jordan and regarded Talal as a necessary, but brief constitutional interim.

Britain's support for Talal's accession has been obscured by the notion that Talal was anti-British. Yet the contemporary evidence suggests this has been exaggerated, and acknowledging this is crucial to understanding British involvement during the royal succession crisis. In their memoirs, both Glubb and Kirkbride dismissed the notion that Talal was anti-British.[51] Avi Shlaim, however, has rejected their claims. He suggests they both played down Talal's anti-British stance in their memoirs because of their 'self-serving' desire to 'protect Britain's reputation'. Shlaim described Talal as completely at odds with his father in regard to their attitudes towards Britain and explains that Talal 'bitterly resented British interference in the affairs of his country'.[52] However, both Glubb and Kirkbride's memoirs were wholly consistent with their contemporary accounts within the archives. Talal's cousin Prince Raad bin Zayd suggested Talal held 'very anti-British' sentiments, and he put this down to anger at Britain's treatment of his grandfather Sharif Husayn at the end of the First World War and its failure to support an independent Arab kingdom.[53] However, Kirkbride was of the opinion that Talal's anti-British tirades were merely an expression of his personal problems with his father that prompted Abdullah to exclude Talal from the line of succession. Kirkbride certainly believed that Talal indulged in criticism of Abdullah's pro-British policies 'in order to make himself as big a nuisance as was possible' and for 'purely personal reasons' related to the tension between father and son.[54] The evidence for Talal's anti-British attitude goes back primarily to the nadir of their relationship,

---

[49] Faysal was just three years old when his father, King Ghazi, died in 1939. Like Hussein, he came of age in 1953. Until then, Abdullah's nephew, Abd al-Ilah, served as regent.
[50] Kirkbride to Furlonge, 23 August 1951, FO371/91837/ET1941/51, TNA.
[51] Glubb, *Soldier*, pp. 281, 293; Kirkbride, *From the Wings*, p. 121.
[52] Shlaim, *Lion of Jordan*, pp. 42–3.
[53] Interview with Prince Raad bin Zayd, 6 September 2002, in: Shlaim, *Lion of Jordan*, pp. 43–4.
[54] Kirkbride to Baxter, 25 March 1947, FO371/62220/E2874, TNA.

during the Second World War, when Talal criticised his father for his pro-British policies. All of the existing studies that refer to Talal's anti-British stance emphasise the same quotation from 1939 in which Kirkbride described Talal as, 'at heart, deeply anti-British'.[55] However, aside from such outbursts during periods of intense disagreement with his father, there is scant evidence – particularly after 1945 – to suggest that Talal was meaningfully anti-British. Talal's strained relations were primarily with his father, with both parties deemed equally to blame for arguments that were deemed often 'entirely childish'.[56]

Given the awful relationship that Talal had with his father, the British offered Talal a sense of security. When he was due to become regent in 1950, while his father was absent from the country, Talal openly expressed his reluctance to accept this honour owing to the teasing that he suffered at the hands of Abdullah's inner circle. In pained words, Talal lamented that those who made fun of him 'enjoy always his [Abdullah's] encouragement and protection'. With fear preying on his mind, it was to Kirkbride that he turned to for 'support' and 'advice'.[57] Moreover, the British Legation in Amman suggested that it 'would not be an exaggeration to say that Talal's only friends in Jordan were British and American'.[58] Back in 1949, Pirie-Gordon reported that Talal had 'many friends amongst the British of his own age' and that he 'much likes being asked back to English homes, usually stipulating that there should be no Arabs among the guests'.[59] Meanwhile, Glubb always maintained that the 'hostile propaganda' regarding Talal's enmity to Britain was 'entirely without foundation'. And as Talal's reign neared its end, Glubb lamented that the king's illness was 'peculiarly poignant', owing to his view that Talal was 'so ideally qualified to be a successful King, had his health permitted'.[60] Glubb described the 'much publicized hatred of King Tellal to Britain' as 'a piece of propaganda with no foundation whatever in fact'.[61] A prime example of this occurred in the spring of 1951, when it was reported in the Egyptian press that Talal had attacked both Glubb and his wife, Rosemary.[62] This story was completely false. However, as with

[55] Shlaim, *Lion of Jordan*, p. 43; Ashton, *King Hussein*, p. 20; Satloff, *Jordan in Transition*, p. 16.
[56] Kirkbride to Furlonge, 27 December 1950, FO371/91836/ET1941/1, TNA.
[57] Talal to Kirkbride, 20 October 1950, FO816/166, TNA.
[58] Walker to Eastern Department (FO), 16 August 1951, FO371/91837/ET1941/43, TNA.
[59] Pirie-Gordon to Burrows, 12 July 1949, FO371/75316/E8782/G, TNA.
[60] 'A Note on the Situation in Jordan', Glubb, 1 July 1952, FO371/98861/ET1081/1, TNA.
[61] 'A Note on the Situation in Jordan', Glubb, 1 October 1951, GP2006, 31.
[62] Wardle-Smith to Chancery, 2 June 1951, FO371/91836/ET1941/8, TNA.

PHOTOGRAPH 1. Glubb Pasha and King Talal, October 1951.
Reproduced from: Middle East Centre Archive, St Antony's College, Oxford.
GB165-0118 Glubb Collection.

any great lie, it was based on a truth. The genesis of the story was the 3
AM attack by Talal on his own wife while she was in hospital just days
after the birth of Princess Basma.[63] The British certainly did not believe
that Talal was anti-British and lamented the fact that this 'canard' of the
extreme Arab press began to creep into British journals, such as the *Daily
Mail* and the *New Statesman*.[64] This misperception served Britain well,
though, because it obscured Britain's true desire and enabled its preferred
outcome to reach fruition without the need for direct intervention.

Talal was eventually brought back to Amman to fill the void left by
Abdullah at the beginning of September. Although there had been no
immediate urgency to confirm Abdullah's successor – thus allowing Talal
time for convalescence and assessment in Europe – as time progressed so
the urgency increased. Talal's continued absence from the country and
the resulting uncertainty fuelled rumours within Jordan and throughout
the Middle East to the effect that Talal was being kept away as part of a
British plot. There were street demonstrations 'calling for Talal to come

[63] Walker to Cairo, 8 June 1951, FO371/91836/ET1941/12, TNA.
[64] Walker to FO, 16 August 1951, FO371/91837/ET1941/43, TNA.

back'.[65] Meanwhile, Glubb and Kirkbride foresaw the possibility that Naif might use the Hashemite Regiment to carry out a coup d'état and proclaim himself king before Talal returned from Geneva. To guard against this Glubb moved the Hashemite Regiment to Mafraq for 'training' while ensuring that two loyal Bedouin regiments were stationed on training exercises in Amman.[66] It thus became increasingly imperative that Talal return as soon as possible and so put an end to the present political vacuum. Talal arrived back in Amman on 6 September and later that day took the required oath.[67] It was believed that Talal's succession would 'kill' the notion that there was a British plot to exclude him.[68] As Furlonge outlined, it was hoped that Talal's presence would breed stability.[69] Initially this proved the case. Maan Abu Nowar recalled that Talal's return prompted 'almost the entire population to come out in demonstrations of joy and happiness'.[70] Meanwhile, the British Embassy in Alexandria reported that the Egyptian press had lost interest in Jordanian affairs as the 'return of King Talal has exploded the favourite theme of a British plot'.[71] Glubb observed: 'Now the country once more feels as secure, stable and contended [*sic*] as before the murder of King Abdullah'.[72] Thus, the British had achieved exactly what they hoped without having to intervene directly. Jordanian stability had been maintained, a pro-British king had succeeded Abdullah, Hussein was confirmed as heir to the throne, and this had all been attained without breaking the constitution and without the suggestion that it was the result of a British plot.

Less than two months after Talal's return, however, the Anglo–Jordanian connection was rocked by another departure when, in late December 1951, Kirkbride transferred to Libya after thirty years' service in Palestine and Jordan. After the prime ministerial and royal successions, this was the third change wrought by the death of Abdullah. Politically, this departure was unnecessary and as such should perhaps have sent a signal to London that the status quo had been irrevocably shaken by the assassination of Abdullah. Indeed, the timing was particularly telling. Just days before Kirkbride's departure was ratified, he reported a serious decline in Talal's mental state that was causing both him and Abu al-Huda

[65] Interview with Ali Abu Nowar, 20 June 1990, Geyelin Papers.
[66] Kirkbride to Furlonge, 3 September 1951, FO371/91837/ET1941/55, TNA.
[67] Kirkbride to Furlonge, 6 September 1951, FO371/91837/ET1941/60, TNA.
[68] Kirkbride to Furlonge, 23 August 1951, FO371/91837/ET1941/51, TNA.
[69] Minute by Furlonge, 12 September 1951, FO371/91797/ET10393/20, TNA.
[70] Abu Nowar, *Jordanian–Israeli War*, p. 432.
[71] Alexandria to FO, 3 October 1951, FO371/91793/ET10316/3, TNA.
[72] 'A Note on the Situation in Jordan', Glubb, 1 October 1951, GP2006, 31.

considerable anxiety. Kirkbride warned: 'One of the dangers of the situation is that Tewfiq and I are the only two people left who can calm the King down in his nervous fits and get him to do things without causing resentment. If the King turns against us [Abu al-Huda and Kirkbride], it *will* be awkward.'[73] Given Kirkbride's utter centrality to the king's trust, it is most curious that only two days later Kirkbride advised that there was no local reason why he should not be redeployed from Amman to Tripoli. Against this, Foreign Secretary Anthony Eden minuted: 'I am very troubled by this.'[74] Abdullah's absence, however, had left Kirkbride with a determined urge to leave. He instigated the Foreign Office's search for a suitable vacancy elsewhere in the Arab world and was determined that he not be held back.[75] Kirkbride's evident desperation to depart, while partly inspired by his personal sense of loss, was an ominous sign for the future of Anglo–Jordanian relations.

Kirkbride's successor as the British minister to Jordan was Geoffrey Furlonge, who arrived in Amman on 14 February 1952.[76] Robert Satloff has argued that this appointment was ill conceived.[77] Yet in many ways he was a logical choice. Not least because he was well acquainted with the situation in Jordan, having been the primary recipient of Glubb and Kirkbride's recent reports in his capacity as head of the Foreign Office's Eastern Department. Furlonge therefore began his post as up to speed as anybody outside Amman could be. The fact of the matter was that Kirkbride was irreplaceable. It was almost inevitable that his successor, whoever that was, would slot into something much closer to a traditional ambassadorial role, and shortly after Furlonge's arrival his job title changed to reflect this – after the British Legation became an embassy in August 1952.[78] What is most evident in contrasting the two is that Furlonge was much more beholden to London. Shortly after Transjordan had assumed independence, Bevin explained that: 'Sir Alec Kirkbride will be responsible for the execution of His Majesty's Government's policy in regard to Transjordan.'[79] Kirkbride's modus operandi was to execute British policy using his own initiative wherever possible, and after the

[73] Kirkbride to Furlonge, 26 November 1951, FO371/91837/ET1941/70, TNA [emphasis in original].

[74] Minute by Strang to Eden, 30 November 1951, ibid.

[75] Kirkbride, *From the Wings*, p. 145.

[76] 'Monthly Situation Report on the Hashemite Kingdom of the Jordan for February, 1952', Walker, 3 March 1952, FO371/98857/ET1013/3, TNA.

[77] Satloff, *Jordan in Transition*, pp. 48–9.

[78] Ibid., p. 179.

[79] Henderson to Under-Secretary of State for Air, 3 July 1946, FO371/52920/E5257, TNA.

immediate turmoil surrounding Abdullah's assassination Kirkbride was praised – by Furlonge – for having 'handled' the situation 'with the minimum of telegraphic references home'.[80] In stark contrast, Furlonge's contact with London gives the distinct impression that he referred almost every problem back to the Foreign Office in London. Furlonge's arrival heralded a significant departure from the level of political power exhibited by his predecessor and it diminished the degree to which the British minister was part of Jordan's inner circle. Kirkbride reported that as a result of their 'long association', Abdullah had 'got in the habit of informing me what he has in mind in both official and private matters with a frankness which is sometimes startling'.[81] Furlonge, however, was significantly reliant on others, particularly the prime minister, with regards to the state of affairs within the palace. By the end of March 1952 Furlonge reported a sharp deterioration in Talal's mental state.[82] Interestingly, Furlonge reported that he had not heard a single whisper from anyone other than Abu al-Huda about this most recent violent episode, which led Furlonge to privately question whether Abu al-Huda 'was telling the truth'. However, Furlonge surmised: 'it seems hardly conceivable that he could have made up the whole thing'.[83] Although Furlonge was evidently more reliant on the prime minister and others for information and intelligence, the prime minister still turned to the new British minister for advice, as was customary in moments of crisis in Jordan for the old guard who were accustomed to Britain's political presence. Furlonge's assumption was that he should advise the same course as last autumn: to stick to the constitution and be guided as far as possible by medical opinion.[84] Furlonge observed that one benefit of Talal's decline was that it had enabled him to 'break the ice' between him and both Abu al-Huda and Talal.[85] The Foreign Office and Eden agreed that this had been a 'welcome effect'.[86] Furlonge's relationship with the king appeared to blossom as Talal expressed a desire to see more of Furlonge, including a regular weekly meeting. According to Furlonge, Talal more than once expressed 'the desire to be "guided by my advice as his father was by Sir Alec"'.[87] This was further evidence that Talal was far from anti-British and

---

80 Minute by Furlonge, 11 August 1951, FO371/91789/ET1015/17, TNA.
81 Kirkbride to Burrows, 16 February 1948, FO371/68819/E2832/G, TNA.
82 Furlonge to Bowker, 31 March 1952, FO371/98898/ET1941/16/G, TNA.
83 Furlonge to Bowker, 5 April 1952, ibid.
84 Furlonge to Bowker, 31 March 1952, ibid.
85 Furlonge to Bowker, 5 April 1952, ibid.
86 Minute by Bowker, 9 April 1952; Minute by Eden, 10 April 1952, ibid.
87 Furlonge to Bowker, 28 April 1952, FO371/98898/ET1941/24/G, TNA.

seemingly justified the British decision to support Talal's accession. The British therefore sincerely hoped Talal's deterioration would blow over.

However, as April turned to May, Talal's health rapidly deteriorated. This shattered the privacy of the king's decline and consequently launched Jordan back into turmoil. With the queen due to return on 3 May 1952 – from convalescence in Europe relating to repeated heart attacks – it was hoped that, thereafter, 'things will be easier'.[88] However, upon her return the Jordanian prime minister reported that Talal repeatedly threatened to kill her and assaulted his children. Abu al-Huda feared that Talal would soon actually murder someone or at the very least cause a huge public scandal. On 14 May Talal, after appearing normal and pleasant in the presence of Furlonge, was reported by Abu al-Huda to have 'assaulted the Queen, the children, and the servants and was really raving against all and sundry'. Abu al-Huda was at a loss for what to do. As such Furlonge arranged a meeting with him and Glubb where they successfully advised the prime minister 'to tell the full Council of Ministers the situation instead of trying to handle it all himself, the time for complete secrecy being completely over'. Consequently Abu al-Huda induced the king to seek treatment abroad. Furlonge was confident that once Talal was safely out of harm's way, 'the country will, after the shock has passed, carry on much the same as before'. Moreover, he noted: 'It is important to remember that in all this we are only playing for a year's respite: Hussein comes of age on May 2nd, 1953.' In short, he stated, 'if we can secure 6 months' treatment and convalescence and 6 more months' relative sanity, we shall be fairly safe'.[89] The Foreign Office considered Talal's mental decline 'disquieting news', but was not panicked as the uncertainty that Abdullah's unexpected death had wrought had been remedied. It was comforted by the fact that: 'The Jordan Constitution, as revised, provides for the steps to be taken if the King becomes ill or insane; and Prince Hussein having been declared the heir, the succession is constitutionally secure.'[90] The British government had already settled on Talal as a mere stopgap, and the constitution had been revised with the specific purpose of providing for 'all eventualities'.[91]

In the meantime, the British remained intent on maintaining a low profile. Talal departed for treatment in France on 17 May 1952, and the British were careful not to lay themselves open to adverse charges

[88] Ibid.
[89] Furlonge to Bowker, 15 May 1952, FO371/98900/ET1941/44/G, TNA.
[90] Minute by Ross, 8 April 1952, FO371/98898/ET1941/16/G, TNA.
[91] Minute by Hunter, 21 May 1952, FO371/98898/ET1941/35, TNA.

of connivance. Consequently the British ensured that Talal travelled via a 'British *civil* aircraft'. An RAF plane was put on standby, but 'in view of possible hostile propaganda' this was very much a last resort.[92] Major Hutson, an Arab Legion intelligence and information officer, nonetheless reported that Amman was still 'seething with a rumour to the effect that the Legion, or the Cabinet, intend handing over West Jordan to Israel, and that King Talal was deported by the British for refusing to agree'.[93] Thus, when Furlonge suggested that Britain should take action necessary to prevent Talal from returning to Amman by forcing him into a French clinic, the Foreign Office was reluctant to do anything that might lead to claims that the British had forced Talal out of Amman.[94] Even when the Talal situation reached its nadir the British were determined not to intervene. During May and June a game of cat and mouse was played out across Europe as Talal chased his fearful wife around the continent. On 29 May Queen Zein arrived at the British Embassy in Paris in a 'frightened' state seeking British protection after Talal 'threatened her with a knife' and 'attempted to kill one of his younger children'. She was therefore offered accommodation at the embassy.[95] When Hussein arrived in Paris on 30 May, he too was attacked by his father before he escorted his mother to Lausanne, where they were subsequently followed, but not found, by Talal.[96] On 11 June Queen Zein reported that 'the present situation has become intolerable'. The king was actively pursuing her in Lausanne, and she was 'seriously apprehensive' for the safety of her youngest son, Prince Hassan, who was still in the care of the king.[97] The entire episode was described by one Foreign Office official as a 'comic opera' and attracted fanciful headlines such as 'Lost Queen Hunt' in the *Evening Standard*.[98] Regarding what to do with Talal, the British were 'reluctant to take action which might be construed as an attempt to keep the King out of Jordan against his will'.[99] The Foreign Office considered, 'the only possible solution seems to be for King Talal to return to Jordan and to be put there under proper restraint'.[100] However, the British preferred not to intervene to ensure this. Thus, the British effectively decided

---

[92] Minute by Ross, 16 May 1952, FO371/98899/ET1941/41, TNA [emphasis added].
[93] G. S. Hutson to Glubb, 21 May 1952, GP2006, 90.
[94] Minute by Ross, 26 May 1952, FO371/98899/ET1941/42/G, TNA.
[95] Paris to FO, 328, 30 May 1952, FO371/98900/ET1941/50/G, TNA.
[96] 'King Talal', Hunter, 3 June 1952, FO371/98900/ET1941/54/G, TNA.
[97] 'Message from Queen Zein to Prime Minister', 11 June 1952, FO816/185, TNA.
[98] Minute by Bowker, 9 June 1952, FO371/98902/ET1941/96/G, TNA.
[99] FO to Amman, 274, 7 June 1952, FO371/98901/ET1941/66/G, TNA.
[100] Minute by Bowker, 9 June 1952, FO371/98902/ET1941/96/G, TNA.

that: 'In [the] circumstances we are inclined to wait and see how things develop.'[101] Maintaining a low profile, however, was becoming increasingly difficult, whatever the British did or did not do.

Despite now favouring the king's return to Amman, the British were still mainly concerned with avoiding the appearance of interfering. To remedy this the Foreign Office opted to 'strongly recommend' two things: firstly, that the Jordanian prime minister immediately send a 'competent emissary to Switzerland ... armed with the necessary medical evidence' to arrange Talal's return to Jordan.[102] Accordingly, Anastas Hanania, Jordan's minister of social welfare, was sent to Switzerland for that purpose within twenty-four hours.[103] Secondly, the Foreign Office recommended that the Jordanian and Swiss governments 'should issue an early statement making it clear that they are handling this affair on their own, entirely uninfluenced by any external pressure'.[104] Wardrop also raised the possibility of making a statement in Parliament 'designed to dispose of the charges that we are intervening'.[105] Eden questioned the logic of this: 'Why need we make [a] statement? Better [to] keep quiet?'[106] Eden quite understandably questioned whether making a statement would merely draw more attention to the issue and provide further fuel to the rumours. Despite claims that Britain was not interfering and only acting as 'a channel of communication', it was not strictly not interfering. Indeed, Hunter later caveated that term when he noted: 'we are still letting the Jordanians work out their own salvation *as far as possible*'.[107]

Britain's attitude towards intervening in Jordanian affairs was neatly illustrated in the aftermath of a curious incident. As Talal's reign was fast coming to an end in the summer of 1952, he was visited in Geneva by his brother, Naif – who had fled Jordan after his failed attempt to claim the throne.[108] In a message to the Jordanian prime minister, Dr Hafiz Abd al-Hadi described the encounter:

The Prince [Naif] had a prolonged audience in a locked room with the King. They asked for paper and a fountain pen. I was told by His Majesty that Na[i]f

[101] FO to Amman, 274, 7 June 1952, FO371/98901/ET1941/66/G, TNA.
[102] FO to Amman, 282, 11 June 1952, FO371/98902/ET1941/99, TNA.
[103] Amman to FO, 263, 12 June 1952, FO371/98902/ET1941/100, TNA.
[104] FO to Amman, 282, 11 June 1952, FO371/98902/ET1941/99, TNA.
[105] Minute by Wardrop, 11 June 1952, ibid.
[106] Furlonge to Amman, 267, 13 June 1952, Annotation by Eden, FO371/98902/ET1941/103, TNA.
[107] 'King Talal of Jordan', Hunter, 24 June 1952, FO371/98903/ET1941/146, TNA [emphasis added].
[108] Troutbeck to Bowker, 4 January 1952, FO371/98898/ET1942/2, TNA.

asked him for money but that he had not given him any. His Majesty would not say anything about the paper and fountain pen but he assured me that he himself had written nothing. ... In carrying out this mission Na[i]f begged me to procure something from His Majesty to the effect that there was no disagreement between him and his brother.[109]

The Foreign Office only found out about this meeting after it had taken place via press reports, resulting in the lamentation that 'we are too late to influence it'.[110] For the British not intervening should not be synonymous with not having influence. With regard to this family matter, Hunter suggested, and Wardrop agreed, that Britain should follow 'a policy of masterly inactivity'.[111] This neatly describes Britain's approach to the yearlong episode that followed Abdullah's death. Britain had a definite vested interest in the outcome of events and ensured that the Jordanian government was imbibed with strong recommendations.[112] The British may not have dictated decisions, but they certainly sought to exert significant influence by subtly pulling the strings behind the scenes.

The British followed a consistent policy of selective non-intervention. After Talal returned to Amman at the start of July 1952, the resultant furore concerned negotiations regarding the queen's potential return to Amman. In handling this matter Wardrop stated: 'our role is limited to that of a post-office'. In that vein, he initially suggested that Queen Zein's message to the prime minister, asking for a written guarantee that she and her family would be protected from Talal if she returned to Amman, be passed on without amendment.[113] However, in actuality the British went beyond the role of mere messenger. A written guarantee was not believed to carry much weight, and it was felt that the queen would be better off staying in Switzerland, from both her and the British point of view.[114] The Foreign Office preferred the queen to remain outside of Jordan as her presence might make it more difficult to maintain the present light restraint of the king.[115] Thus the Foreign Office believed it would be 'justified in "shading" our message in such a way as to avoid the suggestion that the Queen would be prepared to go home to Jordan provided she were given the written guarantee she asked for'. Consequently, Wardrop, Bowker, and Furlonge agreed to pass on the queen's message to the Jordanian

[109] Geneva to FO, 26, 16 June 1952, FO371/98902/ET1941/104/G, TNA.
[110] Minute by Hunter, 16 June 1952, FO371/98902/ET1941/110, TNA.
[111] Minute by Hunter, 16 June 1952; Minute by Wardrop, 16 June 1952, ibid.
[112] FO to Amman, 282, 11 June 1952, FO371/98902/ET1941/99, TNA.
[113] Minute by Wardrop, 7 July 1952, FO371/98903/ET1941/156, TNA.
[114] Minute by Wardrop, 8 July 1952, ibid.
[115] FO to Amman, 403, 8 July 1952, ibid.

prime minister expressing her anxiety about returning to Amman, 'but omitting any intimation that she would do so on receipt of a written guarantee'.[116] Meanwhile the queen was led to believe that Furlonge would 'discuss the matter fully with the Jordan Prime Minister'.[117] Again the British had secured their wish via subtle manipulation rather than direct intervention.

While the queen's return was being discussed, Talal's reign was visibly coming to an end and the British kept a watchful eye on Prime Minister Abu al-Huda's own manipulation of events. Talal himself was expressing his desire to abdicate, but he was being staved off from doing so by the prime minister until all the necessary arrangements could be made – not least the grooming of Hussein. The prime minister therefore refused two written abdication requests from the king. The Jordanian government, like the British, 'were playing for time in the King Talal affair. They wanted to keep him out of harm until his eldest son came of age, when his abdication could be arranged.'[118] For that reason the prime minister stated his intention to inform the Egyptian doctors, who were arriving to assess the king, that Talal 'should not (repeat not) be forced to abdicate until Hussein came of age'.[119] In a letter handed to the Egyptian doctors on their arrival he wrote:

It is important for me to let you know that the Jordan government does not, as a result of the medical advice, wish to make any constitutional arrangements (changes) which concern H.M. the King, as it is determined that he should retain his Kingdom without obstruction of his powers until his heir becomes of age.[120]

The prime minister had requested Talal be assessed by Egyptian doctors to 'stifle criticism in this or any other Arab country by pointing out that the arrangements made for Talal are based on reports from Egyptian doctors and that an Egyptian is in charge'. However, with the knowledge of the British, he actively sought to influence the doctors' assessment of Talal's condition in order to manipulate a particular outcome. Abu al-Huda sought to ensure that the Egyptian doctors recommend that Talal remain on the throne, regardless of his medical condition, until Hussein came of age. In light of the Egyptian doctors' report, however,

---

[116] Minute by Wardrop, 8 July 1952, ibid.
[117] FO to Geneva, 78, 8 July 1952, ibid.
[118] MacDermott [British Legation, Berne] to Wardrop, 25 June 1952, FO371/98903/ ET1941/140, TNA.
[119] Amman to FO, 339, 13 July 1952, FO371/98904/ET1941/166, TNA.
[120] Abu al-Huda to Kamel Bey al-Khuly and Yusef Bey Barada, 14 July 1952, FO371/ 98907/ET1941/216, TNA.

Abu al-Huda changed his mind. The Egyptian doctors told the Jordanian prime minister that it was 'a miracle' that he had 'not already murdered the Queen or someone else'.[121] The British also now believed that abdication was probably the best solution; far easier, politically, for arrangements to be made for Talal, including the possibility of him living in the Saudi-controlled Hijaz – which was now the king's desire – if he was no longer king.[122] By the end of July both the prime minister and the British had become reconciled to the benefits of Talal's abdication – the days of light restraint of the king being over.

In a final twist, however, Abu al-Huda had to resort to enforcing Talal's departure. To avoid suspicion of foul play, the prime minister wanted Talal to confirm in writing that he had made several abdication requests, but that he had dissuaded him.[123] Instead, Talal subjected the prime minister to a bitter reproach stating that he 'had no intention of abdicating'. The prime minister received reports that Talal was denouncing the government and attempting, in vain, to seek assistance from 'private individuals' and 'an officer in the Arab Legion'. The prime minister concluded 'that he had now lost all influence over Talal' and the Council of Ministers therefore summoned 'both Houses of the Majlis to an extraordinary session on 11th August at which they would be asked to approve a motion deposing Talal on the grounds of insanity'.[124] The Jordanian prime minister submitted Talal's medical reports to the two houses and said: 'Much though I hate to say so, I fear that there is little use in waiting for His Majesty's recovery from his schizophrenia.'[125] Patrick Coghill, the Arab Legion's director of general intelligence, reported that when Parliament met on 11 August 1952, during the lunch break

several deputies from both Banks … all said that the deposition of the King for medical reasons was a certainty, but in view of the importance of the decision they felt that they had to go through the motions of a long and careful examination so that the outside world would be led to believe that they had not reached so serious a decision after a brief, cursory examination of the problem.

Later that day, after a 'unanimous vote' that the king be deposed, Talal was informed of the decision, which he accepted 'quietly and with great dignity'. Talal was recorded as saying: 'I have been expecting this for

[121] Amman to FO, 348, 19 July 1952, FO371/98905/ET1941/176, TNA.
[122] Minute by Hunter, 31 July 1952; Minute by Bowker, 1 August 1952, FO371/98905/ET1941/188, TNA.
[123] Amman to FO, 365, 30 July 1952, FO816/186, TNA.
[124] Amman to FO, 375, 5 August 1952, FO371/98906/ET1941/190, TNA.
[125] Hussein, *Uneasy Lies the Head*, p. 31.

a week. If it is in the best interests of my country I accept it.' And in Coghill's words: 'So ends Act I of the tragedy of King Talal.'[126] Talal lived out the rest of his life in a private home in Istanbul, where he died in 1972.[127]

Talal's deposition passed without incident. Glubb was in Britain when Abu al-Huda announced his intention to summon the houses, but was not at all concerned that this present situation would lead to anything untoward that would 'endanger security and cause his recall'.[128] And so it proved. As Furlonge reported: 'Extensive security precautions were taken but there are no signs of disorder.'[129] Coghill reported to Glubb that both banks of the Jordan had received the news of their king's deposition with 'complete calm'.[130] Furlonge even suggested that Glubb's absence from Jordan on leave at this time was 'perhaps fortunate' from Britain's point of view, as he 'can hardly be accused of having staged it'. For that same reason, Furlonge recommended the postponement of General Robertson's proposed visit to the Arab Legion on the day after the Parliament was scheduled to meet.[131] If the commander of the British Middle East forces was to visit Jordan the day after the king was deposed, this might have fuelled unwelcome rumours. It remained important that Britain not lay itself open to charges of imperial interference.

Between Talal's deposition on 11 August 1952 and Hussein's formal accession to the throne on 2 May 1953 Prime Minister Tawfiq Abu al-Huda effectively ruled the Hashemite Kingdom. Even before his deposition, Talal's political reticence was such that it created a power vacuum in Jordan filled by the prime minister.[132] The prime minister ruled in an almost dictatorial manner, which was reassuring for the British as it neatly filled the void left by Abdullah. In Glubb's opinion, Arab countries were still presently 'unfit for full democracy on the British model', and the most stable Arab countries were those ruled by one man, as Abdullah had done. Given Talal's incapacity, Glubb felt 'the next best thing may well be to have a Prime Minister dictator'.[133] Abu al-Huda was a suitable dictator from the British perspective because, as Glubb pointed out, he was part of the old guard. He had served for thirty years under Abdullah

[126] Coghill to Glubb, 12 August 1952, GP2006, 2.
[127] Ashton, *King Hussein*, p. 31.
[128] Minute by Hunter, 6 August 1952, FO371/98906/ET1941/190, TNA.
[129] Amman to FO, 390, 11 August 1952, FO371/98906/ET1941/197, TNA.
[130] Coghill to Glubb, 12 August 1952, GP2006, 2.
[131] Furlonge to Bowker, 7 August 1952, FO371/98907/ET1941/213, TNA.
[132] Satloff, *Jordan in* Transition, pp. 58–72.
[133] 'A Note on the Situation in Jordan', Glubb, 10 December 1951, WO216/747, TNA.

and was therefore accustomed to the existing system and the relationship with Britain. Despite the prime minister's dictatorial approach, Furlonge reasoned: 'I do not think we are in a position to criticise methods which have given, and are apparently continuing to give, such generally satisfactory results.'[134] Indeed, the Foreign Office concurred, with Hunter noting: 'We need not shed too many tears over the continued presence of a firm hand at the Jordanian tiller.'[135] This position sat well with two principal tenets of British policy in Jordan: firstly, that Britain simply wanted to see Jordan remain stable; and, secondly, Britain's preference for non-interference.

Britain's non-interference policy was selective, however. The British were not prepared to give the prime minister unrestricted authority. The policy of non-interference was a means of storing influence for when it mattered most. As James Wardrop noted and James Bowker echoed, there was only so much 'influence we can safely exercise in Jordan. Undoubtedly we have some influence here, but if we abuse it ... we shall merely risk losing it altogether'.[136] On matters of 'lesser importance' the Foreign Office was happy for the prime minister to 'have his own way'. However, on matters of greater importance it was stated that 'we must insist on ours'. The difficulty was distinguishing between matters of greater or lesser importance.[137] As a general rule it was matters relating to foreign policy that Britain was most keen on influencing. Thus, when Abu al-Huda began seeking an independent line on foreign policy that appeared to depart from Abdullah's – including moves closer to the Arab League and away from Iraq – Britain decided to act.[138] In January 1952 Abu al-Huda entered Jordan into the Arab League Collective Security Pact, which was something Abdullah had previously refused to sign.[139] The Foreign Office understood: 'We shall of course have to make allowances for Jordan's wish to get on with the other Arab states.' However, Abu al-Huda was venturing into realms that impinged on direct British interests, as it moved Jordan closer to Britain's enemies. It was therefore deemed crucial that the prime minister be made aware of this, lest he

[134] Furlonge to Bowker, 17 September 1952, FO371/98859/ET1015/9, TNA.
[135] Minute by Hunter, undated [approximately late September 1952], FO371/98859/ET1015/9, TNA.
[136] Minute by Wardrop, 3 March 1952, FO371/98865/ET10393/9/G; 'Iraq–Jordan Relations', Bowker, 13 May 1952, FO371/98865/ET10393/15, TNA.
[137] Minute by Hunter, 27 March 1952, FO371/98862/ET1022/1, TNA.
[138] Furlonge to Bowker, 17 March 1952, ibid.
[139] Satloff, *Jordan in Transition*, p. 45; Abdullah, *Al-Takmilah*, pp. 8–9.

gain encouragement to go further.[140] A crucial component of Britain's non-interference policy was to ensure that the spectre of British authority remained over the decision makers. As such, Hunter noted that it would be in Britain's interest to have a brief 'showdown' with the prime minister lest he 'become too accustomed to British complaisance'.[141] Against this comment, Foreign Secretary Anthony Eden minuted 'yes', and went on to note that 'Tawfiq should be given an early reminder' of Jordan's reliance on Britain and the need for consultation.[142] This facet of Britain's relationship with the prime minister is important because it confirms the extent to which he was subject to British pressure. And if we return to the question of why he came to support Talal as Abdullah's successor, this surely exacerbates the extent to which the British desire to see Talal accede the throne was crucial to this outcome. Moreover, it demonstrates that Britain hoped to steer the Jordanian hierarchy and acknowledging this attitude is important, looking ahead to Britain's and Glubb's relationship with King Hussein.

In the two years that followed Abdullah's death the British sought to act as puppeteer in Jordan, because during the course of this trying period Jordan's strategic significance continued to increase. After the abrogation of the Anglo–Egyptian Treaty in October 1951 and the prospect of British troops having to withdraw from Egypt, Jordan was considered an option for stationing a brigade group of British forces.[143] Moreover, the military coup that overthrew King Farouk in July 1952 further destabilised Britain's relationship with Egypt, which in turn exacerbated the importance of the connection with Jordan. Meanwhile, the Arab Legion maintained the level of importance that it had been awarded since the onset of the Korean War. Having been subjected to a significant three-year reorganisation and expansion plan, which began less than four months before Abdullah's assassination, the British sought to maintain the Arab Legion at this new level. Inevitably the 1951 reorganisation scheme was adjusted to some extent, but this was largely due to a recognition that the original reorganisation plan had been hurriedly compiled in the wake of the Korean War and had not been fully thought out.[144] The

---

[140] Bowker to Furlonge, 29 March 1952, FO371/98862/ET1022/1, TNA.

[141] Minute by Hunter, 27 March 1952, ibid.

[142] Minute by Hunter, 6 April 1952, ibid.

[143] Ross to Fitzgeorge Balfour, 20 February 1952, FO371/98884/ET1204/1/G, TNA.

[144] Brian Robertson to Under-Secretary of State (WO), 27 September 1951, Melville Papers, 1/8.

War Office, for example, increased its financial contribution to provide for approximately 1,200 extra men, after it was realised that for the Arab Legion to perform the Cold War role it was now designed for, it would require a greater reserve than previously agreed.[145] Despite some tinkering with the Arab Legion's reorganisation plan, the general principle of the Arab Legion's post-Korea wartime role in conjunction with British forces remained unchanged.[146] The departure of Abdullah did nothing to alter Britain's thinking regarding the role of the Arab Legion in its Cold War defence strategy. Indeed, the Arab Legion was still considered 'our "cornerstone" in the Middle East'.[147] Jordan remained a valuable investment. The returns were primarily threefold: firstly, Britain could count on, in the event of war, an efficient division of troops already based in the Middle East, and the peacetime cost of this was much less than that of a British division; secondly, Britain had firm possession for another fifteen years, under treaty rights, of two air bases (Amman and Mafraq), which was particularly valuable given the increasing possibility of having to relinquish similar rights elsewhere in the region; and finally, it provided Britain with a foothold of goodwill and influence in the Middle East at a time when this was slipping away elsewhere in the region. Furlonge concluded that British expenditure in Jordan 'could justifiably be regarded as the essential price to be paid for retention of advantages which already seem great and which might well prove essential for the maintenance of our position in the Middle East'.[148] Abdullah's death did not, therefore, devalue the Jordanian connection or the Arab Legion in British eyes.

Abdullah's death did, however, strengthen the argument for avoiding the appearance of imperial influence. As with the previous year the question of exactly which Whitehall department should finance the Arab Legion was raised by the chancellor. The previous year the Labour chancellor, Hugh Gaitskell, had requested that the subsidy be switched from the Foreign Office to the War Office budget, and at the end of 1951 the new Conservative chancellor, Richard Austin Butler, made the same demand because he considered it a constituent part of British strategy. He exclaimed: 'I am convinced that, whatever may have been the situation in the past, it is the military aspect which is paramount now.'[149] However,

[145] 'Development of the Arab Legion', 4 October 1951, ibid.; FO to Amman, 22, 16 January 1952, FO371/98882/ET1202/1, TNA.
[146] 'Expansion of the Arab Legion', WO, 16 September 1952, Melville Papers, 3/40.
[147] Minute by Brownjohn to Mcleod, 13 December 1951, WO216/454, TNA.
[148] Furlonge to Eden, 144, 24 December 1952, FO371/98857/ET1013/14, TNA.
[149] Butler to Head, 10 December 1951, FO371/91823/ET1201/93/G, TNA.

the political situation was now even more sensitive. Secretary of State for War Antony Head referred Butler to Bevin's argument against this back in January. And Eden added:

> In my opinion the objections raised by Bevin when this proposal was put to him by Gaitskell early this year have even more force now than they had then. We are no longer dealing with an absolute monarch, but with a Cabinet which is responsible to Parliament, and has to take account of popular feeling. As you yourself recognise, it would be politically undesirable to suggest openly that the Legion was a mere adjunct of the British Army.[150]

Priya Satia has argued that because of the significance of political ideologies and perceptions, after the First World War 'covert empire came into its own in the Middle East'.[151] And the covert aspect of empire became even more important during the increasingly anti-imperial, good-versus-evil climate of the Cold War era.

In the grand scheme of things, Abdullah's assassination did not affect the role of Jordan or the Arab Legion in British strategy. On the contrary, external events, such as the situation in Egypt, increased the significance of the Anglo–Jordanian relationship. For that reason Britain paid considerable attention to maintaining a malleable pro-British regime in Jordan. Britain recognised that it could no longer rely on Abdullah's steadying hand and there could be 'no return to the benevolent autocracy exercised by Abdullah until the promulgation of the present constitution'.[152] Yet that did not stop it attempting to direct Jordan's royal and political future.

Despite obtaining independence five years earlier, King Abdullah and the Jordanian government continued to look towards Britain in moments of crisis – the 1948 War being a prime example. With Abdullah gone, Britain stood out even more as the real powerbroker in Jordanian politics as all those interested in Jordanian affairs looked towards Britain as the arbiter of Jordan's future. Abdullah, Samir al-Rifai, Abu al-Huda, Naif, Talal, Queen Zein, and the Iraqis all turned to Britain for assistance – for advice, protection, or in pursuit of support for their own designs. It is therefore unsurprising that post-Abdullah Jordan emerged largely according to the template desired by the British, taking into account Britain's own limitations regarding direct intervention. Despite the ignominy of

---

[150] Eden to Butler, 29 December 1951, ibid.
[151] Satia, *Spies in Arabia*, pp. 8, 335.
[152] 'Assassination of King Abdulla of Jordan', 22 July 1951, FO371/91839/ET1942/40, TNA.

Talal's departure from Jordan, his reign had effectively served its purpose. As Furlonge reflected, the country had to readjust 'itself to the new conditions created by the disappearance from the scene, first of all of King Abdullah and, later, of my predecessor [Kirkbride]'. And this process was aided by the 'steadying and stabilising influence' of having Talal on the throne and in Jordan.[153] King Hussein concurred, later reflecting that, 'if my father, with my mother by his side, had not stepped in after the murder of my grandfather, the history of Jordan might have been very different'.[154] Despite the tragic turmoil behind the scenes caused by Talal's mental illness, his royal presence had provided a semblance of stability and proper constitutional practice.

This episode demonstrates that, despite independence, Britain still had a desire and the capability to exert influence at the highest level of Jordanian politics. Hunter summed up Britain's attitude when he remarked that: 'since we pay the piper we are entitled to call the tune'.[155] While wary that they should not – and could not – dictate internal Jordanian affairs, the British had a definite vested interest in Jordan's general stability, its pro-British leaning, and the reliability of the Arab Legion. The Cold War climate and the rise of Arab republicanism had increased Britain's dependence on the Hashemite connection in Jordan. In pursuit of these interests, the British were prepared to intervene – often via subtle manipulation – when deemed necessary. Behind the scenes the British quietly and selectively pulled the strings in an attempt to ensure that Jordan and its hierarchy remained stable and pro-British. In some respects, this goes against the grain of L. Carl Brown's contention that the idea of a great power puppeteer directing a small puppet state is a 'myth' and that the so-called puppet usually drove events rather than the so-called puppeteer.[156] Whether or not the succession crisis would have played out differently without Britain's guiding hand will forever remain counterfactual. What is certain, however, is that the succession process broadly followed Britain's desire, though it is true that Britain was all the time responding to events being driven on the ground: Abdullah's assassination; popular support for Talal; and the king's mental illness. In that respect, therefore, this account is not so far removed from Brown's theory.

[153] Furlonge to Eden, 63, 22 May 1952, FO816/184, TNA.
[154] Hussein, *Uneasy Lies the Head*, pp. 10–11.
[155] Minute by Hunter, 2 August 1951, FO371/91839/ET1942/40, TNA.
[156] Brown, *International Politics and the Middle East*, pp. 197–252.

The real significance of this episode, though, relates not to identifying a master puppeteer – the overarching author of events – but acknowledging that this is the role that Britain was trying to cultivate. Regardless of the significance to the outcome of events, the British acted like a puppeteer in search of a puppet and they hoped that Hussein would fulfil that role.

7

The Glubb Paradox and King Hussein's Quest for Control of the Arab Legion

After the assassination of Abdullah the British pinned their hopes on Hussein as the best option for maintaining the 'special' relationship with Jordan. Yet Hussein had no intention of playing the pliant puppet role the British had intended for him. Less than three years after he acceded the throne – on 2 May 1953 – the young king proved this when he broke free of British constraints in a manner that could not have been imagined during the era of his grandfather. On 1 March 1956 Hussein unceremoniously dismissed Glubb and several other British officers from the Arab Legion. Hussein described it as 'a surgical operation that had to be done brutally. ... Though I knew General Glubb would be upset by the brusqueness, it had to be done the way I did it.'[1] In public Glubb maintained that he had 'no complaints'.[2] In private, however, he could not hide his regret 'that King Hussein did things in such an unnecessarily high-handed manner'.[3] The process that led to this fait accompli was a complex one, and the purpose of this chapter is to explore the events that led to this move – to reassess the early years of Hussein's reign and the final years of Glubb's.

Perhaps unsurprisingly, the existing historiography detailing Glubb's dismissal has focused primarily on King Hussein and his rationale. Gaining an accurate appreciation of any individual's thought process is inherently difficult – especially in this case, given the scarcity of Arab sources. It is perhaps for this reason that Glubb's dismissal, as Robert

[1] Hussein, *Uneasy Lies the Head*, pp. 114–17.
[2] http://news.bbc.co.uk/onthisday/hi/dates/stories/march/2/newsid_2514000/2514379.stm (accessed: 4 January 2014).
[3] Glubb to Harold MacMichael, 10 March 1956, MacMichael Papers, 1/4, MECA.

Satloff observed, has assumed 'almost mythical dimensions'.⁴ While a broad consensus exists that Hussein dismissed Glubb to consolidate his position, there are two principal variances on this theme. The first is that it was a matter of survival. Uriel Dann considers the decision primarily a reaction to Cairo's propaganda campaign directed against Glubb. The king's survival was endangered by association, hence Glubb's removal.⁵ The second suggests it was a question of authority – personal and/or political. Nigel Ashton concludes that it was an expression of the king's desire to assert his personal authority and was compounded by his attachment to Arab nationalism.⁶ Avi Shlaim views it more broadly as an expression of Jordanian independence.⁷ Other contributors have accentuated Glubb and Hussein's personal differences, with Philip Robins emphasising the generational divide.⁸ All these factors contributed to Hussein's decision to some extent. Yet they were unified by a single common denominator: British obstinacy. Hussein's action, as this chapter illustrates, was primarily a reaction against being ignored by the British and restricted as a result of Britain's apparent desire to control. And Glubb symbolised this rebuke.

In analysing the events that led to Glubb's dismissal it is important to consider two contingent components: the trigger and the trail. The first part of this chapter will examine the trail that led to the eventual trigger moment, tracing the nature and evolution of Hussein's relationship with Glubb and Britain. The second part will hone in on the months immediately preceding the dismissal to reveal exactly what triggered the decision. Regarding the trigger, one of the most intriguing questions, as posed by Robert Satloff, is: 'why March 1?' Satloff pointed to a mounting fear of renewed fighting between Israel and the Arab states.⁹ Surprisingly, subsequent studies have overlooked this pertinent observation. Based on significant new evidence, this chapter will further emphasise the threat of renewed Arab–Israeli conflict as an explanation for the abrupt manner of the dismissal and yet simultaneously posit that this trigger merely brought forward and added a grievous touch to a process of vanquishing British control that had already been set in motion by October 1955. Unpacking the timing of the decision is crucial to understanding the motive, and in

---

⁴ Satloff, *Jordan in Transition*, p. 135.
⁵ Dann, *Challenge of Arab Radicalism*, pp. 32–3.
⁶ Ashton, *King Hussein*, p. 53.
⁷ Shlaim, *Lion of Jordan*, p. 99.
⁸ Robins, *History of Jordan*, pp. 93–4.
⁹ Satloff, *Jordan in Transition*, pp. 140–2.

order to comprehend why Glubb was dismissed, it is imperative that the trigger and the trail are considered together. In so doing, this chapter finds that the British were, in some respects, the architects of their own – and Glubb's – downfall. Several studies note that Britain should not have been surprised that Glubb was dismissed. However, perhaps because the British angle was not their primary focus, these studies have tended to acknowledge this aspect in passing reference, with a wry smile at Britain's misplaced confidence, and have neither fully appreciated its significance nor acknowledged how it contributed to the dismissal of Glubb and several other British officers from the Arab Legion. Philip Robins, for example, remarked that 'in retrospect, Glubb and others should not have been so sure of themselves'.[10] However, as this chapter illustrates, British complacency was conversely borne out of its uncertainty rather than vice versa. This precluded Britain from attending to Hussein's increasing frustrations, which in turn prompted the king to take decisive action.

Hussein's decision to fracture the British connection less than three years after acceding the throne was exactly what Britain had tried to guard against in the wake of Abdullah's assassination. Having decided on Talal as a mere stopgap until Hussein came of age, the British immediately turned their attention towards grooming Hussein to be a pro-British ruler akin to his grandfather. Hussein switched schools from Alexandria, Egypt, to Harrow, London, where it was hoped he could form personal bonds that would encourage him to maintain the British connection. While the year that Hussein spent at Harrow was thought useful, it was shorter than considered necessary to integrate Hussein into the British world.[11] Upon finishing his schooling Hussein was therefore sent to Sandhurst. The Foreign Office was anxious about Hussein's stint at the military academy, where cadets 'must expect to put up with some pretty rigorous discipline'. The concern was that: 'There is, of course, always the risk that either the general treatment he receives or some (possibly imagined) slight may make an unfortunate impression on the King such as to prejudice him against this country for the rest of his days.'[12] His housemaster at Harrow reported that Hussein reacted badly when disciplined for breaking school rules, such as driving his car without permission.[13]

[10] Robins, *History of Jordan*, pp. 93–4; Tal, *Politics, the Military, and National Security*, pp. 28–9; Dann, *Challenge of Arab Radicalism*, p. 31.
[11] Minute by Seton Dearden, 21 August 1952, FO816/187, TNA.
[12] Wardrop to Furlonge, 2 September 1952, FO371/98908/ET1941/229/G, TNA.
[13] 'The Emir Hussein of Jordan', Furlonge, 10 July 1952, FO371/98904/ET1941/171/G, TNA.

The last thing Britain wanted was to frustrate and rile Hussein with military discipline. The Foreign Office was anxious that 'he should derive the greatest possible benefit from his short course at the College and go home with the happiest possible recollections of it'.[14] The future king was thus afforded some privileges at Sandhurst. He had a room to himself, complete with modern conveniences; he had a shared servant to clean his equipment; and he was afforded leniency to account for his inexperience.[15] When Hussein left Sandhurst the Foreign Office was satisfied with the result. He was believed to have 'both enjoyed his course and profited by it, not only in his military instruction but in the many friends he has made and the aspects of British life' that had been revealed to him.[16] Indeed, in his memoirs Hussein reflected positively on all aspects of his Sandhurst experience.[17] This was considered a boost to Britain's future relationship with Jordan, with James Bowker noting: 'The continuance of good relations between the United Kingdom and the Kingdom of Jordan is of great importance, and in this the friendship of the young King, in whose education the six months at Sandhurst have virtually taken the place of three years at a university, will play an essential part.'[18]

Despite the apparent success of Hussein's Sandhurst stint, Britain's relationship with the new king got off to an ominous start as a result of discussions concerning how best to occupy Hussein after his Sandhurst course finished in February 1953. In anticipation of a several-month gap until his accession to the throne in May, his mother, Queen Zein, asked the Foreign Office to consider options for his occupation during this interim period. However, in what Bowker described as a 'regrettable accident', Hussein 'got wind' of British 'ideas for his occupation after February' prematurely. The Foreign Office consulted several departments and the War Office proposal was an attachment to the Royal Horse Guards at Windsor. It was rumours regarding this option that reached Hussein. The idea that the British planned for him to spend time in a 'British "Royal Regiment"' led Hussein to express 'indignation at such a suggestion which he said he would never accept'.[19] Upon Hussein's premature discovery they 'did not (repeat not) reveal that this was done

[14] Wardrop to Furlonge, 2 September 1952, FO371/98908/ET1941/229/G, TNA.
[15] 'King Hussein', Hunter, 8 September 1952, FO371/98909/ET1941/238/G, TNA.
[16] Bowker to Major-General Dawnay, 4 February 1953, FO371/98909/ET1941/238/G, TNA.
[17] Hussein, *Uneasy Lies the Head*, pp. 36–7.
[18] Bowker to Major-General Dawnay, 4 February 1953, FO371/98909/ET1941/238/G, TNA.
[19] Bowker to Furlonge, 1 December 1952, FO816/187, TNA.

in accordance with Queen Zein's or the Jordan Government's wishes'. Instead the British decided to halt such talks until guided further by his mother.[20] The British were resolved to keep the queen's secret because ultimately she was believed to be 'a helpful power behind the throne and worth cultivating'.[21] Behind the scenes Zein was an astute political operator and a 'rock of stability' for both her husband and son.[22] The Foreign Office therefore deemed it more important to keep Queen Zein onside rather than appease Hussein, and hoped 'this unhappy affair ... will not cause any lasting trouble'.[23] However, this incident ignited the notion that Britain sought to control Hussein and put Britain's relationship with the king-in-waiting off on the wrong foot.

While the British were attempting to groom Hussein in London, Glubb was endeavouring to quell the threat of nationalism that had emerged within the Arab Legion. The 1948 War was a key turning point in this regard, as it was for armies throughout the Middle East. It led to a successful military coup in Syria in 1949 and helped consolidate the Free Officers movement that overturned the Egyptian monarchy in 1952.[24] Similar aspirations flourished within the Arab Legion, where a Free Officers movement also emerged, though it was less united than its Egyptian counterpart on which it was modelled.[25] One of its leading members – though not one of its founders – was Ali Abu Nowar, who had fought in Jerusalem in 1948 and been a member of the marginalised armistice delegation sent to Rhodes. He described himself as the 'the anti-British number one in the Jordanian Army', and explained that his political inclination 'came all from Palestine'.[26] Prior to 1948, anti-British nationalism in the Arab Legion was considered non-existent. As Lieutenant-Colonel Melville explained: 'There weren't the Ali Abu Nowar's in those days – as far as one knew. They may have been cooking in the background, but they hadn't emerged.'[27] Indeed, in October 1948 'Teal' Ashton described Abu Nowar as 'an exceptionally good man', and when he was transferred back to divisional headquarters, Ashton lamented: 'We shall miss him sadly as he held our strangely cosmopolitan

[20] FO to Amman, 707, 27 November 1952, ibid.
[21] Minute by Hunter, 19 September 1952, FO371/98867/ET10393/61, TNA.
[22] Ashton, *King Hussein*, p. 20.
[23] Wardrop to Furlonge, 1 December 1952, FO816/187, TNA.
[24] Shlaim, *Lion of Jordan*, p. 64; Gamal Abd al-Nasser, *Egypt's Liberation: The Philosophy of the Revolution* (Washington, DC, 1956), pp. 19–24.
[25] Massad, *Colonial Effects*, p. 178.
[26] Interview with Ali Abu Nowar, 20 June 1990, Geyelin Papers.
[27] Author interview with Robert K. Melville, 13 March 2013, London.

family together in an incredible way.'[28] The 1948 War ruptured this affinity, though it was not until the 1950s that the nationalist movement really came to prominence. During Abdullah's reign Jordan had been ruled by a small group of 'king's men', which made it difficult for nationalists to gain political influence. The succession crisis therefore provided an opportunity for nationalists to exploit. Glubb observed that it was during the uncertain period after Abdullah's assassination that Ali Abu Nowar 'suddenly emerged as an extremist politician'.[29] Glubb alleged that after Talal became king, Abu Nowar sought a private interview with Jordan's new ruler and fruitlessly tried to convince Talal that Glubb had murdered Abdullah.[30] This is somewhat ironic given Abu Nowar's own admission, in a private meeting with Major-General Benson, that at the time of Abdullah's murder he himself was involved in a separate plot, which was almost complete, to assassinate the king.[31] This, though, is at odds with Abu Nowar's retrospective complaint that Abdullah was unjustly 'talked about in an unfavourable way' and his praise for Abdullah opposing Britain and therefore saving Jerusalem in 1948.[32] What is certain is that Abu Nowar sought to exploit the political upheaval created by Abdullah's assassination and that Glubb was equally determined to thwart him. Describing Abu Nowar, and other nationalist elements within the Arab Legion, Melville explained: 'They were perfectly polite, but you could tell that they had an agenda that wasn't the same as ours.'[33] This politeness, however, did not prevent Abu Nowar and Glubb from locking horns. At a meeting of Arab Legion officers the two men 'had a very hot argument', in which both parties accused the other of politicising the Arab Legion. Abu Nowar explained that as a result of this:

All the officers hated me. Glubb was checked for the first time in Jordan, his authority was checked and he was sick! He had to have lunch at my brigade headquarters. He was at the end of the table and I was at the other end. All the time, all he did was gaze at me and I gaze at him, not talk. When he finished his lunch, we said goodbye to him. He shook hands with everybody. When I stretched my arm to shake his hand, he withdrew it.[34]

---

[28] Ashton to Glubb, 14 October 1948, GP2006, 85.

[29] 'King Husain & the Arab Legion', Glubb, 11 October 1955, FO371/115683/VJ12011/2, TNA; Salibi, *Modern History of Jordan*, p. 189.

[30] 'King Husain & the Arab Legion', Glubb, 11 October 1955, FO371/115683/VJ12011/2, TNA.

[31] 'Report by Major-General E. R. Benson in Amplification of the Minutes of the 10th Meeting of the AJJDB', 24 July 1956, FO371/121534/VJ1192/91/G, TNA.

[32] Interview with Ali Abu Nowar, 20 June 1990, Geyelin Papers.

[33] Author interview with Robert K. Melville, 13 March 2013, London.

[34] Interview with Ali Abu Nowar, 20 June 1990, Geyelin Papers.

In a variation on Laleh Khalili's theme of confinement and 'incarceration of civilians and combatants' being used as a counterinsurgency tactic,[35] Glubb's primary means of nullifying the threat of adverse political influence infiltrating the Arab Legion was to isolate potential threats from positions of influence, to confine them to roles, preferably outside Jordan, where they would be unable to spread their ideas. For political reasons Glubb proposed that Ali al-Hiyari, commander of the 5th Regiment, be removed from Jordan for six months.[36] And recognising the threat Ali Abu Nowar posed, in September 1952 Glubb had him transferred to Paris as military attaché, where it was hoped he would be beyond doing harm in Jordan and the Arab Legion.[37]

This move backfired, though, as it was during his exile in Paris that Ali Abu Nowar got to know the London-based Hussein.[38] They met when Hussein stopped in the French capital while travelling from London to Amman, and the roots of their political outlook made it easy for them to find common ground. Abu Nowar's anti-British attitude was entrenched in a sense of perpetual betrayal. As he explained: 'In the First World War, we joined you [Britain] and the Arab world is stabbed in the back of King Husayn. In the Second World War, we joined you and we Arabs lost to Israel. In the third war, if we join you again you may give us all to Israel.'[39] Similarly, Hussein's political outlook was rooted in the issue of Britain's 'broken' promises to the Arabs after the First World War.[40] He was particularly influenced by George Antonius's account of this event based on Hashemite sources.[41] Hussein was therefore well disposed to find accord with Ali Abu Nowar during their first meeting, which Abu Nowar recounted:

I opened the Arab-British fight. From there to Palestine, to the intentions of his grand-grandfather [Sharif Husayn], to the intentions of his grandfather [Abdullah], to the intentions of his father, to our aspirations as people, to how much we cling to his family.[42]

[35] Khalili, *Time in the Shadows*, pp. 6, 239.
[36] Qiada [Hutton] to TJL [Melville], 31 October 1953, Melville Papers, 10/70.
[37] 'King Husain & the Arab Legion', Glubb, 11 October 1955, FO371/115683/VJ12011/2, TNA.
[38] Shlaim, *Lion of Jordan*, pp. 64–5.
[39] Interview with Ali Abu Nowar, 20 June 1990, Geyelin Papers.
[40] Hussein, *Uneasy Lies the Head*, p. 73.
[41] Ibid., pp. 1, 73; Ashton, *King Hussein*, pp. 13–15; George Antonius, *The Arab Awakening: The Story of the Arab National Movement* (London, 1938).
[42] Interview with Ali Abu Nowar, 20 June 1990, Geyelin Papers.

This would have chimed with Hussein, who had a strong sense of his Hashemite heritage and dynastic duty.[43] They convened again in London where they discussed,

how to be an independent state, and how to defend our country. ... What would be the relations between us and the other Arab countries? We ended this by having a program of what should be done – starting by finishing the army command from the British, terminating the treaty, having an Arab alliance, having a new parliament and government. ... We did not put them in a real order of priority, except for one, the freeing of the Jordanian Army from the British command. That was priority number one and that was very clear.[44]

When Hussein finally arrived in Jordan to accede the throne, he did so not only with a degree of resentment from his personal experience of British attempts to control him, but also with the nationalist indignation of the exiled Ali Abu Nowar.

Hussein's early resentment of British control, particularly in relation to the Arab Legion, was further compounded just a few months after his accession when he was faced with his first significant test: a devastating attack by the IDF on the Jordanian village of Qibya on 14 October 1953. Since the end of the 1948 War the Jordan–Israeli border had been beset by tension. The general pattern was incidents of infiltration from Jordan into Israel, which subsequently prompted retaliatory raids by the IDF on villages inside the West Bank. As the Israeli foreign minister, Moshe Sharett, acknowledged, retaliatory action 'had become routine'.[45] According to Benny Morris, at least 90 per cent of Arab infiltration was economically or socially motivated, including farmers harvesting crops.[46] Sometimes, however, infiltration took the form of deliberate acts of sabotage, which Glubb believed was often sponsored by anti-Hashemite elements, including Egypt and Saudi Arabia. The Israeli raid on Qibya was preceded by a murderous attack of this ilk. On 13 October infiltrators from Jordan entered the Israeli settlement of Yehuda, where a grenade was thrown into a house, killing a mother and two of her children. As ever, the Arab Legion did all it could to bring the infiltrators swiftly to justice. The Arab Legion immediately invited Israeli trackers with dogs to follow the perpetrators into Jordan. According to Morris, Glubb was so concerned by

[43] Interview with Zeid al-Rifai, 3 March 1994, ibid.
[44] Interview with Ali Abu Nowar, 20 June 1990, ibid.
[45] Walid Khalidi and Neil Caplan (eds.), 'The 1953 Qibya Raid Revisited: Excerpts from Moshe Sharett's Diaries', *Journal of Palestine Studies*, 31:4 (2002), p. 83.
[46] Morris, *Israel's Border Wars*, p. 428.

the potential ramifications of the Yehuda incident that he was compelled to do this for the 'first time'.[47] Newly available evidence reveals that this was not new, however. After a previous murderous incident in June 1953 Glubb had 'immediately offered [to] permit Israel police with dogs [to] follow tracks into Jordan with a view [to] arrest [the] murderer'.[48] Thereafter this agreement was left in place as a means of dealing with infiltration.[49] It was therefore invoked during the Yehuda incident, but the scent of the infiltrators was lost and the perpetrators escaped.[50] The following day the Israeli–Jordanian Mixed Armistice Commission met. The Jordanian representatives denounced the attack and promised to do everything possible 'to prevent such atrocities in the future'. Moshe Sharett welcomed this conciliatory gesture. However, Israeli plans for a 'retaliation operation' were already in place.[51] That night future Israeli prime minister Ariel Sharon led a special forces unit of the IDF in a merciless attack on the village of Qibya, leaving between sixty and seventy Arab villagers – men, women, and children – dead.[52] The Chief of Staff of the UN Truce Supervision Organisation, Major General Vagn Bennike, reported to the UN Security Council that: 'Bullet ridden bodies near the doorways and multiple hits in the doors of the demolished homes indicated that the inhabitants had been forced to remain inside while their homes were blown up over them.'[53] Because of the international condemnation, Ben-Gurion denied any official IDF involvement.[54] He claimed that it was an ad hoc retaliation by inhabitants of the local Israeli settlements and insisted that 'all responsibility must rest with the Transjordan Government which for many years tolerated and thereby encouraged attacks ... against Israeli citizens'.[55] However, much to Moshe Sharett's disgust, the retaliation had been sanctioned at the highest level, as a means of deterring future attacks on Israel.[56]

The Qibya incident was indicative of the dilemma facing the Arab Legion. On one hand, it was doing all it could to prevent infiltration emanating from Jordan and bringing the perpetrators to justice. Yet on the

[47] Ibid., p. 257.
[48] Qiada [Hutson] to TJL [Melville], 20 June 1953, Melville Papers, 10/70.
[49] Qiada [Glubb] to TJL [Melville], 23 June 1953, ibid.
[50] HQ Arab Legion [Hutson] to unknown, 15 October 1953, GP2006, 51.
[51] Khalidi and Caplan (eds.), 'Moshe Sharett's Diaries', pp. 81–2.
[52] Ibid., pp. 79–82; Morris, *Israel's Border Wars*, pp. 260–1; Glubb, *Soldier*, p. 313; Shlaim, *Iron Wall*, pp. 90–1.
[53] Quoted in: Khalidi and Caplan (eds.), 'Moshe Sharett's Diaries', p. 80.
[54] Shlaim, *Iron Wall*, pp. 91–2.
[55] *SWB, Part IV*, 23 October 1953, p. 27.
[56] Khalidi and Caplan (eds.), 'Moshe Sharett's Diaries', pp. 79, 81–2; Shlaim, *Iron Wall*, p. 92.

other hand, it was responsible for defending against Israeli retaliation. As a consequence of a rise in attacks by Israeli forces in January 1953, including prominent attacks on Falama and Rantis, all villages along the frontier were put on a 'state of defence'.[57] Moreover, Glubb issued a Special Order to all officers of the Arab Legion, which made abundantly clear that any breach of the border from Israel should be met with force. He stated:

Incidents continue to occur from time to time, in which officers or O.R.'s [other ranks] of the Arab Legion fail to fire upon enemy patrols or forces which enter the Kingdom, and subsequently excuse themselves on the grounds that they had no orders to fire. It is hereby notified once again, that it is the duty of every officer and man of the Arab Legion to open fire on any enemy force which enters the Kingdom of Jordan, on the sole condition that he is sure that the enemy has crossed the border and entered the Kingdom.

He added: 'In future any commander who fails to seek out and attack an enemy who has entered the Kingdom within reach of his position, will be liable to trial by Court Martial.'[58] After Qibya, Glubb reissued this Special Order because the local Arab Legion units had not been deployed, and this was exactly the kind of situation the Special Order was designed to counter.[59] Long-serving British officer 'Teal' Ashton was in command of the local Arab Legion brigade that night, and in a Court of Inquiry he was found to have been negligent.[60] As a result of the inquiry, one Arab officer was imprisoned, one was pensioned off, another Arab officer was demoted, and Ashton was dismissed.[61]

Ashton's dismissal may have been influenced by the political fallout created by the Qibya incident, as the Arab Legion came under intense criticism throughout the country for not defending Qibya. This put the Arab Legion and the British connection under extreme scrutiny.[62] The Jordanian press and pamphlets distributed on behalf of the 'Free Officers in Jordan' demanded the dismissal of Glubb and those British officers responsible for failing to protect Jordan's border villages.[63] Demonstrations in Amman – organised by the political opposition – made similar demands and had to be suppressed by the Arab Legion.[64]

[57] 'A Directive for Putting Villages in a State of Defence', 8 February 1953, GP2006, 78.
[58] 'Special Order', Glubb, 19 February 1953, GP2006, 2.
[59] Glubb to 'All British Officers', 2 November 1953, ibid.
[60] Bromage, *Soldier in Arabia*, pp. 61–2.
[61] *SWB, Part IV*, 13 December 1953, p. 50.
[62] Amman to FO, 508, 16 October 1953, FO371/104788/ER1091/365, TNA.
[63] *SWB, Part IV*, 3 November 1953, p. 35; Anderson, *Nationalist Voices*, p. 151.
[64] Anderson, *Nationalist Voices*, p. 151; Young, *Arab Legion*, p. 12.

Egypt's *Voice of the Arabs* radio programme complained that, like the 1948 War, the Arab Legion had been hampered by its British officers and therefore called on Jordan to Arabise command of its army and 'make it clear to Britain that she will not accept the arbitrary control of the British command over the Arab Legion'.[65] Glubb reported that the 'whole [of] Jordan [was] strongly shaken', resulting in 'extremist politicians and agitators' visiting front-line villages 'preaching intense hatred of Britain'. When he and other officers drove through villages on the West Bank, they were subjected to 'curses and insults'.[66] Britain presented Israel with a note of protest after Qibya, which Israel's foreign minister described as 'a scathing and most severe denunciation of the dreadful act in the village of Qibya'.[67] However, the Jordanian government considered it inadequate and requested that Britain sever diplomatic relations with Israel or prohibit trade and transfer of currency. The Jordanian government also requested – in a document drafted in Glubb's handwriting – the expansion of the Arab Legion on the basis that this incident proved that Britain could not provide rapid assistance to Jordan and therefore it was necessary for the Arab Legion to be sufficiently strengthened so that it could resist attack on its own.[68]

However, this demand to expand the Arab Legion came at a time when Britain was once again looking to scale back expenditure on this force. Although a three-year expansion plan had been initiated in 1951, by the end of 1952 the international situation was perceived to have 'changed owing to the progress of Western Re-armament, and a major war within the next few years' was no longer considered likely. It was therefore deemed necessary to overhaul the Arab Legion's plans 'to suit the new World situation'. Given Britain's worsening financial status, this effectively meant that the Arab Legion's expansion would be brought to a halt – if not subject to reductions.[69] Even before Qibya, Glubb was adamant that the subsidy needed to be increased to help the Arab Legion cope with Israeli belligerence. However, despite War Office support, the Treasury refused the Foreign Office's request for a £1 million increase in

---

[65] *SWB, Part IV*, 30 October 1953, p. 32.
[66] Qiada [Glubb] to TJL [Cruickshank], FO, and WO, 16 October 1953, FO371/104789/ER1091/385, TNA.
[67] Khalidi and Caplan (eds.), 'Moshe Sharett's Diaries', p. 82.
[68] Jordan Government to HMG, 17 October 1953, GP2006, 34, 40; 'Memorandum on the Defence of Jordan', 7 November 1953, GP2006, 2.
[69] 'Build up of Reserves for the Arab Legion', Glubb, 19 October 1952, Melville Papers, 2/ 22.

the subsidy for 1954/5.[70] As before, the Israeli emphasis regarding the Arab Legion's role was not sufficient justification for Treasury approval. Instead the Foreign Office subsidy remained at £7.5 million, supplemented by £1.8 million contributed by the War Office for the reservist scheme and the Mobile Desert Force.[71] Thereafter the Foreign Office annual subsidy plateaued at £7.5 million for every year between 1953 and 1956. Additional targeted subsidies (e.g., for an anti-tank unit and the Dead Sea Flotilla) meant that Britain's total annual expenditure on the Arab Legion during this period was between £9.3 million and £10.2 million.[72] The Arab Legion had only experienced rapid growth in 1951 because of its new role in Britain's global defence plans, and the Treasury was not prepared to sanction increases in the Arab Legion merely to deal with Israel – despite high-profile incidents such as Qibya.

The Qibya incident did, however, prompt Hussein to take a more active political role.[73] In particular, it drew his attention to the Arab Legion and therefore to the limitations on his authority imposed by Britain. The failure to obtain any expansion of the Arab Legion was a bitter blow – which Glubb shared – but perhaps more galling than the subsidy amount was the method of its payment, which was paid directly to Glubb and the Arab Legion. The Jordanian government queried this setup in 1950, but it was agreed that while payments to the War Office and other British departments should be deducted at source, the balance of the subsidy should be paid direct to the Arab Legion.[74] The issue was raised again in August 1953 and then again during the Anglo–Jordanian financial talks in October/November – immediately after Qibya. The Jordanians claimed it was contrary to the treaty, but the British were concerned that 'we cannot trust the Jordan Government to deal fairly by the Legion once they get their hands on the subsidy'.[75] After a brief period of silence on this issue the British opted to assume that the Jordanians had dropped this request.[76] However, Hussein returned to the matter with renewed vigour when he visited London in December 1954. At the end of the visit, the British again believed – or at least hoped – that the Jordanian

---

[70] Minute by Thompson, 24 February 1954, FO371/110924/VJ1201/6, TNA.
[71] Furlonge to Stephenson, 5 April 1954, FO371/110924/VJ1201/20, TNA.
[72] Falla to Bredin, 25 August 1954, FO371/110925/VJ1202/16/G; 'The Arab Legion', 13 September 1955, FO371/115682/VJ12010/1, TNA.
[73] Ashton, *King Hussein*, p. 41; Shlaim, *Lion of Jordan*, p. 76.
[74] Drake to Falla, 28 April 1954, FO371/110924/VJ1201/19, TNA.
[75] 'Method of Payment of Arab Legion Subsidy', Thompson, 24 March 1954, FO371/110924/VJ1201/18, TNA.
[76] Russell Edmunds to Thompson, 5 July 1954, FO371/110924/VJ1201/26, TNA.

delegation had returned to Amman having 'agreed (reluctantly) to drop their demand for the Arab Legion subsidy to be paid direct'.[77] The use of the term 'reluctantly' is telling. Whatever the Jordanian delegation said – or whatever the British heard – Hussein was not satisfied with this outcome. Moreover, at least one Foreign Office official recognised this and counselled:

I do not feel very happy about the way we have left this. The Jordanians will never be satisfied with the present method of payment, and we shall have recurrent trouble over it. Are we really sure that we have been into their case thoroughly and that there is nothing more we can do?[78]

True to this portent, Hussein was left frustrated and resentful.

The outcome of these talks proved undesirable to both parties. The British failed to listen to the Jordanians' main concerns, they reciprocated, and as a result, neither side achieved its desired ends. During this visit the Jordanian delegation raised three primary issues: It initiated exploratory discussions to elicit British views on revising the treaty; it requested additional financial assistance for the National Guard; and it suggested that the Arab Legion subsidy be paid directly to the Jordanian government. At the end of this visit, the Jordanian delegation handed over an aide memoire, and it was the method of payment for the Arab Legion that received by far the most detailed attention.[79] This was Jordan's primary objective. Meanwhile Britain's principal target was to obtain permission to move a British armoured regiment from Aqaba, in the south of Jordan, to Mafraq, in the north. Britain's regional defence strategy was now based on securing the northern tier, from Turkey to Pakistan. It was deemed vitally important to this strategy to have British forces stationed in north Jordan so that they could be deployed quickly into Iraq in the event of war with the Soviet Union.[80] To that end, Britain offered to accede partially to one of Jordan's lesser requests. During the December talks the British had inferred that the Jordanians would look favourably on their request if additional funding for the National Guard were forthcoming.[81] Despite deep ministerial and Treasury reluctance, Britain therefore offered an additional £350,000 per annum to support the National Guard for the next five years. This was a fraction of the

[77] Eden to Butler, 31 December 1954, FO371/115670/VJ1192/1/G, TNA.
[78] Minute by [indecipherable signature], 1 January 1955, FO371/115670/VJ1192/2, TNA.
[79] 'Aide-Memoire', 30 December 1954, FO371/115670/VJ1192/2, TNA.
[80] BMEO to Richmond, 17 January 1955; Head to Eden, 2 February 1955, FO371/115672/ VJ1194/1–2, TNA.
[81] FO to Amman, 11, 11 January 1955, FO371/115671/VJ1193/2, TNA.

£1 million annual commitment the Jordanians had requested.[82] However, the British believed this would be enough to convince the Jordanians to give permission to station an armoured regiment from the British Army at Mafraq.[83] This was not an agreed quid pro quo, however, and although the Jordanians accepted the additional subsidy for the National Guard, they repeatedly refused to respond to Britain's request to station troops at Mafraq until they received a full reply to their aide memoire.[84] This therefore prompted Britain to reconsider the method of payment of the Arab Legion subsidy.[85] However, this matter required careful consideration and much debate. In the meantime, the British continually deferred responding to the aide memoire and, in turn, the Jordanians delayed replying to Britain's request to station British troops at Mafraq. Thus neither side secured its objective.[86]

Hussein's request that the subsidy be paid directly to the Jordanian government was effectively a first attempt to release – or at least loosen – the shackles of British control. And his failure in this effort led him to contemplate a first attempt to remove Glubb. A document released via a Freedom of Information request reveals that in the spring of 1955 Hussein made, as Glubb explicitly recorded, a 'first attempt to get rid of me and some of the senior British officers'.[87] Documents previously available meant that it was already apparent that Hussein was frustrated with Glubb in the spring of 1955, and Robert Satloff put this down 'ostensibly' to Glubb's plans for the defence of the West Bank and the pace of Arabisation.[88] This indeed correlates with Hussein's explanation in his memoirs for the eventual dismissal in March 1956.[89] In April 1955 Hussein did indeed rave against Glubb on these points. In what Charles Duke, who replaced Furlonge as British ambassador in November 1954, described as a 'remarkable' episode, King Hussein lambasted Glubb's defence plans during a meeting of the Jordan

[82] Eden to Butler, 31 December 1954, FO371/115670/VJ1192/1/G, TNA.
[83] FO to Amman, 11, 11 January 1955; Brewis to Richmond, 15 January 1955; FO to Amman, 26, 18 January 1955, FO371/115671/VJ1193/1–7, TNA.
[84] 'Move Northwards of the British Armoured Regiment', Rose, 7 February 1955, FO371/115672/VJ1194/2, TNA.
[85] Rose to Richmond, 25 February 1955, ibid.
[86] Duke to Rose, 3 March 1955, FO371/115672/VJ1194/4; BMEO to Shuckburgh, 3 May 1955, FO371/115672/VJ1194/9; Hadow to Duke, 24 September 1955, FO371/115673/VJ1194/28; Duke to Rose, 2 November 1955, FO371/115673/VJ1194/34, TNA.
[87] 'Note on King Husain and the Police', Glubb, 19 May 1955, FO371/115706/VJ1641/1, TNA.
[88] Satloff, *Jordan in Transition*, p. 136.
[89] Hussein, *Uneasy Lies the Head*, pp. 107–8.

Supreme Council on 9 April. After Glubb explained his defence plans in detail he invited questions and the king responded by excitedly reading out a pre-prepared speech in which, among other things, he announced that the number of British officers should be reduced and expressed his utter disagreement with Glubb's plan, even though, according to Glubb, the king had not seen the plans before, which suggested that the attack on Glubb had other underlying causes.[90] These issues indeed masked a much deeper frustration regarding Hussein's general lack of control over the Arab Legion, which was exacerbated by Hussein's fruitless visit to London in December 1954 and was entangled in the request to have the Arab Legion subsidy paid to the Jordanian government. This is where Hussein's frustrations with Glubb truly emanated. The aide memoire handed over in December contained a veiled attack on Glubb as it lamented that the only reason Britain wanted the subsidy paid directly to the Arab Legion was because it was commanded by a British officer.[91] Hussein made an almost identical attack on Glubb in his Cabinet speech on 9 April. Here, he remarked that the subsidy was being misspent and that 'it was all wrong that the loyalty of the Arab Legion should be to "one man"'.[92] Hussein returned from the December 1954 visit to London with a 'frigid and obstructive attitude' towards Glubb.[93] Duke apprised that the reason for this was that the king 'had been told that the reason why the Jordan Mission's visit to London last December had not been more successful was because their proposals had not been discussed and cleared first with General Glubb'.[94] This was not strictly true. Prior to Hussein's visit Glubb did warn Britain in no uncertain terms that the Arab Legion would disintegrate into an unreliable and inefficient rabble if the Jordanian Ministry of Finance obtained control of the subsidy.[95] However, at this point the British were equally opposed. The British blocked Hussein's attempt to acquire some degree of control over the Arab Legion, and as a result Glubb became the focus of Hussein's frustration. This was the crux of Hussein's first attempt to remove Glubb. He was frustrated at effectively being ignored by Britain, and Glubb symbolised this rebuke.

[90] Duke to Shuckburgh, 16 April 1955, FO371/115674/VJ1201/8/G; Glubb to WO, 29 April 1955, FO371/115674/VJ1201/16/G, TNA.
[91] 'Aide-Memoire', 30 December 1954, FO371/115670/VJ1192/2, TNA.
[92] Duke to Shuckburgh, 16 April 1955, FO371/115674/VJ1201/8/G, TNA.
[93] Duke to Shuckburgh, 14 July 1955, FO371/115719/VJ1941/110, TNA.
[94] Duke to Shuckburgh, 20 May 1955, FO371/115715/VJ1941/43, TNA.
[95] Drake to Falla, 28 April 1954, FO371/110924/VJ1201/19, TNA.

This breakdown in relations did partially open Britain's eyes to Hussein's primary frustrations. However, it also reaffirmed Britain's reliance on Glubb and in the final analysis the latter trumped the former. The Foreign Office surmised that:

The long-term answer to all this is, we believe, gradually to transfer as much as possible of our control over the Arab Legion to the Jordanians themselves, i.e. financial control, by paying our subsidy to the Jordan Government and not direct to the Legion and administrative control by a gradual process of 'Arabisation' of the Legion to place greater responsibility in the hands of the Arab officers.[96]

Moreover, it was acknowledged within Whitehall that the legal argument was in favour of Hussein's request.[97] However, this appreciation jarred with Britain's increasing reliance on Glubb as the guardian of British interests in Jordan. When consulted about the future of British officers in the Arab Legion, the War Office was adamant that British officers should be retained and that Glubb must continue in command. Otherwise it would no longer be worth subsidising the Arab Legion at the present level.[98] Glubb wanted advice from London as to what action he should take in the event that a sudden crisis should arise regarding his position.[99] If Glubb felt the need for a 'showdown' with the king, the Foreign Office was resolved to give Glubb its 'wholehearted support', and as a 'last resort' the Foreign Office was prepared to consider threatening to withdraw the subsidy.[100] Although the Foreign Office recognised the likely benefits of giving Hussein greater control over the Arab Legion, it was recommended that no change be made without first giving full consideration to Glubb's opinion.[101] He, however, was utterly against relinquishing any control over the Arab Legion. As was explained in a Foreign Office memo: 'For political reasons we are anxious to do what we can to meet the Jordanians on this: but General Glubb is opposed to any change.'[102] Glubb now assumed the omnipotent presence that

---

[96] 'King Hussein's Attitude to General Glubb and the Arab Legion', Rose, 7 May 1955, FO371/115674/VJ1201/17/G, TNA.
[97] Somerville (DMO) to MELF, 'Method of Payment of Arab Legion Subsidies', 23 May 1955, Melville Papers, 5/54.
[98] 'Sharif Nasser Ibn Jamal, King Hussein of Jordan's Uncle', Rose, 27 April 1955, FO371/115674/VJ1201/8/G, TNA.
[99] BMEO to FO, 151, 2 May 1955, FO371/115674/VJ1201/10/G, TNA.
[100] 'King Hussein's Attitude to General Glubb and the Arab Legion', Rose, 7 May 1955, FO371/115674/VJ1201/17/G, TNA.
[101] Somerville to MELF, 'Method of Payment of Arab Legion Subsidies', 23 May 1955, Melville Papers, 5/54.
[102] 'The Arab Legion', 13 September 1955, FO371/115682/VJ12010/1, TNA.

Hussein had attributed to him in December. Yet more significantly, the Foreign Office was determined to support Glubb 'to the hilt' if the king tried to direct a move against him.[103] This tense period during the spring of 1955 served to consolidate Glubb's position and Britain's reliance on him. Supporting Glubb was more important than appeasing Hussein.

What is particularly interesting – as revealed by a series of recently released documents – is how Britain therefore sought to deal with the king's animosity towards Glubb. According to Glubb, the principal cause of tension between himself and the king was Hussein's maternal uncle, Sharif Nasser.[104] Hussein was certainly close to his uncle, whom he described as 'a very kindly and wise man'.[105] Glubb believed that Sharif Nasser was trying to turn Hussein against the British in order to remove obstacles – principally Glubb – to his alleged smuggling of arms and hashish.[106] After Glubb was informed by one of his Arab officers that Sharif Nasser had told him that 'British officers were about to be removed', Glubb and Duke agreed that it was time to make a 'serious effort to get Nasser out of the country for good'.[107] While Glubb's 'age and personality' were thought to play a part, the Foreign Office surmised that, 'clearly … the King's attitude towards Glubb and the Legion generally can be attributed to the influence of his uncle Sharif Nasser'.[108] The Foreign Office therefore decided: 'Our main objective is to get rid of Nasser.'[109] Thereafter the British believed they would be free 'to convince the King that his personal dynastic interests demand the closest relations with the British and the maintenance of a British-officered Arab Legion under Glubb'.[110] To achieve this the British discussed two options. He could be removed 'by force (i.e., talking tough to the King, *demanding* Nasser's removal, threatening to withhold supplies from the Legion, casting doubts on our willingness to implement the Anglo-Jordan Treaty,

---

[103] Minute by Summerhayes, 3 May 1955, FO371/115674/VJ1201/10/G, TNA.
[104] 'King Husain & the Arab Legion', Glubb, 11 October 1955, FO371/115683/VJ12011/2, TNA.
[105] Hussein, *Uneasy Lies the Head*, pp. 35, 46.
[106] 'King Husain & the Arab Legion', Glubb, 11 October 1955, FO371/115683/VJ12011/2, TNA.
[107] Amman to FO, 166, 19 April 1955; Minute by Summerhayes, 20 April 1955, FO371/115674/VJ1201/7/G, TNA.
[108] Minute by Hadow, 22 April 1955, FO371/115674/VJ1201/8/G; 'King Hussein of Jordan's Attitude to Glubb and the Arab Legion', Hadow, 2 May 1955, FO371/115674/VJ1201/9/G, TNA.
[109] 'King Hussein of Jordan's Attitude to Glubb and the Arab Legion', Hadow, 2 May 1955, FO371/115674/VJ1201/9/G, TNA.
[110] Minute by Hadow, 22 April 1955, FO371/115674/VJ1201/8/G, TNA.

etc.)'. Alternatively, Britain would need to 'discredit Nasser' before getting Hussein to remove him, possibly with offers of further assistance,
such as the supply of Vampire jets for the Arab Legion Air Force.[111] In a
continuation of Britain's policy of selective non-intervention, as enacted
during the aftermath of Abdullah's assassination, the British sought to
remove Nasser as a means of maintaining the pro-British tendency of the
Jordanian hierarchy. As this was threatened, the British were prepared to
intervene. However, the British remained intent on avoiding obvious interference. The danger was that Britain risked turning Sharif Nasser into a
'martyr' and consolidating the king's anti-British stance if any attempt to
oust him was unsuccessful.[112] Rather than confronting the king directly,
it was deemed preferable to work through the prime minister, who was
also known to be opposed to Sharif Nasser, Hussein's wife, Dina, or the
crown prince of Iraq, with a view to 'discrediting' Sharif Nasser in the
king's eyes. The British proposed using them to point out the threat Sharif
Nasser would pose to Hussein if he gained control of the Arab Legion.[113]
However, it soon became apparent that the king's family could not be
used to engineer his removal, so the Foreign Office questioned how else
they could 'implant doubts in the King's mind about Nasser's loyalty?'[114]
Finding a subtle means of removing Sharif Nasser without obvious British
interference ultimately proved elusive. Nonetheless, despite Britain's failure to appease Hussein, or remove his uncle, this first attempt to remove
Glubb and some of the senior British officers petered out, and the British
therefore clung to Glubb's assertion that Hussein 'had ceased his efforts
in this direction for the moment'.[115]

This episode left a bitter taste in Glubb's mouth and caused him
to become increasingly frustrated with the king's interference. Glubb
resented that Hussein attempted to bypass his advice. In order to reassert
his position, Glubb explained that it would 'be of considerable assistance
to me if someone of importance in H.M.G. could drop two points into
the King's ear'. Firstly, Glubb wanted it made clear that he had already
discussed the issue of gradual Arabisation of the Arab Legion and that
they therefore saw eye to eye on this issue. Secondly, he wanted Hussein

---

[111] 'King Hussein of Jordan's Attitude to Glubb and the Arab Legion', Hadow, 2 May 1955,
FO371/115674/VJ1201/9/G, TNA [emphasis in original].
[112] Minute by Hadow, 22 April 1955, FO371/115674/VJ1201/8/G, TNA.
[113] 'King Hussein of Jordan's Attitude to Glubb and the Arab Legion', Hadow, 2 May 1955,
FO371/115674/VJ1201/9/G, TNA.
[114] Shuckburgh to Duke, 13 May 1955, FO371/115674/VJ1201/17/G, TNA.
[115] 'Note on King Husain and the Police', Glubb, 19 May 1955, FO371/115706//VJ1641/
1, TNA.

to be informed that 'my long experience probably makes me the best judge of how quickly the process can be carried out'. He added: 'My object in venturing to suggest the above is to make the King see that I am his correct military adviser, and that in the long run he will get more by working through me, than by concocting plots with his boy friends.'[116] Glubb resented anybody's interference in the running of the Arab Legion. When the Arab Legion Air Force was formed, the British Air Ministry wanted it to be independent of the main Arab Legion with its own British commander with direct access to the Jordanian minister of defence. Glubb, however, was opposed to this system, which would effectively bypass him.[117] Patrick Coghill also experienced Glubb's reluctance to give up any degree of control when he was appointed as the Arab Legion's director of general intelligence in April 1952. After the assassination of Abdullah the Jordanian government requested that Britain supply an officer to organise a 'Special Branch' as it was most concerned about internal security. Although Coghill only agreed to take on the role if he had Glubb's blessing, when he arrived he had a 'puzzling' and 'disappointing' first meeting with Glubb. Evidently he was not especially welcomed. Coghill described his first few weeks in the job as 'hell'. He found it impossible to find out how anything operated, and the only answer he received when he asked who did what was: '"It is for the Pasha" – i.e. Glubb.'[118] As Kirkbride observed, Glubb tended 'to regard himself and the Legion as being something of an autonomous organisation inside the Jordan state'.[119] Under the Abdullah regime this system worked, but with Hussein this led to a clash of wills and mutual frustration. Indeed, according to Farhan Shbeilat, the minister of defence, Hussein's principal complaint with Glubb was that he 'tried to keep everything in his own hands and had his own favourites'.[120] This contributed to the emerging power struggle. Hussein resented Glubb's authority and Glubb resented Hussein's interference.

Hussein's resentment towards Glubb was further fuelled by two unlikely sources – in addition to Ali Abu Nowar and the Free Officers movement. One was Abdullah al-Tall. This connection is surprising, given he had been convicted of involvement in the assassination of Hussein's grandfather. However, in the 1970s Hussein pardoned Tall

[116] Glubb to Duke, 5 June 1955, FO371/115674/VJ1201/21, TNA.
[117] Pundik, *Struggle for Sovereignty*, p. 266.
[118] Coghill, *Before I Forget*, unpublished memoir, MECA.
[119] Kirkbride to Furlonge, 29 April 1950, FO371/82752/ET1202/23, TNA.
[120] Duke to Shuckburgh, 6 October 1955, FO371/115683/VJ12011/1, TNA.

and enabled his return to Jordan from exile. Presumably, therefore, the king did not believe him to be guilty.[121] According to Glubb's intelligence sources, Hussein engaged in covert correspondence with Tall. This included 'a secret meeting' in Cairo during Hussein's state visit to Egypt in the early summer of 1955. Glubb was informed that Abdullah al-Tall told Hussein that 'the British had killed King Abdullah, and that I [Glubb] had "fixed" the Court which tried the case, so that he, Abdulla al-Tell, was condemned to death'.[122] The British ambassador's own sources did not confirm Glubb's report of secret contact between Hussein and Abdullah al-Tall. However, Glubb remained adamant that his information was correct.[123]

A second, more concrete influence was Wing-Commander 'Jock' Dalgleish, a British RAF pilot seconded to command the Arab Legion Air Force. The two became close friends after Dalgleish evacuated Hussein from Jerusalem immediately after Abdullah's assassination.[124] Like so many of Hussein's close associates, Dalgleish was also unsupportive of Glubb. In particular Dalgleish was frustrated that newly trained pilots were regularly dismissed because Glubb considered their 'political sympathies ... uncertain'.[125] Despite Dalgleish being considered a 'king's man', neither Glubb nor Britain believed he exercised a suitable influence on Hussein.[126] Partly as a result of this, but also because his secondment period was legitimately expiring, it was announced in September 1955 that Dalgleish would have to leave Jordan. While Glubb's relationship with Hussein improved after the failure of his first attempt to remove Glubb in May, Glubb had always been concerned that things would deteriorate when the king was informed of British plans to replace Dalgleish. And so it proved after this was announced. When Hussein's antagonism towards Glubb resurfaced in the autumn of 1955, Court Minister Fawzi al-Mulki, Minister of Defence Farhan Shbeilat, Duke, Glubb, and the Foreign Office all attributed the king's poor relations with Glubb – at least in part – to his irritation over the decision to replace Dalgleish and believed that Dalgleish probably stoked the king's animosity towards

---

[121] Ashton, *King Hussein*, p. 25.
[122] 'King Husain & the Arab Legion', Glubb, 11 October 1955, FO371/115683/VJ12011/ 2, TNA.
[123] Duke to Shuckburgh, 20 October 1955, FO371/115683/VJ12011/2, TNA.
[124] Royle, *Glubb Pasha*, pp. 443–5.
[125] Fisher to Glubb, 26 July 1952; Dalgleish to Fisher, 26 July 1952, GP2006, 1.
[126] Minute by Laurence, 12 October 1955, FO371/115683/VJ12011/1; Summary of points discussed between Glubb and Minister of State, Shuckburgh, 11 August 1954, FO371/ 110928/VJ1208/5, TNA.

Glubb.[127] This was not the sole reason for Hussein's renewed ire, but it was a factor, and acknowledging this reveals two salient points. Firstly, Hussein was not avowedly anti-British personnel purely because they were British. What he resented were those who threatened and challenged his control. Secondly, Hussein was not merely surrounded by Arab nationalists. Instead, he was subject to anti-Glubb influence from several different quarters with varying motives.

Nationalism was nevertheless a significant pressure, and Hussein's relationship with Glubb was put under further strain by the 'challenge of Arab radicalism' that emanated from Egypt.[128] In July 1952, just a few weeks before Talal was deposed in Jordan, a group of officers within the Egyptian Army launched a successful coup against King Farouk. The dominant figure of the movement, who became president in February 1954, was Gamal Abd al-Nasser. Thereafter Egypt became an increasing threat to both Hussein and Britain as the Nasser regime became 'regionally interventionist and globally activist'.[129] Nasser sought Arab independence and in June 1954 concluded an Anglo–Egyptian treaty that involved Britain's military withdrawal from the Suez base within two years. Nasser also sought Arab unity.[130] He thought in terms of a 'common struggle' throughout the Middle East and saw 'imperialism' as 'the great force that is imposing a murderous, invisible siege upon the whole region'.[131] In his view, Jordan's relationship with Britain was typical of the Arab world's imperial plight. Nasser described the deposed King Farouk as a 'masked stooge'.[132] Abdullah had been the subject of similar criticism, and the danger for Hussein was that he would be seen in the same light and might suffer the same fate.

It was in 1955 when Nasser's pan-Arabism rose to the fore and became a particular problem for Hussein, Glubb, and Britain. Hussein later reflected that this was the beginning of 'three dangerous years in which Jordan as a country nearly perished'. He apprised that: 'If the cold war between Egypt and Jordan was born well before my grandfather's assassination,

---

[127] Duke to Shuckburgh, 6 October 1955; Minute by Laurence, 12 October 1955; Duke to Shuckburgh, 26 October 1955, FO371/115683/VJ12011/1; Duke to Shuckburgh, 20 October 1955, FO371/115683/VJ12011/2, TNA.
[128] Dann, *Challenge of Arab Radicalism.*
[129] Adeed Dawisha, 'Egypt', in: Sayigh and Shlaim (eds.), *Cold War*, p. 29.
[130] Ali E. Hillal Dessouki, 'Nasser and the Struggle for Independence', in: William Roger Louis and Roger Owen (eds.), *Suez 1956: The Crisis and Its Consequences* (Oxford, 1989), pp. 31–4.
[131] Nasser, *Egypt's Liberation*, p. 103.
[132] Ibid., p. 41.

it came to boiling point in 1955.'[133] Nasser's influence was particularly telling during Britain's failed attempt to secure Jordanian accession to the Baghdad Pact. Although arguably opposed to what had begun as America's 'northern tier' project, Britain became the principal champion of the pact as a result of the belief that it could be used as a vehicle to uphold British interests in the region.[134] Britain joined Iraq, Turkey, Pakistan, and Iran in the pact on 4 April 1955 and hoped to extend its membership to other Arab states, principally Jordan. Britain wanted to promote Hashemite Iraq as its bastion in the Middle East. And bringing Hashemite Jordan into the pact was seen as a way of strengthening Iraq's position.[135] Nasser, however, was utterly opposed to the Baghdad Pact. He believed it was a means for Britain to control the Arab world and isolate Egypt.[136] Nasser publicly attacked the pact and when he met Anthony Eden in Cairo in February 1955, he warned the British foreign secretary not to encourage Jordan to join.[137] After Iraq joined the pact, Hussein recalled that: 'Night after night Cairo Radio fulminated against "this traitor to the Arab cause" and "the catspaw of Imperialists".'[138] Cheap, portable transistor radios gave Nasser unprecedented access to the masses throughout the Arab world.[139] Particularly effective was *Voice of the Arabs*, which began as a thirty-minute programme on Radio Cairo in 1953, before it evolved into its own twenty-four hour station.[140] The *Voice of the Arabs* denounced Iraqi Prime Minister Nuri al-Said's 'betrayal of Arabism'.[141] And when Britain joined the pact, the *Voice of the Arabs* sarcastically congratulated Britain on 'her success in obtaining control once more over Iraq'.[142] At the end of October 1955 Egypt signed mutual defence pacts with Syria and Saudi Arabia. This, combined with Egypt's procurement of Soviet arms via Czechoslovakia in September, made Nasser very popular in Jordan. Radio Cairo lauded Nasser for throwing off 'the shackles of the West' and portrayed him as the 'best bet for the future against Israel'. According to

---

[133] Hussein, *Uneasy Lies the Head*, p. 83.
[134] Blackwell, *British Military Intervention*, pp. 20–5.
[135] Nigel Ashton, *Eisenhower, Macmillan and the Problem of Nasser* (Basingstoke, 1996), pp. 62–3.
[136] Mohamed Heikal, *Nasser: The Cairo Documents* (London, 1972), p. 56.
[137] Ibid., pp. 80–4; Pappé, 'British Rule in Jordan', pp. 211–12.
[138] Hussein, *Uneasy Lies the Head*, pp. 84–5.
[139] Salibi, *Modern History of Jordan*, p. 183.
[140] Jarice Hanson and Uma Narula, *New Communication Technologies in Developing Countries* (London, 1990), p. 137.
[141] *SWB, Part IV*, 25 February 1955, p. 37.
[142] Ibid., 13 April 1955, p. 22.

Hussein: 'The ordinary people of Jordan rejoiced, and I took in my stride
the increasing abuse hurled at me for continuing to let my Army be run
by Glubb and other British officers.'[143] Egypt's growing popularity consequently increased Britain's desire to secure Jordanian accession to the
Baghdad Pact.[144] Yet owing to the success of Egyptian propaganda, the
Jordanian government was 'afraid to sign' without an obvious quid pro
quo.[145] Glubb sent frequent signals to Melville in November, vehemently
requesting that Britain make a 'really generous' offer to expand the Arab
Legion as a means of securing Jordan's accession to the pact.[146] Glubb
was assured by the chief of the imperial general staff, Sir Gerald Templer,
that this matter was currently the top priority and that the prime minister
had seen his signals, which were 'most effective'.[147] Glubb's demand for
an extra division – which would cost £10 million on top of the existing
subsidy – was deemed 'unreasonable', but Britain was willing to make a
'package offer'.[148] Thus, Templer was sent to Amman to persuade Jordan
to make a public statement of its intention to join the Baghdad Pact by
offering material and financial assistance to the Arab Legion and a promise to replace the 1948 Treaty with a Special Agreement. It is pertinent to
note that the British once again sought to obtain a quid pro quo by partially adhering to one of Hussein's lesser requests from Jordan's aide memoire of the previous year. Hussein later reflected that the financing issue
helped fuel the propaganda emanating from Egyptian radio broadcasts
and therefore made his task of trying to keep order much harder.[149] On 13
December the Jordanians therefore handed Templer a counter-proposal
of conditions for Jordan to join the Baghdad Pact, which included paying
the subsidy to the Jordanian government rather than directly to the Arab
Legion.[150] It is arguable that offering Hussein more control over the Arab
Legion – particularly over its finances – would have been a more valuable
quid pro quo to counter Egyptian and nationalist criticism. However, the
British were not prepared to go that far, and on 14 December Templer left
Jordan empty-handed.[151]

---

[143] Hussein, *Uneasy Lies the Head*, p. 88.

[144] Ashton, *King Hussein*, p. 47.

[145] Qiada [Glubb] to TJL [Melville], 17 November 1955, Melville Papers, 7/61.

[146] See Melville Papers, 7/61.

[147] TJL [Hutton] to Qiada [Glubb], 26 November 1955, ibid.

[148] Harold Macmillan to Eden, 25 November 1955, FO371/115532/VJ1073/1336/G, TNA.

[149] Hussein, *Uneasy Lies the Head*, p. 88.

[150] Dann, *Challenge of Arab Radicalism*, pp. 27–8.

[151] 'Report by General Sir Gerald Templer', 16 December 1955, PREM11/1418; FO to
       Amman, 815, 3 December 1955, FO371/115654/VJ1051/51/G, TNA.

The following day the Foreign Office tried to change tack and resolved to use propaganda as a weapon to persuade Jordan to join the Baghdad Pact. Glubb and Duke were asked to try to get articles published in the Jordanian press.[152] However, on 16 December, before any such action could be taken, anti-Baghdad Pact riots broke out in Jordan.[153] Britain believed Hussein still wanted to join the pact.[154] However, politically it was not possible. As a close confidant of Nasser's explained, the Egyptian president believed that Eden, who was now prime minister, had broken his promise not to encourage Jordan to join the pact: 'The Templer mission therefore marked the start of a period of all-out propaganda against the British, the Baghdad Pact, and all other policies in the Middle East.'[155] Consequently, Jordan was beset by riots, which left Hussein with 'no alternative but to call out the Legion', who, with the aid of tear-gas, 'met force with force'.[156] However, the disturbances that plagued Jordan in December and January were only lastingly quelled when Samir al-Rifai led a new government – the third new government in three weeks – on the premise that Jordan would not join the Baghdad Pact.[157] Popular opinion against the pact, as manifested in the disturbances on the street in Jordan – egged on by Egypt – was too well established, and no amount of propaganda or material assistance for the Arab Legion would be able to reverse this.

At the beginning of 1956 both Britain and Glubb stepped up their efforts in the field of propaganda. Hitherto, British propaganda activities in the Middle East had focused on countering communism and the Soviet Union. Now the British concerted their efforts against Nasser and the threat of Arab nationalism.[158] To that end, Kirkbride returned to Jordan. Having first been approached by Eden in June 1955, he arrived in mid-February 1956. The 'ostensible purpose' of his visit was 'archaeological research', but he was actually sent to 'help forward' British interests.[159] It was a preliminary visit prior to a six-month mission in

---

[152] TJL [Melville] to Qiada [Glubb], 15 December 1955, Melville Papers, 2/21.

[153] Shlaim, *Lion of Jordan*, pp. 86–7.

[154] Amman to FO, 699, 22 December 1955, FO371/115659/VJ1015/130, TNA; Hussein, *Uneasy Lies the Head*, p. 92.

[155] Heikal, *Cairo Documents*, p. 84.

[156] Hussein, *Uneasy Lies the Head*, pp. 92–3.

[157] Amman to FO, 51, 8 January 1956, FO371/121491/VJ1051/13, TNA.

[158] James Vaughan, '"Cloak Without Dagger": How the Information Research Department Fought Britain's Cold War in the Middle East, 1948–1956', *Cold War History*, 4:3 (2004), p. 74.

[159] Kirkbride to Eden, 26 June 1955; Lloyd to Eden, 'Sir A. Kirkbride', 10 February 1956, PREM11/1443, TNA.

which he would 'conduct pro-British and anti-Egyptian propaganda in Jordan, Syria and the Lebanon under cover of his work in the Palestine Archaeological Museum'.[160] During the visit Kirkbride 'dropped a lot of anti-Egyptian poison' amongst his contacts on both banks of the Jordan and reported that he found 'many ready listeners'.[161] Meanwhile Glubb created a new branch of twenty people within the Arab Legion head-quarters tasked with tackling the problem of propaganda in Jordan, with plans for a sister branch to be created in London.[162] These efforts included the jamming of Egyptian radio broadcasts.[163] And on 25 January a new broadcasting station in Amman began to rival Radio Cairo. In stark contrast to its Egyptian counterpart, this new station described Jordan as 'the Arab world's first line of defence' and the Arab Legion as 'its victorious Arab army the strongest bulwark of Arab free-dom'. It called on the Arab world to 'rally round Hussein and his brave, victorious army'.[164] For Radio Cairo and Egyptian newspapers such as *Al-Ahram*, this new station was merely further evidence of Glubb and Britain's imperialist dominance in Jordan. 'It is Glubb, the repre-sentative of the British, who injects the poison into that broadcasting station's commentaries', commented Ahmad Said on *Voice of the Arabs*, adding:

Colonialism is imposing Glubb on Jordan to dominate her and rend the Arab nation. ... Glubb is the one who organises plots against Arabs. Glubb is the one who slays our martyrs. Glubb is the one who arrests many of you. Glubb is the one who imposes fines on you. Arabs, Glubb must go.[165]

In response to the Egyptian press attacks on Glubb, a commentator on the Amman station countered:

We wish to say with full confidence to these newspapers and to the people behind them that the only powers enjoyed by General Glubb are those required by his official post, which are similar to those enjoyed by officers of his rank in other countries. Furthermore, he is only an officer of the Arab Legion of the Hashemite Kingdom, and is subject to laws and regulations as well as to the orders and instructions of the Defence Minister.[166]

---

[160] Logan to Bishop, 19 April 1956, PREM11/1443, TNA.
[161] 'Note by Sir A. Kirkbride on Visit to Jordan', 4 April 1956, PREM11/1420, TNA.
[162] Young to Melville, 30 January 1956, Melville Papers, 4/44.
[163] Glubb to Templer, 28 March 1956, GP2006, 77; *SWB, Part IV*, 13 January 1956, p. 2; *SWB, Part IV*, 3 February 1956, p. 25.
[164] *SWB, Part IV*, 31 January 1956, pp. 1, 32–3.
[165] Ibid., 21 February 1956, pp. 24–7.
[166] Ibid., 24 February 1956, p. 28.

These counterclaims had little impact, though, and just four weeks after Glubb's new propaganda department was established, he was summarily dismissed. For the past seven years Glubb had lamented Britain's failure to devote more resources to propaganda.[167] The problem, though, was that British propaganda failed to hit the right note.[168]

It would be short-sighted to portray the dismissal of Glubb simply as a direct consequence of the Baghdad Pact disturbances and the Egyptian propaganda campaign. But it put huge pressure on Hussein and it was within the atmosphere of pan-Arabism that he was compelled to take dramatic action against Glubb. The specific context was the gathering possibility of Jordan's Arab allies becoming embroiled in renewed conflict with Israel. Abu al-Huda had already committed Jordan to the Arab League Collective Security Pact before Hussein's accession, but thereafter the king repeatedly confirmed Jordan's commitment to pan-Arab solidarity. In response to a rumour that Israel intended to attack Syria and Lebanon in 1954 Hussein assured both Arab states 'that Jordan would assist in this event'.[169] After a rise in incidents in Gaza throughout 1955, including a major Israeli raid in February, an official Jordanian statement emphasised that any breach of the armistice line would be regarded as a breach of the entire front with all Arab states.[170] This belligerent attitude deeply concerned Glubb. Since Qibya he firmly believed the Israelis were deliberately creating tension with the object of initiating a preventative war designed to extend Israel's eastern frontier to the River Jordan.[171] The dilemma the Arab Legion faced was that if it became involved, it would almost inevitably be defeated and lose the West Bank (which is exactly what happened in the 1967 War), but if it stood by and did nothing, it would lay itself open to the charge of treachery throughout the Arab world and would significantly damage the British connection.[172] Moreover, Hussein would have been acutely aware that to abandon his Arab neighbours would be to risk not only his political survival, but also

---

[167] Qiada [Glubb] to TJL [Melville], 18 December 1955, Melville Papers, 2/21.
[168] For a broader account of propaganda in the Middle East, see: James Vaughan, *The Failure of American and British Propaganda in the Arab Middle East, 1945–1957: Unconquerable Minds* (Basingstoke, 2005).
[169] Melville to Glubb, repeating signal from Hutton, 24 August 1954, Melville Papers, 7/61.
[170] Qiada [Hutton] to TJL [Glubb], 5 September 1955, ibid.
[171] 'Need for Increases to Arab Legion as a Result of Russian Penetration into Egypt', 30 October 1955, Melville Papers, 3/28; Qiada [Glubb] to TJL [Melville], 20 November 1953, Melville Papers, 10/70.
[172] Qiada [Glubb] to TJL [Melville], 8 April 1955; Glubb to Melville, 9 April 1955, Melville Papers, 7/61.

his life. Indeed, he had witnessed the assassination of his grandfather for allegedly betraying his Arab allies during the 1948 War.

In February 1956 these fears reached a crescendo, and detailed consideration of the timing indicates that this proved the trigger that compelled Hussein to take the desperate action of dismissing Glubb. One explanation for the timing of Glubb's dismissal was that Hussein acted in a fit of anger at an article published in the *Illustrated* magazine, which stated: 'The real ruler of Jordan is a short, blue-eyed soldier named John Bagot Glubb.'[173] Yet while this might have rankled, it hardly seems commensurate with the abrupt manner of the dismissal.[174] Hussein himself described this suggestion as 'nonsense'.[175] A much more convincing trigger for Glubb's dismissal was the urgent threat of a second Arab–Israeli war. After the Jordanian government pledged its support for Egypt in September 1955, if it were attacked by Israel, Glubb, who was in Britain at the time, replied that the view in London was that the tension in Gaza was designed to create a *casus belli* for an Israeli offensive against Jordan, and he urged that this be explained to Hussein, the prime minister, and the minister of defence.[176] 'Sam' Cooke, the Arab Legion divisional commander, duly advised the king and the prime minister against taking any action to assist Egypt without first consulting Britain, and this was accepted.[177] True to this promise, when a specific threat of conflict arose, the Jordanian government consulted Britain. The Jordanians first expressed their concerns of a specific threat of renewed conflict between Israel and the Arab states to Britain on 24 January.[178] It was anticipated that hostilities would break out when Israel was set to begin work on the Jisr Banat Yaqub Canal to divert waters away from the River Jordan in the demilitarised zone between Israel and Syria.[179] The Israelis threatened to start work on 1 March – the same day that Glubb was dismissed – or any day thereafter.[180] The Jordanian prime minister was convinced that if Israel did resume work on the canal, then the Syrian Army would intervene.[181] The Arab News Agency reported that 'a great

173 'A Flying Scot Keeps the Jets Over Jordan', *Illustrated*, 25 February 1956, GP2006, 35.
174 Philip Geyelin, *Hashemite: The Story of King Hussein of Jordan* (unpublished manuscript), Chapter 19, pp. 2–3, Geyelin Papers.
175 Hussein, *Uneasy Lies the Head*, p. 115.
176 TJL [Glubb] to Qiada [Ahmad Sudqi and Cooke], 5 September 1955, Melville Papers, 7/61.
177 Qiada [Hutton] to TJL [Glubb], 5 September 1955, ibid.
178 Amman to FO, 156, 25 January 1956, PREM11/1418, TNA.
179 Amman to FO, 255, 25 February 1956, ibid.
180 Amman to FO, 239, 21 February 1956, ibid.
181 Amman to FO, 21 February 1956, ibid.

wave of anxiety has swept Syria since Israel threatened to resume diversion of the River Jordan ... and since the reports about Israel's intentions to embark upon an attack on the Arab states in the spring'. The Egyptian and Syrian armies held 'urgent talks', and the Syrian defence minister issued a statement confirming that the country was prepared to counter a spring offensive.[182] Glubb, who was 'extremely anxious' about the prospect of conflict, reported that 'King Hussein declared yesterday that if fighting begins between Egypt or Syria and Israel he will immediately order the Arab Legion to attack'.[183] The Jordanians were anxious to know what degree of support they would receive under the terms of the treaty if Jordan became embroiled in war as a result of having to fulfil its obligations under the Arab League Collective Security Pact.[184]

In the absence of a reply to his request for support from Britain on 24 January, Hussein faced the daunting prospect of being unable to send his own army to war. Glubb would not countenance the use of the Arab Legion in the event of fighting breaking out between Israel, Egypt, and Syria. Glubb believed: 'If we obey the King's orders the Arab Legion will be destroyed and Israel [will] occupy the west bank.' Thus, as Glubb saw it: 'The only way to avoid this would be for me and British officers to refuse.' Just as Jordan had asked Britain to clarify its position, Glubb also pleaded for counsel. Glubb warned: 'We are drifting towards disaster with no plan and no (repeat no) advice from Her Majesty's Government.'[185] The Jordanians considered the prospect of Arab–Israeli hostilities breaking out a matter of 'extreme urgency'.[186] However, because Ben-Gurion had publicly renounced any intention of causing trouble at Banat Yaqub, the British explained to Glubb: 'We do not believe, however, that the immediate situation is as black as you fear. We have no indications that the Israelis intend to attack in the near future.'[187] However, the Syrian authorities warned that any attempt by Israel to divert the course of the River Jordan would be answered with force.[188] Glubb therefore pleaded that it was 'absolutely essential (repeat absolutely essential) [that] Her Majesty's Government immediately inform us of their proposed action in the event of Israeli-Syrian hostilities on March 1'.[189] Yet owing to the lack

---

[182] *SWB, Part IV*, 17 February 1956, p. 29.
[183] Glubb to Templer, Amman to FO, 218, 17 February 1956, PREM11/1418, TNA.
[184] Amman to FO, 251, 23 February 1956, ibid.
[185] Amman to FO, 218, 17 February 1956, ibid.
[186] Amman to FO, 251, 23 February 1956, ibid.
[187] Brownhill (VCIGS) to Glubb, FO to Amman, 271, 18 February 1956, ibid.
[188] *SWB, Part IV*, 28 February 1956, p. 27.
[189] Glubb to Templer, Amman to FO, 240, 21 February 1956, PREM11/1418, TNA.

of urgency that it attached to this threat, Britain laboured.[190] Britain's response was not given until Duke met Jordanian Prime Minister Samir al-Rifai on the morning of 1 March, by which time the process of Glubb's dismissal had been set in motion.[191] Duke described it as an 'ironical coincidence' that as he left the prime minister's office having given the reply to the question of Britain's response to an Israeli attack on Syria, 'King Hussein was on his way to instruct the Prime Minister to dismiss General Glubb'.[192] Perhaps, though, it was too little too late.

The prospect of a second Arab–Israeli war almost certainly explains the timing and the manner of the dismissal. However, new evidence indicates that Hussein's decision to dispense with Glubb's services and limit British interference had seemingly been made several months earlier. A light is shined on this aspect when we look beyond Glubb and consider another victim of the March 1956 purge of the Arab Legion. On 1 March King Hussein not only removed Glubb, but he dismissed Glubb's Chief of Staff, Brigadier W. M. Hutton, four senior Arab officers, eight British commanding officers, and four other Arab officers deemed particularly loyal to Glubb.[193] The second most significant departure was Arab Legion Director of General Intelligence Patrick Coghill.[194] However, a document released via a Freedom of Information request reveals that Coghill's dismissal was only a partial surprise. His departure had already been arranged months in advance. The Jordanian government notified Coghill in early October 1955 that his contract would not be renewed when it expired on 31 March 1956 and that his present Arab assistant would replace him.[195] However, in the event, Coghill was dismissed along with Glubb on 1 March, despite his already imminent departure. This surely confirms that something made the removal of Glubb and British control of the Arab Legion an urgent matter. Satloff previously queried why Hussein dismissed Glubb on 1 March when he could have let his contract expire on 31 March, to emphasise apparent

---

[190] Shuckburgh, *Descent*, p. 337.
[191] Amman to FO, 272, 1 March 1956, PREM11/1418, TNA; Satloff, *Jordan in Transition*, p. 142.
[192] Amman to FO, 315, 3 March 1956, PREM11/1419, TNA.
[193] 'The Arab Legion: between 1 March and 1430 Hours 6 March 56', Nigel Bromage, 6 March 1956, Melville Papers, 2/21; 'Officer Situation', undated [but 1956 after dismissal], GP2006, 54.
[194] Amman to FO, 274, 1 March 1956, FO371/121540/VJ1201/8/G, TNA; Dann, *Challenge of Arab Radicalism*, p. 31.
[195] Duke to Shuckburgh, 20 October 1955, FO371/115683/VJ12011/2, TNA; J. K. Heisch to CGS, Appendix B, GP2006, 54.

urgency.[196] The case of Coghill is much more significant in this regard, though, because unlike the Glubb scenario – which was circumstantial speculation by Satloff – Coghill had, in fact, already been informed that his contract would not be renewed.

The Coghill scenario is all the more informative when we consider two other factors. Firstly, at the end of September the Arab Legion Air Force was renamed the Royal Jordanian Air Force.[197] Similarly, four months after Glubb's dismissal the Arab Legion was renamed the Jordan Arab Army. This would seem to indicate that the gradual process of reducing the British connection and rebranding the Jordanian military had already begun in September 1955. Secondly, when questioned why he dismissed Glubb, Hussein was adamant that he had warned Britain of his grievances with Glubb in October 1955. On the day he dismissed Glubb, Hussein explained that despite warning London in October, 'nothing seemed to be done'.[198] The crucial exchange was a private conversation on 24 October between Hussein and Evelyn Shuckburgh, the under-secretary in charge of Middle Eastern affairs for the Foreign Office. It was Shuckburgh who raised the topic of Glubb with Hussein. He did so in response to a memorandum from Glubb, which detailed the dire state of his relationship with the king. In this document, released via a Freedom of Information request, Glubb reported: 'For the moment we must assume that the King is intent on getting rid of me.' After speaking to Hussein, the minister of defence informed Glubb that

the King's mind had been completely poisoned against the Arab Legion and myself [Glubb]. He said that the King had said with some heat that the Arab Legion was a mob without organization. That he felt the time had come when he must intervene himself and insist on a higher standard of efficiency, and so on.[199]

In passing on Glubb's '*cri de coeur*', Duke counselled that he did not believe that a major crisis over Glubb was imminent. However, he explained, 'it does seem that the process has started of making life as difficult for Glubb as possible in the hope that he will soon resign and the question

---

[196] Satloff, *Jordan in Transition*, p. 140. As a point of fact it should be acknowledged that Glubb's contract was actually due to expire on 16 May 1956: Heisch to CGS, Appendix A, GP2006, 54.

[197] 'King Husain & the Arab Legion', Glubb, 11 October 1955, FO371/115683/VJ12011/2, TNA.

[198] Amman to FO, 278, 1 March 1956, FO371/121540/VJ1201/6/G, TNA.

[199] 'King Husain & the Arab Legion', Glubb, 11 October 1955, FO371/115683/VJ12011/2, TNA.

is therefore what we are to do about it'.[200] As it turned out, the British did virtually nothing. The striking feature of the meeting is the disparity with which the two participants seemed to perceive the results of this discussion.[201] Shuckburgh came away believing that if Hussein ever lost full confidence in Glubb that he would let Britain know.[202] Meanwhile, Duke reported that when the king returned to Amman, he said that he had confidence in Glubb, but he did so 'without much warmth', leaving Duke with the 'impression that he had made up his mind to carry out some changes in the administration of the Arab Legion'.[203] This suggests that just like the situation a year earlier, in December 1954, the British underestimated Hussein's frustration, resentment, and vulnerability to attack from Arab nationalists. Considered in tandem with the Coghill situation, it would seem fairly certain that Hussein did indeed have Glubb's departure – if not dismissal – in mind at least as early as October 1955.

The British response to Hussein's concerns in October mirrored its response to Hussein's desire to remove Glubb in the spring. In reporting on the meeting, Shuckburgh noted that it was 'still clear that the King has considerable reservations in his attitude to Glubb and that we must do our best to clear them up'.[204] As in the spring, the British had no intention of appeasing Hussein in his complaints against Glubb and his lack of control over the Arab Legion. Instead, the British sought to *clear things up* by once again attempting to remove perceived undesirable influences. Just days after his meeting with Hussein, Shuckburgh reignited the previously halted campaign against the king's uncle. Because of the 'malign influence' that Sharif Nasser was deemed to exercise on the king, the Foreign Office became re-determined that 'he should be removed'. The British regretted that hitherto 'no feasible method has presented itself'. However, the removal of Sharif Nasser once again became a firm Foreign Office objective, and Shuckburgh therefore requested the advice of Duke and Glubb 'on the best way to tackle this very tricky business'.[205] The Foreign Office believed that it had become 'increasingly apparent that most of the trouble we are having with the King derives from the poison which Sherif Nasser and others are continually pouring into the King's ear and that we shall see our best efforts frustrated unless we can bring

[200] Duke to Shuckburgh, 20 October 1955, FO371/115683/VJ12011/2, TNA.
[201] Satloff, *Jordan in Transition*, p. 136.
[202] Shuckburgh to Ivone Kirkpatrick, 24 October 1955, PREM11/1418, TNA.
[203] Duke to Shuckburgh, 28 November 1955, WO216/891, TNA.
[204] Shuckburgh to Duke, 5 November 1955, FO371/115683/VJ12011/4, TNA.
[205] Shuckburgh to Poett (DMO), 27 October 1955, FO371/115683/VJ12011/2, TNA.

about his removal'.[206] While Hussein departed London in October 1955 believing that Britain would act against Glubb, instead they were more intent on acting against his uncle. Once again, the British decided that the best way to solve Hussein's frustrations with Glubb was not to appease him, but to attempt to eliminate what they perceived as a malign influence.

Britain's failure to deal with Hussein's frustrations regarding Glubb and control of the Arab Legion was a symptom of the Glubb paradox that was created by the assassination of Abdullah and compounded by the departure of Kirkbride soon after. The departure of Abdullah and Kirkbride meant that Glubb was hoisted into the role of elder statesman within the Hashemite Kingdom. Abdullah's absence meant that Britain's position in Jordan had been weakened, and as the influence of Jordanian and Arab nationalists increased, Britain became ever more reliant on Glubb. The paradox this created was that by the time Hussein came to power Glubb was increasingly becoming both indispensable and detrimental to Britain's position in Jordan. Glubb's position posed a dilemma. On one hand, it was believed that 'a successful campaign for his dismissal would be the final blow to our prestige in Jordan'.[207] Britain might be expected, therefore, to have taken remedial action to avoid compelling Hussein to take drastic action. Yet on the other hand, removing Glubb even on British terms was deemed equally undesirable. For, as Shuckburgh reflected, such a retreat would have been seen as 'another case of "scuttle"'.[208] With Britain in the process of withdrawing from Egypt, it was deemed imperative that its position in Jordan appeared strong. Given the undesirability of Glubb's departure, whether forced or voluntary, the British clung to signs of improvement. At the start of 1956 Michael Rose, the head of the Foreign Office Eastern Department, accepted Duke's appraisal that the January riots in Jordan had drawn 'the King and Glubb much closer together', meaning Glubb would hopefully 'be able to carry on for some while yet'.[209] In truth, however, Glubb's relationship with Hussein had experienced no such renaissance. Months before the dismissal it was suggested by a Northern Ireland MP, based on the views of former Arab Legion officer, and King Abdullah's former ADC and close friend, Ronnie Broadhurst, that Glubb 'may now, in

---

[206] Shuckburgh to Duke, 5 November 1955, FO371/115683/VJ12011/4, TNA.
[207] Minute by Summerhayes, 28 December 1955, FO371/115683/VJ12011/6, TNA.
[208] Shuckburgh, *Descent*, p. 292, n. 1.
[209] Duke to Rose, 1 February 1956; Rose to Poett, 13 February 1956, FO371/121560/VJ1206/4, TNA.

spite of his good work in the past, prove to be an embarrassment to our interests'.[210] Foreign Secretary Selwyn Lloyd dismissed this, however. He countered that he had 'complete confidence' in Glubb, noting: 'naturally he is sniped at by Communists, Egyptians and anti-Western elements in Jordan. But I do not think that makes him a liability.'[211] This was despite the belief that Britain's position in Jordan depended 'quite considerably on General Glubb's prestige'.[212] Given the Arab nationalist pressure on Hussein, Glubb *was* a liability to the king. However, the British did not take this into consideration and talked themselves into accepting criticism of Glubb as par for the course.

The Glubb paradox was evident in the fruitless discussions concerning Glubb's potential successor after the murder of Abdullah made Glubb the number one target for assassination. It was adjudged that Glubb's successor would require two prerequisites. In Glubb's view: 'My successor wants two (almost incompatible) qualifications – a capable Arabist and an efficient soldier.'[213] He also required 'considerable political acumen'.[214] These criteria posed a problem because no such candidate existed. Ultimately, the problem was that 'the Pasha [Glubb] did everything' and no one else could do 'everything' like Glubb did.[215] When the issue was discussed after the 1948 War Glubb and Kirkbride both recommended Gawain Bell from the Sudan Political Service as a potential replacement.[216] Although he had spent time on secondment with the Arab Legion during the Second World War and had the required skills as an Arabist, he had no meaningful military experience. He was therefore discounted. In 1951 'Sam' Cooke, the Arab Legion divisional commander, came to the fore as a candidate. However, despite Glubb initially putting his name forward, both he and Kirkbride quickly established that Cooke was a mirror opposite of Bell. While he was militarily very capable he was deemed not to have the required political acumen. Nonetheless Cooke was earmarked as the best immediate replacement in the event of Glubb's sudden unexpected departure, but it was deemed necessary to begin the search for a more suitable 'long term successor'.[217] It was established that a suitable officer

[210] Currie to Lloyd, 3 January 1956, FO371/121491/VJ1051/21, TNA; Royle, *Glubb Pasha*, pp. 450–1.
[211] Lloyd to Currie, 16 January 1956, FO371/121491/VJ1051/21, TNA.
[212] Shuckburgh to Duke, 5 November 1955, FO371/115683/VJ12011/4, TNA.
[213] Glubb to Crocker, 6 November 1949, GP2006, 44.
[214] Furlonge to Kirkbride, 21 November 1951, FO371/91823/ET1201/78, TNA.
[215] Author interview with Robert K. Melville, 13 March 2013, London.
[216] Walker to Wardrop, 19 December 1951, FO371/91823/ET1201/94, TNA.
[217] Kirkbride to Furlonge, 28 November 1951, FO371/91823/ET1201/86, TNA.

would need to spend several years inside Jordan to get to know and be known by all the leading personalities.[218] However, no candidate was ever found. Nor, it seems, were they meaningfully searched for. MELF and Glubb agreed that the 'correct procedure' for finding a successor was to install potential candidates in the Arab Legion as and when vacancies occurred.[219] Glubb apprised that 'my successor ought to have "gone native" like me!' Not least because 'we want the Jordan Government to welcome my successor', as opposed to accepting him 'unwillingly' in response to threats to stop the subsidy.[220] Yet several years later, when Glubb was dismissed, Britain was still dependent on him to plough a lone furrow, with no replacement in sight. In October 1955 Cooke was still being bandied about as a potential immediate replacement in the event of Glubb's unexpected dismissal, even though he was still considered little more than a 'simple soldier' who would be out of his depth politically.[221] The War Office collected names of potential successors, but did not believe that anyone could fully replace Glubb.[222] The problem was that Glubb was deemed 'irreplaceable; not only as regards his Arab experience, but also as regards the loyalty which has enabled him to carry on, despite the occasional rumbles of discontent'. Glubb 'grew' with the role, but a replacement of the required rank would have to jump straight into the fire; he would need a 'concrete' reward for leaving the British Army mid-career and to ensure he became 'a contented and efficient servant of the Jordan Government'.[223] The British were dependent on Glubb's loyalty to the role – to what had effectively become the *Glubb role*. Consequently, the British found it almost impossible to look beyond Glubb. The British took advantage of the scant reward and heavy price that he was prepared to accept because of his loyalty to the role, and when faced with the prospect of his removal, the British effectively buried their heads in the sand, almost as if they hoped Glubb would continue forever. In so doing they broke one of the tenets of British imperial strategy. As Edward Said noted, during the nineteenth century it became commonplace for British colonial administrators to be retired off by the age of fifty-five to avoid the Oriental subjects seeing the Western superiors age and degenerate.[224]

[218] Furlonge to Kirkbride, 21 November 1951, FO371/91823/ET1201/78, TNA.
[219] Robertson to Brownjohn, 3 April 1952, WO216/767, TNA.
[220] Glubb to Crocker, 6 November 1949, GP2006, 44.
[221] Duke to Shuckburgh, 20 October 1955, FO371/115683/VJ12011/2, TNA.
[222] Poett to Shuckburgh, 28 October 1955, FO371/115683/VJ12011/3, TNA.
[223] Hunter to Major Newall, 5 October 1951, FO371/91822/ET1201/63/G, TNA.
[224] Edward Said, *Orientalism: Western Conceptions of the Orient* (London, 1995), p. 42.

Born in 1897, Glubb hit the magic number of fifty-five in 1952 – shortly before Hussein's accession – and thereafter he was perceived as increasingly anachronistic and irksome in the eyes of the younger generation of Jordanians entering the political scene – not least the king himself.

Ultimately it was this Glubb paradox that precluded Britain from satisfying any of the king's requirements in his quest for control of the Arab Legion. In the wake of Glubb's dismissal Duke questioned whether the 'action taken against Glubb was (a) directed against him personally or (b) intended as a blow against British influence and position in Jordan generally'.[225] The king's action does not fit neatly into either of these categories. Ultimately Hussein's decision was not simply about striking a blow against Britain. Rather, it was about reacting against British obstinacy, breaking free of British constraints, and Glubb was the perceived personification of this problem. Referring to questions about the details of his dismissal in a television interview less than a year after the event, Glubb remarked: 'In reality the details of the crisis were unimportant. It was the build up [over several years] that was important. Once the crisis arises, it is probably too late to do anything.'[226] Indeed it was the build-up of frustration over a number of years that fed Hussein's desire to be rid of Glubb. The British declined to expand the Arab Legion after Qibya; they failed to reply to the aide memoire of December 1954 and to acknowledge Hussein's vehemence regarding the method of paying the subsidy; and they failed to appease Hussein's frustrations with Glubb in the spring and then again in the autumn of 1955. Time and again the British decided that appeasing Hussein was not the answer. When he was irked by plans for his occupation before acceding the throne, the British favoured appeasing his mother. When he sought to obtain greater control over the Arab Legion, the British preferred to plot against his uncle. This approach was borne partly out of Britain's original belief that it could act as puppeteer. But it was also because Britain had become increasingly reliant on Glubb. The British therefore clung to the fiction that they could mould Hussein to work with Glubb. They did this not out of misplaced sureness, but out of the ominous uncertainty of a Glubbless Jordan.

After a brief lull in the friction between Glubb and Hussein during the summer of 1955, Hussein set in motion a process of Arabising the Arab Legion in the autumn, as evidenced by the change of name to the Arab

[225] Amman to FO, 339, 5 March 1956, FO371/121492/VJ1051/47/G, TNA.
[226] Transcript of Glubb's interview with Richard Dimbleby on the TV programme: *At Home: Glubb Pasha*, 23 January 1957, GP2006, 47.

Legion Air Force, the notice that Coghill would be replaced by his Arab assistant when his contract expired, and Hussein's evident – and now public – displeasure with Glubb, which led Glubb to believe that Hussein was intent on replacing him. This gradual process of Arabisation, however, was expedited when the threat of a renewed Arab–Israeli conflict raised its head. Indeed, we know this process was expedited because why else would Hussein dismiss Coghill when he was already scheduled to leave just a few weeks later? In February 1956 Hussein's frustrations with Glubb and Britain collided with a sense of urgency. Added to the increasingly anti-British, Arab nationalist atmosphere, this proved a potent mix. The trigger for dismissing Glubb was the urgent threat of renewed Arab–Israeli fighting. However, the underlying cause of removing Glubb was the king's lack of authority over the Arab Legion, which was compounded by Britain repeatedly ignoring Hussein's concerns and requests. Just as Glubb's dismissal was indicative of the king's need to exert his authority, it was indicative of Britain's struggle to adapt to evolving global conditions. As Samir al-Rifai astutely apprised, Britain had been 'unable [to] adjust traditionalist thinking to new circumstances'. It hoped that through 'waiting and patience all will turn out well'.[227] As it turned out, Britain's policy of waiting and patience frustrated Hussein and therefore resulted in change being thrust on it. The British were hostage to the Glubb paradox. That is why Britain failed to remedy the king's complaints and in turn why Hussein decided that Glubb must go.

---

[227] Mallory to State Department, 26 January 1956, *FRUS, 1955–57, XIII*, pp. 21–3.

8

Behind the Veil of Suez: Glubbless Jordan and the Termination of the Treaty

In his memoirs Hussein described the dismissal of Glubb and other officers from the Arab Legion as a 'strictly Jordanian affair'.[1] Glubb, after
all, was contracted to the Jordanian government with no official link
to Britain. Moreover, the removal of seconded British officers was not
contrary to the Anglo–Jordanian Treaty, as Britain was only obligated to
supply officers if requested. However, the British deemed that the manner
of the dismissals – given the lack of consultation – broke the spirit of the
treaty, if not the letter.[2] Moreover, the removal of Glubb was a crushing
blow not only to British dominance of the Arab Legion, but also to British
prestige throughout the Middle East.[3] Glubb's dismissal was a headline
event. Yet hitherto its consequences have largely avoided critical analysis.
Within the existing literature Glubb's dismissal has been considered primarily within the context of King Hussein's political survival, or, within
the British context, as a component part of the Suez Crisis later that year,
which culminated in a botched collusion between Britain, France, and
Israel at the end of October after the Egyptian president, Gamal Abd
al-Nasser, nationalised the Suez Canal Company in July. The purpose of
this chapter is to explore the relationship between Glubb's dismissal, the
Suez Crisis, and the termination of the Anglo–Jordanian Treaty in March
1957. In so doing this chapter fills a crucial gap in the Anglo–Jordanian

---

[1] Hussein, *Uneasy Lies the Head*, p. 107.
[2] 'Sir Anthony Eden's Statement in the House of Commons on 5th March, 1956',
'Supplementary Questions', GP2006, 54; 'Jordan', 2 March 1956, PREM11/1419, TNA.
[3] The Arab Legion was formally rebranded as the Jordan Arab Army on 12 July 1956.
For ease of reference, though, this chapter will continue to refer to this force as the Arab
Legion.

historiography, but also the broader historiographical debates concerning the Suez Crisis and Britain's Middle East retreat.

In assessing the impact of Glubb's dismissal, it is necessary to break the analysis down into two aspects: the reaction and the response. The bulk of this chapter will focus on the practicalities of the British response, assessing how Britain sought to cope with the dismissal and exploring the process that led to the termination of the treaty almost exactly twelve months after Glubb was dismissed. Hitherto the veil of Suez has obscured analysis of this process. As A. J. Stockwell reminds us: 'It is readily claimed that the Suez crisis marked the end of the British Empire.'[4] Both Peter Hahn and Scott Lucas, for instance, contend that Suez was a watershed moment that marked the end of British influence in the Middle East.[5] Nigel Ashton has convincingly countered the watershed argument by emphasising Britain's continued involvement in the region after 1956, particularly British military intervention in Jordan in 1958 and Kuwait in 1961.[6] Stephen Blackwell, like Ashton, posits that the British military intervention in Jordan was more than just the 'brief Indian summer' that Keith Kyle dismissed it as.[7] Similarly, Simon Smith and Ashley Jackson have emphasised Britain's continued commitments and influence even after the 1971 withdrawal from East of Suez.[8] Lucas, though, has remained unconvinced by those who 'cling to tangible markers of continuing but limited British presence'.[9] It is beyond the scope of this chapter to explore Britain's continued relationship with Jordan beyond 1957. However, it nonetheless contributes to the Suez watershed debate by revealing the insignificant role that Suez played in Britain's retreat from Jordan. Stephen Blackwell, for example, considers the British abandonment of Jordan one of the results of the Suez debacle.[10] This notion supports the template that Suez was a watershed that heralded

---

[4] A. J. Stockwell, 'Suez 1956 and the Moral Disarmament of the British Empire', in: Simon C. Smith (ed.), *Reassessing Suez 1956: New Perspectives on the Crisis and Its Aftermath* (Aldershot, 2008), p. 227.

[5] Scott Lucas, *Divided We Stand: Britain, the US and the Suez Crisis* (London, 1991); Peter Hahn, *The United States, Great Britain, and Egypt, 1945–1956: Strategy and Diplomacy in the Early Cold War* (Chapel Hill, 1991), p. 240.

[6] Ashton, 'Microcosm of Decline', pp. 1069–83; Ashton, 'Special Relationship', pp. 221–44.

[7] Blackwell, *British Military Intervention*, p. 1; Keith Kyle, *Suez: Britain's End of Empire in the Middle East*, 2nd edn (London, 2003), p. 582.

[8] Simon C. Smith, *Britain's Revival and Fall in the Gulf: Kuwait, Bahrain, Qatar, and the Trucial States, 1950–71* (London, 2004), pp. 5–6; Philip Murphy, 'Britain as a Global Power in the Twentieth Century', in: Andrew Thompson (ed.), *Britain's Experience of Empire in the Twentieth Century* (Oxford, 2012), p. 69.

[9] Scott Lucas, 'Conclusion', in: Smith (ed.), *Reassessing Suez*, p. 242.

[10] Blackwell, *British Military Intervention*, pp. 50–1.

the end of Britain's moment in the Middle East. Blackwell argues that the Suez Crisis 'wrecked' Britain's attempt to renew the Anglo–Jordanian relationship.[11] As this chapter reveals, though, the Suez Crisis did not significantly contribute to the termination of the Anglo–Jordanian Treaty. Although the formal termination discussions took place after Suez, the re-evaluation process had been initiated by Glubb's dismissal – and was delayed, rather than caused, by the Suez Crisis. Suez was undoubtedly a significant aspect of Britain's moment in the Middle East, but it was not the all-defining watershed it is often portrayed as. In that regard, this chapter supports Stockwell's contention that 'the ebb and flow of empire washed over the supposed Suez watershed'.[12]

In the first instance, though, this chapter will hone in on the immediate British reaction – where Suez has again dominated the historiographical analysis. Within the existing literature it is generally accepted that British Prime Minister Anthony Eden was initially furious at the decision to dismiss Glubb. Even one of Eden's most sympathetic biographers concedes that the initial telegrams suggest that Eden 'initially overreacted'.[13] It is accepted as an almost undisputed fact that the British – and Eden in particular – blamed the Egyptian president for engineering the dismissal.[14] The significance of this, as Nigel Ashton has contended, is that Glubb's dismissal marked 'the point at which the British Government abandoned the strategy of trying to work with Nasser'.[15] By paying close attention to the nuances of the reaction and with the aid of three recently released documents, this chapter challenges this hitherto accepted contention that Eden blamed Nasser. Instead it posits an altered understanding of the link between Glubb's dismissal and the origins of the Suez Crisis.

The traditional appreciation of the British reaction has its origins in the memoirs of Minister of State for Foreign Affairs Anthony Nutting. In 1967, after a self-imposed ten-year wait and amidst much government debate, Nutting published his memoirs of the Suez Crisis.[16] In the very first line he pinpointed Glubb's dismissal as being where the 'drama that was to become the Suez disaster actually began'. He added, in notably unequivocal terms:

[11] Ibid., p. 31.
[12] Stockwell, 'Moral Disarmament of the British Empire', p. 238.
[13] Robert Rhodes James, *Anthony Eden* (London, 1986), p. 432.
[14] For example: Aburish, *Nasser*, p. 97; Ashton, *King Hussein*, pp. 56–7; Blackwell, *British Military Intervention*, p. 28; Bradshaw, *Glubb Reports*, p. 131; Dann, *Challenge of Arab Radicalism*, p. 31; Shlaim, *Lion of Jordan*, p. 104.
[15] Ashton, *Eisenhower, Macmillan*, p. 72.
[16] Philip Murphy, 'Telling Tales Out of School: Nutting, Eden and the Attempted Suppression of *No End of a Lesson*', in: Smith (ed.), *Reassessing Suez*, pp. 195–213.

As one who spent the evening and half of the night after Glubb's dismissal arguing with Eden, I can testify that, at the time, he put all the blame on Nasser. ...
And on that fatal day he decided that the world was not big enough to hold both
him and Nasser.[17]

This appreciation is reinforced by the initial reaction of British Foreign
Secretary Selwyn Lloyd, who had been dining with Nasser at the time of
Glubb's dismissal. When Lloyd first heard news of the incident – after
leaving his engagement with Nasser – he sent a telegram to Eden stating that he found 'it difficult to believe that Nasser did not know, but
he [Nasser] gave no hint'.[18] This has been unanimously interpreted as
evidence that Lloyd blamed Nasser for engineering Glubb's dismissal.[19]
Within the existing literature Eden is deemed to have shared this opinion
and become intent on revenge.

However, new evidence and close attention to the timing of correspondence during the twenty-four hours after Glubb's dismissal posit an
alternative interpretation of the British reaction. When news of Glubb's
dismissal first reached London, the initial reaction was consistent with
the pre-dismissal policy hampered by the Glubb paradox; instinctively
the British hoped that the decision could be reversed and the status quo
maintained. It was mooted that Britain should 'try to preserve the fiction
that he has gone to Cyprus on leave while we work on the King ... to
modify his view'.[20] In his first message to the king – sent before receipt of
Lloyd's telegram – Eden warned Hussein that if he did not reverse Glubb's
dismissal, 'the resentment in Britain at this action will be widespread and
deep. I cannot foretell its final consequences upon the relations between
our two countries.' Eden tempered this warning, though, by explaining
that it was being made, 'in the insterests [*sic*] of the friendship of our two
countries'.[21] In his memoirs Nutting claimed that Eden's first instinct was
'to telegraph to the King personally to say that if he persisted in removing
Glubb our relations with Jordan would be at an end', but that Nutting
'managed to dissuade him'.[22] Eden's initial message to the king perhaps
reads, therefore, like a threat tempered by Nutting. However, a document

---

[17] Anthony Nutting, *No End of a Lesson: The Story of Suez* (London, 1967), pp. 17–18, 29.
[18] Cairo to FO, 413, 2 March 1956, FO371/121243/V1071/85, TNA.
[19] Steven Freiberger, *Dawn Over Suez: The Rise of American Power in the Middle East,
1953–1957* (Chicago, 1992), pp. 246–7; Tal, *Politics, the Military, and National Security*,
pp. 29–30; Kyle, *Suez*, p. 94; Monroe, *Britain's Moment*, p. 190; Shlaim, *Lion of Jordan*,
pp. 105–6.
[20] FO to Amman, 347, 2 March 1956, FO371/121540/VJ1201/11/G, TNA.
[21] FO to Amman, 346, 2 March 1956, ibid.
[22] Nutting, *No End of a Lesson*, pp. 28–9.

released in 2007 posits another interpretation to explain the construction of this message. The preceding telegram to London, from the British
ambassador, Charles Duke, contained the following passage:

Reverting to the subject of Anglo–Jordan relations the Prime Minister [Samir
al-Rifai] said, speaking personally to me as a friend, that he suggested that Her
Majesty's Government should make clear to the King the gravity of his action but
should not allow it to damage those mutual interests which were served by the
maintenance of cooperation between the two countries.[23]

In light of this telegram Eden's message to the king reads like a considered
response which heeded the Jordanian prime minister's advice – rather
than, or perhaps in addition to, Nutting's counsel – to demonstrate *the
gravity of the king's action*, while simultaneously protecting *the maintenance of cooperation between the two countries*. Indeed, this interpretation is supported by a minute written by Foreign Affairs Private Secretary
Phillip de Zulueta, who stated that Eden simply wanted to avoid giving the impression that the 'British will always accept a fait accompli'.[24]
This, indeed, is consistent with Eden's approach as foreign secretary after
Abu al-Huda signed Jordan up to the Arab League Collective Security
Pact in 1952. Given the general tone of Nutting's memoirs, there is a
distinct possibility that he exaggerated the extent of Eden's anger some-
what.[25] Although deeply stunned, Eden was seemingly more pragmatic
than Nutting, and much of the subsequent literature has given him credit.
Perhaps, though, this equates to little more than a diluted version of
Nutting's account.

Yet what of Nutting's claim that Eden turned his attention towards
Nasser? Here a more significant reappraisal emerges. Notably, this contention is not supported by the Cabinet secretary's notebook – released
in 2008. These notebooks had been previously withheld on the basis that
they revealed the contribution of individual members to Cabinet debates
and so might have undermined collective responsibility. According to the
notes taken during the 5 March Cabinet meeting, when the dismissal of
Glubb was discussed, Eden apparently made no mention of Nasser. In
fact, Eden's comments – although possibly diluted by their note form –
appeared to be pragmatically concerned with establishing the future
course of policy towards Jordan. Richard Austen Butler, the Lord Privy
Seal and Leader of the House of Commons, indicated that measures

should not be confined to Jordan and suggested that Britain 'may have to move closer to Israel and ... *[perhaps] unseat Nasser*'. Yet even after Butler had brought Nasser into the debate, Eden seemingly dismissed this suggestion, stating only that: 'We are more likely to transfer support elsewhere – e.g. reinforce [the] P.[ersian] Gulf.'[26] Not only did Eden not mention Nasser himself, but he dismissed claims by others to act against him. This belies the notion that Eden wanted Nasser destroyed as a consequence of Glubb's dismissal.

So how do we explain the change in Eden's attitude from anger directed at Nasser on the night of Glubb's dismissal – as Nutting claimed – and his rebuttal of linking this incident to Nasser a few days later in the Cabinet meeting? Or does the Cabinet secretary's notebook merely mask Eden's anger towards Nasser? The answer to the second question is seemingly: no. It is reasonable to accept that Eden did rage against Nasser to Nutting during the twilight hours following Glubb's dismissal. Perhaps this was fuelled by Lloyd's euphemistic report that he found it hard to believe that Nasser did not know – which is not quite the same as saying he believed Nasser was to blame. Eden's apparent change of heart can be explained by the third recently released document. On the morning after Glubb's dismissal Lloyd met Nasser again at breakfast, at which point both believed the other was responsible. Recounting the meeting, Nasser lamented: 'I was not able to convince him of my innocence and at the same time I was unable to stop myself from laughing at what had happened and the way he looked.'[27] However, Nasser's fears were seemingly unfounded, because after this meeting – the first time the pair had met since hearing news of Glubb's dismissal – Evelyn Shuckburgh, assistant under-secretary at the Foreign Office in charge of Middle East affairs, informed Sir Ivone Kirkpatrick, the permanent under-secretary of state, that 'the Secretary of State had been with Colonel Nasser last night and had derived the impression that *Nasser knew nothing about it*'.[28] Lloyd's suspicion, it seems, was at most an instinctive reaction, which lasted for one night only. It is therefore wholly plausible that Eden's alleged indignation directed at Nasser in the early hours of 2 March was placated, in the cold light of day, by Lloyd's better-informed and unequivocal appraisal that Nasser was not involved.

[26] Cabinet Secretary's Notebook, 5 March 1956, CAB195/14, TNA [emphasis added].
[27] Heikal, *Cairo Documents*, p. 86.
[28] Shuckburgh to Kirkpatrick, 2 March 1956, FO371/121542/VJ1201/57, TNA [emphasis added].

British indignation against Nasser did increase in early March 1956. However, an important nuance must be acknowledged. On 8 March Shuckburgh recorded that: 'Today both we and the Americans really gave up hope of Nasser and began to look around for means of destroying him.'[29] The question, therefore, is: what explains this sudden change on 8 March if the widely held turning point – Glubb's dismissal – had occurred a week previously? The United States' frustration with Nasser was a result of Robert Anderson's failed mission to secure Nasser's support for an Arab–Israeli rapprochement.[30] After Israeli Prime Minister Ben-Gurion refused to accept the territorial concessions proposed by Project Alpha – a secret Anglo-American peace initiative for the Arab–Israeli conflict – the United States sent Anderson to negotiate support from Egypt.[31] The mission failed, however. Partly because of the conditions set by Ben-Gurion and the failure to provide contiguous land between Egypt and the rest of the Arab world in the Negev; but also because Nasser baulked at the United States' apparent attempt to buy peace by linking any settlement to the financing of the Aswan Dam project.[32] The United States remained pragmatic in its attitude towards Nasser, but the failed Anderson mission prompted the United States to move from a 'carrot' to a 'stick'-based approach to dealing with the Egyptian president.[33] Britain's increasingly belligerent stance, meanwhile, can be explained by another incident, to which Glubb's dismissal was related: the House of Commons debate on Glubb's dismissal on 7 March. Evelyn Shuckburgh immediately predicted that Eden would be 'jeered at in the house' and that this was 'his main concern'.[34] And so it proved. Eden's winding-up speech received heavy parliamentary criticism.[35] Consistent with the pragmatism displayed thus far, Eden was not criticised for over-reacting, but for under-reacting.[36] When Lloyd tackled Nasser over Glubb's dismissal, he remarked that,

---

[29] Shuckburgh, *Descent*, p. 345.
[30] Clea Bunch, 'Supporting the Brave Young King: The Suez Crisis and Eisenhower's New Approach to Jordan, 1953–1958', in: Smith (ed.), *Reassessing Suez*, pp. 114–15.
[31] Nigel Ashton, 'Hitler on the Nile? Britain and American Perceptions of the Nasser Regime, 1952–70', in: Lawrence Freedman and Jeffrey H. Michaels (eds.), *Scripting Middle East Leaders: The Impact of Leadership Perceptions on US and UK Foreign Policy* (New York, 2013), pp. 54–5.
[32] Kennett Love, *Suez: The Twice-Fought War* (New York, 1969), pp. 307–10; Aburish, *Nasser*, p. 99; Heikal, *Cairo Documents*, pp. 64–5.
[33] Ashton, 'Hitler on the Nile?' p. 55.
[34] Shuckburgh, *Descent*, p. 340.
[35] Sue Onslow, 'Julian Amery and the Suez Operation', in: Smith (ed.), *Reassessing Suez*, pp. 69–70.
[36] Anthony Howard, *RAB: The Life of R.A. Butler* (London, 1988), p. 228.

as a result of Egypt's vociferous propaganda campaign against Glubb, it would 'rightly or wrongly be attributed to Egypt in large measure'.[37] It was this kind of ill-informed assumption – predicted by Lloyd – that contributed to the parliamentary criticism that Eden received. Several MPs asserted that 'the finger points to the influence of Nasser and none other'.[38] If a decisive turning point linking Glubb's dismissal to the Suez Crisis exists, this was surely it. Glubb's dismissal itself did not rouse Eden's antagonism against Nasser, but the parliamentary criticism concerning this event did. Glubb's dismissal might have assisted the abandonment of working with Nasser, but he was not believed to be behind the decision by those in the know. The subsequent policy towards Nasser seemingly had more to do with Eden's temperament, parliamentary wrangling, and Anglo–Egyptian relations than events in Jordan.

Beyond this initial reaction, the response to Glubb's dismissal was more concerned with repairing the Anglo–Jordanian relationship in the short term, while the future value of the relationship was re-evaluated. During the 5 March Cabinet meeting Richard Austen Butler and Lord President of the Council Lord Salisbury were in favour of immediately ending the subsidy and the treaty. Others, such as Harold Macmillan, wanted to save what they could in Jordan, lest it fall under Egyptian control, which in turn might 'lead to the collapse of the Hashemite regime in Iraq'.[39] All those best placed to make an informed judgement regarding the situation in Jordan – Glubb, Kirkbride, and Duke – advised against pressing Hussein too hard or too fast.[40] There was nothing to be gained by acting hastily, and this was the line that was followed. It was deemed necessary to re-evaluate the value of the alliance and carefully consider the implications of any change to the existing arrangement. Instinctively the Foreign Office questioned whether the subsidy was still a worthwhile investment.[41] Meanwhile, the War Office and the Chiefs of Staff had consequently 'written the Legion off as a military body in which they have any serious interest'.[42] The War Office had always justified its portion of the subsidy on the basis that it could rely on

---

[37] Bahrain to FO, 156, 2 March 1956, FO371/121540/VJ1201/24, TNA.

[38] Parliamentary Debate, 7 March 1956, Hansard, vol. 549, http://hansard.millbanksystems .com/commons/1956/mar/07/ [accessed: 3 May 2016].

[39] Peter Caterall (ed.), *The Macmillan Diaries: The Cabinet Years, 1950–1957* (London, 2003), pp. 540–1; Shuckburgh, *Descent*, p. 343.

[40] Nicosia to FO, 139, 2 March 1956, FO371/121540/VJ1201/14/G; Amman to FO, 289, 2 March 1956, FO371/121540/VJ1201/18/G; 'My Conclusions and Queries', Kirkbride, 8 March 1956, PREM11/1419, TNA.

[41] Kirkpatrick to Levant Department, 5 March 1956, FO371/121541/VJ1201/51/G, TNA; Pappé, 'British Rule in Jordan', p. 217.

[42] Hadow to Mason, 13 June 1956, FO371/121549/VJ1201/216, TNA.

Arab Legion assistance in the event of a global war. After Glubb's departure this was no longer the case, and the War Office believed it could no longer justify any expenditure on the Arab Legion.[43] Nonetheless, the Foreign Office appraised that cutting the subsidy abruptly would further damage relations. The whole value of the relationship would have to be considered first.[44] Thus, instead of fixing the annual subsidy for the new financial year as normal, Britain continued to pay the subsidy on a month-by-month basis at the same level as the previous year while the long-term future of the relationship with Jordan was reconsidered.[45]

In the meantime, the British had to deal with two more immediate and interconnected problems created by the dismissal of Glubb: the future of seconded British officers within the Arab Legion and the impact that the recent changes would have on Britain's treaty obligations. Regarding the former, not only were there now fewer British officers, but also those who remained had their authority extinguished overnight. Technical and training officers continued as normal, but executive officers were now in the awkward position of holding command without authority.[46] When Lieutenant-Colonel Dingwall, commander of the 3rd Tank Regiment, inspected his men on 3 March, while 'the larger and better part' of his regiment were on guard duties elsewhere, only about five per cent 'raised a salute, some turned their backs, some got behind vehicles, and others found similar excuses. A few laughed.' Although Dingwall was still officially in command of the regiment, authority now rested with Adeeb Abu Nowar, Ali Abu Nowar's cousin. Over the next few days Dingwall reported that 'a truly remarkable number of officers' visited the regiment, but instead of going to see Dingwall, they all visited Adeeb Abu Nowar.[47] British officers 'as a whole' were keen to leave Jordan 'as quickly as possible'. They were angry at the events of 1 March, but they also felt that it was 'extremely dangerous' for them to serve in executive command of fighting units as they would be blamed for any defeat in war.[48] As the

[43] 'Arab Legion Subsidy', Rose, 20 April 1956, FO371/121557/VJ1205/15/G, TNA.

[44] Minute by Horley, 6 April 1956, FO371/121557/VJ1205/17/G, TNA.

[45] Rose to Duke, 17 May 1956, FO371/121558/VJ1205/25; FO to Amman, 2750, 30 November 1956, FO371/121500/VJ1051/252/G, TNA.

[46] 'Notes on Meeting with Brigadier Mead', VCIGS to CIGS, 12 March 1956, WO216/912, TNA.

[47] 'Report by Lt-Col. J. J. Dingwall, Commanding 3 Tank Regiment Arab Legion, upon the Events Which Took Place on 1 March 1956 as They Affected Him', 8 March 1956, GP2006, 54.

[48] 'The Arab Legion: Between 1 March and 1430 hours 6 March 56', Nigel Bromage, 6 March 1956, Melville Papers, 2/21.

chief of the imperial general staff, Gerald Templer, appraised, British officers were now in an 'impossible position'.[49] In the first instance, Britain's
'main object' was to 'maintain the cohesion and stability of the Arab
Legion as a whole'. Thus, the remaining British officers were instructed by
the British government to 'obey the orders' given by their new superiors
and if any officers of Bedouin battalions protested about the replacement
of the British commanding officer, then the displaced officer was told he
'must do all in his power to prevent trouble'.[50] In the second instance,
Britain was intent on revising the nature of British involvement in the
Arab Legion, to remove the dilemma of British officers being blamed for
reverses in a war with Israel when they had no control over operations.[51]
The impossible position in which the remaining British officers were now
placed meant that some change was needed.

The nature of this change has hitherto been misunderstood, or at
least misrepresented, within the existing literature. Avi Shlaim stated
that: 'The British officers on secondment to the Arab Legion were withdrawn, but those, like Glubb, under contract to the Jordanian government were allowed to stay.'[52] Meanwhile Stephen Blackwell asserted
that British officers seconded to the Arab Legion were converted into
a 'military mission' in May.[53] Both these statements are incorrect.
Instantaneously the British concluded that British officers could not 'be
asked to continue in positions of responsibility without authority'. As
Eden stated in the Commons: 'We have therefore asked that such officers should be relieved of their commands.'[54] Ironically, the Jordanians
were less keen on such a swift process of complete Arabisation. They
wished to maintain a number of seconded British officers in command
positions, including Cooke and Dingwall, in order to allow time for an
orderly transition.[55] It appeared to Hutton – who was asked to stay on
for a couple of weeks, despite his dismissal, in order to hand over to
his replacement as Chief of Staff, Ali al-Hiyari – that the Jordanians
now expected to run the Arab Legion themselves, but with all the same
benefits of British support in terms of men, money, and materials.[56] The

[49] FO to Amman, 494, 12 March 1956, GP2006, 54.
[50] FO to Amman, 353, 2 March 1956, FO371/121540/VJ1201/9/G, TNA.
[51] FO to Amman, 494, 12 March 1956, FO371/121542/VJ1201/73/G, TNA.
[52] Shlaim, *Lion of Jordan*, p. 105.
[53] Blackwell, *British Military Intervention*, p. 41.
[54] 'Sir Anthony Eden's Statement in the House of Commons on 5 March, 1956', GP2006, 54.
[55] Amman to FO, 399, 12 March 1956, FO371/121542/VJ1201/73/G; Amman to FO, 410
and 411, 13 March 1956, FO371/121542/VJ1201/74/G, TNA.
[56] Amman to FO, 290, 2 March 1956, FO371/121540/VJ1201/19/G, TNA.

Foreign Office was adamant that in the interest of preventing future friction, Britain could not adhere to the king's request for British officers to remain in executive command positions at any level. However, it was vital that this rejection did not encourage Hussein to turn to his Arab neighbours because, in an advisory capacity, the British were keen to provide the Arab Legion with as much 'unobtrusive British assistance and guidance as possible at all levels'.[57] The presence of British officers was still required in order to limit any decline in the Arab Legion's efficiency and 'thereby prevent the disruption of Jordan'.[58] The War Office wanted 'all British officers in command' positions 'withdrawn from the Legion and reconstituted as a Military Mission'. From the Foreign Office perspective, this would 'satisfy Jordanian aspirations to command' and enable British officers to maintain some influence.[59] To that end, Brigadier Brooke, who had experience setting up a military mission in Burma, was sent to Amman to advise Duke in his negotiations with the Jordanian government.[60] The Jordanians, however, were utterly opposed to a military mission, which would be a separate British team. They wanted British officers to continue as integrated members of the Arab Legion under the same terms as before Glubb's dismissal, albeit performing training and advisory functions.[61] This was not the first time Britain had faced opposition to installing a military mission in an Arab army because it implied control and therefore provided a target for hostile propaganda. For that reason British military advisers in Iraq were labelled 'British Loaned Personnel' (BLPI).[62] The BLPI was a War Office establishment, much like a military mission, but as far as the Iraqis were concerned, it was 'simply a number of British service personnel integrated in Iraqi forces'.[63] The War Office suggested doing the same in Jordan, although it preferred a straightforward military mission.[64] However, the Jordanians were equally opposed to a loan system as this would also involve a change to the present system and therefore

[57] FO to Amman, 518, 15 March 1956, FO371/121543/VJ1201/79, TNA.
[58] Bishop to Forward, 1 April 1956, FO371/121545/VJ1201/143, TNA.
[59] FO to Amman, 495, 12 March 1956, FO371/121563/VJ1208/6, TNA.
[60] FO to Amman, 512, 15 March 1956, FO371/121543/VJ1201/79; 'Directive for Brigadier F. M. Brooke', Templer, 15 March 1956, FO371/121543/VJ1201/86, TNA.
[61] Amman to FO, 466, 21 March 1956, WO32/16704; Amman to FO, 478, 22 March 1956, FO371/121543/VJ1201/96/G, TNA.
[62] 'British Officers for Jordan', 22 March 1956, FO371/121543/VJ1201/100, TNA.
[63] FO to Amman, 574, 22 March 1956, FO371/121543/VJ1201/88, TNA.
[64] 'British Officers for Jordan', 22 March 1956, FO371/121543/VJ1201/100, TNA.

imply a lack of confidence in Arab officers and the new command of the Legion. Brooke concluded that there was 'definitely no chance' of the Jordanians accepting a military mission and that rather than compel the Jordanians to seek advisers from elsewhere, they should 'provisionally accept their proposals as the lesser evil'.[65] Having British officers serving solely under the control of Jordanians was deemed highly undesirable, but if it was the only option for maintaining British influence and Arab Legion efficiency, Duke felt, and Eden agreed, Britain had to accept.[66] The two parties therefore agreed to maintain British officers within the same framework as before. Seconded officers were neither withdrawn, because both Britain and Jordan required their stabilising presence and expertise, nor converted into a military mission, because the Jordanians would not accept a change to the existing arrangement. Yes it was agreed that seconded British officers would be employed 'exclusively in training and technical duties'. However, seconded British officers would continue to wear the Jordanian uniform and to hold the king's commission.[67] This was formalised in an agreement eventually published by the Jordanians on 14 October.[68]

The continued presence of British officers was pursued to offset the potential reduction in the Arab Legion's efficiency. However, it did not solve the problem of reliability. With no British officers in positions of executive authority, the Arab Legion was now deemed liable to take offensive or defensive action contrary to British policy. The British therefore pursued two means of maintaining influence over the Arab Legion's command. The first was to collaborate with the currents of Jordanian nationalism that had overturned the Glubb regime, which was indicative of Britain's pragmatic response to the Glubb crisis. While the British did not believe Nasser had engineered the decision to dismiss Glubb, they did believe that Ali Abu Nowar had heavily influenced Hussein.[69] Yet despite this, he did not become the subject of any British retribution. Rather, the British were prepared to support him. Glubb's immediate replacement was Radi Innab. However, the British believed Ali Abu Nowar held real authority and it was deemed only a matter of

[65] Amman to FO, 478, 22 March 1956, FO371/121543/VJ1201/96/G, TNA.
[66] Amman to FO, 479, 22 March 1956; Cairncross to Sinclair, 23 March 1956, FO371/121543/VJ1201/97/G, TNA.
[67] Duke to Lloyd, 28 April 1956, FO371/121565/VJ1209/19, TNA.
[68] W. G. A. Lawrie to DMO, 23 November 1956, FO371/121562/VJ1207/44, TNA.
[69] Amman to FO, 277, 1 March 1956, FO371/121540/VJ1201/9/G, TNA.

time before he assumed the top job within the military. This was not unfounded. As Abu Nowar explained:

the Jordanians will think that a young King and a young commander-in-chief, both young – so let's put Brigadier Innab there who had all grey hair.... We will do the job but we want Rabhi Innab at our head.[70]

Ali Abu Nowar was the real power behind the army, and when Major Kawwar approached the British Embassy in an attempt to enlist British support for him, Duke surmised that Abu Nowar himself was 'angling for British political and possibly financial support'. Duke therefore suggested that Britain should give Abu Nowar 'discreet support for [the] position of Chief of the General Staff' and offer him £2,000 of 'personal financial assistance'.[71] Templer distrusted Abu Nowar and was against Britain having dealings with him. Similarly Eden questioned the logic of bribing 'the least reputable military character'.[72] However, based on the judgement of Duke and, crucially, Kirkbride, that Britain should swim with the tide and embrace his approach, Duke was given authorisation to offer Abu Nowar 'discreet support'.[73] In the event, Duke 'decided not to' offer him the bribe. Nonetheless, the British had opted to work with, rather than against the current of Jordanian nationalism, and when Abu Nowar finally became chief of the general staff on 24 May, Selwyn Lloyd was once again 'anxious that we should try to establish some relationship with him'.[74]

Two other recent studies have commented on Britain's willingness to support Abu Nowar. However, there is scope to reinterpret the rationale behind this move. Nigel Ashton has suggested that, 'in hindsight it seems to have been a misjudgement on the part of the British government to extend "personal financial assistance" to Ali Abu Nowar, who proved an unreliable guarantor of anyone's interests, except his own'.[75] Abu Nowar's involvement in a failed coup against the king in April 1957 is evidence of his eventual unreliability. Meanwhile Stephen Blackwell suggested that the British 'decided to place their bets on Abu Nuwar as the future of Jordanian politics'.[76] However, contrary to Ashton's assertion of hindsight the British were under no illusion about Abu Nowar's unreliability. It was noted that: 'Nuwar is essentially pro-Nuwar, and King Hussein is taking a considerable risk with him.'[77]

[70] Interview with Ali Abu Nowar, 20 June 1990, Geyelin Papers.
[71] Amman to FO, 570, 7 April 1956, PREM11/1420, TNA.
[72] Eden to Lloyd, 15 April 1956, ibid.; Ashton, *King Hussein*, p. 55.
[73] Lloyd to Eden, 14 April 1956; FO to Amman, 782, 17 April 1956, PREM11/1420, TNA.
[74] 'Ali Abu Nuwar', Rose, 31 May 1956, FO371/121549/VJ1201/212/G, TNA.
[75] Ashton, *King Hussein*, p. 56.
[76] Blackwell, *British Military Intervention*, p. 41.
[77] Minute by Holmer, 25 June 1956, FO371/121548/VJ1201/203, TNA.

The British were concerned that a power struggle between Abu Nowar and the king might eventually occur. However, Britain's acceptance of Abu Nowar was a means of keeping a lid on the immediate turmoil created by Glubb's dismissal and the consequent upheaval within the Arab Legion. It was believed that: 'King Hussein, Abu Nuwar and senior officers in the Legion constitute a power complex of which component parts provide support for each other.'[78] To disrupt that power complex would have been to risk further destabilising the kingdom. The British recognised that Hussein would not be receptive to any complaints being made against one of his close allies.[79] Support for Abu Nowar within Jordan was not unanimous and there was an opportunity to intrigue against him. There was some dissension against Abu Nowar within the Arab Legion. Moreover, Queen Zein was known to be 'intriguing hard' against him. However, opposition was not believed to be 'as united or well organised as Queen Zein' asserted.[80] The British were comforted by the belief that Abu Nowar gave the impression of being a 'Jordanian nationalist' rather than a 'disciple' of Nasser.[81] Therefore it was deemed not 'the moment to throw a rock into the pool by trying to shake the King's confidence in him'.[82] Britain supported Abu Nowar not because he was the future, as Blackwell suggested, but because he was the present. Britain was hedging its bets with Abu Nowar. Britain had not thrown its lot in with him, but accepted his primacy as a short-term remedy to the upheaval created by Glubb's departure, partly because he was considered a Jordanian nationalist, but mostly because he was in a position of power and had the support of the king. This was in stark contrast to the pre-dismissal approach of ignoring Hussein – thus frustrating him – and intriguing against those believed to be influencing him. In the absence of Glubb's control, collaboration with those deemed close to Hussein was now considered the best means of exerting influence.

In order to ensure a smooth relationship with Abu Nowar and in light of the breakdown in relations with Glubb during the eighteen months prior to his dismissal, the British became increasingly pre-emptive regarding the personality of the senior British officer (SBO) – a position that the Jordanians reluctantly, and privately, agreed to recognise merely as a point

[78] Amman to FO, 626, 19 April 1956, PREM11/1420, TNA.
[79] Cabinet Minutes, 27 March 1956, CAB128/30; Amman to FO, 617, 17 April 1956, PREM11/1420, TNA.
[80] Amman to FO, 1058, 2 August 1956, FO371/121550/VJ1201/245/G; Amman to FO, 617, 17 April 1956, PREM11/1420, TNA.
[81] Amman to FO, 570, 7 April 1956, PREM11/1420, TNA.
[82] FO to Damascus, 484, 9 June 1956, FO371/121568/VJ12013/1, TNA.

of contact for British officers on welfare matters.[83] After Glubb's departure Cooke was by default the most senior British officer. However, he had no desire to remain, and it was generally considered preferable for the new SBO to be a fresh face not tainted by the previous regime. In his stead the War Office seconded Brigadier Mackenzie, who was appointed head of the Infantry Training Team.[84] Mackenzie did not last long in this role, though. Duke quickly became concerned that he lacked the required tact. Duke warned Mackenzie of the 'delicacy' of his task. Yet while he provided reassuring replies, Duke cautioned: 'I have a premonition, which I hope will prove unfounded, that he may through excessive zeal and a tendency to look on Arabs as "wogs", land us in trouble and open up once again the whole question of British officers in the Legion.'[85] General Templer agreed that Mackenzie 'appears to be a complete bull in a china shop'. He added: 'I am very doubtful indeed of the wisdom of allowing such a person to continue to serve in Jordan today. It seems to me much better to grasp the nettle now rather than wait until he has blotted his copy book properly.'[86] Shuckburgh believed this was sound advice, noting: 'With things as they are we cannot afford to take risks in our military relations with Jordan.'[87] Completely unprompted, Abu Nowar informed Duke that the Jordanians were happy with Mackenzie.[88] Nonetheless, it was deemed necessary to remove Mackenzie as a precaution because: 'Since the dismissal of General Glubb, the position of the senior British officer in the Arab Legion has become an extremely delicate one.'[89] Mackenzie was deemed 'obviously not fitted for a quasi-diplomatic post'.[90] He was therefore replaced as SBO by Lieutenant-Colonel Strickland. Duke suggested that because Strickland was deemed 'flexible in his approach to the Jordanians ... [and] sensitive to political undercurrents within the army', he was the man through whom Britain could 'exercise the greatest influence upon the Jordan army and its present Chief of the General Staff [Ali Abu Nowar]'.[91] Mackenzie was therefore removed from Jordan and Strickland was promoted to the rank of brigadier, thus making him the senior British officer attached to the Arab

[83] Amman to FO, 485, 24 March 1956, WO32/16704, TNA.
[84] 'British Officers in the Arab Legion: Record of a Meeting in the Jordan Prime Minister's Office – 24 March, 1956', FO371/121544/VJ1201/121, TNA.
[85] Duke to Shuckburgh, 6 June 1956, FO371/121549/VJ1201/223/G, TNA.
[86] Templer to Shuckburgh, 14 June 1956, ibid.
[87] Shuckburgh to Duke, 16 June 1956, ibid.
[88] Duke to Shuckburgh, 6 June 1956, ibid.
[89] Ross to Lt.-Gen. Euan Miller, 11 July 1956, FO371/121550/VJ1201/236/G, TNA.
[90] Ross to Kirkpatrick, 9 July 1956, FO371/121550/VJ1201/236/G, TNA.
[91] Amman to FO, 1220, 5 September 1956, FO371/121551/VJ1201/256/G, TNA.

Legion.[92] It was hoped that Abu Nowar would now gravitate towards Strickland for advice, given his new rank.

Placating Ali Abu Nowar and the tide of Jordanian nationalism was one avenue Britain pursued for maintaining influence over the Arab Legion. The second means by which Britain sought to exercise control was via the Anglo-Jordan Joint Defence Board (AJJDB), which the British had hitherto been reluctant to utilise. The AJJDB had been created at Britain's instigation in 1948 for two reasons: firstly, to 'give expression to the idea of equal status as between Great Britain and Transjordan'; and, secondly, it was hoped that it would 'be a first step towards setting up similar boards in all other Arab States'.[93] With the onset of the 1948 War, however, the first meeting of the AJJDB was delayed until 1950.[94] Consequently, it never became an effective machine. The private directive given to the original British delegation was that the AJJDB should meet at least quarterly. However, when Glubb was dismissed it had not met since November 1954. The British felt that they gained little from the AJJDB and so made no effort to instigate any meetings. Less than two weeks prior to his dismissal Glubb suggested an AJJDB meeting be arranged to allay Jordanian fears over British adherence to its obligation to defend Jordan in the event of an attack by Israel.[95] For 'security reasons', though, the Ministry of Defence did not want to discuss its plan for defending Jordan – Operation Cordage – with the AJJDB.[96] Operation Cordage was not even discussed with Glubb, except in the 'broadest' terms.[97] A meeting would have provided some operational advantages in the event of Cordage being implemented, as it would have ensured that the efforts of the Arab Legion and the British forces were coordinated. However, while Glubb was in charge this was not considered a major problem. The British could rely on Glubb to cooperate fully from the outset – even if he was not fully briefed in advance.

Glubb's dismissal changed this. After his departure the Jordanians made the first move in asking Britain for an early meeting of the AJJDB. However, the British were no longer reluctant to agree.[98] MELF believed that the security risks and the political dangers of discussing Britain's

---

[92] Bill Oliver to Rose, 12 September 1956, ibid.
[93] 'Private Directive from Chiefs of Staff for the British Members of the Anglo-Transjordan Joint Defence Board', 19 June 1948, FO816/113, TNA.
[94] Pundik, *Struggle for Sovereignty*, pp. 262–3.
[95] MELF to MOD, 16 February 1956, FO371/121531/VJ1192/17/G, TNA.
[96] MOD to MELF, 17 February 1956, ibid.
[97] MELF to MOD, MECOS 128, 11 April 1956, FO371/121531/VJ1192/30/G, TNA.
[98] 'Draft Report to Minister of Defence: The Implications of the Anglo-Jordan Defence Treaty', Note by the Chiefs of Staff, 19 April 1956, FO371/121532/VJ1192/36/G, TNA.

defence plans with the AJJDB were even greater since Glubb's dismissal.[99] However, the British were now prepared 'to disclose to the Jordanians at least in part our plan to come to her aid in the event of aggression by Israel'.[100] This was because the AJJDB was now considered Britain's only means of 'exercising any control over Arab Legion planning'.[101] The British were 'anxious to hold it as soon as possible'.[102] After the Jordanians kept postponing, much to Britain's frustration, the AJJDB eventually convened on 23–24 July.[103] Given Britain's reluctance to reveal details about its own defence plans, the British used this as an opportunity to listen. This had the dual benefit of giving the Jordanians the impression that they were being consulted rather than dictated to, but primarily it enabled Britain to discover how closely Jordanian plans corresponded with Operation Cordage without needing to divulge any secrets. During the early stages of the meeting the Jordanians outlined their requirements for British aid to expand and strengthen the Arab Legion. Having taken this on board, the British then directed the Jordanian delegation to outline its plans for the defence of Jordan, given its existing strength.[104] Under Jordan's plan for defence against Israeli attack, it required only air and naval support from Britain; the Jordanians did not want British land forces in the West Bank or the north.[105] This chimed with Britain's revised plans.[106]

The existence of Operation Cordage and British concerns over its obligation to defend Jordan against Israeli attack has become a point of contention within the historiographical debate exploring the causes of the Suez Crisis. The infamous British, French, and Israeli collusion to evict Nasser from the Suez Canal was concocted during a secret meeting held in the French city of Sèvres between 22 and 24 October and was laid bare in a secret document that became known as the 'The Protocol of Sèvres'.[107]

[99] MELF to MOD, MECOS 128, 11 April 1956, FO371/121531/VJ1192/30/G, TNA.

[100] MOD to MELF, SECME 78, 10 April 1956, FO371/121544/VJ1201/118/G, TNA.

[101] 'Anglo/Jordan Defence Board', Rose, 12 April 1956, FO371/121531/VJ1192/30/G, TNA.

[102] FO to Amman, 947, 12 May 1956, FO371/121531/VJ1192/30/G; 'Anglo/Jordan Joint Defence Board', Rose, 11 May 1956, FO371/121532/VJ1192/45/G, TNA.

[103] MOD to MELF, COSME 120, 13 July 1956, FO371/121533/VJ1192/66, TNA.

[104] 'Anglo Jordan Joint Defence Board: Minutes of a Meeting Held on 23rd and 24th July, 1956', FO371/121534/VJ1192/91/G, TNA.

[105] Abu Nowar to Maj.-Gen. E. R. Benson, Appendix B to: ibid.

[106] 'Draft Report to Minister of Defence: The Implications of the Anglo–Jordan Defence Treaty', Note by the Chiefs of Staff, 19 April 1956, FO371/121532/VJ1192/36/G; 'Meeting of the Anglo/Jordan Joint Defence Board: Brief for British Representatives', 4 May 1956, FO371/121532/VJ1192/50/G, TNA.

[107] 'The Protocol of Sèvres', in: Kyle, *Suez*, pp. 587–9.

The basic timetable of the conspiracy, which was faithfully followed, was that Israel would invade the Sinai on the evening of 29 October, and the following day Britain and France would issue an ultimatum to Israel and Egypt, including a demand that both parties withdraw ten miles from the Canal. If the Egyptians did not agree within twelve hours, this would provide the European powers with the *casus belli* they required to intervene militarily against Nasser on 31 October. In article 5 of the Sèvres Protocol, Israel agreed not to attack Jordan – an act that would have invoked the Anglo–Jordanian Treaty and therefore Operation Cordage. Equally, Britain agreed not to aid Jordan if it should attack Israel during this operation. This has led Scott Lucas to suggest that protecting Jordan was a primary motivation for Eden's adherence to the Suez collusion. Lucas argues that the French encouraged Israel to create tension on the border with Jordan as a means of encouraging Britain to join their collusion against Egypt. He posits that this was one possible reason for the Israeli attack on the West Bank village of Qalqilya on the night of 10/11 October.[108] Led by Ariel Sharon, this retaliation for the murder of two Israeli farmers was the most serious Arab–Israeli clash since the 1948 War.[109] Yet regardless of whether the Qalqilya attack was calculated for that reason, Lucas is adamant that the French used this to pressure Britain to join the collusion and that this is what explains Eden's decision to join the tripartite coalition against Nasser.[110] As Zeid Raad has illustrated, being called on to defend Jordan while military operations were ongoing against Egypt was the 'nightmare' scenario for Eden.[111] Britain could not implement Operation Cordage concurrent with Operation Musketeer Revise – the British plan, eventually enacted, for attacking Egypt. The problem was that both operations relied on the same forces stationed in Cyprus. It was therefore incumbent upon the prime minister to eliminate that conundrum. Yet that does not necessarily mean that it was the raison d'être for attacking Egypt or for joining forces with France and Israel. As Ashton has convincingly countered, Eden had plenty of existing reasons to join the coalition against Nasser without contriving to portray British involvement as designed to prevent Israel from attacking Jordan.[112] This aspect of the Suez Crisis has recently been revisited

---

[108] Lucas, *Divided We Stand*, pp. 227–37.
[109] Shlaim, *Lion of Jordan*, p. 110.
[110] Lucas, *Divided We Stand*, pp. 227–37.
[111] Zeid Raad, 'A Nightmare Avoided: Jordan and Suez 1956', *Israel Affairs*, 1:2 (1994), pp. 296–7.
[112] Ashton, *Eisenhower, Macmillan*, pp. 93–4.

by Eric Grove, who appears to confuse policy and planning. His general argument corresponds with the implication in his title that Britain had a choice of enemies and that, at the last minute, 'a new choice of enemy was made'.[113] While it is true that Operations Cordage and Musketeer could not be executed simultaneously, Cordage was not evidence of a British policy to attack Israel. Rather it was a contingency plan to meet its treaty obligation to defend Jordan in the event of an attack on Britain's Hashemite ally.

The Anglo–Jordanian Treaty did not deepen British involvement in the Suez Crisis. Rather the situation in Egypt impacted the process of revising the treaty, as the uncertainty the Suez Crisis created delayed Britain's desire to alter the status quo. Having individually reconsidered the value of the Jordanian alliance during the months immediately following Glubb's dismissal, all of the interested Whitehall departments eventually gathered to discuss Britain's future relationship with Jordan on 17 July. The purpose of the meeting was to discuss a draft Cabinet paper produced by the Foreign Office. The meeting was chaired by the Treasury and framed around the fact that the £12.5 million [£10.2 million for the Arab Legion and £2.25 million for development] a year spent by Britain in Jordan was 13 per cent 'of the cost of all Foreign Office, Colonial Office and the Commonwealth Relations Office activity and two-thirds of what was put into the Colonies each year by way of development'. From the Treasury perspective: 'This situation was objectionable in every way.'[114] This meeting did not culminate with an agreed future policy, but it was essentially established that a way had to be found to reduce Britain's financial commitment to Jordan and that an agreed paper should be put to ministers for consideration in the Cabinet soon. Less than ten days later, however, the problem of Britain's future relationship with Jordan was overshadowed by events in Egypt. In response to the United States' decision to withdraw the offer of Anglo-American funding for Egypt's Aswan Dam project, on 26 July Nasser nationalised the Suez Canal Company. Although Nasser was legally entitled to do this, the Company's principal shareholder, Britain, was aghast. The most worrying aspect of nationalisation was that Nasser now had control of a vital artery of Britain's world system. Thus, Eden immediately created

---

[113] Eric Grove, 'Who to Fight in 1956, Egypt or Israel? Operation Musketeer versus Operation Cordage', in: Smith (ed.), *Reassessing Suez*, pp. 79–85.

[114] 'Note of a Meeting Held in the Treasury on the 17th July to Discuss the Foreign Office Draft of a Cabinet Paper on Jordan Circulated under Cover of a Treasury Letter of 10th July 1956', FO371/121529/VJ1153/7/G, TNA.

the Egypt Committee, which comprised a small group of ministers, with the primary objective of attaining the downfall of the Nasser regime.[115] But for the Suez Crisis, Michael Rose, the head of the Eastern and Levant Department at the Foreign Office, admitted, Britain might have risked halting expenditure on Jordan.[116] However, given the uncertainty over Suez it was deemed advisable to have as few changes as possible during this period.[117] Consequently, Britain's internal review of the treaty was halted. The impending Jordanian elections, scheduled for October, did not help as this meant Britain could not effectively discuss a revision of the treaty until the new government was in place.[118] However, it was the deterioration of the Suez Crisis that meant the draft Cabinet paper was never circulated to the Cabinet and on 18 September Eden agreed with Lloyd that Britain should 'delay forming a view on the question until we could see how developments over the Suez dispute proceeded'.[119] Nonetheless, the British had effectively concluded that the subsidy had become an undesirable expense, but vanquishing this burden was put on hold, given the uncertainty created by the Suez Crisis.

In the meantime, tension along the border with Israel continued to increase, and this raised the ominous question of Britain's obligation to defend Jordan in accordance with the treaty. The British may not have joined the tripartite collusion against Nasser for the purpose of averting an Israeli attack on Jordan, but they were nonetheless anxious to avoid becoming embroiled in an Israeli–Jordanian dispute. This prompted the Foreign Office to ask the Chiefs of Staff to advise whether it could seize the first opportunity to liquidate the treaty and the subsidy, if and when it should become politically convenient to do so. The Foreign Office requested the Chiefs of Staff's assessment of the military importance of the treaty on 5 October and after the Jordanians made a number of military requests in the wake of the Qalqilya incident, during which the Jordanians unsuccessfully attempted to invoke the treaty, the Foreign Office asked if this assessment could be expedited.[120] With increasing pressure from Jordan for Britain to intervene militarily, the British became ever more eager to vanquish this unwanted and burdensome

[115] Keith Kyle, 'Britain and the Crisis, 1955–1956', in: Louis and Owen (eds.), *Suez 1956*, pp. 112–13.
[116] 'Anglo-Jordan Joint Defence Board', Rose, 13 August 1956, FO371/121534/VJ1192/106/G, TNA.
[117] Rose to Duke, 16 August 1956, FO371/121550/VJ1201/248/G, TNA.
[118] Rose to Peck, 21 August 1956, FO371/121529/VJ1153/9/G, TNA.
[119] 'Jordan Treaty Revision', Rose, 19 October 1956, FO371/121499/VJ1051/211/G, TNA.
[120] Ross to Dickson, 22 October 1956, FO371/121535/VJ1192/115/G, TNA.

responsibility. At the very least, the British had a decision to make. The dilemma, as Kirkpatrick spelled out, was that: 'If we do not give some satisfaction to the Jordanians, we risk compromising the Treaty. But if we do give them satisfaction this involves us in political and military complications.' Before giving the Jordanians a clear indication of the level of support that Britain would provide Jordan against Israeli belligerence, the British needed to decide whether it was worth maintaining its treaty rights.[121] Britain benefited from two principal military assets in Jordan. Firstly, the treaty provided Britain with overflying and staging rights. The Chiefs of Staffs' view was that these rights provided advantages, but they were 'not militarily essential'. They were certainly considered 'not of such importance as to make essential the continuance of our present commitments to Jordan'.[122] Secondly, the British had RAF bases at Amman and Mafraq. The Chiefs of Staff were already examining relinquishing rights to Amman airfield and withdrawing the RAF squadron there.[123] At the inter-departmental meeting in July the Air Ministry expressed its desire to pull out of Amman as soon as possible.[124] The airfield itself was not part of Britain's global war strategy or Operation Cordage, and since the events of 1 March, the RAF fighter squadron stationed there was considered 'a hostage to fortune'. The chief of the air staff therefore wanted to transfer this squadron to Cyprus, where it would be available for a 'strike role against Egypt'.[125] Mafraq was more valuable, however. It was important to Britain's strategic requirements as a medium-range bomber base. In July the Air Ministry advised that an alternative would have to be found if Britain was denied access to Mafraq and warned that Iraq was too close to Russia and Habbaniya was not suitable.[126] However, as part of the October assessment the Chiefs of Staff concluded that Mafraq was deemed 'highly desirable but not vital'. The conclusion, therefore, was that if the Foreign Office deemed it politically necessary to terminate the treaty, 'there would be

---

[121] Minute by Kirkpatrick, 18 October 1956, ibid.

[122] 'Strategic Importance of Jordan', 26 October 1956, FO371/121499/VJ1051/220/G, TNA.

[123] 'Jordan', 3 July 1956, FO371/121529/VJ1153/5/G, TNA.

[124] 'Note of a Meeting Held in the Treasury on the 17th July to Discuss the Foreign Office Draft of a Cabinet Paper on Jordan Circulated under Cover of a Treasury Letter of 10th July 1956', FO371/121529/VJ1153/7/G, TNA.

[125] F. Cooper (Air Ministry) to Rose, 2 August 1956, FO371/121576/VJ1226/4/G, TNA.

[126] 'Note of a Meeting Held in the Treasury on the 17th July to Discuss the Foreign Office Draft of a Cabinet Paper on Jordan Circulated under Cover of a Treasury Letter of 10 July 1956', FO371/121529/VJ1153/7/G, TNA.

no overriding military objection'.[127] Thus, by the time the Suez Crisis reached its climax, it had already been established that financially and militarily the British were in favour of terminating, or at the very least, substantially revising, the treaty. Acting on this desire was put on hold, however, until the Suez Crisis was over.

While the gathering crisis over Suez primarily served to delay the process of treaty revision, it certainly did not help Anglo–Jordanian relations. Hussein's statement of support for Nasser after he nationalised the Suez Canal riled the British, resulting in Duke being instructed to tell Hussein that his statement had produced the 'most deplorable impression'.[128] The mounting dispute with Egypt also led to a deterioration in the relationship between British and Arab officers within the Legion.[129] Moreover, British military intervention in November put Anglo–Jordanian relations further under strain, prompting Hussein to sarcastically enquire whether Britain expected the Arab Legion to assist in its current operations against Egypt.[130] The British even feared that 'the Jordanians may well break off diplomatic relations', prompting London to obtain Italy's agreement to take charge of British interests in Jordan should that occur.[131]

The most notable contribution that the Suez Crisis made to the process of terminating the treaty, though, was that it ended the fallacy of attempting to maintain the presence of seconded British officers on the same basis as before. On 29 October – shortly before Israel launched its initial strike on Egypt later that evening – RAF Amman commenced evacuation to Mafraq in a move that took the Jordanians by surprise. This left the seconded officers in the Royal Jordanian Air Force (RJAF) more exposed. Thus, on 30 October, Strickland, British Military Attaché W. G. A. Lawrie, and Wing-Commander Dobree-Bell – who had been replaced as commander of the RJAF, at Ali Abu Nowar's request, by Major Ibrahim Othman the previous day – made plans for the withdrawal of British officers in the Arab Legion and the RJAF to Mafraq in case the political situation in the Middle East should deteriorate further. In the early hours of the 31 October Othman telephoned Dobree-Bell to insist that all seconded RAF personnel remain in their quarters due to rising anti-British feeling among the Arab officers,

[127] 'Strategic Importance of Jordan', 26 October 1956, FO371/121499/VJ1051/220/ G, TNA.

[128] FO to Amman, 1326, 28 July 1956, PREM11/1422, TNA.

[129] Amman to FO, 1084, 9 August 1956, FO371/121550/VJ1201/245/G, TNA.

[130] Duke to Rose, 2 November 1956, FO371/121500/VJ1051/235, TNA.

[131] 'Jordan Arab Army Requests for Money from the Subsidy', Rose, 2 November 1956, FO371/121500/VJ1051/230; Rome to FO, 764, 2 November 1956, FO371/121599/ VJ1905/4, TNA

as a result of the attacks on Egypt. Nonetheless, at Dobree-Bell's request, and with Ali Abu Nowar's approval, all officers seconded to the RJAF were evacuated to Mafraq on 31 October.[132] On Abu Nowar's recommendation, all British officers attached to the Arab Legion soon followed for their own safety.[133] Because of restricted accommodation and water access, by 9 November nearly all of the seconded and contracted British officers in the Arab Legion and the RJAF had withdrawn from Mafraq to Britain or Cyprus, without the knowledge of the Jordanians.[134] As far as Abu Nowar was concerned, this evacuation was supposed to be only temporary.[135] However, less than two weeks after their departure, Duke appraised: 'I think we must now regard this chapter of Anglo–Jordan military relations as closed.' He explained that confidence in the British training teams was already dire and after they had evacuated, the British officers had their houses looted, 'probably by their own servants'. This compounded the British officers' desire not to return.[136] Moreover, the new terms of service, published on 14 October, were unacceptable to most of the British officers who would not have remained after the March dismissals had they known that this is what the War Office would agree to.[137] After the evacuation from Mafraq it was considered that, 'notwithstanding our obligation under the Anglo–Jordan Treaty to provide personnel on request, we are never likely to return to the old arrangement whereby British officers hold King Hussein's commission and wear Jordanian uniform'.[138] The British were now convinced that officers could no longer be seconded to the Arab Legion on the old basis. They could only return as a military mission or something akin to the BLPI.[139] The evacuation of British officers from Jordan thus marked the end of attempts to continue as before. The most significant correlation between the climax of the Suez Crisis and the eventual termination of the treaty, though, was simply that the crisis had reached a conclusion, thus ending the uncertainty.

[132] 'Extract from Letter from Wing-Commander Dobree-Bell to Air Ministry', 6 November 1956, FO371/121576/VJ1226/10, TNA.
[133] Amman to FO, 1605, 1 November 1956, FO371/121562/VJ1207/35, TNA.
[134] FO to Amman, 2455, 9 November 1956, FO371/121562/VJ1207/35; Amman to FO, 1718, 10 November 1956, FO371/121562/VJ1207/38, TNA.
[135] Amman to FO, 1605, 1 November 1956, FO371/121562/VJ1207/35, TNA.
[136] Amman to FO, 1725, 10 November 1956, FO371/121562/VJ1207/37, TNA.
[137] W. G. A. Lawrie to DMO, 23 November 1956, FO371/121562/VJ1207/44, TNA.
[138] 'British Army Personnel in Jordan', Rose, 13 November 1956, FO371/121562/VJ1207/42, TNA.
[139] Lawrie to DMO, 23 November 1956, FO371/121562/VJ1207/44; Hamilton (DMO) to Rose, 7 December 1956, FO371/121562/VJ1207/46, TNA.

The Jordanians were also ready to end the treaty in advance, and regardless, of Suez. Their formal request to do so was merely delayed by the process of forming a new government. Jordan's first free and fair elections were scheduled for October, and despite calls from former associates of Abdullah to cancel them, in light of the deepening crisis over Suez, Hussein pressed ahead as planned.[140] The results demonstrated an overwhelming show of public support for the Jordanian national movement, leading Hussein to appoint the leader of the National Front, Sulayman al-Nabulsi, to serve as prime minister in Jordan's first nationalist government. Like the other parties within the movement, terminating the British connection was central to Nabulsi's campaign.[141] And on 27 November the new government followed through on this pledge, issuing a ministerial statement announcing its intention to terminate the 'unequal Treaty' with Britain.[142] With the new government in place and the uncertainty surrounding Suez over, both allies were ready to begin the process of terminating the treaty.

Neither side was in an immediate rush, however. From conversations between Nabulsi and the new British ambassador, Charles Johnston, the Foreign Office garnered the impression that the Jordanians had in mind a 'leisurely long drawn out process'. This meant Britain believed it could hold on in Jordan for some time, if it wanted to.[143] The British, though, had no interest in clinging onto the treaty, having already decided that the costs outweighed the benefits. However, they were eager not to withdraw abruptly, thus leaving a vacuum for what they considered undesirable elements – notably Egypt or Russia – to fill.[144] Thus, the British opted not to hasten the termination process.

It was in Britain's interest to allow time to seek a replacement. The ideal successor was its most reliable ally: the United States, which ever since Glubb's dismissal had shown signs that it was prepared to support British interests in Jordan in a way that it had previously avoided. The situation in Jordan was symptomatic of an Anglo–American relationship defined by what David Reynolds described as 'competitive cooperation'.[145]

---

[140] Massad, *Colonial Effects*, p. 191.

[141] Anderson, *Nationalist Voices*, pp. 168–72.

[142] Amman to FO, 1854, 27 November 1956, FO371/121500/VJ1051/246, TNA.

[143] 'Anglo–Jordan Treaty', Rose, 5 December 1956, FO371/121501/VJ1051/279/G, TNA.

[144] Minute by Shuckburgh, 24 April 1956, FO371/121557/VJ1205/15/G; Minute by H. N. Shepherd, 9 July 1956, FO371/121529/VJ1153/5/G; 'Strategic Importance of Jordan', 26 October 1956, FO371/121499/VJ1051/220/G, TNA.

[145] David Reynolds, *The Creation of the Anglo–American Alliance, 1939–1941: A Study in Competitive Cooperation* (Chapel Hill, 1981).

Prior to Glubb's dismissal the United States erred on the side of competition. During the Baghdad Pact disturbances at the end of 1955, the United States was happy to see Britain flounder, in the hope this would cause 'the British to re-think their policy in the Middle East and perhaps to put greater weight on the necessity for securing a peace between Israel and Egypt'.[146] The US ambassador in Amman, Lester Mallory, was concerned by Washington's 'tendency to feel that there was no need to worry about Jordan as it was safely in the British bag on account of' the Arab Legion subsidy and the presence of British officers. He therefore wanted 'to administer something of a jolt' to Washington.[147] Yet despite Mallory's concerns that British influence was 'steadily declining and if tested might be found insufficient', this had little impact on US policy.[148] Yet where Mallory's warnings failed, Glubb's dismissal succeeded. It nudged the United States into a change of attitude because it exposed a perceived weakness in the Western bloc. After the Baghdad Pact turmoil, the director of the CIA, Allen Dulles, expressed the view that this represented Britain's 'most humiliating diplomatic defeat in modern history'.[149] Douglas Little has taken this to show that the United States believed Britain might soon be driven out of Jordan altogether.[150] Yet, in a passage that Little omitted, Dulles maintained that he was comforted by the belief 'that General Glubb would probably be able to maintain the situation against the extremists'.[151] Glubb's presence reassured the United States that the Arab Legion would remain a 'source of order, unless unpredictable events develop'.[152] His dismissal proved the unpredictable event that broke US comfort. It now feared that 'not only may Jordan soon be lost to the West', but that this might influence the future of Lebanon and Iraq as well.[153] In a subsequent paper on US policy it was acknowledged that, as a result of Glubb's dismissal, the Arab Legion had been weakened and that British influence had receded and was 'bound to decline' further. Moreover, the United States appraised that 'neutralist and pre-communist sentiment' had 'increased'. The upshot of these

---

[146] Memorandum of 272nd NSC meeting, 12 January 1956, FRUS, 1955–57, XIII, p. 19.
[147] Duke to Shuckburgh, 27 October 1955, FO371/115653/VJ1051/22, TNA.
[148] Mallory to State Department, 22 October 1955, FRUS, 1955–57, XIII, pp. 6–7.
[149] Memorandum of 272nd NSC meeting, 12 January 1956, FRUS, 1955–57, XIII, p. 19.
[150] Douglas Little, 'A Puppet in Search of a Puppeteer? The United States, King Hussein, and Jordan, 1953–1970', International History Review, 17:3 (1995), p. 520.
[151] Memorandum of 272nd NSC meeting, 12 January 1956, FRUS, 1955–57, XIII, p. 19.
[152] Mallory to State Department, 10 January 1956, FRUS, 1955–57, XIII, pp. 16–17.
[153] Operations Coordination Board Intelligence Notes, 4 April 1956, Declassified Documents Reference System (accessed: 25 March 2009).

observations was a proposal that future US policy should be to 'support the British position in the country'.[154] This amounted to a minor yet significant change in US policy. Gone was the passive acceptance that Britain had Jordan in the bag and gone was the American avoidance of support for what was previously considered British imperial interests. If Britain no longer had Jordan under control, there thus existed the danger that communist elements might take advantage. As a result of Glubb's dismissal, the need to cooperate superseded America's desire to compete. Or as one journalist rather colourfully put it, 'the Americans can no longer take a malicious delight in the failures of their British rivals. The victory of the liberation movement of the Arabs does not bode well for them either.'[155]

When Jordan announced its intention to terminate the treaty at the end of November, US Assistant Secretary of State Herbert Hoover Jr. asked the British ambassador in Washington 'point blank' whether Britain would wish the United States to take on the subsidy if the Anglo–Jordanian Treaty was terminated.[156] The United States made no promises, but by merely asking this question, the British were encouraged that US assistance for Jordan was a real possibility. When the foreign secretary met US Secretary of State John Foster Dulles on 14 December, Selwyn Lloyd explained that Britain hoped the United States could subsidise Jordan, either directly, or indirectly via Saudi Arabia, to prevent it from collapsing.[157] Thereafter the British sought time to encourage the United States to 'relieve' Britain of the 'burden of the subsidy' and to allow 'time to work out the details of the hand-over'.[158] Britain's intention was to try to 'persuade the United States to relieve us of the responsibility for financial and military support of Jordan'.[159] Britain did consider 'the possibility that future financial support to Jordan might be shared' with the United States. But as the existence of a British contribution was deemed unlikely to alter Jordan's membership of the sterling area, Britain preferred to hand over the entire financial burden.[160]

[154] 'Future United States Policy Toward Jordan', 19 April 1956, *FRUS, 1955–57, XIII*, pp. 37–9.
[155] G. Mirski, 'The End of General Glubb's Career', Trud, 8 March 1956, FO371/121542/VJ1201/76, TNA.
[156] Washington to FO, 2414, 4 December 1956, FO371/121529/VJ1153/15, TNA.
[157] FO to Washington, 1 January 1957, FO371/121900/VJ1051/16/G, TNA.
[158] Commander Allan Noble to Henry Brooke, 13 December 1956, FO371/121501/VJ1051/270/G, TNA.
[159] FO to Amman, 2925, 21 December 1956, FO371/121501/VJ1051/273, TNA.
[160] 'Jordan', 11 January 1957, FO371/121900/VJ1051/22/G, TNA.

The British were encouraged by the United States' stance, but they were not dependent on the United States formally agreeing to take over the burden. The treaty had become a financial and military obligation with no vital return. For that reason the British were eager to end the treaty without too prolonged a delay.[161] Despite announcing its intention to terminate the treaty in November, at the start of 1957 the Jordanians had still not approached the British government to begin negotiations.[162] However, Britain wanted the treaty terminated by 31 March at the latest; they did not want the subsidy to continue into the new financial year.[163] Thus, Ross advised: 'Since we are prepared to accept the risk of Jordan getting her money from the Arabs the sooner we tell the Jordan Government that we are as sick of the treaty as they, the better.'[164] The British were particularly eager to set this process in motion before Hussein met his Arab allies on 19 January, lest Britain's offer to negotiate look like 'capitulation' if, as anticipated, Jordan accepted financial support from Nasser.[165] Thus, on 16 January Johnston informed the Jordanian government of Britain's readiness to discuss termination of the treaty.[166] Three days later Jordan did indeed sign an Arab Solidarity Agreement with Saudi Arabia, Syria, and Egypt, which offered financial support roughly equivalent to the British subsidy.[167] In the event, though, only Saudi Arabia made any financial contribution.[168] When Britain notified Jordan of its intention to begin negotiations to terminate the treaty, the British simultaneously informed the United States in the hope that it would agree to take over the financial commitment.[169] Dulles replied that the United States could not assume Britain's present obligation, as it stood, but he gave enough hope that the United States could and would be able to provide Jordan with financial aid in some form.[170] There was no firm Anglo–American agreement to handover financial responsibility for Jordan, but Britain agreed to terminate the treaty with the belief that

[161] FO to Baghdad, 24, 4 January 1957, FO371/121900/VJ1051/5/G, TNA.
[162] 'Anglo–Jordan Treaty', C. C. B. Stewart, 2 January 1957, FO953/1831/PG1808/1, TNA.
[163] 'Future Relations with Jordan: Brief for Meeting of the Cabinet on January 3', 2 January 1957, FO371/121900/VJ1051/16/G, TNA.
[164] 'Anglo–Jordan Treaty', Ross, 11 January 1957, FO371/121900/VJ1051/20, TNA.
[165] Ibid.; Cabinet Minutes, 15 January 1957, CAB128/31/1, TNA.
[166] Johnston to Lloyd, 28 January 1958, FO371/134006/VJ1011/1, TNA.
[167] Dann, *Challenge of Arab Radicalism*, p. 43.
[168] D. K. Fieldhouse, *Western Imperialism in the Middle East 1914–1958* (Oxford, 2006), p. 241.
[169] FO to Washington, 218, 16 January 1957, FO371/121900/VJ1051/20, TNA.
[170] Washington to FO, 89, 18 January 1957, FO371/121900/VJ1051/23, TNA.

the United States would prevent Jordan from collapsing or succumbing to other external influences.

Once formal negotiations for terminating the treaty began on 4 February, the process was largely straightforward. The first few weeks were hindered by a dispute over missing British Army stores, which the Jordanians had taken after the British officers departed in November, and vast differences of opinion over the valuation of facilities to be handed over to Jordan. However, these differences were ironed out by the beginning of March, and the negotiations, in the end, were swift.[171] On 13 March, just over a month after formal negotiations began, the Anglo–Jordanian Treaty was terminated. The British were relieved that the Jordanians did not complicate the negotiations by raising the issue of future development loans or Jordan's place in the sterling area.[172] Instead, the negotiations were confined to the task of dealing with the remnants of Britain's military presence. The termination of the treaty stipulated that all British forces would be withdrawn from Jordan within six months. Johnston suggested protracting the military withdrawal in order to give time for a favourable emerging coalition between Jordan and Saudi Arabia to flower and therefore keep the Egyptians out.[173] London, however, felt that the military withdrawal had to be as swift as possible.[174] In the event, Britain's military withdrawal from Jordan was smooth and ahead of schedule, with the final evacuation of British troops from Aqaba completed on 6 July.[175] As part of the termination agreement the Jordanian government agreed to pay Britain £4.25 million. In return the Jordanians received RAF stations at Amman and Mafraq and the military camps at Zerqa, Aqaba, and Maan, along with ammunition and other stores.[176] Britain also wrote off the £1.5 million debt owed since the 1948 War.[177] Britain's main failure from the termination negotiations concerned overflying, landing, and staging rights. On this they managed only to obtain an agreement in principle, subject to future negotiations.[178]

---

[171] Johnston to Lloyd, 28 January 1958, FO371/134006/VJ1011/1, TNA.

[172] Johnston to Lloyd, 20 March 1957, FO371/127905/VJ1051/136, TNA.

[173] Amman to FO, 188, 4 February 1957, FO371/121902/VJ1051/63, TNA.

[174] 'Jordan', Rose, 6 February 1957, FO371/121902/VJ1051/70, TNA.

[175] Johnston to Lloyd, 9 July 1957, FO371/127930/VJ1192/41, TNA; Johnston to Lloyd, 28 January 1958, FO371/134006/VJ1011/1, TNA.

[176] Johnston to Lloyd, 20 March 1957, FO371/127905/VJ1051/136, TNA.

[177] 'Exchange of Notes between the Government of the United Kingdom ... and the Government of the Hashemite Kingdom of Jordan Terminating the Treaty of Alliance of March 15, 1948', 13 March 1957, FO371/121905/VJ1051/128, TNA.

[178] Johnston to Lloyd, 20 March 1957, FO371/127905/VJ1051/136, TNA.

Nonetheless, the foreign secretary thanked Johnston for securing an agreement that was 'better' than he had hoped.[179] The British secured a satisfactory sum for the facilities they left behind, but most importantly they had rid themselves of the ongoing financial burden of the subsidy and the military obligation to defend Jordan against attack.

Despite the departure of Glubb and the termination of the treaty, Jordan's internal structure and its international alignment remained relatively unchanged. Adnan Abu Odeh, an anti-British, anti-government member of the Communist Party, who later became an adviser to Hussein, described the Arabisation of the Arab Legion and the dismissal of Glubb as 'the completion of independence. Official independence was in '46, but independence was completed in February '56.'[180] In many respects, though, this simply marked a continuing shift towards neo-colonial governmentality.[181] Typical of Joseph Massad's contention that independence does not lead to a radical overhaul of the former imperial institutions of control, the Arab Legion merely emerged with new leaders.[182] In the immediate aftermath of Glubb's dismissal, the Arab Legion continued to rely on British officers' technical expertise. They now lacked executive authority, but Britain sought to circumnavigate this obstacle via collaboration with Ali Abu Nowar and the resurrection of the AJJDB. Massad did emphasise Abu Nowar's efforts to de-Bedouinise the Arab Legion by altering the uniforms, creating promotion barriers based on academic qualifications, and integrating them with the *hadari*.[183] Yet even these changes were short-lived. Merely a month after the treaty was terminated, Jordan's liberal experiment went into reverse. Hitherto, the Jordanian national movement had been united around the demand for greater independence, but once the treaty with Britain had been terminated, its divisions began to surface and by the end of 1957, the 'old' political order had been restored.[184] After a series of confrontations between the king and the prime minister, including disagreement over whether to align with the United States or the Soviet Union, on 10 April 1957 Hussein dismissed Nabulsi's nationalist government and with the backing of his mother initiated the return of politicians from the Abdullah regime, such

[179] FO to Amman, 645, 15 March 1957, FO371/127904/VJ1051/119, TNA.
[180] Interview with Adnan Abu Odeh, 6 March 1989, Geyelin Papers.
[181] For a critique of neo-colonialism, see: Kwame Nkrumah, *Neo-colonialism: The Last Stage of Imperialism* (London, 1965), p. xi.
[182] Massad, *Colonial Effects*, pp. 1, 9.
[183] Ibid., pp. 186–7.
[184] Anderson, *Nationalist Voices*, p. 171; Massad, *Colonial Effects*, p. 197.

as Samir al-Rifai and Ibrahim Hashim.[185] This was followed by the exile of Ali Abu Nowar and other nationalist army officers after an attempted coup against the king a few days later. Details of the alleged coup remain opaque.[186] The outcome, though, demonstrated that the Free Officers movement in Jordan had failed to obtain the kind of control of the army that nationalists had in Egypt and Syria.[187] It also illustrated the robust nature of the Arab Legion created by Glubb and its enduring loyalty to the Hashemite regime, as Hussein came to rely on the Bedouin units of the army – that Glubb had favoured – for his security.

The failed coup also served to consolidate Hussein's burgeoning relationship with the United States.[188] Just as Britain wanted the United States to provide financial support to Jordan, so did King Hussein. Britain's departure did not end Jordan's dependence on external financial support. Rather, it made economic aid even more important to the security of the country and the Hashemite regime, as Jordan no longer had the military insurance of the Anglo–Jordanian Treaty. For that reason, Hussein made an informal request for US arms shortly after Glubb's dismissal.[189] And the Jordanian government made a formal approach to the United States on 9 November, two weeks before announcing its intention to terminate the treaty. As Joseph Massad pointed out, the United States' stance over Suez helped make it a welcome ally.[190] In that regard, Anglo–American discord over Suez might be said to have strengthened the transatlantic alliance. Suez is often portrayed as the moment when Britain became subservient to the United States in the Middle East.[191] However, if we prioritise the cooperative, rather than the competitive, element of the relationship, the Suez Crisis arguably helped make the Anglo–American alliance more robust. Because the United States was not negatively associated with the Suez collusion, it was easier for it to replace Britain as Jordan's principal backer, thus securing the Hashemite Kingdom's stability and its continued association with the West. Hussein was predisposed to support the West anyway, but Suez helped avoid any complications. Jordan did not formally sign up to the Eisenhower Doctrine – the US

[185] Bunch, 'Supporting the Brave Young King', pp. 117–18; Ashton, *King Hussein*, pp. 62–6.
[186] Dann, *Challenge of Arab Radicalism*, pp. 56–9; Ashton, *King Hussein*, pp. 63–4; Massad, *Colonial Effects*, pp. 192–7.
[187] Dann, *Challenge of Arab Radicalism*, pp. 57–8.
[188] Bunch, 'Supporting the Brave Young King', pp. 117–18; Ashton, *King Hussein*, pp. 65–6.
[189] 'Daily Intelligence Abstracts of Interest to Working Groups No. 611', 27 April 1956, *Declassified Documents Reference System* (accessed: 25 March 2009).
[190] Massad, *Colonial Effects*, p. 191.
[191] Scott, *Divided We Stand*, p. 324.

strategy launched in January 1957 for combatting Soviet expansion by offering economic and military aid to Middle Eastern countries. But the United States did become Jordan's new patron. On 29 April 1957 Jordan received a $10 million US grant and further sums followed: $10 million at the end of May, $30 million during the summer, and in September a US shipment of arms arrived.[192] Fortunately for Hussein, Glubb's dismissal not only convinced Britain to depart, it also helped convince the United States that it should step in. In practical terms this meant that Jordan merely moved from being dependent on Britain to being dependent on the United States.

Existing accounts of the British reaction and response to Glubb's dismissal have been largely unanimous. It has been generally accepted that Eden was furious, that the British blamed Nasser, that they therefore resolved to destroy the Egyptian president, and that Britain initially sought to cling on to its predominant position in Jordan until the Suez Crisis shattered this hope. As this chapter has illustrated, however, each of these apparent truisms needs to be adjusted to some extent. Eden was certainly rattled by the action taken against Glubb and initially refused to accept the finality of the decision. Moreover, it is not an exaggeration to suggest that he was angry and anxious as he considered the implications during the night following Glubb's dismissal. However, the notion that Eden blamed Nasser for engineering the dismissal does not hold water. The principal substance to this claim comes from the memoirs of Anthony Nutting. Despite the evident bias of Nutting's account, it surely has to be accepted that Eden did express indignation against Nasser during the uncertain late night hours that followed Glubb's dismissal. However, in the cold light of day, any words uttered in anger against Nasser were quickly supplanted. Contrary to the prevailing account, new evidence reveals that Selwyn Lloyd did not believe that Nasser was to blame. While a few hard-line members within the Cabinet may have linked the dismissal to Nasser and called for a dramatic cutting of the ties with Jordan, Eden, Lloyd, Macmillan, and the Foreign Office responded much more pragmatically than the prevailing accounts suggest. This pragmatic reaction fuelled an equally pragmatic British response, where far from blaming Nasser for Glubb's dismissal and therefore seeking retribution against him, the British were much more convinced that Ali Abu Nowar was significantly involved in the plot to oust Glubb and yet they opted to work with, rather than against, him. At face value,

---

[192] Ashton, *King Hussein*, pp. 68–9; Dann, *Challenge of Arab Radicalism*, p. 71.

this perhaps confirms the notion that Britain was trying to cling onto its position of influence within Jordan. In part this is true. It is evidence of the British having learned lessons from their previous policy, which had helped contribute to the king's decision to dismiss Glubb in the first place. However, Britain's decision not to take abrupt action against Jordan or any of the perceived conspirators in the wake of Glubb's dismissal was a short-term policy designed to avoid any hasty action until the long-term future value of the alliance with Jordan had been thoroughly re-evaluated. This reappraisal of the alliance unanimously concluded that it was in Britain's interest to rid itself of the disproportionate financial and military burden of the treaty. The Suez Crisis did not prompt this reappraisal. Rather, it delayed it. Avi Shlaim has argued that the dismissal of Glubb – in combination with the election of Nabulsi and the Suez debacle – caused the subsidy 'to become a costly white elephant'.[193] It is perhaps more accurate to suggest that Glubb's dismissal exposed, rather than rendered, the subsidy as such. While the election of Nabulsi and the Suez Crisis certainly did not help Anglo-Jordanian relations, neither did they make the subsidy any less palatable to Britain than it already was. Glubb's dismissal prompted Britain to evaluate the cost-benefit ratio of the treaty and its conclusion was that the costs outweighed the benefits. What Britain gained from the treaty – from a practical perspective – was desirable, but non-vital military rights. In return, Britain was obligated to defend Jordan against Israeli attack and committed to spending a disproportionate amount of its foreign budget on the small Hashemite Kingdom. Meanwhile, any remaining notion that Britain's prestige would suffer if the Anglo–Jordanian connection were severed was shattered by the events of 1 March. On that day, Hussein garnered Jordanian control of the armed forces from Britain. A year later the British, in agreement with the Jordanians, rid themselves of the ongoing financial and military burden of the treaty. Hitherto British policy making had been obscured by the Glubb paradox. With that filter removed, the British were able to see more clearly the pragmatic value of the existing treaty relationship.

[193] Shlaim, *Lion of Jordan*, p. 125.

Conclusion

The termination of the treaty was not the end of Britain's relationship with Jordan. It was merely the end of a particular phase of the relationship characterised by British control of the Arab Legion. As Nigel Ashton has detailed, Britain continued to count on Jordan as one of its most important Arab allies, and the Jordanians also 'strove to sustain "special" relations with London'.[1] Indeed, almost exactly a year after the last British troops exited Jordan, King Hussein requested they return in order to help protect himself and his kingdom in light of the coup in Iraq, during which his cousin, King Faysal II, his uncle, Abd al-Ilah, and the Iraqi prime minister, Nuri al-Said, were murdered, and an Iraqi republic was created.[2] The British duly agreed to intervene because Jordanian stability and the Hashemite dynasty remained important. As Nigel Ashton asserted, the fundamental reason for British intervention in Jordan in 1958, as well as in Kuwait three years later, was 'to maintain in power a regime friendly to British interests'.[3] The events of 1958 even led to the return of British involvement with the Jordan Arab Army in the form of a military mission, which included former SBO of the Arab Legion, Lieutenant-Colonel Strickland, Nigel Bromage, and Hussein's good friend, Wing-Commander Jock Dalgleish. The British ambassador emphasised, however, that this

[1] Ashton, 'Special Relationship', p. 240.
[2] For an account of Britain's military intervention in 1958, see: Shlaim, *Lion of Jordan*, pp. 155–73; William Roger Louis, 'Britain and the Crisis of 1958', in: William Roger Louis and Roger Owen (eds.), *A Revolutionary Year: The Middle East in 1958* (London, 2002), pp. 15–76; Lawrence Tal, 'Britain and the Jordan Crisis of 1958', *Middle Eastern Studies*, 31:1 (1995), pp. 39–57; Blackwell, *British Military Intervention*; Ashton, 'Microcosm of Decline', pp. 1069–83; Ashton, 'Special Relationship', pp. 221–44.
[3] Ashton, 'Microcosm of Decline', p. 1070.

did 'not in itself mean a return to the Glubb system'.[4] Nonetheless, it was indicative of the enduring nature of the relationship.

While the 'special' relationship endured at the diplomatic level, Hussein's personal connection with Glubb also survived, despite the abrupt manner in which they parted ways professionally. They remained in direct correspondence for the rest of Glubb's life.[5] Hussein visited Glubb at his home in Mayfield, and when Glubb died, the king read out a touching address at his memorial service.[6] Glubb never returned to Jordan, though. He explained that the Arabs are such 'frenziedly hospitable people' that if he ever returned, he would be invited to 'breakfast, lunch, tea and dinner at a different place every day, and I couldn't take it at my age'.[7] This was no doubt Glubb demonstrating his innate British stoicism. As his daughter suspected, 'he felt it would be too painful to go back. My father told us that he dreamt about Jordan almost every night.' Given that Glubb spent the best part of his adult life in the Middle East, including twenty-six years in Jordan, this is hardly surprising. Glubb's attachment to Jordan – to the land he inhabited and the people he lived and served with for most of his life – never diminished, and he was 'devastated' when it lost the West Bank during the 1967 War.[8] This, indeed, was exactly what Glubb had attempted to guard against since 1949, most notably during the month leading up to his dismissal.

Despite enforced retirement, Glubb – who was knighted for his service shortly after his return to Britain – remained committed to the mission that had motivated him throughout his career in Jordan: the consolidation of the British Empire and the stability of the Middle East. Glubb therefore maintained his penchant for advising the British government of the day. In 1970, for example, Foreign Secretary Alec Douglas-Home and US Assistant Secretary of State Joseph J. Sisco both politely thanked Glubb for offering suggestions on how to settle the Arab–Israeli conflict.[9] His musings during retirement, however, had even less bearing on high policy than they had in the 1940s when Glubb lamented his lack of political influence. At the end of the Second World War Glubb was full of regret regarding the trajectory of his career, but he must surely have

---

[4] Amman to FO, 1888, 16 October 1958, DEFE11/174, TNA; Bromage, *Soldier in Arabia*, p. 74.
[5] For correspondence in the 1980s, see: GP2006, 93.
[6] Private correspondence with Glubb's daughter.
[7] Desert Island Discs, www.bbc.co.uk/programmes/p009msyv (accessed: 9 July 2013).
[8] Private correspondence with Glubb's daughter.
[9] Douglas-Home to Glubb, 29 December 1970; Sisco to Glubb, 8 January 1971, GP2006, 5.

reflected, during his dying days, on an ambition ultimately fulfilled. In 1920 Glubb put his dream of being a writer on hold. When he left the region thirty-six years later, Glubb now had the experiences required to devote himself to the career he craved. The result was a plethora of written words – twenty-two published books and countless articles.[10]

Glubb is ultimately remembered, however, not for his written work, but for his pivotal role in the history of the Middle East and his greatest contribution, certainly beyond 1945, was to the shaping of the 1948 War. Glubb was not the architect of the Greater Transjordan scheme, as Maureen Norton claimed, but he was nonetheless crucial to its implementation. After Bevin approved the scheme in February 1948 – and new evidence detailed here corroborates this – Glubb actively sought to cultivate the conditions that would allow the Arab Legion to peacefully occupy the areas of Palestine allotted to the Arab state by the United Nations. In his assessment of Glubb's role in the Arab–Israeli conflict, Benny Morris asserted that: 'If Israel and Jordan entered the 1948 War with a secret, unwritten understanding of mutual non-belligerence, it was primarily Israel that violated it in May and June and then again in July and October 1948, not Jordan.'[11] It is beyond the scope of this book to provide a thorough analysis of Israel's war aims, but this assessment of the Arab Legion's conduct in 1948 suggests that Transjordan's adherence to this pact owed more to Glubb than Abdullah. The king's negotiations with the Jewish Agency were certainly important, providing the two parties with a good comprehension of each other's aims and objectives. The key feature of the Abdullah–Meir meeting in November 1947 was that the Zionists confirmed they would favour and accept Transjordan's occupation of the Arab areas of Palestine and emphasised their intention to work within the parameters of the UN resolution. This was the foundation on which the Greater Transjordan scheme was built. This gave Abdullah confidence that his dynastic ambitions could be realised in Palestine and prompted him to seek British approval to use the Arab Legion to that end. As the situation in Palestine deteriorated during the final few months of the mandate, Abdullah began to have second thoughts about the original scheme. This is where Glubb's command of the Arab Legion was pivotal. The rank and file of the Arab Legion, both British and Arab, were eager to fight, and it is unlikely that Abdullah would or could have stopped them in the face of pan-Arab pressure. However, Glubb

---

[10] Glubb's published books are listed in: Royle, *Glubb Pasha*, pp. 500–1.
[11] Morris, *Road to Jerusalem*, p. 241.

and the other British officers in executive command positions, such as Lash, Goldie, and Ashton, ensured that the Arab Legion remained on the defensive. At no point did the Arab Legion seek to destroy the enemy. Even when the Arab Legion did plan offensives, such as the victory in Qula, and the discarded 'Operation Glucose', the attacks were politically motivated; they were designed to provide the appearance that the Arab Legion was fighting for the purpose of justifying, in the eyes of the Arab world, Jordan's annexation of the Arab areas of Palestine and the value of the British connection. Glubb's management of the war effort should not be construed as the actions of a complete lone ranger, or those of a British stooge. Abdullah and the prime minister remained in favour of the Greater Transjordan scheme, but were under political pressure not to be seen breaking ranks from the rhetoric of Arab unity. In this way, it becomes clear that the Arab Legion's conduct during the 1948 War was less about Abdullah faithfully fulfilling a promise to the Zionists – even if he maintained that desire – but more about Glubb fulfilling the Greater Transjordan objective coveted by Abdullah and approved by Britain.

The principal flaw in the Greater Transjordan scheme was that it did not have an exit strategy. A full-blown war involving the Arab states was not originally anticipated, and it was hoped that the Arab Legion's occupation of the areas of Palestine assigned to the proposed Arab state would be accepted as the new *natural* order. Indeed, the Greater Transjordan scheme was effectively in accordance with the UN partition plan. It merely sought to exploit the Arab Higher Committee's unwillingness to accept partition and its inability to secure an independent Palestinian Arab state. Once the territorial objectives of the Greater Transjordan scheme had been achieved, both Britain and the Jordanians sought to manipulate an end to the conflict. The key to consolidating Greater Transjordan and withdrawing from the conflict was to avoid being the first to negotiate publicly with the Israelis. To that end, the British sought to starve the Arab states into submission by proposing an arms embargo. Far from being evidence of Britain thwarting the Greater Transjordan scheme, as Bradshaw has argued, this was consistent with Britain's desire to minimise the level of conflict and to see Greater Transjordan emerge from Palestine. Similarly, the Jordanians suggested, during the first truce, the imposition of UN sanctions against the Arab states, including themselves. This was to no avail, however, and Transjordan was compelled to follow the Arab consensus of renewing the fight. By October Abdullah had returned to his more forthright pursuit of his dynastic objectives and he was keen to establish a peace accord with the Israelis. However, under the auspices of British guidance, he was persuaded not to risk ostracising himself from the rest of the Arab world. Accordingly, Abdullah avoided being the first to negotiate. To that end, Glubb was again pivotal as he successfully helped push the Egyptians into a corner that forced them to become the first Arab state to negotiate with Israel. Contrary to the traditional Zionist narrative of the conflict, the Arabs were far from a united coalition. This had been the case from the outset, but it was particularly telling during the final stages of the conflict as it was here when the Arab Legion and the Egyptian Army were actively working against each other. As the incident in Falluja illustrated, they were beset by mutual suspicions. Had it not been for the political jockeying amongst the Arab states, then partition would likely have been much smoother, and Israel much smaller. Inter-Arab rivalries made the process much more difficult for the Arab Legion and created the conditions for the Zionists to exploit. The Arab Legion's limited objectives and the inter-Arab rivalries thus debunk the traditional David versus Goliath narrative. This study has shown that the 1948 War was heavily influenced by the Greater Transjordan scheme, the eventual success of which owed much to Glubb, who was integral to its preparation, its implementation, and its eventual consolidation in the form of the 1949 armistice.

The Arab Legion proved a valuable tool for the British in 1948, but this did not alter its role in Britain's imperial defence system. Contrary to Vatikiotis's portrayal of the Arab Legion's progression, the British did not seek to expand the Arab Legion after the Second World War, or after 1948. When the 1946 Treaty was signed, Britain planned to drastically reduce the Arab Legion back to its pre-war size. It was only maintained at its Second World War level on an ad hoc basis because the situation in Palestine required replacement units to be raised within the TJFF first, in order to allow for a gradual handover of responsibility. The Arab Legion was not deemed an imperial defence asset in its own right; it was primarily considered the cost for securing strategic rights in Transjordan and was funded merely for the purpose of maintaining internal security. As the end of the Palestine mandate drew near, the Arab Legion assumed a more practical purpose in the pursuit of Britain's geostrategic interests. The Arab Legion became a useful tool for securing an alternative form of partition more favourable than that proposed by the United Nations. It was therefore consolidated via an increased subsidy. During the course of 1948, the Arab Legion exceeded its approved size, and the intention in 1949 was for the Arab Legion to revert to its pre-war setting. Again, however, the Palestine problem – the ongoing tension on the new West

Bank border with Israel – precluded extensive reduction. It was only in 1951, in response to the Korean War, that Britain actively sought to expand the Arab Legion as an imperial defence asset in its own right – capable of supporting the British Army in Cold War countermeasures. Even this expansion was short-lived, though. Despite initiating a three-year reorganisation scheme, by the end of 1952 fears of a global war had receded and the British once again sought to cut the cloth of the Arab Legion – or at least to cease further expansion. Ultimately, between 1945 and 1957 the British funded the Arab Legion primarily as a quid pro quo for keeping Jordan on side and stable.

Understanding how and why the Arab Legion was designated this role provides a useful insight into the process of policy-making at the centre of the British world system. The War Office and the Chiefs of Staff were certainly keen for the Arab Legion to be expanded for the purpose of contributing to Britain's imperial defence needs, and the Foreign Office was generally willing to acquiesce. If they had had a free hand, the Arab Legion would probably have expanded at a much greater rate. However, its imperial defence role was very much kept in check by the Treasury. This supports George Peden's assessment that the Treasury played a vital role ensuring 'that strategists were thinking clearly about priorities'.[12] The Whitehall structure meant that despite the military's desire to build the Arab Legion for imperial defence purposes, Treasury restrictions prompted the War Office to prioritise its budget towards the British Army. Consequently, the Arab Legion's contribution to imperial defence was incidental rather than integral. This identifies a self-regulating Whitehall system with its own checks and balances. We should be wary of over-emphasising the efficacy of this systemic structure, however. Indeed, there was also a distinct lack of coordination between the various Whitehall departments. The construction of the 1946 Treaty was a case in point. The Arab Legion, Jordan, and the Middle East were all the subject of interest from numerous Whitehall departments. Yet the treaty was drafted almost exclusively by the Colonial Office – the department about to relinquish its interest in Transjordan. This resulted in a distinctly bilateral treaty unrelated to the process of treaty revision the Foreign Office was simultaneously exploring with Egypt and Iraq.

Understanding the construction and sustenance of the treaty-based relationship is crucial to explaining its demise. Otherwise we risk losing

---

[12] George Peden, 'The Treasury and Defence of Empire', in: Greg Kennedy (ed.), *Imperial Defence: The Old World Order, 1856–1956*, paperback edn (London, 2014), p. 87.

perspective. By simply emphasising Glubb's dismissal one might conclude, as Pappé does, that the British were bowled out of Jordan by nationalists. Certainly Hussein's frustrations with Glubb and the British were formulated within a toxic atmosphere stoked by Nasser's anti-Glubb and anti-British diatribe. We also cannot deny that nationalists such as Ali Abu Nowar, and even, it seems, Abdullah al-Tall, had the ear of the king. However, this portrayal ignores the fact that Hussein received anti-Glubb encouragement from non-nationalists, including Wing-Commander Dalgleish, and that Hussein wanted to maintain the British connection despite dismissing Glubb. By emphasising the termination of the treaty it would be easy to appraise that Britain's withdrawal from Jordan was the result of a loss of will, on the basis that the British no longer had the stomach to rail against the forces that had removed Glubb, particularly after the Suez catastrophe. However, this would seem to ignore the fact that Britain maintained the will to intervene in 1958. Even Britain's pragmatic attitude towards Ali Abu Nowar after Glubb's dismissal negates the loss of will argument, for as William Roger Louis has argued: 'it demanded just as great an "act of will" to treat the Arabs as equals as it did just to sit on them'.[13] More convincing is the idea that imperial overstretch and economic constraints prompted Britain to retreat. Certainly the British willingly terminated the treaty after a post-Glubb reappraisal of the relationship established that the costs of the treaty – politically, financially, and militarily – outweighed the benefits. If the 1946 Treaty was constructed as a wide-ranging insurance policy, then the 1957 termination was based on a realisation that the premiums were too high. However, the British would not have conducted the re-evaluation that led them to this conclusion had it not been for Glubb's dismissal and the subsequent loss of control of the Arab Legion. This therefore drags us back to the process that led to Glubb's dismissal.

Ultimately it is imprudent to pinpoint one single factor to explain the sustenance or the demise of the Anglo–Jordanian treaty relationship. As Gallagher has pointed out, the historian's task is not to rank the causes, but to join up the dots, 'to identify ways in which one set of forces worked on the other in critical situations'.[14] The key to piecing together the puzzle of Britain's withdrawal from Jordan – to join those dots – is to identify the relative balance of dependence. With the Arab Legion at the heart

[13] Louis, *British Empire in the Middle East*, p. 737.
[14] Gallagher, *Decline, Revival and Fall*, p. 74.

of the treaty – as a quid pro quo – the Anglo–Jordanian relationship was founded on a system of mutual dependence, and it was a shift in the balance of this system that caused the Anglo–Jordanian relationship to deteriorate and ultimately resulted in the treaty's termination and Britain's withdrawal. Transjordan was dependent on Britain financially and militarily, and Abdullah accepted this. The 1948 War is particularly illustrative of this feature of the relationship. Abdullah's pursuit of Greater Transjordan and his subsequent desire for an armistice with Israel were both subject to British approval. Because of his personal dependence, Abdullah willingly worked within the parameters of a dominant British presence over Jordanian foreign policy and the Arab Legion. In some respects Abdullah's assassination was therefore a turning point. In a letter to Attlee, written shortly before the king's death, Abdullah explained: 'few are the people who comprehend that independence is a gradual affair and take into consideration the necessity of allowing a time lapse from the moment of its inception to its maturity'.[15] Abdullah accepted his dependence on Britain in a way that Hussein, regardless of the pan-Arab fervour that threatened his kingdom, would not – as his outburst against serving with the British Army prior to acceding the throne in 1953 indicated. The underlying cause, though, was the changing international climate within which Britain and Jordan were operating. The treaty began to break down as the balance of dependence shifted. Britain's withdrawal from Palestine; its increasingly fraught relationship with Egypt; and the Cold War with the Soviet Union; all these factors increased Britain's dependence on Jordan as a geostrategic safe haven. These same factors, however, made Jordan less reliant on Britain. The British had hoped that Greater Transjordan would be tied to Britain by even greater dependence than the pre-1948 state, and materially it was. However, the impact the 1948 War had on Arab nationalism within Jordan and the Arab Legion, and the rise of Nasserism after 1952, made British dominance, including Glubb's presence, an increasing liability. Consequently, both parties sought to exert more control. In response to the Soviet threat the British Anglicised the Arab Legion, but this merely added fuel to the fire of anti-British Arab nationalists, which in turn encouraged the Jordanians to establish greater control of the Arab Legion. The British acknowledged that control would have to be transferred to Jordan in the long term and that Glubb would eventually have to be replaced. Yet because of their

---

[15] Abdullah to Attlee, 10 July 1951, FO371/91799/ET1052/1, TNA.

dependence on maintaining their position in Jordan, the British nonetheless failed to make any positive moves in either direction. From a practical point of view, the British were comforted that they could rely on Glubb's influence if and when Jordanian or Arab Legion support was required. And from a prestige perspective, the British were concerned that Glubb's departure, whether forced or voluntary, would look like scuttle. Glubb had become symbolic of British power, and his departure was anticipated to be worse than the propaganda attacks he was the target of. In that respect, because of the perceived significance of prestige, Arab nationalism encouraged the British to stay, rather than forcing them to depart. Yet this merely exacerbated the tensions within the relationship. Meanwhile, Jordan's dependence on the British connection was further weakened by Britain's failure to assist in its struggle against Israel, including attempts to invoke the treaty in relation to Qibya in October 1953, Qalqilya in October 1956, and the tension surrounding Banat Yaqub in February 1956, which proved the trigger for Glubb's dismissal.

What this study has demonstrated is that British policy cannot be apprised simply as a rational balance sheet calculation of material interests, or as a mere psychological capitulation. British policy makers were prey to a number of competing considerations, influences, and afflictions, including external factors beyond their control. British policy in Jordan, as this appraisal of Glubb and the Arab Legion has demonstrated, was indeed a product of this melting pot. The foundation of British policy towards Jordan was to consolidate Britain's strategic interests. The transition towards a treaty-based relationship in 1946 was testament to Britain's recognition that mandatory control could no longer be justified; it would damage Abdullah's and Britain's reputations. Equally, however, the maintenance of British interests also inculcated an imperialist character to the treaty. As with Britain's support for Abdullah's Greater Transjordan option when the Palestine mandate ended, and Britain's policy of selective non-intervention during the royal succession crisis, Britain was motivated by the perceived need to secure the lines of communication across the globe, to protect its oil interests, and to provide freedom of access in the event of global war with the Soviet Union. Maintaining predominance in Jordan and Palestine was considered a key component of this system of British imperial defence. The Arab Legion itself was not considered a part of this system, except to the extent that it was capable of maintaining internal security within and the goodwill of a strategically located ally. The Arab Legion was primarily the price – a cheap one – for maintaining these rights. The international climate made Britain ever more dependent on the alliance with Jordan. The Korean War, for example, made the Arab Legion a direct asset to imperial defence. Moreover, Britain's deteriorating relationship elsewhere in the Arab world, particularly in Egypt where the Suez base was located, made Jordan an increasingly important geostrategic asset. Because of this rising significance the British felt compelled to exert greater control. However, increased British dominance jarred with the rise of anti-British Arab nationalism. Hussein was therefore simultaneously prompted to assert more authority in order to vanquish the puppet tag associated with the British connection. The Anglo–Jordanian treaty relationship was built and sustained by a system of mutual dependence. Its demise can be explained by a gradual shift in the balance, and mutual recognition that this system of dependence no longer existed. Piers Brendon described the mandate system as 'a continuation of imperialism by other means'.[16] Meanwhile, the first moves towards independence have been characterised as 'empire by treaty'.[17] These are apt portrayals of British attempts to maintain control of geostrategic assets within a changing international climate. The ending of the treaty was another example of the British world system evolving in response to the global conditions that it adapted to and was shaped by.

As a final thought, it seems pertinent to reflect on Glubb's legacy. Towards the end of the Second World War, in a moment of personal despair, Glubb complained: 'I am unlikely to play any part at all in the future of the Arab countries'.[18] Yet twelve years later, shortly before his departure, Melville appraised, with all sincerity:

I don't think that one would be exaggerating to say that the majority of what British influence still remains in the Middle East, is a result of Glubb's lifelong work out there. I do not think his unique position can be overstressed or his enormous services to the British, as well as the Arabs, exaggerated.[19]

In some respects, given Glubb's dismissal less than three weeks later, Melville's eulogy is tinged with a degree of irony. It is nonetheless utterly apt. Between 1945 and 1956 Glubb was central to Britain's position in

---

[16] Brendon, *Decline and Fall*, p. 317.
[17] Fitzsimons, *Empire by Treaty*.
[18] Glubb to Foot, 28 February 1944, GP2006, 83.
[19] 'Glubb Pasha', Melville to Stanley Priddle (Reuters), 9 February 1956, Melville Papers, 4/ 45.

the Middle East – for good and for bad. While his time may have been up, that does not detract from the fact that, for many years, Glubb had been a unique servant of Anglo-Arab interests. This period of Middle Eastern history would have been quite different, but for his presence, and both Britain and Jordan would find life without him at the helm of the Arab Legion very, very different.

Bibliography

PRIMARY SOURCES

Archival Collections

Official Government Records

The Haganah Archives, Israel
Israel State Archives, Israel
The National Archives, London (TNA)
    Air Ministry (AIR)
    Cabinet (CAB)
    Colonial Office (CO)
    Foreign Office (FO)
    Ministry of Defence (DEFE)
    Prime Minister's Office (PREM)
    Treasury (T)
    War Office (WO)

Private Papers

Avi Shlaim's Private Collection
    Desmond Goldie
Bodleian Library, University of Oxford
    Clement Attlee
    Harold Macmillan
Liddell Hart Military Archive, King's College London
    Geoffrey Furlonge
    Charles Johnston
    Harold Pyman

Middle East Centre Archive, St Antony's College, University of Oxford (MECA)
    Patrick Coghill
    Cecil Edmonds
    Philip Geyelin
    John Glubb
    James Lunt
    Harold MacMichael
    Robert Melville
    Harry Philby
Rhodes House Library, University of Oxford
    Arthur Creech Jones
    Trafford Smith

Sound Recordings

    Imperial War Museum
    Gawain Bell
    John Glubb

Official Publications (Print and Online)

Declassified Documents Reference System.

Documents on the Foreign Policy of Israel, 1950–7 (Jerusalem: Israel State Archives, various dates of publication).

Foreign Relations of the United States [FRUS], 1945–57 (Washington, DC: U.S. Government Printing Office, various dates of publication).

Hansard Parliamentary Debates, http://hansard.millbanksystems.com

The Hashemite Documents: Papers of King Abdullah (Amman: Ministry of Information, 1995).

Political and Diplomatic Documents, December 1947–May 1948 (Jerusalem: Israel State Archives, 1979).

Edited Document Collections

Boyle, Peter G. (ed.), *The Eden–Eisenhower Correspondence, 1955–1957* (Chapel Hill: University of North Carolina Press, 2005).

Khalidi, Walid (ed.), 'Selected Documents on the 1948 Palestine War', *Journal of Palestine Studies,* 27:3 (1998), pp. 60–105.

Laqueur, Walter (ed.), *The Israel–Arab Reader: A Documentary History of the Middle East Conflict,* 2nd edn (Harmondsworth: Penguin Books, 1970).

Memoirs and Diaries

Abdullah, King, translated by Philip P. Graves, *Memoirs of King Abdullah of Transjordan* (London: Jonathan Cape, 1951).

Abdullah, King, translated by Harold W. Glidden, *My Memoirs Completed: 'Al-Takmilah'* (London: Longman, 1978).

Ben-Gurion, David, translated by Nechemia Meyers and Uzy Nystar, *Israel: A Personal History* (London: New English Library, 1972).

Bromage, Nigel, *A Soldier in Arabia: A British Military Memoir from Jordan to Saudi Arabia* (London: Radcliffe Press, 2012).

Catterall, Peter (ed.), *The Macmillan Diaries: The Cabinet Years, 1950–1957* (London: Macmillan, 2003).

Coghill, Patrick, *Before I Forget* (unpublished memoirs, 1970; available at the Middle East Centre Archive, St Antony's College, Oxford).

Dayan, Moshe, *Story of My Life* (London: Weidenfeld and Nicolson, 1976).

Eden, Anthony, *Full Circle* (London: Cassell, 1960).

Elpeleg, Zvi (ed.), translated by Rachel Kassel, *Through the Eyes of the Mufti: The Essays of Haj Amin Translated and Annotated*, paperback edn (Elstree: Vallentine Mitchell, 2015).

Glubb, John Bagot, *The Story of the Arab Legion* (London: Hodder and Stoughton, 1948).

A Soldier with the Arabs (London: Hodder and Stoughton, 1957).

Britain and the Arabs (London: Hodder and Stoughton, 1959).

Arabian Adventures: Ten Years of Joyful Service (London: Cassell, 1978).

Into Battle: A Soldier's Diary of the Great War (London: Book Club Associates, 1978).

The Changing Scenes of Life: An Autobiography (London: Quartet Books, 1983).

Heikal, Mohamed H., *Nasser: The Cairo Documents* (London: New English Library, 1972).

Cutting the Lion's Tail: Suez Through Egyptian Eyes (London: Andre Deutsch, 1986).

Hussein of Jordan, H. M. King, *Uneasy Lies the Head: An Autobiography* (London: William Heinemann, 1962).

Johnston, Charles, *The Brink of Jordan* (London: Hamish Hamilton, 1972).

Khalidi, Walid, and Caplan, Neil (eds.), 'The 1953 Qibya Raid Revisited: Excerpts from Moshe Sharett's Diaries', *Journal of Palestine Studies*, 31:4 (2002), pp. 77–98.

Kirkbride, Sir Alec, *A Crackle of Thorns: Experiences in the Middle East* (London: John Murray, 1956).

From the Wings: Amman Memoirs 1947–1951 (London: Frank Cass, 1976).

Lloyd, Selwyn, *Suez 1956: A Personal Account* (London: Jonathan Cape, 1978).

Macmillan, Harold, *Tides of Fortune, 1945–1955* (London: Macmillan, 1969).

Riding the Storm, 1956–1959 (London: Macmillan, 1971).

Meir, Golda, *My Life*, 2nd edn (London: Futura, 1989).

Nasser, Gamal Abd al-, *Egypt's Liberation: The Philosophy of the Revolution*, 2nd printing (Washington, DC: Public Affairs Press, 1956).

Nasser, Gamal Abd al-, and Khalidi, Walid (ed.), 'Nasser's Memoirs of the First Palestine War', *Journal of Palestine Studies*, 2:2 (1973), pp. 3–32.

Nutting, Anthony, *No End of a Lesson: The Story of Suez* (London: Constable and Company, 1967).

Qawuqji, Fawzi al-, 'Memoirs, 1948. Part I', *Journal of Palestine Studies*, 1:4 (1972), pp. 27–58.

'Memoirs, 1948. Part II', *Journal of Palestine Studies*, 2:1 (1972), pp. 3–33.

Shuckburgh, Evelyn, *Descent to Suez, Diaries 1951–56* (London: Weidenfeld and Nicolson, 1986).

Wishah, Um Jabr, 'Palestinian Voices: The 1948 War and Its Aftermath', *Journal of Palestine Studies*, 35:4 (2006), pp. 54–62.
Young, Peter, *Bedouin Command: With the Arab Legion 1953–1956* (London: William Kimber, 1956).
The Arab Legion (Reading: Osprey, 1972).

Media Outlets and Monitoring Services

British Broadcasting Corporation (BBC)
Desert Island Discs
On This Day
Summary of World Broadcasts (SWB)
Evening Standard
Mideast Mirror
New York Times

Interviews

Robert Kenneth Melville, 13 March 2013, London.

PRINTED SECONDARY SOURCES

Abidi, Aqil Hyder Hasan, *Jordan: A Political Study, 1948–1957* (London: Asia Publishing House, 1965).
Abu Nowar, Maan, *The Struggle for Independence 1939–1947: A History of the Hashemite Kingdom of Jordan* (Reading: Ithaca Press, 2001).
The Jordanian–Israeli War 1948–1951: A History of the Hashemite Kingdom of Jordan (Reading: Ithaca Press, 2002).
Aburish, Said K., *Nasser: The Last Arab* (London: Gerald Duckworth & Co, 2004).
Alon, Yoav, 'Tribal Shaykhs and the Limits of British Imperial Rule in Transjordan, 1920–1946', *Journal of Imperial and Commonwealth History* 32:1 (2004), pp. 69–92.
The Making of Jordan: Tribes, Colonialism and the Modern State (London: I.B. Tauris, 2007).
'Historiography of Empire: The Literature on Britain in the Middle East', in: Zach Levey and Elie Podeh (eds.), *Britain and the Middle East: From Imperial Power to Junior Partner* (Eastbourne: Sussex Academic Press, 2008), pp. 33–47.
'British Colonialism and Orientalism in Arabia: Glubb Pasha in Transjordan, 1930–1946', *British Scholar*, 3:1 (2010), pp. 105–26.
Anderson, Betty S., 'Review Essay: The Evolution of Jordanian Studies', *Critique: Critical Middle Eastern Studies*, 12:2 (2003), pp. 197–202.
Nationalist Voices in Jordan: The Street and the State (Austin: University of Texas Press, 2005).

Anderson, David M., 'Guilty Secrets: Deceit, Denial, and the Discovery of Kenya's "Migrated Archive"', *History Workshop Journal*, 80:1 (2015), pp. 142–60.

Antonius, George, *The Arab Awakening: The Story of the Arab National Movement* (London: Hamish Hamilton, 1938).

Aruri, N. H., *Jordan: A Study in Political Development, 1921–1965* (Hague: Nijhoff, 1972).

Ashton, Nigel, *Eisenhower, Macmillan and the Problem of Nasser: Anglo–American Relations and Arab Nationalism, 1955–59* (Basingstoke: Macmillan, 1996).

'A Microcosm of Decline: British Loss of Nerve and Military Intervention in Jordan and Kuwait, 1958 and 1961', *The Historical Journal*, 40:4 (1997), pp. 1069–83.

'"A 'Special Relationship' Sometimes in Spite of Ourselves": Britain and Jordan, 1957–73', *Journal of Imperial and Commonwealth History*, 33:2 (2005), pp. 221–44.

King Hussein of Jordan: A Political Life (New Haven: Yale University Press, 2008).

'Hitler on the Nile? British and American Perceptions of the Nasser Regime, 1952–70', in: Lawrence Freedman and Jeffrey H. Michaels (eds.), *Scripting Middle East Leaders: The Impact of Leadership Perceptions on US and UK Foreign Policy* (New York: Bloomsbury, 2013), pp. 47–61.

Bar-Joseph, Uri, *The Best of Enemies: Israel and Transjordan in the War of 1948* (London: Frank Cass, 1987).

Barr, James, *A Line in the Sand: Britain, France and the Struggle for the Mastery of the Middle East*, paperback edn (London: Simon & Schuster, 2012).

Blackwell, Stephen, *British Military Intervention and the Struggle for Jordan: King Hussein, Nasser and the Middle East Crisis, 1955–1958* (New York: Routledge, 2009).

Bradshaw, Tancred, 'History Invented: The British–Transjordanian "Collusion" Revisited', *Middle Eastern Studies* 43:1 (2007), pp. 21–43.

Britain and Jordan: Imperial Strategy, King Abdullah I and the Zionist Movement (London: I.B. Tauris, 2012).

(ed.), *The Glubb Reports: Glubb Pasha and Britain's Empire Project in the Middle East 1920–1956* (Basingstoke: Palgrave Macmillan, 2016).

Brendon, Piers, *The Decline and Fall of the British Empire, 1781–1997* (London: Jonathan Cape, 2007).

Brown, L. Carl, *International Politics and the Middle East: Old Rules, Dangerous Game* (London: I.B. Tauris, 1984).

Bunch, Clea Lutz, 'Supporting the Brave Young King: The Suez Crisis and Eisenhower's New Approach to Jordan, 1953–1958', in: Simon C. Smith (ed.), *Reassessing Suez 1956: New Perspectives on the Crisis and Its Aftermath* (Aldershot: Ashgate, 2008), pp. 107–22.

'Invitation to Intervene: British and American Relations with Jordan in the 1950s', in: Tore T. Petersen (ed.), *Challenging Retrenchment: The United States, Great Britain and the Middle East* (Trondheim: Tapir Academic Press, 2010), pp. 95–113.

Cain, P. J. and Hopkins, A. G., *British Imperialism: Crisis and Deconstruction, 1914–1990* (London: Longman, 1993).

Caplan, Neil, *Futile Diplomacy, Volume II: Arab–Zionist Negotiations and the End of the Mandate* (London: Frank Cass, 1986).

Carlton, David, *Anthony Eden: A Biography* (London: Allen and Unwin, 1986).

Cohen, Michael, J., *Palestine: Retreat from the Mandate: The Making of British Policy, 1936–45* (London: Paul Elek, 1978).

Palestine and the Great Powers 1945–1948 (Princeton: Princeton University Press, 1982).

Fighting World War Three from the Middle East: Allied Contingency Plans, 1945–1954 (London: Frank Cass, 1997).

'The Strategic Role of the Middle East after the War', in: Michael J. Cohen and Martin Kolinsky (eds.), *Demise of the British Empire in the Middle East: Britain's Responses to Nationalist Movements, 1943–55* (London: Frank Cass, 1998), pp. 23–40.

Collins, Larry and Lapierre, Dominique, *O Jerusalem!* (London: History Book Club, 1972).

Cronin, Stephanie, *Armies and State-Building in the Modern Middle East: Politics, Nationalism and Military Reform* (London: I.B. Tauris, 2014).

Dann, Uriel, 'The Beginnings of the Arab Legion', *Journal of Middle Eastern Studies*, 5:3 (1969), pp. 181–91.

Studies in the History of Transjordan, 1920–1949: The Making of a State (London: Westview Press, 1984).

'The Foreign Office, the Baghdad Pact and Jordan', *Asian and African Studies*, 21:3 (1987), pp. 247–61.

'Glubb and the Politicization of the Arab Legion: An Annotated Document', *Asian and African Studies*, 21:3 (1987), pp. 213–20.

King Hussein and the Challenge of Arab Radicalism: Jordan, 1955–1967 (Oxford: Oxford University Press, 1989).

King Hussein's Strategy of Survival (Washington, DC: The Washington Institute for Near East Policy, 1991).

Darby, Philip, *British Defence Policy East of Suez 1947–1968* (London: Oxford University Press, 1973).

Darwin, John, 'British Decolonization since 1945: A Pattern or a Puzzle?' *Journal of Imperial and Commonwealth History*, 12:2 (1984), pp. 187–209.

Britain and Decolonisation: The Retreat from Empire in the Post-war World (Basingstoke: Macmillan, 1988).

'Imperialism and the Victorians: The Dynamics of Territorial Expansion', *English Historical Review*, 112:447 (1997), pp. 614–42.

'Decolonization and the End of Empire', in: Robin W. Winks (ed.), *The Oxford History of the British Empire, Volume V: Historiography* (Oxford: Oxford University Press, 1999), pp. 541–57.

'Was there a Fourth British Empire?', in: Martin Lynn (ed.), *The British Empire in the 1950s: Retreat or Revival?* (Basingstoke: Palgrave Macmillan, 2006), pp. 16–31.

The Empire Project: The Rise and Fall of the British World System 1830–1970 (Cambridge: Cambridge University Press, 2009).

Dawisha, Adeed, 'Egypt', in: Yezid Sayigh and Avi Shlaim (eds.), *The Cold War and the Middle East* (Oxford: Clarendon Press, 1997), pp. 27–47.

Dearden, Ann, *Jordan* (London: Robert Hale, 1958).

Dessouki, Ali E. Hillal, 'Nasser and the Struggle for Independence', in: William Roger Louis and Roger Owen (eds.), *Suez 1956: The Crisis and Its Consequences* (Oxford: Clarendon Press, 1989), pp. 31–42.

Devereux, David R., *The Formulation of British Defence Policy Towards the Middle East, 1948–1956* (Basingstoke: Macmillan, 1990).

Dockrill, M. L., 'The Foreign Office, Anglo–American Relations and the Korean War, June 1950–June 1951', *International Affairs*, 62:3 (1986), pp. 459–76.

Feldman, Ilana, *Governing Gaza: Bureaucracy, Authority, and the Work of Rule, 1917–1967* (London: Duke University Press, 2008).

Fieldhouse, D. K., *Western Imperialism in the Middle East 1914–1958* (Oxford: Oxford University Press, 2006).

Fitzsimons, M. A., *Empire by Treaty: Britain and the Middle East in the Twentieth Century* (London: Ernest Been, 1965).

Flapan, Simha, *The Birth of Israel: Myths and Realities* (New York: Pantheon, 1987).

Fletcher, Robert S. G., *British Imperialism and 'The Tribal Question': Desert Administration and Nomadic Societies in the Middle East, 1919–1936* (Oxford: Oxford University Press, 2015).

Fraser, T. G., *The Arab–Israeli Conflict*, 3rd edn (Basingstoke: Palgrave Macmillan, 2008).

Freiberger, Steven Z., *Dawn Over Suez: The Rise of American Power in the Middle East, 1953–1957* (Chicago: Ivan R. Dee, 1992).

French, David, *Army, Empire, and Cold War: The British Army, Military Policy, 1945–1971* (Oxford: Oxford University Press, 2012).

'The British Army and the Empire, 1856–1956', in: Greg Kennedy (ed.), *Imperial Defence: The Old World Order, 1856–1956*, paperback edn (London: Routledge, 2014), pp. 91–110.

Gallagher, John, *The Decline, Revival and Fall of the British Empire: The Ford Lectures and Other Essays* (Cambridge: Cambridge University Press, 1982).

Gelber, Yoav, *Jewish–Transjordanian Relations 1921–1948* (London: Frank Cass, 1997).

Gerges, Fawaz A., 'Egypt and the 1948 War: Internal Conflict and Regional Ambition', in: Eugene Rogan and Avi Shlaim (eds.), *The War for Palestine: Rewriting the History of 1948*, 2nd edn (Cambridge: Cambridge University Press, 2007), pp. 151–77.

Geyelin, Philip, *Hashemite: The Story of King Hussein of Jordan* (unfinished and unpublished manuscript; available at the Middle East Centre Archive, St Antony's College, Oxford).

Grose, Peter, 'The President versus the Diplomats', in: William Roger Louis and Robert W. Stookey (eds.), *The End of the Palestine Mandate* (London: I.B. Tauris, 1986), pp. 32–60.

Grove, Eric, 'Who to Fight in 1956, Egypt or Israel? Operation Musketeer versus Operation Cordage', in: Simon C. Smith (ed.), *Reassessing Suez 1956: New Perspectives on the Crisis and Its Aftermath* (Aldershot: Ashgate, 2008), pp. 79–86.

Hahn, Peter, *The United States, Great Britain, and Egypt, 1945–1956: Strategy and Diplomacy in the Early Cold War* (Chapel Hill: University of North Carolina Press, 1991).

'Discord or Partnership? British and American Policy toward Egypt, 1942–56', in: Michael J. Cohen and Martin Kolinsky (eds.), *Demise of the British Empire in the Middle East: Britain's Responses to Nationalist Movements, 1943–55* (London: Frank Cass, 1998), pp. 30–2.

Hampshire, Edward, '"Apply the Flame More Searingly": The Destruction and Migration of the Archives of British Colonial Administration: A Southeast Asia Case Study', *Journal of Imperial and Commonwealth History*, 41:2 (2013), pp. 334–52.

Hanson, Jarice, and Narula, Uma, *New Communication Technologies in Developing Countries* (London: Lawrence Erlbaum Associates, 1990).

Heller, Joseph, *The Birth of Israel, 1945–1949: Ben-Gurion and His Critics* (Gainesville: University Press of Florida, 2000).

Herzog, Chaim, *The Arab–Israeli Wars: War and Peace in the Middle East* (London: Arms and Armour Press, 1982).

Howard, Anthony, *RAB: The Life of R.A. Butler* (London: Papermac, 1988).

Hughes, Matthew, 'Collusion across the Litani? Lebanon and the 1948 War', in: Eugene Rogan and Avi Shlaim (eds.), *The War for Palestine: Rewriting the History of 1948*, 2nd edn (Cambridge: Cambridge University Press, 2007), pp. 204–27.

'British Private Armies in the Middle East? The Arab Legion and the Transjordan Frontier Force, 1920–1956', *The RUSI Journal*, 153:2 (2008), pp. 70–5.

Hyam, Ronald, 'The Primacy of Geopolitics: The Dynamics of British Imperial Policy, 1763–1963', in: R. D. King and R. W Kilson (eds.), *The Statecraft of British Imperialism: Essays in Honour of Wm. Roger Louis* (London and Portland, OR: Frank Cass, 1999), pp. 27–52.

Britain's Declining Empire: The Road to Decolonisation 1918–1968 (Cambridge: Cambridge University Press, 2006).

Jackson, Ashley, 'Imperial Defence in the Post-Imperial Era', in: Greg Kennedy (ed.), *Imperial Defence: The Old World Order, 1856–1956*, paperback edn (London: Routledge, 2007).

Distant Drums: The Role of Colonies in British Imperial Warfare (Brighton: Sussex Academic Press, 2010).

James, Robert Rhodes, *Anthony Eden* (London: Weidenfeld and Nicolson, 1986).

Jevon, Graham, 'The Arab Legion and the 1948 War: The Conduct of "Collusion"?', *English Historical Review*, 130:545 (2015), pp. 907–33.

Jones, Martin, *Failure in Palestine: British and United States Policy after the Second World War* (London: Mansell, 1986).

Karsh, Efraim, 'Rewriting Israel's History', *Middle East Quarterly*, 3:2 (1996), pp. 19–29.

'Historical Fictions', *Middle East Quarterly*, 3:3 (1996), pp. 56–60.

Fabricating Israeli History: The 'New Historians' (London: Frank Cass, 1997).

'The Collusion That Never Was: King Abdullah, the Jewish Agency and the Partition of Palestine', *Journal of Contemporary History*, 34:4 (1999), pp. 569–85.

Kent, John, 'The Egyptian Base and the Defence of the Middle East, 1945–54', in: Robert Holland (ed.), *Emergencies and Disorder in the European Empires after 1945* (London: Frank Cass, 1994), pp. 45–65.

'Britain and the Egyptian Problem, 1945-48', in: Michael J. Cohen and Martin Kolinsky (eds.), *Demise of the British Empire in the Middle East: Britain's Responses to Nationalist Movements, 1943–55* (London: Frank Cass, 1998), pp. 142–61.

'Informal Empire and the Defence of the Middle East, 1945–56', in: Roy Bridges (ed.), *Imperialism, Decolonization and Africa* (Basingstoke: Macmillan, 2000), pp. 114–52.

'The Foreign Office and Defence of the Empire', in: Greg Kennedy (ed.), *Imperial Defence: The Old World Order, 1856–1956*, paperback edn (London: Routledge, 2014), pp. 50–70.

Khalidi, Rashid, *The Iron Cage: The Story of the Palestinian Struggle for Statehood* (Oxford: Oneworld Publications, 2007).

'The Palestinians and 1948: The Underlying Causes of Failure', in: Eugene Rogan and Avi Shlaim (eds.), *The War for Palestine: Rewriting the History of 1948*, 2nd edn (Cambridge: Cambridge University Press, 2007), pp. 12–36.

Khalidi, Walid, 'The Arab Perspective', in: William Roger Louis and Robert W. Stookey (eds.), *The End of the Palestine Mandate* (London: I.B. Tauris, 1986), pp. 104–36.

Khalili, Laleh, *Time in the Shadows: Confinement in Counterinsurgencies* (Stanford: Stanford University Press, 2013).

Killingray, David, 'Imperial Defence', in: Robin W. Winks (ed.), *The Oxford History of the British Empire, Volume V: Historiography* (Oxford: Oxford University Press, 1999), pp. 342–53.

Kimche, Jon and Kimche, David, *Both Sides of the Hill: Britain and the Palestine War* (London: Secker and Warburg, 1960).

Kingston, Paul W. T., *Britain and the Politics of Modernization in the Middle East, 1945–1958* (Cambridge: Cambridge University Press, 1996).

Kyle, Keith, 'Britain and the Crisis, 1955–1956', in: William Roger Louis and Roger Owen (eds.), *Suez 1956: The Crisis and Its Consequences* (Oxford: Clarendon Press, 1989), pp. 103–30.

Suez: Britain's End of Empire in the Middle East, 2nd edn (London: I.B. Tauris, 2003).

Landis, Joshua, 'Syria and the Palestine War: Fighting King Abdullah's "Greater Syria Plan"', in: Eugene Rogan and Avi Shlaim (eds.), *The War for Palestine: Rewriting the History of 1948*, 2nd edn (Cambridge: Cambridge University Press, 2007), pp. 178–205.

Lapping, Brian, *End of Empire* (London: Granada, 1985).

Levenberg, Haim, *Military Preparations of the Arab Community in Palestine 1945–1948* (London: Frank Cass, 1993).

Lias, Godfrey, *Glubb's Legion* (London: Evans Brothers, 1956).

Little, Douglas, 'A Puppet in Search of a Puppeteer? The United States, King Hussein, and Jordan, 1953–1970', *International History Review*, 17:3 (1995), pp. 512–44.

Louis, William Roger, *The British Empire in the Middle East 1945–1951: Arab Nationalism, the United States, and Postwar Imperialism* (Oxford: Clarendon Press, 1985).

'British Imperialism and the End of the Palestine Mandate', in: William Roger Louis and Robert W. Stookey (eds.), *The End of the Palestine Mandate* (London: I.B. Tauris, 1986), pp. 1–31.

'The Tragedy of the Anglo–Egyptian Settlement of 1954', in: William Roger Louis and Roger Owen (eds.), *Suez 1956: The Crisis and Its Consequences* (Oxford: Clarendon Press, 1989), pp. 43–72.

'Britain and the Crisis of 1958', in: William Roger Louis and Roger Owen (eds.), *A Revolutionary Year: The Middle East in 1958* (London: I.B. Tauris, 2002), pp. 15–76.

'Robinson and Gallagher and Their Critics', in: William Roger Louis, *Ends of Imperialism: The Scramble for Empire, Suez and Decolonisation* (London: I.B. Tauris, 2006), pp. 907–54.

Love, Kennett, *Suez: The Twice-Fought War* (New York: McGraw-Hill Book Company, 1969).

Lucas, Scott W., 'Redefining the Suez "Collusion"', *Middle Eastern Studies*, 26:1 (1990), pp. 88–112.

Divided We Stand: Britain, the US and the Suez Crisis (London: Hodder and Stoughton, 1991).

'Conclusion', in: Simon C. Smith (ed.), *Reassessing Suez 1956: New Perspectives on the Crisis and Its Aftermath* (Aldershot: Ashgate, 2008), pp. 239–42.

Lunt, James, *Imperial Sunset: Frontier Soldiering in the 20th Century* (London: Macdonald Futura Publishers, 1981).

Glubb Pasha: A Biography (London: Harvill Press, 1984).

Hussein of Jordan: A Political Biography (London: Macmillan, 1989).

The Arab Legion (London: Constable, 1999).

Massad, Joseph A., *Colonial Effects: The Making of National Identity in Jordan* (New York: Columbia University Press, 2001).

Mattar, Philip, *The Mufti of Jerusalem: Al-Hajj Amin al-Husayni and the Palestinian National Movement* (New York: Columbia University Press, 1988).

Mawby, Spencer, *British Policy in Aden and the Protectorates, 1955–67: Last Outpost of a Middle East Empire* (London: Routledge, 2005).

Meyer, Karl E. and Brysac, Shareen Blair, *Kingmakers: The Invention of the Modern Middle East* (New York: W. W. Norton & Company, 2008).

Monroe, Elizabeth, *Britain's Moment in the Middle East, 1914–1956*, 2nd edn (London: Chatto & Windus, 1981).

Morewood, Steve, 'Prelude to the Suez Crisis: The Rise and Fall of British Dominance over the Suez Canal, 1869–1956', in: Simon C. Smith (ed.), *Reassessing Suez 1956: New Perspectives on the Crisis and Its Aftermath* (Aldershot: Ashgate, 2008), pp. 13–34.

Morris, Benny, *The Birth of the Palestinian Refugee Problem, 1947–1949*, paperback edn (Cambridge: Cambridge University Press, 1989).

1948 and After: Israel and the Palestinians (Oxford: Clarendon Press, 1990).

Israel's Border Wars, 1949–1956 (Oxford: Oxford University Press, 1993).

The Road To Jerusalem: Glubb Pasha, Palestine and the Jews (London: I.B. Tauris, 2003).

Murphy, Philip, 'Telling Tales Out of School: Nutting, Eden and the Attempted Suppression of *No End of a Lesson*', in: Simon C. Smith (ed.), *Reassessing Suez 1956: New Perspectives on the Crisis and Its Aftermath* (Aldershot: Ashgate, 2008), pp. 195–214.

'Britain as a Global Power in the Twentieth Century', in: Andrew Thompson (ed.), *Britain's Experience of Empire in the Twentieth Century* (Oxford: Oxford University Press, 2012), pp. 33–75.

Musa, Sulayman, *Jordan: Land and People* (Amman: The Hashemite Kingdom of Jordan Ministry of Culture and Information, undated).

Cameos: Jordan and Arab Nationalism (Amman: Hashemite Kingdom of Jordan Ministry of Culture and Information, 1997).

Nachmani, Amikam, *Great Power Discord in Palestine: The Anglo-American Committee of Inquiry into the Problems of European Jewry and Palestine, 1945–1946* (London: Frank Cass, 1987).

Nevo, Joseph, 'Abdallah's Memoirs as Historical Source Material', in: Asher Susser and Aryeh Shmuelebitz (eds.), *The Hashemites in the Modern Arab World: Essays in Honour of the Late Professor Uriel Dann* (London: Frank Cass, 1995), pp. 165–82.

King Abdallah and Palestine: A Territorial Ambition (Basingstoke: Macmillan, 1996).

Nkrumah, Kwame, *Neo-colonialism: The Last Stage of Imperialism* (London: Thomas Nelson and Sons, 1965).

Onslow, Sue, 'Julian Amery and the Suez Operation', in: Simon C. Smith (ed.), *Reassessing Suez 1956: New Perspectives on the Crisis and Its Aftermath* (Aldershot: Ashgate, 2008), pp. 67–78.

Oren, Michael B., 'A Winter of Discontent: Britain's Crisis in Jordan, December 1955–March 1956', *International Journal of Middle East Studies*, 22:2 (1990), pp. 171–84.

Ovendale, Ritchie, *Britain, the United States, and the Transfer of Power in the Middle East, 1945–1962* (London: Leicester University Press, 1996).

Pappé, Ilan, *Britain and the Arab–Israeli Conflict, 1948–51* (Basingstoke: Macmillan, 1988).

'Sir Alec Kirkbride and the Anglo-Trans-Jordanian Alliance, 1945–50', in: John Zametica (ed.), *British Officials and British Foreign Policy, 1945–50* (Leicester: Leicester University Press, 1990), pp. 121–55.

'British Rule in Jordan, 1943–55', in: Michael J. Cohen and Martin Kolinsky (eds.), *Demise of the British Empire in the Middle East: Britain's Responses to Nationalist Movements, 1943–55* (London: Frank Cass, 1998), pp. 198–219.

The Making of the Arab-Israeli Conflict, 2nd edn (London: I.B. Tauris, 2001).

Parsons, Laila, 'Soldiering for Arab Nationalism: Fawzi al-Qawuqji in Palestine', *Journal of Palestine Studies*, 36:4 (2007), pp. 33–48.

Peden, George, 'The Treasury and Defence of Empire', in: Greg Kennedy (ed.), *Imperial Defence: The Old World Order, 1856–1956*, paperback edn (London: Routledge, 2014), pp. 71–90.

Petersen, Tore T., 'Post-Suez Consequences: Anglo–American Relations in the Middle East from Eisenhower to Nixon', in: Simon C. Smith (ed.), *Reassessing Suez 1956: New Perspectives on the Crisis and Its Aftermath* (Aldershot: Ashgate, 2008), pp. 215–26.

'Introduction: End of Empire?' in: Tore T. Petersen (ed.), *Challenging Retrenchment: The United States, Great Britain and the Middle East* (Trondheim: Tapir Academic Press, 2010), pp. 1–8.

Podet, Allen Howard, *The Success and Failure of the Anglo-American Committee of Inquiry, 1945–1946: The Last Chance in Palestine* (Lewiston: E Mellen Press, 1986).

Pundik, Ron, *The Struggle for Sovereignty: Relations between Great Britain and Jordan, 1946–1951* (Oxford: Blackwell, 1994).

Raad, Zeid, 'A Nightmare Avoided: Jordan and Suez, 1956', *Israel Affairs*, 1:2 (1995), pp. 288–308.

Rabinovitch, Itamar, *The Road Not Taken: Early Arab–Israeli Negotiations* (Oxford: Oxford University Press, 1991).

Radai, Itamar, 'Jaffa, 1948: The Fall of a City', *Journal of Israeli History*, 30:1 (2011), pp. 23–43.

Reynolds, David, *The Creation of the Anglo–American Alliance, 1939–1941: A Study in Competitive Cooperation* (Chapel Hill: University of North Carolina Press, 1981).

Robins, Philip, *A History of Jordan* (Cambridge: Cambridge University Press, 2004).

Robinson, Ronald and Gallagher, John, with Denny, Alice, *Africa and the Victorians: The Official Mind of Imperialism*, 2nd edn (London: Macmillan, 1981).

'Wm. Roger Louis and the Official Mind of Decolonization', in: Robert D. King and Robin Kilson (eds.), *Statecraft of British Imperialism: Essays in Honour of Wm. Roger Louis* (London: Frank Cass, 1999), pp. 1–12.

Robinson, Ronald and Gallagher, John, 'The Imperialism of Free Trade', *Economic History Review*, 6:1 (1953), pp. 1–15.

Rogan, Eugene, 'Jordan and 1948: The Persistence of an Official History', in: Eugene Rogan and Avi Shlaim (eds.), *The War for Palestine: Rewriting the History of 1948*, 2nd edn (Cambridge: Cambridge University Press, 2007), pp. 104–24.

The Fall of the Ottomans: The Great War in the Middle East, 1914–1920 (London: Penguin Books, 2016).

Royle, Trevor, *Glubb Pasha* (London: Little, Brown and Company, 1992).

Said, Edward, *Orientalism: Western Conceptions of the Orient*, 2nd edn (London: Penguin Books, 1995).

Salibi, Kamal, *The Modern History of Jordan* (London: I.B. Tauris, 1993).

Satia, Priya, 'The Defense of Inhumanity: Air Control and the British Idea of Arabia', *American Historical Review*, 111:1 (2006), pp. 16–51.

Spies in Arabia: The Great War and the Cultural Foundations of Britain's Covert Empire in the Middle East (Oxford: Oxford University Press, 2008).

Satloff, Robert B., *From Abdullah to Hussein: Jordan in Transition* (Oxford: Oxford University Press, 1994).

Sato, Shohei, 'Britain's Decision to Withdraw from the Persian Gulf, 1964–68: A Pattern and a Puzzle', *Journal of Imperial and Commonwealth History*, 37:1 (2009), pp. 99–117.

Schneer, Jonathan, *The Balfour Declaration: The Origins of the Arab–Israeli Conflict* (London: Bloomsbury, 2010).

Schulze, Kirsten E., *The Arab–Israeli Conflict*, 2nd edn (London: Pearson Education, 2008).

'The 1948 War: The Battle over History', in: Joel Peters and David Newman (eds.), *The Routledge Handbook on the Israeli–Palestinian Conflict* (London: Routledge, 2013), pp. 45–55.

Segev, Tom, *One Palestine, Complete: Jews and Arabs under the British Mandate* (London: Little, Brown and Company, 2000).

Sela, Avraham, 'Transjordan, Israel and the 1948 War: Myth, Historiography and Reality', *Middle Eastern Studies*, 28:4 (1992), pp. 623–88.

Shlaim, Avi, *Collusion across the Jordan: King Abdullah, the Zionist Movement, and the Partition of Palestine* (Oxford: Clarendon Press, 1988).

The Politics of Partition: King Abdullah, the Zionists and Palestine 1921–1951 (Oxford: Oxford University Press, 1990).

'The Debate about 1948', *International Journal of Middle East Studies*, 27:3 (1995), pp. 287–304.

'A Totalitarian Concept of History', *Middle East Quarterly*, 3:3 (1996), pp. 52–5.

'The Protocol of Sevres, 1956: Anatomy of a War Plot', *International Affairs*, 73:3 (1997), pp. 509–30.

The Iron Wall: Israel and the Arab World (London: Penguin Books, 2001).

'Israel and the Arab Coalition in 1948', in: Eugene Rogan and Avi Shlaim (eds.), *The War for Palestine: Rewriting the History of 1948*, 2nd edn (Cambridge: Cambridge University Press, 2007), pp. 79–103.

Lion of Jordan: The Life of King Hussein in War and Peace (New York: Alfred A. Knopf, 2008).

Shryock, Andrew, 'Review of Colonial Effects', *International Journal of Middle East Studies*, 38:3 (2006), p. 479.

Sluglett, Peter, 'Formal and Informal Empire in the Middle East', in: Robin W. Winks (ed.), *The Oxford History of the British Empire, Volume V: Historiography* (Oxford: Oxford University Press, 1999), pp. 416–36.

Slyomovics, Susan, 'The Rape of Qula, a Destroyed Palestinian Village', in: Ahmad H. Sa'di and Lila Abu-Lughod (eds.), *Nakba: Palestine, 1948, and the Claims of Memory* (New York: Columbia University Press, 2007).

Smith, Simon C., *Britain's Revival and Fall in the Gulf: Kuwait, Bahrain, Qatar, and the Trucial States, 1950–71* (London: Routledge, 2004).

Ending Empire in the Middle East: Britain, the United States and Post-war Decolonization, 1945–1973 (London: Routledge, 2012).

Stockwell, A. J. 'Suez 1956 and the Moral Disarmament of the British Empire', in: Simon C. Smith (ed.), *Reassessing Suez 1956: New Perspectives on the Crisis and Its Aftermath* (Aldershot: Ashgate, 2008), pp. 227–38.

Susser, Asher, *On Both Banks of the Jordan: A Political Biography of Wasfi al-Tall* (London: Frank Cass, 1994).

Tal, Lawrence, 'Britain and the Jordan Crisis of 1958', *Middle Eastern Studies*, 31:1 (1995), pp. 39–57.

'Jordan', in: Yezid Sayigh and Avi Shlaim (eds.), *The Cold War and the Middle East* (Oxford: Clarendon Press, 1997), pp. 102–24.

Politics, the Military, and National Security in Jordan, 1955–1967 (Basingstoke: Palgrave Macmillan, 2002).

Thornhill, Michael T., 'Eden, Churchill and the Battle of the Canal Zone, 1951–1954', in: Simon C. Smith (ed.), *Reassessing Suez 1956: New Perspectives on the Crisis and Its Aftermath* (Aldershot: Ashgate, 2008), pp. 35–52.

Tidrick, Kathryn, *Heart Beguiling Araby: The English Romance with Arabia*, 2nd edn (London: I.B. Tauris, 1990).

Vatikiotis, P. J., *Politics and the Military in Jordan: A Study of the Arab Legion 1921–1957* (London: Frank Cass, 1967).

Vaughan, James, '"Cloak Without Dagger": How the Information Research Department Fought Britain's Cold War in the Middle East, 1948–56', *Cold War History*, 4:3 (2004), pp. 56–84.

The Failure of American and British Propaganda in the Arab Middle East, 1945–1957: Unconquerable Minds (Basingstoke: Palgrave Macmillan, 2005).

Wilson, Mary C. *King Abdullah, Britain and the Making of Jordan* (Cambridge: Cambridge University Press, 1988).

Yitzhak, Ronen, 'The Formation and Development of the Jordanian Air Force: 1948–1967', *Middle Eastern Studies*, 40:5 (2004), pp. 158–74.

'The Question of Arab Solidarity in the 1948 War: Political Interests versus Military Considerations', *Mediterranean Quarterly*, 19:2 (2008), pp. 19–46.

'A Small Consolation for a Big Loss: King Abdullah and Jerusalem during the 1948 War', *Israel Affairs*, 14:3 (2008), pp. 398–418.

'Fawzi al-Qawaqji and the Arab Liberation Army in the 1948 War toward the Attainment of King Abdullah's Political Ambitions in Palestine', *Comparative Studies of South Asia, Africa and the Middle East*, 28:3 (2008), pp. 459–66.

'The Assassination of King Abdullah: The First Political Assassination in Jordan: Did It Truly Threaten the Hashemite Kingdom of Jordan?' *Diplomacy and Statecraft*, 21:1 (2010), pp. 68–86.

'Jordanian Intelligence Under the Rule of King Abdullah I (1921–1951)', *Intelligence Journal of Intelligence and Counterintelligence*, 23:4 (2010), pp. 647–62.

'Transjordan's Attack on the Etzion Bloc during the 1948 War', *Middle Eastern Studies*, 17:2 (2011), pp. 194–207.

Abdullah al-Tall – Arab Legion Officer: Arab Nationalism & Opposition to the Hashemite Regime (Brighton: Sussex Academic Press, 2012).

'British Military Supplies to Jordan during the 1948 War: How the Anglo–Jordanian Treaty Was Put to the Test', *Middle East Critique*, 24:4 (2015), pp. 345–54.

Unpublished Theses

Jevon, Graham, '*Jordan, Palestine and the British World System, 1945–57: Glubb Pasha and the Arab Legion*' (University of Oxford, DPhil thesis, 2014).

Norton, Maureen, '*The Last Pasha: Sir John Glubb and the British Empire in the Middle East, 1920–1949*' (Johns Hopkins University, PhD thesis, 1997).

Sarairah, Hatem Ahmed al-, '*A British Actor on the Bedouin Stage: Glubb's Career in Jordan, 1930–1956*' (Indiana University, PhD thesis, 1989).

Index